CONGRESS

POWERS, PROCESSES, AND POLITICS

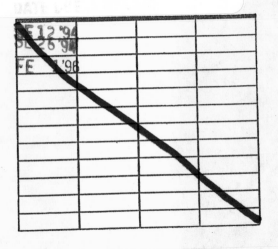

CONGRESS

POWERS, PROCESSES, AND POLITICS

Alan L. Clem
University of South Dakota

 Brooks/Cole Publishing Company
Pacific Grove, California

Brooks/Cole Publishing Company
A Division of Wadsworth, Inc.

Printed in the United States of America

10   9   8   7   6   5   4   3   2   1

Library of Congress Cataloging in Publication Data

Clem, Alan L., [date]
   Congress : powers processes and politics / Alan L. Clem
     p. cm.
   Bibliography: p.
   Includes index.
   ISBN 0-534-09222-5
   1. United States. Congress—Powers and duties. 2. Legislative power—United States. 3. United States—Politics and government.
4. Politics, Practical—United States. 5. United States. Congress.
I. Title.
JK1061.C5825 1988
328. 73'074—dc19

88-14477
CIP

Sponsoring Editor *Cynthia C. Stormer*
Editorial Assistant: *Mary Ann Zuzow*
Production Editor: *Linda Loba*
Manuscript Editor: *Evelyn Mercer Ward*
Permissions Editor: *Carline Haga*
Interior and Cover Design: *Kelly Shoemaker*
Cover Photo: *Architect of the Capitol*
Art Coordinator: *Sue C. Howard*
Interior Illustration: *Maggie Stevens-Huft*
Typesetting: *Kachina Typesetting, Tempe, Arizona*
Printing and Binding: *The Maple-Vail Book Manufacturing Group*

PREFACE

A century ago, William Allen White, a Kansas newspaper editor, stung by widespread negative attitudes about his state, wrote an editorial entitled "What's the Matter with Kansas?" Americans today, who are by and large proud of their nation's democratic heritage and institutions, complain frequently and loudly about Congress, prompting the question, "What's the matter with Congress?"

White attempted to convince his fellow Kansans that they had a state of which they should be proud. But defenders of Congress today would have to argue in the face of abundant and persistent evidence that there is much that is the matter with the legislative branch. Congress exhibits myriad unhealthy symptoms, as noted by many journalists and scholars. Congress is said to be cumbersome, slow, and inconsistent in policy making. Among its members are too many "showhorses" interested in their personal image and not enough "workhorses" interested in solving important national problems. At taxpayer expense, members send hundreds of thousands of pretentious, self-serving newsletters to constituents. They use mysterious, arcane procedures to secure higher salaries and perquisites for themselves. They denounce special interests but write campaign finance laws in such a way as to help incumbents and discourage challengers.

Some members behave in wasteful, selfish, and even immoral ways. One flies to Brazil as the only passenger on an Air Force plane. Another hires a female typist whose services do not include typing or anything else likely to benefit the public. A few use information obtained in the course of congressional investigations to make personal investment decisions. Several accept trips and vacations from interests that have a stake in pending legislation. A few accept direct bribes in return for promising to promote or kill particular bills. All in all, this side of Congress is not a pretty sight.

Such bad habits and aberrations understandably disturb Americans. Naturally, we all have a stake in the honesty and effectiveness of our national representatives. But there is a broader perspective from which to evaluate the performance of Congress. Its success or failure as a powerful, popularly chosen lawmaking institution may well determine the ultimate fate of representative democracy, a modern development that flowered in the nineteenth century and by the middle of the twentieth century had come to dominate the First World (North America, Western

Europe, Japan, Australia, New Zealand) and some parts of the Third World. Events of the next few decades may reveal whether representative democracy will survive and spread or decline and even disappear.

This book deals with the underlying reality that Congress is, as the framers of the Constitution intended it to be, a responsible body with limited powers. Congress was designed to determine policy and thereby to set the direction of the nation, but its policy making powers are significantly limited by the Constitution. The general objectives of the government of the United States—to establish justice, ensure domestic tranquility, provide for the common defense, promote the general welfare, and secure the blessings of liberty for future generations—were stated in the Constitution's preamble. Enactment of wise laws by Congress was to be the principal means of achieving these goals. In Section 8 of Article I, Congress is given certain specified powers, which are somewhat enlarged by the "necessary and proper" clause at the end of Section 8. But Sections 1 and 9 of Article I, as well as the Bill of Rights, considerably limit and define the extent of Congress's lawmaking power. Congress is restrained not only by constitutional limitations but also by what might be called practical and political limits. The phrase *practical limits* applies to those problems that are beyond the power of the federal government to solve; *political limits* designates those problems that involve such divisive, controversial issues that even their discussion creates intense internal tension.

These considerations lead to two fundamental lessons: first, that the Constitution and our own attitudes about personal freedom and private enterprise continue to act as restraints on Congress, and second, that if new governmental initiatives are to emerge, they must come from Congress or at least have Congress's specific assent.

Conflict, division, pressure, and tension pervade and affect every significant thing Congress does and are a recurring motif in this book. Emphasis on tension, however, should not obscure the fact that Congress as an institution constantly seeks and usually reaches agreement and consensus on important policy questions. Consensus building and consensus holding, in fact, are probably Congress's most impressive and important continuing achievements.

Congress is a complex institution with a complex role in a complex political system. Thus to reduce its character to a single theme risks misinterpreting relevant facts. Theories, conceptual frameworks, and integrative themes, in an attempt to be encompassing, can be misleading. The writer Ruth Rendell has described this problem in *Murder Being Once Done* (Doubleday & Co.: N.Y., 1972, pp. 62–63): "Inspector Baker was one of those men who, like certain too eager philosophers and scientists, form a theory and then force the facts to fit it. Anything which disturbs the pattern, however relevant, must be rejected, while insignificant data are magnified."

Specific illustrations, examples, or cases involving congressional personalities, groups, procedures, issues, and decisions are presented to convey the reality and immediacy of Congress. These vignettes are intended to fill the need for more richly detailed observation of legislative life, an idea forcefully expressed by

Richard Fenno in his presidential address to the American Political Science Association, "Observation, Context, and Sequence in the Study of Politics" (*American Political Science Review* Vol. 80 [March 1986]: 13–14). Fenno believes that too few political scientists are engaged in observation and discusses his own study of how six senators reached their respective personal decisions on the question of selling AWACS planes to Saudi Arabia.

> It should not be thought that I have told the story of AWACS. Far from it. At best I have told six little stories to feed into the larger story of AWACS. But the six stories suggest how complex the study of any large legislative decision must be, and how many different decision contexts and decision sequences are involved. They further suggest how much research room yet remains for the microscopic, observation-based analyses of the governing activity of legislative politicians.

Hopefully, this book's vignettes will enrich the reader's understanding of this powerful, complex, and altogether remarkable institution. These illustrations of policy-making processes do more than merely describe actors and actions in the congressional environment. They can also suggest to students ways they can develop empirical data and sharpen integrative skills that can help in critically assessing current congressional events.

A book such as this, which so briefly surveys so much territory, inevitably uses and summarizes much previous research, and the extent of such obligations is suggested by the footnotes and bibliographical citations. As will be seen, considerable use has been made of information published in the *Congressional Quarterly Weekly Report,* the *Almanac of American Politics* (the 1986 edition by Michael Barone and Grant Ujifusa, published by the *National Journal*); the *Congressional Directory;* the *Congressional Record;* and *Vital Statistics on Congress* (the 1984–1985 edition by Norman J. Ornstein, Thomas E. Mann, Michael J. Malbin, Allen Schick, and John F. Bibby, published by the American Enterprise Institute).

Several other acknowledgements are in order. First, I am indebted to the many students whose questions and comments over the years have helped shape my perceptions of what is important about Congress. Thanks are also due to Professor Barbara Bardes, Loyola University, Chicago; Dr. David Cingranelli, State University of New York; Dr. Robert Craig, University of New Hampshire; Dr. Burdett Loomis, University of Kansas; Professor Wayne Peak, Colorado State University; Professor Joseph Pika, University of Delaware; Professor William Shaffer, Purdue University, Indiana; and Professor Elizabeth Warren, Loyola University, Chicago, who have reviewed several draft chapters and suggested ways of improving them, and to Deans Galen Hadley and Joe Cash and Professors Howard Coker and Donald Dahlin of the University of South Dakota for expediting a data-gathering trip to Capitol Hill in early 1986.

Walter Kravitz, an old friend from graduate school at the American University in Washington and long-time legislative expert with the Library of Congress, taught me all I know (certainly not all he knows) about the amendment tree and congressional procedure. With great consideration, Ray Nedrow, a knowledgeable and dedicated administrative assistant who served a series of Nebraska representatives (Robert Simmons, Karl Stefan, and Robert Harrison) over four decades, shared his understanding with his co-workers.

Several persons have helped me gather information for particular illustrations and cases, and their understanding of their own functions have strengthened these examples: Nancy Allison, Melinda Plaisier, and Chris Sautter, associated with Rep. Frank McCloskey of Indiana; Margaret Ford and Stephen Nix, associated with McCloskey's rival, Rick McIntyre; Steve Berg of the Washington bureau of the *Minneapolis Star and Tribune;* Carole Hansen of the staff of the Senate Committee on Foreign Relations; James Mack, public affairs director of the National Machine Tool Builders Association; Diana Marino, administrative assistant to Rep. Leon Panetta of California; Doug Miller and Kevin Schieffer of the staff of Sen. Larry Pressler of South Dakota; Senator Pressler; Pete Stavrianos, administrative assistant to former Rep. (now Sen.) Tom Daschle of South Dakota; and Jim Whittinghill, administrative assistant to Rep. Tom Loeffler of Texas.

My appreciation also goes to Mildred Hendricks and Mary Jane Malthesen, who typed parts of this manuscript; to Julie Anderson, Stewart Flannery, Jill Gebaugh, Scott Henderson, and James Hieb, who performed helpful tasks cheerfully; and to my colleague, Robin Russel, who read and commented constructively on a chapter whose organization was giving me trouble. Finally, my thanks to Marie Kent and Cindy Stormer, former and present political science editors at Brooks/ Cole, who at different stages have given me important encouragement and advice. All have helped make this a better book.

Alan L. Clem
Vermillion, South Dakota

CONTENTS

III

REPRESENTATION AND APPORTIONMENT   36

IV

CONSTITUENCIES AND
THE ELECTORAL SETTING   59

VII

CONGRESSIONAL LEADERSHIP   121

VIII

CONGRESSIONAL COMMITTEES   142

IX

CONGRESSIONAL PROCEDURE   168

X

CONGRESSIONAL VOTING BEHAVIOR   193

XI

GOVERNMENTAL CONNECTIONS   208

XII

INTEREST GROUPS AND THE MEDIA   224

XIII

ETHICS, PERFORMANCE, AND REFORM   243

LIST OF
TABLES, FIGURES, AND MAPS

LIST OF TABLES

LIST OF FIGURES

LIST OF MAPS

I FOUNDATIONS, STRUCTURE, AND FUNCTIONS

Congress, our nation's representative, policy-making institution, is in the problem-solving business. Problems are one commodity of which we seem to have an inexhaustible supply. Attempting to solve them is not only difficult but hazardous to the political health of the problem solvers.

Should we raise the highway speed limit to 65 miles per hour? Send surplus wheat to the Soviet Union? Raise tariffs on imported automobiles and appliances? Send troops, weapons, or food to Central America? Ban tobacco smoking in public places? Enact a plan to cover catastrophic medical costs? Cut off trade with the Union of South Africa? Pass a constitutional amendment to allow prayers in public schools? Prohibit abortions? Raise taxes or cut spending to reduce the deficit?

Congress is constantly confronted by an immense, bewildering, shifting collection of problems impatiently waiting to be addressed and solved. Solutions require decisions, and Congress cannot make important decisions without forcing its members to make uncomfortable choices, choices that often threaten members' political careers.

Such dangers to political ambitions are not imaginary or remote. One example of the hazards of congressional life occurred in September 1987 when a coalition of church, labor, and peace groups in Iowa declared, "There is no good reason for any Iowa congressional member to continue to support Contra aid. If they vote for Contra aid one more time . . . we will work to remove them from office." This message was directed toward Sen. Charles Grassley (R.–Iowa) and Rep. Fred Grandy (R.–Iowa), who could have viewed the threat as a mild one, coming as it did from a group that represented traditionally Democratic interests. Nonetheless, the statement served as a reminder that a member's every vote is watched and that one misstep might be politically fatal.

Policy problems change from time to time. Over the past forty years, our national attention has shifted from Korea to Soviet missiles in Cuba, to Vietnam, to school desegregation, to urban unrest, to soaring oil prices, to galloping inflation, to hostages in Tehran, to international terrorism, to the collapse of the farm economy, to arms control negotiations, to imbalances in American foreign trade, to illegal immigration, to how best to encourage democracy and justice in Central America.

1

While the issues on the congressional agenda change over time, their intensity is constant. No matter what today's political problems may be, they have great potential for change, controversy, and tension. They challenge Congress to its foundations.

It is appropriate to begin the study of Congress by considering how much is expected of that institution. Let us start by considering how much the Founding Fathers expected of Congress when they defined its constitutional role.

CONGRESS AND THE AMERICAN SYSTEM

Most people regard governmental authority as a matter of administering policy, particularly of enforcing compliance and prosecuting lawbreakers. While it is of course true that any government must be able to enforce its laws, the Founding Fathers were more concerned about authority of a broader and more positive sort. In specifying the new constitutional system, the Founders first addressed two questions concerning the power of making laws: What kind of institution would enact the laws? What kinds of laws would be permitted and what kinds would be prohibited?

The European governments in existence at the time of the American Revolution were for the most part entrenched long before anyone considered the question of how laws would be enacted. In contrast, the basic rules of the American lawmaking system were established from the beginning in the Constitution.

The writers of the Constitution wanted a stronger national government than had existed under the Articles of Confederation, and they intended that Congress would be the central element of this stronger government. Congress would be elected by and responsible to the people, and it would have sufficient but limited powers. *The Federalist* (Hamilton, Madison, and Jay, 264–265) expressed these ideas.

> In framing a government which is to be administered by men over men, the great difficulty lies in this; you must first enable the government to control the governed; and in the next place oblige it to control itself. . . . But it is not possible to give to each department an equal power of self-defense. In republican government, the legislative authority necessarily predominates. The remedy for this inconveniency is to divide the legislature into different branches; and to render them, by different modes of election and different principles of action, as little connected with each other as the nature of their common functions and their common dependence on the society will admit.

Although many would argue that the presidency is more visible, innovative, and powerful than the legislative branch, the Founders believed that Congress should and would occupy the central place in the nation's government.

Preeminence of the Legislature

To the men who wrote the U. S. Constitution in 1787, the national legislature was the most central and important element of the government they were working to establish. The legislative branch of the new national government therefore became the subject of the Constitution's first article, which is the longest and most detailed segment of the Constitution. From the care given to writing this article as well as from notes and accounts of the proceedings of the constitutional convention, it is clear that the Founding Fathers were conscious of the crucial role the powers and functions assigned to Congress would play in determining the new government's success.

The Founders were fearful of the dangers inherent in an improperly constituted Congress. They were more worried by the threat that would be posed by an unlimited, unregulated Congress than they were by the threat of a tyrannical president or court. If the government was to have limited powers, it was the Congress particularly that would have to be restrained. Having managed to throw off the yoke of British government, the newly independent people of America did not wish to replace a foreign oppressor with a domestic one. The Founders wanted sufficient but clearly limited power for the government, for Congress, and for the populace.

Article I of the Constitution clearly expresses these anxieties about a too-powerful government, particularly a too-powerful Congress. At the very beginning of Article I, the Founders attempted to hedge the power of Congress. "All legislative powers herein granted," begins the first article, "shall be vested in a Congress of the United States." Notice is served at once that many kinds of legislative power would be beyond the reach of Congress. As much attention is given in Article I to what Congress (and the several state legislatures) may *not* do as to what they may do. Both the denials of legislative power and the positive grants of power serve to define and restrain Congress's role.

Among the most important positive legislative powers granted to Congress are the powers "to lay and collect taxes . . . and pay the debts" (Article I, Section 8), "to make appropriations" (Section 9), to regulate interstate and foreign commerce (Section 8), to declare war and provide for the armed forces (Section 8), to regulate immigration and naturalization of citizens (Section 8), and to regulate the appellate jurisdiction of the courts (Article III) and establish additional federal courts under the Supreme Court (Article I, Section 8). At the end of Section 8, Congress is given the general power "to make all laws necessary and proper for carrying into execution the foregoing powers, and all other powers vested by this Constitution in the government of the United States, or in any department or officer thereof." This "necessary and proper" clause has been the basis for broadening the scope of congressional authority. Finally, Article IV gives Congress jurisdiction over the territory and property of the United States and the power to admit new states.

On the negative side, the Bill of Rights (Amendments I through X) and Section 9 of Article I specify a large number of important areas where Congress may not act. It is significant that the Bill of Rights, regarded as the cornerstone of individual liberties and civil rights, begins with a set of prohibitions against legislative action by Congress.

The Constitution's first three articles develop one of the most fundamental principles of the American Constitution: the separation of powers. Congress, the president, and the courts are each given fairly explicit areas of action and responsibility. The legislative branch is to write the laws and oversee their administration. Powers given to the president and the courts generally are less specific. In the early years of the republic, there were several clashes as each branch tried to establish its turf, or area of constitutional jurisdiction. These adjustments somewhat diminished the independence of Congress. The executive branch is to carry the laws into effect and to recommend new laws to Congress. The judicial branch is to apply the law to specific controversies. These separate legislative, executive, and judicial functions and operations are modified to some extent by checks and balances designed to prevent any one branch from dominating the other branches and to force a degree of cooperation and compromise among the branches.

There has never been a fundamental change made in Article I of the Constitution, but there have been some amendments that have affected Congress in one way or another.

The Sixteenth Amendent (1913) gives Congress power to levy a direct income tax, thereby affecting the part of Section 9 of Article I that prohibited a capitation or other direct tax. The Seventeenth Amendment (also 1913) provides for direct election of U. S. senators, taking that power away from the respective state legislatures. The Twentieth Amendment (1933) changes the date of the beginning of presidential terms and of each Congress from the traditional date of March 4 to January, thereby eliminating the lame duck sessions of Congress that ran from December to March. In the Twenty-Fifth Amendment (1967), Congress is given a role in installing and later removing an acting president in the event of a temporary presidential inability; the same amendment also assigns to Congress the role of approving a president's nomination of a person to fill a vacancy in the vice-presidency. In addition to these specific references to Congress, Congress is also given authority to carry out the intent of constitutional amendments, as is evident in the final section of the Twenty-Sixth Amendment (1971): "The Congress shall have the power to enforce this article by appropriate legislation."

Divisions of Congress

As we have seen, the Founding Fathers intended to establish a national legislature with limited powers. To establish these limitations, the Founders sometimes specified certain policy areas where laws were not to be written, such as in the establishment of a religion or in the imposition of a direct tax. But many of the limitations on Congress are embedded in the complex organization of Congress itself. The Constitution requires that Congress be a divided body, meaning that Congress has difficulty acting clearly, quickly, or decisively.

There are three structural divisions of Congress: by chamber (House and Senate), by party (Democratic and Republican), and by committee.

The most obvious division of Congress is its bicamerality: The House and the

Senate are separate. They have no common leader, both generally have equal constitutional status, and both must pass a bill in identical form if the bill is to become law. This duplication of process gives the opportunity for double deliberation of legislative proposals, allowing a cooling period that may improve the final product.

The Federalist held that both chambers would be unlikely to agree on undesirable policies (Hammond and Miller, 1987, 1157–1158); an advantage of the Senate, in The Federalist's words, "is the additional impediment it must prove against improper acts of legislation" (Hamilton, et. al. 316). Proponents of legislation must satisfy both bodies if their bill is to become law; opponents get at least two chances to kill a bill or to amend it more to their liking.

Two features of the Constitution should be noted, since they affect the relative functions of the two chambers. Article I states that revenue bills must originate in the House. To this constitutional mandate may be added the tradition that appropriations (spending) measures are also initiated in the House. As a consequence, the House has augmented powers and responsibilities with respect to fiscal matters. On the other hand, the Constitution gives to the Senate the exclusive power of "advice and consent" in the matters of treaties with foreign countries (in which case a two-thirds vote is required for approval) and of presidential nominations of federal judges, ambassadors, and top administrative officials (in which case a simple majority vote is required). This gives the Senate extra influence with respect to the conduct of American foreign policy and of the judiciary.

Several other differences between the two chambers are noteworthy. The House is obviously a much larger body than the Senate. The "iron law of oligarchy" holds that the larger a body is, the smaller the group that controls it. Thus power in the House is more centralized and unevenly distributed than in the Senate. Representatives serve shorter terms than do senators, and, except in the six one-member states (Alaska, Delaware, North Dakota, South Dakota, Vermont, and Wyoming), representatives serve fewer constituents than do senators. For this reason representatives are often more concerned with parochial matters. All representatives are elected on the same day, whereas with the Senate's system of staggered six-year terms, in a given November election only one-third of the Senate seats are contested. These electoral circumstances are thought to give senators a broader, longer-range point of view. The fact that there are fewer than one-fourth as many senators as representatives may add to the greater prestige generally associated with senators.

The relative size of the House and Senate also has consequences—for the exercise of leadership, for the role of committees, and for the conduct of floor debate; these matters will be elaborated in Chapters 7, 8, and 9 respectively.

The second structural division in Congress involves political parties. Parties were not anticipated in the Constitution, but they did evolve in Congress and soon became central to its operation and leadership. In each chamber each party makes most of its internal leadership decisions in caucus. Naturally enough, the majority party in each chamber makes the more significant of these leadership choices. Majority party caucus decisions apply not only to floor leaderships, whips (number two members for their party), and chairs of committees and subcommittees but also to the staffs of the committees as well as the staffs of a host of Capitol Hill offices (clerks, sergeants-at-arms, parliamentarians, chaplains, physicians, superintendents of documents, and the like).

The third structural division of Congress is represented by its standing committees. Particularly in the House, these committees are powerful, entrenched, and jealous of their turf. If a farm bill is to be debated in the House, it will have been shaped by the House Agriculture Committee. If an arms reduction treaty is to be debated in the Senate, it will first have been reviewed by the Senate Foreign Relations Committee. To a great extent congressional power is divided by jurisdictional claims of competing committees within and between the chambers. Other less formal groups—including groups concerned with regional interests, ethnicity, individual policy issues, and ideology—have emerged in Congress over the past two centuries and serve to further disperse the powers of Congress.

There is, in short, no unity of power in Congress. Not even the speaker of the House or the majority leader of the Senate, the most powerful leaders of the two chambers, can presume to speak for Congress. Furthermore, there is no unity of congressional action. On a particular administrative action, the president or his subordinate is capable of acting quickly. On a particular court case, the Supreme Court hears the arguments, considers its options, and issues its decision. But Congress acts on a typical legislative proposal in many arenas and over an extended period of time. At each place and stage there is adequate opportunity to kill the entire proposal or to amend it so drastically that it bears little resemblance to the original proposal.

Even after Congress finally enacts a bill, that bill is subject to administrative discretion in the executive branch and may be challenged and then adjudicated in the courts. All of this makes it difficult to follow and fix responsibility for congressional actions.

FUNCTIONS OF CONGRESS

Congress performs five paramount functions.

1. It writes laws.
2. It levies taxes and spends money to carry laws into effect.
3. It represents citizens.
4. It oversees the administration of the laws it passes.
5. It approves or rejects presidential nominations and treaties.

Each of these fundamental functions merits a brief explanation.

Making Laws

The first and foremost of these functions is the power of Congress to make laws, thereby establishing governmental policy. This lawmaking power includes the power to regulate commerce and the economy; to encourage the health, education, and welfare of the people; to conserve resources; and to maintain the armed forces to protect the nation's security. A law ordinarily does four important things. It provides rules of conduct, setting forth things that must be done (driving an automobile carefully) as well as things that may not be done (stealing). A law carefully describes the individuals and organizations to be affected; some laws apply to all persons while others are directed at particular categories of people or organizations (such as physicians or airlines). A law explains what kinds of relief are to be granted, providing for the distribution of costs and benefits. Finally, a law provides a procedure for its implementation: Specified problems are to be settled in a preordained way.

Congress's power to write laws, as already noted, is somewhat limited by Article I of the Constitution. But occasionally Congress takes giant steps in establishing new government programs. The New Deal of the 1930s and the Great Society of the 1960s were particularly fruitful periods for congressional lawmaking. The former produced the Tennessee Valley Authority, the National Recovery Act, the Agricultural Adjustment Act, the Social Security Act, the Securities and Exchange Act, the Federal Communications Act, the Wagner Act (concerning labor-management relations), and many more. The latter produced fundamental, far-reaching legislation on civil rights, equal opportunity, medical care, housing, and antipoverty programs. Several hundred new laws are enacted each year, but many of them are of an incremental nature, merely extending or making minor adjustments in ongoing federal programs.

It is in the shaping of major controversial legislation that we see Congress in its characteristic partisan, contentious work.

The distinction made by Vogler and Waldman (1985, 3–4) between adversary and unitary models of Congress harkens back to more primitive times, before the maturation of national representative policy-making bodies, when unanimity (or at least very strong institutional consensus) was sought on policy questions. In adversary democracy, representatives are elected to protect the district, and Congress is involved in a bargaining process carried on by district agents; the policy that results is a compromise that satisfies enough of the district representatives to produce a majority. In unitary democracy, legislators characteristically engage in face-to-face deliberation, debate is based on the different views of the common or national interest, and conflicts are resolved by consensus.

Congress does not attempt to solve all of the nation's problems at once. Problems are necessarily taken up one by one, and many problems are avoided because they are believed to be insoluble or beyond Congress's constitutional powers. The problems Congress does wish to address are thoroughly studied by specialists and discussed within the standing committees having jurisdiction over the problem area. For any proposal, alternative solutions are presented, considered, amended, and refined. Then the proposed solutions to all of these problems are presented in order for floor consideration.

For a proposal to become law requires careful planning, exact timing, and considerable persistence on the part of legislative strategists. Barbara Nelson (1984) has divided the policy process into four distinct stages: (1) issue recognition—the issue is noticed by legislators; (2) issue adoption—the decision is made whether or not to respond; (3) issue prioritization—the new issue is placed on the legislative agenda, often at the expense of other issues awaiting legislative attention; and (4) issue maintenance—effort is expended to keep the issue on the agenda until there is sufficient support for it to pass.

Raising and Spending Money

To support the programs established by its laws, Congress must raise money (revenue) and then specifically provide for its spending (appropriation). Congress accomplishes these fiscal functions by means of three kinds of statutes. Tax or revenue laws, which must originate in the House, include taxes on individual and corporate income, tariffs on imported goods, and excise taxes on such products as tobacco, automobile tires and fuel, and liquor. Authorization bills establish programs and authorize the expenditure of specified amounts of money on these programs over a specified period of years. Appropriations bills formally set aside the money to carry out particular authorized programs. No money may be withdrawn from the U. S. Treasury unless it has been appropriated by Congress (Article I, Section 9).

The power over money is a most crucial power in any government. As a number of scholars have noted, modern legislative institutions developed into significant political institutions in modern Europe only as they gained power over the national purse. The early English experience is the classic example. In the thirteenth century most of the English national government's income came from feudal dues and land rents rather than from taxes and parliamentary subsidies to the king. The king largely decided how the revenues were to be spent since much of the revenue was considered royal possession. But as royal spending increased, new sources of revenue beyond the king's immediate capacity were needed. These sources could best be tapped by means of parliamentary approval, since Parliament represented the classes likely to bear the brunt of taxes. The nobility and higher clergy were represented in the House of Lords; the land owning farmers and townsmen were represented in the House of Commons. Parliament provided for these new taxes on a quid pro quo basis: what Parliament gave up in short-run revenues granted to support the king's adventures it recovered in long-run power to determine policies for which the revenues were needed. In other words, money power and legislative, or statutory, power grew hand in hand in Parliament (Pollard 1938, 43). Hanna Pitkin (1969, 3) notes the connection between granting taxes and representing the grievances of the realm: "And so, gradually, they began to use the threat of refusing consent to taxes as a lever against the king, to force him to consider their petitions and grievances."

Representing People and Groups

Historically, national lawmaking bodies such as the English Parliament were representative and advisory bodies before their legislative functions were well developed. The king made requests for money, troops, or other support, and Parliament presented the attitudes of the nobles, clergy, and common folk. In the legislatures that endured, it was the representative element (such as the House of Commons in England rather than the House of Lords) that became more powerful and popular. One of the basic problems for the American Founding Fathers was how to make Congress representative. The House of Representatives was designed to be as representative as possible, given many antidemocratic circumstances of the times, such as slavery and the property requirement to vote. Each state's allotment, or apportionment, of seats in the House was based on its population relative to the national population, and each member was to be chosen by popular election. No federal standards for voting eligibility for U. S. representatives are set forth in the Constitution; whoever voted for members of the state legislatures was eligible to vote for U. S. representatives. Mathematically, the Senate was less representative than the House in that each state was awarded the same number of senators irrespective of relative state population. Politically, the Senate was less representative in that a state's two senators were to be chosen by the state legislature rather than by the general voters. Direct popular election of U. S. senators did not occur until the Seventeenth Amendment was adopted in 1913. The Constitution thus provides that the American people are equitably represented in the House of Representatives and that the American states are equitably represented in the Senate. Both House and Senate are elected by and may be considered representative of the people. Each representative is elected by the voters of one particular congressional district and is their sole representative in the House. Each senator is elected by and represents his or her entire state.

More indirectly, members of Congress reflect the dominant features of their constituencies. In industrial states, labor organizations are powerfully represented. In more rural states, farm organizations and small-town business associations will be the interests emphasized. Many interest groups exert influence on Congress through the representatives and senators who serve areas where these groups are large, well organized, and vocal. Congressional representation is essentially parochial rather than national; the sum of all these parochial interests, however, does not necessarily add up to the national interest.

Congress tries to represent the forces, demands, and pressures arising in a diverse country. We as a nation expect Congress to represent us in a way and to a degree that presidents, administrators, and judges cannot. Congress is a place where the nation can bring its important problems for discussion and resolution. Yet

Congress is not a microcosm of the nation; its members are not a cross section of the American public. Higher percentages of whites, males, wealthy, and educated people are found in Congress than in the general public. But Congress is expected— and tries—to give voice to and listen to all meaningful factions. Congress is thereby able to weigh the relative merits of various demands and to play off one interest or set of interests against other interests to find compromise solutions that are likely to please the largest number of concerned people while displeasing the fewest. While not everyone or every group can be satisfied, Congress usually finds a way to resolve even the bitterest, most intractable disputes in such a way that the political system can endure to work out other compromises as necessity requires.

In the following prepared statement by a member of Congress, Sen. Larry Pressler (R.–S. D.), vocalizes the interests of a particular constituency, in this case small prairie cities (Pressler 1987, 25).

Defending Constituents:
The Essential Air Service Program

Access to air service is one of the key elements of South Dakota's economic development plans. Businesses looking to relocate in South Dakota cities almost always cite adequate air service as a crucial factor in their decision. However, we are now experiencing the harmful consequences of the Airline Deregulation Act of 1978. As I predicted when I voted against airline deregulation, we are seeing loss of service and increased prices to rural America, safety deterioration, and dominance by a handful of carriers. True to my fears, the ill effects of deregulation abound.

The Airline Deregulation Act of 1978 included a ten-year phase-out period for the Essential Air Service (EAS) program, which was created to guarantee that our smaller cities and towns would not lose air service. Since passage of the 1978 Act, the EAS program has continued to dwindle and is scheduled to terminate at the end of September 1988. During the decline of the EAS program, we have seen the gradual demise of air service to small cities. If we allow this program to terminate completely, it will result in certain death for air service to the affected communities.

South Dakota has seven EAS points at Pierre, Aberdeen, Watertown, Mitchell, Huron, Brookings, and Yankton. Were it not for the EAS program, each of these cities would be in danger of losing air service.

Airline deregulation has had a drastic impact on South Dakota's air service. In 1978 there were 104,801 outbound passengers fron the seven South Dakota EAS designations. By 1986 that number had decreased to 56,687. During that same time, EAS support decreased by approximately 75 percent. If

Congress does not act soon, the results will be even more detrimental to South Dakota's air service and its program of economic development.

I am committed to retaining adequate air service in America's smaller cities and have joined in sponsoring legislation which will not only extend the current EAS program for ten more years, but also enhance it by increasing service and improving aircraft.

I am well aware of the importance of air transportation to the municipalities and communities of South Dakota and will continue fighting for the Essential Air Service program. Please feel free to let me know your views.

Overseeing the Administration

Congress has an obvious interest in seeing to it that the laws it passes are executed promptly and properly. Therefore, a good deal of its time is spent in legislative oversight, that is, reviewing the work of executive agencies.

Much legislative oversight is done through the congressional standing committees, which have jurisdiction over the activities of particular departments (for instance the Armed Services Committee oversees the Defense Department, and so on). In committee hearings and reports and in the offices of members of Congress, there are abundant opportunities to monitor administrative activities, to criticize and modify executive behavior, and to see that the agencies satisfactorily address constituents' problems.

Congress's control over the administration is even more extensive than is suggested by the foregoing. Congress establishes programs and departments and appropriates the money needed to operate them. This power affords Congress considerable opportunity to assert legislative oversight. Further, Congress by law has established the civil service system, which governs the conditions under which most executive branch employees work.

Providing Advice and Consent

As noted earlier, the advice and consent function is performed only by the Senate. A large part of the Senate's work involves reviewing the conduct of U. S. foreign policy. Treaty and appointment confirmation hearings and debates give the Senate abundant opportunity to challenge the president in a highly visible way, as evident in 1977–1978 in the debate over the Panama Canal treaties presented by President Jimmy Carter and in 1979–1980 in the review of the ill-fated Strategic Arms Limitation Treaty (SALT II).

Whether the White House and Congress are controlled by the same party or by different parties has a major effect on congressional ratification of presidential nominations and treaties. However, cooperation between branches of government can occur even if branches are controlled by different parties, just as confrontation can occur if only one party is in charge. Since World War II, party discord between the White House and the Senate has existed in 1947–1948, 1955–1960, 1969–1976, and 1987–1988 (a total of eighteen years), while party concord has existed in 1949–1954, 1961–1968, and 1977–1986 (a total of twenty-four years). (Table 1-1 shows presidential and congressional party control for each postwar biennium.)

In addition to the five essential functions, Congress has potential but seldom exercised power with respect to (1) declaring war; (2) proposing amendments to the Constitution; (3) redefining the jurisdiction of the federal courts; (4) electing the president and vice-president in case the electoral college voting is inconclusive (as happened in the wake of both the 1800 and 1824 elections); (5) approving the appointment of a new vice-president when there is a vacancy in that office (as in Congress's approval of Gerald Ford in 1973 and of Nelson Rockefeller a year later); and (6) removing presidents, other administrative officers, and judges from office through the impeachment process.

As it performs these functions, Congress at the same time educates the public as to the details of various policy proposals, thereby hopefully raising the level of public discourse on public questions. Congress also, while representing the general public, performs services for individual constituents and groups who have established access to their respective members.

In summary, Congress is a central institution of American government. It has all the strengths and all the flaws associated with democracy, individuality, ambition, diversity, and freedom. We should not be surprised to find in Congress greed and generosity, patriotism and pomposity, intelligence and intransigence, statesmanship and stubbornness, sensitivity and selfishness, virtue and venality.

CONFLICT AND TENSION

Congress is thus an institution confronted at every turn by conflict. The Founders knew that conflict was inevitable in human society and believed management of this conflict to be the main role of government in general, and of Congress in particular. These conflicts are imposed on an institution that is seriously divided in its structure and, as we have seen, has tremendous responsibility but limited power under the Constitution.

Congress receives unremitting pressure from several sources, each of which

Table 1-1. Party control of executive and legislative branches following each biennial election since the end of World War II

Control of Congress	Control of the presidency		
	Democratic	Republican	Total
Democratic	1948, 1950, 1960, 1962, 1964, 1966, 1976, 1978	1954, 1956, 1958, 1968, 1970, 1972, 1974, 1986	16
Split	—	1980, 1982, 1984	3
Republican	1946	1952	2
Total	9	12	21

has expectations that produce divergent, contradictory directions. The most notable sources of pressure are the president; national and state political party leaders; ethnic, economic, and ideological groups; and the individual constituencies.

Conflict, division, and pressure inevitably result in tension. Congress as an aggregate institution and its members as individual politicians are constantly forced to make choices that are not easy; whatever choice is made, an important individual or group is likely to be offended.[1] Some of the more obvious and critical tensions besetting Congress follow. (Numbers following each item refer to the chapters wherein each topic is treated.)

- Congress versus the president (1, 11)
- the House versus the Senate (1, 2, 8, 9)
- long-range, general policy concerns versus short-range, specific policy concerns (or what the economic historian Thomas Sowell [1987] has referred to as conflicts of vision as opposed to conflicts of interest) (1, 13)
- demands of the member's office versus demands of the member's home (6)
- demands of the member's district versus demands of Capitol Hill (4, 6)
- the Democratic party versus the Republican party (10)
- the national interest versus the constituency's interest (3)
- the common good versus special group interests (1, 3, 12)
- the member's personal convictions and judgment versus the constituency's preferences (3)
- conservative interests (often but not always seen as buttressing the status quo) versus liberal interests (often seen as attempting to redistribute wealth and influence) (1, 10)
- doing the job (and forgetting the credit) versus getting reelected (and forgetting the duties) (4, 5, 6, 12)
- being an independent member versus following the leaders (or going along to get along) (7)
- concentrating on constituency work versus concentrating on policy and committee work (4, 6)
- devoting time to lobbyists or press versus devoting time to party, committee, or constituent work (6, 12)
- being conventional, habitual, incremental, and stable versus being original, innovative, creative, and unstable (1, 6, 13)
- operating in a consensual, accommodative style versus operating in a polarizing, adversarial style (1, 7)
- being objective-oriented (if necessary changing or defying the rules and conventions in order to reach important goals) versus being rule-oriented (using the rules and playing by the book) (9)
- Making policy versus overseeing the execution of policy (1, 8, 11)

These are the chief tensions confronting congressional members that are explored throughout this book. Tension is a pervasive aspect of Congress's organization, rules, and tasks. While tension exists in other vocations, congressional tension is notable for its persistence over time, its visibility to other political actors, its intensity, and its public and official nature. Tension is not necessarily bad; it can be creative and positive as well as destructive and negative. The determining factor in whether tension is positive or negative depends on how effectively Congress handles the pressures that confront it.

SUMMARY

The Constitution establishes Congress as a policy-making body responsible to the people, a body having considerable but not unlimited powers and a divided structure. Congress has great potential, but usually its important decisions can be made only with a great deal of internal cooperation, coordination, compromise, and consensus. Writing laws and representing people are Congress's two most obvious and significant functions. The oft-chronicled weaknesses and failures of Congress are caused in part by the ways the Constitution constrains Congress and by the fact that Congress is an institution composed of men and women who are, like the rest of humanity, imperfect and fallible.

NOTE

1. For an interesting view of the tensions endured by members as they cast votes almost every day "in ways that hurt them," see Hendrik Hertzberg, "The Education of Mr. Smith: A Wise Politician Exchanges His Idealism for the Morality of Pragmatism" (1986). The article recalls the popular, simplistic movie "Mr. Smith Goes to Washington" (1939), starring Jimmy Stewart.

REFERENCES

DE GRAZIA, ALFRED (ed.). *Congress: The First Branch of Government*. Garden City, N. Y.: Doubleday/Anchor, 1967.

DODD, LAURENCE C., and OPPENHEIMER, BRUCE I. (eds.). *Congress Reconsidered*. 3rd ed. Washington, D. C.: Congressional Quarterly Press, 1985.

HAMILTON, ALEXANDER, MADISON, JAMES, and JAY, JOHN. *The Federalist* or *The New Constitution*. Everyman's Library ed. New York: E. P. Dutton and Company, 1911. (Originally published 1787–1788)

HAMMOND, THOMAS H., and MILLER, GARY J. "The Core of the Constitution." *American Political Science Review* 81 (December 1987):1155–1174.

HERTZBERG, HENDRIK. "The Education of Mr. Smith: A Wise Politician Exchanges His Idealism for the Morality of Pragmatism." *Esquire* 105, no. 2 (February 1986): 37–38, 40.

JONES, CHARLES O. *The United States Congress*. Homewood, Ill.: Dorsey Press, 1982.

MANN, THOMAS E., and ORNSTEIN, NORMAN J. (eds.). *The New Congress*. Washington, D. C.: American Enterprise Institute, 1981.

NELSON, BARBARA. *Making an Issue of Child Abuse: Political Agenda Setting for Social Problems*. Chicago: University of Chicago Press, 1984.

NICHOLS, ROY F. *Blueprints for Leviathan: American Style*. New York: Atheneum, 1963.

PITKIN, HANNA. *Representation*. New York: Atherton Press, 1969.

POLLARD, A. F. *The Evolution of Parliament*. London: Longmans, Green, 1938.

PRESSLER, LARRY. "Defending Constituents: The Essential Air Service Program." In *South Dakota Municipalities* (September 1987): 25.

SOWELL, THOMAS. *A Conflict of Vision: Ideological Origins of Political Struggles*. New York: Morrow, 1987.

VOGLER, DAVID J. and WALDMAN, SIDNEY. *Congress and Democracy*. Washington, D. C.: Congressional Quarterly Press, 1985.

II EVOLUTION AND VARIATION

Lawmaking assemblies did not appear at the same time in the various nations of Europe, evolve in the same pattern, or follow a standard timetable. Legislative institutions and democracy matured irregularly and haphazardly, if at all. The evolution of these political institutions in Europe over the past millenium helped set the stage for American independence and influenced the organization and functions of our Congress.

The term *representative legislative assemblies* seems unnecessarily cumbersome, but the verbiage is important in conveying three important ideas about these institutions. First, the institutions in a real sense represent and take serious account of the needs, desires, and interests of the people. Second, the institutions produce the laws that govern the state rather than being mere "rubber stamps," or advisory bodies without any real power. Third, the members assemble regularly and visibly and reach their decisions among themselves with a minimum of outside interference.

Robert Dahl (1966, xi), noting the close relationship among representative legislative bodies, political parties, and public elections, writes of "the three great milestones in the development of democratic institutions—the right to participate in governmental decisions by casting a vote, the right to be represented, and the right of an organized opposition to appeal for votes against the government in elections and in parliament."

All this should be familiar to American students, but what is not often realized is that these principles applied in the United States long before they did in most European nations and have become common in the Western world only in the past century. Furthermore, it is not necessarily true that representative democracy is more just, honest, wise, efficient, or equitable than other systems. While there is considerable basis for an argument defending the superiority of representative government, the success of such governments depends on the time and place. Representative democracy, like any system, has advantages and disadvantages.

This chapter presents a brief survey of the evolution of national legislatures from the ancient world to our modern Congress. The last half of the chapter places Congress in clearer perspective by comparing its organization and powers to those of foreign and American state legislatures.

16

ANCIENT AND MEDIEVAL ASSEMBLIES

Deliberative bodies originated in antiquity, but Greek and Roman civilizations, for all their merit, did little to create powerful national legislatures as we know them today. Councils and forums existed, but no permanent, powerful, and popular body had authority to make laws. Greek and Roman councils could not halt the concentration of political power in leaders such as Alexander the Great, Julius Caesar, and Augustus Caesar, who built their vast empires by means of military power. As J. A. O. Larson (1955, 157) notes: "From the time of Alexander the Great to Theodosius the Great and beyond, the world relied too exclusively on strong men for salvation." The Greeks believed that "the collective judgment of the masses" was superior to "the judgment of experts" and were loath to give power to representative institutions (Larson 1955, 1).

Our culture relies on the superiority of a government of laws rather than a government of men. Inherent in this form of government is the fact that laws are intended to affect each person equally and are to be applied neutrally and without favoritism or prejudice. In ancient and medieval times, law had a much different character. The idea of the law as specific published statements that guide the systematic actions of governmental officials would have been beyond the understanding of most people in those times.

In primitive tribal societies, law was thought to be divinely established and thus beyond the power of human beings to change. Canon law developed in Europe as the first modern legal system in the West and defined and affected not only ecclesiastical powers and jurisdictions but also criminal law, marriage, inheritance, property, and contracts. Secular law evolved side by side with canon law and included feudal law, manorial law, mercantile law, and urban law; each of these divisions affected certain limited classes of people. At the end of the medieval period, royal, or national, systems of law grew under the aegis of great early lawgivers such as Roger II of the Norman kingdom of Sicily (1112–1154), Philip Augustus of France (1180–1223), Frederick Barbarossa of the Holy Roman Empire (1152–1190), and Henry II of England (1154–1189).

Scholars have summarized the evolution of legislatures in Europe since medieval times by identifying four distinct stages of development of national representative assemblies (Beard and Lewis 1932, 223–240).

First, parliaments representing "estates of the realm" (nobility, clergy, landed gentry, town officials) met to vote taxes for the royal treasury;

Second, parliaments began also to present grievances to the king and began to debate legislative proposals;

Third, gradually, culminating in revolutions in England in the seventeenth century which deposed Charles I and James II, Parliament wrested lawmaking and tax-voting power from the king; and

Fourth, representation was extended beyond the traditional privileged groups to include, finally, universal adult suffrage.

Only gradually and irregularly, if at all, did popular or common assemblies in particular places attain sufficient permanence, information and intelligence, and independence to be considered significant lawmaking assemblies. In England, almost alone of European nations and almost by chance, Parliament proved to be a persistent and adaptable institution. It became a nationalizing rather than a parochial or class-oriented force as were national assemblies in most other countries, and it grew in influence as the nation grew in power.

THE ENGLISH EXPERIENCE

The origins of modern Parliament may be traced to the thirteenth century. In 1265 the king summoned to confer with him not only nobles and bishops but also two knights from each shire (county) and two burgesses from each borough (town). Nobles and bishops were "lords," knights and burgesses were "commons." Thirty years later (a long lapse between legislative sessions!) Edward I convened the Model Parliament, similarly constituted. To be called to parley with the king was a doubtful honor; usually the king wanted more money to carry on his wars and other projects, which necessitated increasing taxes. Taxes were no more popular then than they are today. Over the years, as it assented to the taxes requested by the king, Parliament gained power over legislation. In effect, Parliament purchased its legislative powers with the taxes it allowed to be levied on the people. As Parliament rather than the King supplied sources of money, there occurred a shift in the locus of political power. Parliament had increasing influence on policy and was frequently able to control who sat on the throne. Parliament deposed Richard II in 1399, replacing him with Henry IV of the House of Lancaster, and twice in the seventeenth century it ousted a reigning monarch (Charles I and James II).

But Parliament was slow to adopt a modern view of its role. It was jealous and protective of its growing powers and privileges, yet it did not regard itself as the central, vital instrument of government. It adopted a passive role, not expecting to be summoned to meet unless there was serious financial trouble, corruption, or mismanagement. It functioned chiefly to rectify mistakes or, as in the fifteenth century, to provide the king, when he desired, with a particularly full and representative council.

The next century was dominated by the intimidating figures of four Tudor monarchs: Henry VII (1485–1509), Henry VIII (1509–1547), Mary (1553–1558), and Elizabeth I (1558–1603). The Tudors generally found the House of Commons to be a "necessary but pliant tool" (Sayles 1974, 135). By the end of the Tudor period, Parliament had reached its status as an essential partner in the lawmaking process. The English historian J. E. Neale (1963, 307) concludes that "the House of Commons reached maturity in Elizabeth's reign." According to Neale (1963, 289, 306) that body included most of the famous men of the Elizabethan age, among them Philip Sydney, Walter Raleigh, Francis Bacon, Edward Coke, and Francis Drake.

Birth and education, expert knowledge, practical experience, and corporate solidarity—all were present in abundant measure in the Elizabethan House of Commons. And so was character. It was an assembly which never failed to display high and independent spirit, moral and religious fervor, and patriotism.

Parliament gained considerable power under the Stuart monarchs who followed the Tudors after the death of Elizabeth in 1603. The early Stuarts, James I (of the King James Bible) and Charles I, believed in the idea of the divine right of kings, but many of their subjects did not. Charles I was executed in 1649, and forty years later Parliament ousted his son, James II, and called to the throne James's daughter, Mary, who had been raised a Protestant, and her husband, William of Orange. The settlement made it abundantly clear that Parliament would control critical matters of state in the future. The Declaration of Rights (1689) made Parliament rather than the king the initiator of policy, outlawed armies raised without Parliamentary consent, and established the policy that money was provided to the monarch only to implement policies agreeable to Parliament (Smith 1971, 273).

In the next century, the tradition was established that the ministry, or cabinet, would fall whenever the Commons by vote failed to support it. As Parliament continued to evolve as the nation's lawmaking assembly, a permanent two-party system became institutionalized in the House of Commons. The two parties in the partisan division of Commons gradually changed over the decades: Tory versus Whig in the eighteenth century, Conservative versus Liberal in the nineteenth century, and Conservative versus Labour by the middle third of the twentieth century. The past three hundred years have witnessed a steady reduction in the powers of the monarch and the House of Lords, a broadening of the suffrage, the maturation of the party system, and the evolution of a cabinet system under which the prime minister and his ministry remain in power only so long as they command the support of a majority in the House of Commons.

In summary, five centuries of English parliamentary experience (roughly the period from 1250 to 1750) offered to the modern world the essential institutions, processes, and habits of representative democracy. These essential contributions include the following ideas:

1. that policy should be made and financed by a particular responsible body
2. that the lawmaking body should be chosen by, responsible to, and representative of a substantial portion of the people
3. that members of the legislature be free of coercion or intimidation by any external element, including not only freedom to speak in debate but freedom to travel to and from legislative sessions
4. that decisions should be made by formal, orderly processes, with the majority ruling
5. that minority interests should always have the right to be heard, particularly

when the minority or its point of view is unorthodox, odious, or out of step
with public opinion
6. that every citizen in voting for a member, and every member in voting on a
legislative question, should have a vote weighted equally with the vote of
other citizens or members (that is, political equality)
7. that debate and division on legislative questions should be conducted with
fair and clearly stated rules
8. that governmental affairs generally, and legislative business particularly,
should be conducted in a reasonably public way

No system ever existed that performed perfectly on all these factors, but the
American Founding Fathers believed that these principles could be achieved and
maintained in a national legislative assembly. The Founders also probably realized
that a good deal of common sense, luck, skill, and understanding would be needed
to sustain the system.

THE EVOLUTION OF CONGRESS

The American Founders modeled the form and functions of Congress on several
institutions: the English Parliament; the colonial legislatures which operated under
British rule; the Continental Congress of the era of the Revolutionary War; the
Congress operating under the Articles of Confederation; and the legislatures of the
thirteen original states. Each body provided its unique lessons and experiences. The
first constitutional Congress convened in early 1789 in New York City, and the date
of March 4 was to become (until the Twentieth Amendment was ratified in 1933)
the traditional day for inauguration of the president and for swearing in the new
Congress. Each chamber developed a procedure for handling bills and performing
other business, appointed standing committees to consider bills in various policy
categories, and evolved political party machinery to choose leaders and plan
legislative strategy. These essential functions and institutions were in place by the
middle third of the nineteenth century, when Henry Clay, Daniel Webster, John C.
Calhoun, and Thomas Hart Benton were among the most prominent congressional
figures. The size of Congress grew with the territorial and population expansion of
the nation until House membership was stabilized at 435 following the census of
1910 (see table 2-1).

In its first century, Congress played a central role in debating and resolving
such fundamental questions as westward expansion (witness the Missouri Com-
promise, the Kansas-Nebraska Act, the annexation of Texas, the wresting of the
Southwest from Mexico, and the purchase of the lands that now comprise Oregon,
Idaho, Washington, and Alaska), the abolition of slavery, and the conduct of the
Civil War and the reconstruction period that followed.

During the nineteenth century, a noteworthy development was the growth of
the power of the speaker of the House. Henry Clay greatly enhanced the power of

Table 2-1.   Growth in U. S. population and size of House of Representatives and Senate for selected census years

Year	Population (millions)	Number of senators	Population per senator (thousands)	Number of repre- sentatives	Population per representative (thousands)
Original (1789)	—	26	—	65	—
1800	5	32	152	141	35
1820	9	48	187	213	42
1840	16	52	306	223	71
1860	30	68	435	241	123
1880	49	76	650	325	152
1900	75	90	828	386	193
1920	106	96	1,101	435	243
1940	131	96	1,365	435	301
1960	179	100	1,786	435	410
1980	227	100	2,265	435	521

Source: U. S. Bureau of the Census, 1975, p. 1084, supplemented by 1980 census data.

the speaker during eleven sessions beginning in 1811 and ending in 1825. The dominance of the office of speaker became more permanently established under the strong leadership of James G. Blaine (1869–1875), Thomas B. Reed (1889–1891, 1895–1899), and Joseph G. Cannon (1903–1911). The Congress of the post–Civil War decades was analyzed by Woodrow Wilson in his doctoral dissertation, later published as *Congressional Government: A Study in American Politics* (1956), and described in Henry Adams's novel, *Democracy: An American Novel* (1952), both important historical sources. During this time, the speaker came to dominate the House Rules Committee and thereby to control the committee assignments of members and to determine the fate of individual bills.

During his term in the early 1900s, Speaker Cannon became particularly domineering and thereby offended a growing number of members. Cannon was brought down by a revolt led by Progressive Republican George Norris, a young representative from Nebraska. The revolt led to permanent reforms and had the general result of decentralizing power in the House. The speaker could no longer dominate the Rules Committee or make assignments to the standing committees. These changes gave the various standing committees real control over the content and progress of their bills and thereby made committee membership a more significant factor in the careers of individual representatives. In effect, the various committees rather than the central majority party leadership became the determining factor in the fate of legislation in the House. Rather than being chosen by the party leaders, committee chairmen were determined automatically by their seniority status. The seniority system, whereby members' committee rank positions de-pended solely on their relative lengths of continuous service on the committee, meant that members could rise to positions of significance without regard for the wishes of the speaker or floor leader of their party.

An important change occurred in 1913 with the adoption of the Seventeenth

Amendment, which provided that U. S. senators in the future were to be elected by popular vote rather than by the respective state legislatures.

The chief political developments of the last decades of the nineteenth century and the first four decades of the twentieth century included (1) the monetary issue and its relation to the financial status of farmers; (2) such progressive issues as direct election of senators, the advent of primary elections to give the population more control over party nominations and party leadership, greater governmental regulation of business, adoption of the income tax, and attempts to stabilize farm income by various government controls and subsidies; and (3) a wide range of regulatory, labor, and social welfare programs brought into being during President Franklin D. Roosevelt's first term (1933–1937).

Another important stage in the evolution of Congress came with the Legislative Reorganization Act of 1946. This reduced the number of committees in Congress from forty-five to twenty in the House and from thirty-three to fifteen in the Senate. This resulted in a reduction of the number of independent sources of power over legislation and simplified jurisdictional assignment of bills to committees in certain policy areas. To a large extent, the system of committee jurisdiction over bills in the two chambers became parallel (for instance, an agriculture committee existed in each chamber).

The 1946 act also increased the staff assistance for committees and for individual members. Whereas before World War II the typical House member might have a staff of one or two persons to handle correspondence and other business, the typical congressional member in the 1950s had a staff of four or five persons. Salaries and retirement plans were made more attractive for members. Provisions of the act designed to improve the budget process and regulate lobbying did not work out very well, however. (These topics are further explored in chapters 11 and 12.)

Congress in the postwar period took a lead in developing U. S. foreign aid programs to rebuild the war-torn world, in planning and financing the interstate highway system, in supporting the space program, in strengthening civil rights, in expanding federal urban renewal and antipoverty programs, in revitalizing state-level initiatives through revenue sharing, and in tax reform.

Even with the ambitious policy initiatives of the 1960s under President Lyndon Johnson, there arose a flood of complaints that Congress hid decision making from public scrutiny, bottled up legislation, and resisted new ideas. Responding to such complaints, Congress established a number of piecemeal but significant changes in its operation. Congressional business began to be conducted in a more open way, with fewer secret committee and caucus meetings and, eventually, with live television coverage of House and Senate sessions. The Democratic caucus removed the chairs of several standing committees, thereby making the committees of the House less independent of the party caucus than before. The Democratic caucus adopted the practice of secret balloting so that leaders who were being challenged could not wreak vengeance on dissident elements of the caucus. Subcommittee chairmanships were divided among a larger number of members, thereby increasing the number of members in significant roles, and subcommittees were made more independent of action from the parent committee. The Rules Committee in the House continued to decline in influence, and since the early 1960s has become less obstructionist and more an arm of the Democratic party leadership. Each chamber attempted, with indifferent success, to regulate lobbying activities more stringently and to establish and enforce higher standards of ethical behavior. (This point will be elaborated more fully in the final chapter.) Congressional budget procedures were fundamentally reformed, new budget committees were added in each chamber, and a Congressional Budget Office was established. In the Senate, changes in the cloture rule made it a little easier to end filibusters. (Chapter 9 will treat the subject of procedure.)

Some of these changes have had unforeseen ramifications. For instance, the growth of television as a national news medium and the televising of congressional proceedings have tended to increase the public's awareness of national issues and personalities at the expense of parochial matters. Oversight is a function that attracts the attention of more and more members. Many bright, young, ambitious members consider oversight activity a better means of gaining notice and prestige than drafting or amending legislation. National attention seems especially easy to capture when members criticize administrative agencies and bureaucrats. Nelson Polsby (in Mann and Ornstein, 1981, 28–30) notes that this increase in public attention has led to more conflict and tension between Congress and the president and other elements of the political system.

CONGRESS IN COMPARATIVE PERSPECTIVE

While Congress in large part was shaped by the experiences of earlier national assemblies, it differs today from most of the world's legislatures in several important ways.

First, the American system of separation of powers affects the way Congress deals with the chief executive and with the execution of policy. The British Parliament chooses the prime minister, who with the ministry is responsible for both enacting and executing policy. In the United States, the president is chosen by the electoral college, not by Congress. Congress writes laws and must zealously watch the executive branch if it is to ensure that the laws are being executed as intended. This watchdog role is critical whether the same or the opposing political party is in power in the executive branch.

Second, parliaments are generally organized by much stronger political parties than either of the major political parties in this country. Members of Congress can vote contrary to the wishes of the party leaders with impunity. A member of the British House of Commons who shows too much independence in debating or voting on bills is not likely to receive his party's nomination at the next general election. Parliamentary governments resign when the leaders lose a test vote, and national elections are called as a consequence, whereas congressional leaders are chosen for the full two-year term and can reasonably expect to be reelected to their same leadership offices for as long as they remain in Congress. (Leadership in Congress is explored in chapter 7.)

The perfect legislature would be one that fits comfortably into the traditions and culture of its country. The American Congress has been reasonably successful and secure as the basic institution of American national government. It has served as something of a model for many regional, national, and international legislative bodies, such as the new European Parliament. But since nations vary, there is no standard model for an effective national legislature, and thus no two legislatures are exactly alike in structure, size, powers, organization, and procedures.

Identifying the essential ways in which legislatures differ can enhance an understanding of legislatures in general and of our Congress in particular. The following comparison of contemporary legislative assemblies is divided into three parts: their general powers, their geographical and architectural environments, and their organizational and procedural arrangements.

Powers

Legislatures are more central and significant in some nations than in others. In authoritarian regimes, popularly elected bodies are usually mere window dressing. In democratic systems, the national legislature is a significant center of power. In most European democracies, the parliamentary system of government prevails, with the prime minister and the entire governmental ministry appointed by and dependent on a majority vote in the assembly. In a multiparty parliamentary system, the ministry often must include members from several different parties, those that happen to make up the current governing coalition. In a two-party parliamentary system or in a multiparty system where one party has won a majority of the legislative seats, all of the ministers may come from one party. Typically in parliamentary systems, a government stays in power as long as it maintains majority support in the legislature. If the government loses a test vote (one on which the ministry promises to dissolve parliament and call for new national elections if the governing party loses) or if it decides the time is ripe for a national election, the prime minister calls for dissolution of the current assembly.

The president of the United States is elected by the people through the mechanism of the electoral college. Having different constituencies, the executive and legislative branches are often controlled by different parties, whereas in parliamentary nations executive and legislative functions are merged. In the American presidential system of government, power is diffused, and it is not easy to fix responsibility for political action (or inaction). This diffusion of power and lessening of legislative authority was precisely what the Founding Fathers had in mind when they provided for the principle of separation of powers.

Geographical Matters

To a lesser but sometimes significant extent, the importance of a national legislature depends in part on the geographical concentration or diffusion of power. Both the

United States and Canada are federal systems in that the states (in the United States) and provinces (in Canada) are semiautonomous and have a good deal of independent legislative authority. These federal systems contrast with unitary systems, such as the United Kingdom where shires are administrative subdivisions that merely carry out national policy, and confederations, such as the United States under the Articles of Confederation where the power of the constituent unit is greater within its own boundaries than the power of the nation. The term *confederation,* according to an eminent political geographer (Pounds 1972, 47), is "reserved for federal organizations of a very loose order."

The exercise of power can also be affected by physical position, such as the arrangement of seats inside the legislative chamber. One basic arrangement is that followed in the U. S. House of Representatives, with the speaker's dais in the middle along one of the long walls of an oblong room, with members seated in semicircular rings, all facing the speaker. The semicircular arrangement has been modified to a horseshoe shape in the legislative chamber of Manitoba, Canada, and in the state senate chamber in the state of Wisconsin. The second basic form is that found in the British (and Canadian) House of Commons, where the speaker's dais occupies one of the short sides of an oblong chamber, with the members seated along the two longer walls, the opposing parties facing one another, and none of the members facing the speaker.

The size, shape, and seating arrangements of legislative chambers are not trivial matters; the atmosphere created by these arrangements has much to do with the way legislative business is conducted. For example, the Vietnam peace talks in Paris were stalled for months in 1969 because of disagreements over the arrangement of tables and chairs for the various delegations. Winston Churchill insisted that, after the House of Commons was damaged by Nazi bombs during World War II, the chamber be rebuilt in its former shape and size, believing that the confrontational arrangement of seats for the government and opposition parties and the limited number of places added to a sense of urgency in conducting parliamentary business. For further examples, consider from your own experience how the conduct of official business by city councils, state legislative committees, and church and fraternal organizations is affected by the relative positions of speakers, members, petitioners, witnesses, staff professionals, clerks, and the public.

Institutional Arrangements

National lawmaking assemblies vary in several siginificant ways. Congress and many other national legislative assemblies are composed of two chambers, each having substantially equal and coordinate powers. In Germany and Japan, one of the chambers has more power than the other. It has been argued that a two-chamber legislature is weaker because of its division into two parts. Bicameralism makes it more difficult for a legislature to pass a bill and easier for executive branch leaders or interest groups to kill a bill. There are a few single-chambered (unicameral) legislatures. The British Parliament, though bicameral in form and theory, is virtually a unicameral body, since the power of the House of Lords even to delay legislation is severely constrained. Israel's Knesset is a unicameral body, as is Nebraska's state legislature. This arrangement means that the legislature can act more quickly, without having to wait for agreement on the part of a companion chamber.

Legislative leaders are chosen in a wide variety of ways, sometimes by some external authority and sometimes internally by the members of the legislature itself. The speaker of the British House of Commons is chosen by the members, as is the American speaker. However, in the House of Commons, the speaker is a neutral presiding officer, whereas in the House of Representatives, the speaker is expected to be a partisan officer upholding the interests of the party. Though often absent, the presiding officer of the U. S. Senate is the vice-president of the United States; the president pro tempore or some other senator usually presides in the vice-president's place. In most American states, the lieutenant governor presides over the upper chamber of the state legislature, and a speaker presides over the lower chamber.

In the United States there is virtually universal adult suffrage; eligibility to serve is restricted only by age (at least twenty-five years of age for the House, thirty for the Senate), citizenship, and residence in the state. Even so, on average over the past generation, a little less than half of the electorate has taken the trouble to vote in congressional elections (Ornstein et al., 1984, 40).

Two parties compete for control of the American Congress. Other legislatures differ in the number of political parties represented. In such legislatures (as in our own) critical areas of evaluation include the relative strength of the parties, how competitive legislative campaigns actually are, how parties nominate candidates, and how frequently party control of the legislature changes.

Other questions when comparing legislatures have to do with limitations on the time served by individual members: How long are the terms in the legislature? Are all members elected at the same time, or are the terms staggered so that only some of the incumbents face reelection in a given year? Are there limits on how many terms a member may serve? In a recent Brazilian national constitution, there was a provision that prevented members from being elected to two consecutive terms. The evident purpose of the provision was to reduce the experience and information of the legislators and thus weaken the power and significance of the legislature as a whole.

The power to convene, dissolve, and adjourn the legislature is certainly of fundamental importance. Legislatures that cannot control the times of their daily meetings and annual sessions are obviously in a weak position. Some constitutions limit the time a legislature may be in session in a given year or give special powers to the executive authority to convene or adjourn the legislature.

The nature of a legislature's committee system is another fundamental matter. Are the jurisdictions over policy areas of the various committees clearly and permanently specified? Are committee decisions crucial or merely suggestive of the final shape of legislation?

The rules of legislative procedure vary considerably. Tightly defined rules of procedure are characteristic of advanced democratic systems. The power of a legislature varies with the maturation of a complex procedural system, at least up to a point. Procedural rules should not hamper the system, frustrate the majority, or stalemate the lawmaking process. Loose rules of procedure are characteristic of new, revolutionary, or totalitarian regimes. In open, powerful, democratic legislative systems, the rules of procedure facilitate rule by the majority while asserting the equality of all members and giving to the minority the right to be publicly heard. The hallmarks of a democratic, representative system are majority rule, minority rights, and political equality.

Legislatures have been quite imaginative in finding different ways to arrange their constituencies. Some systems require that a candidate receive an absolute majority of the constituents' votes to be elected, while other systems require only a mere plurality (receiving more votes than any other candidate). Some systems feature single-member districts, while others make use of multimember districts. For multimember district systems, a wide variety of proportional representation methods have been developed. Among the more interesting varieties of election systems are the following: (1) the list system, which gives to each party a percentage of legislative seats approximating its share of the popular votes cast; (2) the single-transferrable vote system, in which voters rank several candidates in order of their personal preference; (3) the Bosnian mandate system, in which certain areas, factions, or interests are given specified numbers of seats before the election takes place; and (4) the Lebanese binomial system, in which names of candidates from two different parties must be paired on the ballot, forcing a degree of cooperation between parties before and, hopefully, after the election.

In view of these complex systems of proportional representation Americans might well appreciate the simplicity of the standard plurality, single-member, first-past-the-post system as generally used in the English-speaking world. But there are trade-offs. Because it enhances the political clout of dominant groups, the single-member district system does not facilitate the expression of fine shadings of party or interest. The voter has two options rather than many, and in the legislative arena, one party will be in control rather than a coalition of several parties as in multiparty parliamentary systems.

The Craxi Government in Italy

An illustration of the general mechanics of a multiparty parliamentary system is found in the coalition government headed for several years by Italian Premier Bettino Craxi. The premier in Italy is the head of the cabinet, and his naming of the cabinet members is the critical step in securing a parliamentary majority.

While in the United Kingdom the cabinet is responsible to the House of Commons only, in Italy the cabinet must receive a vote of confidence in both chambers (Senate and Chamber of Deputies) of the national legislature.

In forming his cabinet, Craxi had to confront the party division in the two chambers following the national general election in June 1983. The two largest parties in both chambers were the Christian Democrats and the Communists (see table 2-2). Typically in Italy, the non-Communist parties unite to achieve a coalition excluding the Communists, and a Socialist such as Craxi may become premier even though he belongs to a comparatively small party. In his center-left coalition, Craxi awarded sixteen of the thirty cabinet positions to the largest party contingent, the Christian Democrats. (See table 2-3 for the list of ministers by party.) Craxi reserved six seats for his own Socialist party. The remaining eight seats were divided among three smaller parties: the Social Democrats, the Republicans, and the Liberals. The five-party coalition held 182 of the 315 seats in the Senate, or 57.8 percent, and 366 of 630 seats in the Chamber of Deputies, or 58.1 percent.

Table 2-2. Results of Italian general election, June 26, 1983

Parties	Seats in Senate	Seats in Chamber of Deputies
Christian Democrats[a]	120	225
Communists	107	198
Socialists[a]	38	73
Italian Social Movement	18	42
Social Democrats[a]	8	23
Republicans[a]	10	29
Liberals[a]	6	16
Radicals	0	11
Other parties	8	13
Total	315	630

[a]Parties belonging to the Craxi coalition.
Source: Paxton, J. *The Statesman's Year-Book 1985–6,* 122 ed.

Table 2-3. Italian cabinet positions, by party, in Craxi coalition, 1983–1986

Party	Cabinet positions held
Christian Democrats (16)	Vice-premier, Foreign Affairs, Interior, Justice, Treasury, Education, Agriculture, Post, Merchant Navy, State Industry, Health, Culture, Public Administration, Scientific Research, Southern Affairs, Civil Protection
Socialists (6)	Premier, Transport, Labor, Foreign Trade, Tourism, EEC Affairs
Social Democrats (3)	Budget, Public Works, Regional Affairs
Republicans (3)	Finance, Defense, Relations with Parliament
Liberals (2)	Industry, Ecology

Source: Paxton, J. *The Statesman's Year-Book 1985–6,* 122 ed.

The Craxi government was Italy's forty-fourth postwar government and was nearing the nation's record for longevity when, in October 1985 after twenty-six months in office, it resigned because of criticism of the way Craxi handled the international crisis involving the hijacking of the Italian cruise liner *Achille Lauro* and the murder by Palestinian pirates of the sixty-nine-year-old American passenger, Leon Klinghoffer.

The Craxi coalition collapsed when Defense Minister Giovanni Spadolini and two fellow members of the Republican party resigned in protest of the Italian government's decision to release Mohammed Abbas, an official of the Palestine Liberation Organization (PLO) whom the United States accused of directing the hijacking. Abbas had joined Egyptian negotiators in obtaining the surrender of the four hijackers who had seized the ship as it neared Port Said, Egypt. Abbas and the four hijackers boarded an Egyptian plane to seek a haven, but the plane was intercepted by U. S. Navy jets and forced to land at a NATO base in Sicily. The United States issued a warrant for Abbas's arrest, but Italian authorities allowed him to fly to Yugoslavia.

Within a few weeks, however, Craxi was able to reconstitute the same five-party coalition, or *pentapartito,* and to receive a new parliamentary vote of confidence. The Craxi government finally ended in national elections held in June 1987. Craxi had forced the election by refusing to abide by an earlier agreement to cede the prime minister position to the Christian Democrats, the largest component of the *pentapartito* that had governed Italy for most of the decade (Rosenthal, 1987).

CONGRESS AND AMERICAN STATE LEGISLATURES

The fifty American state legislatures are, in effect, the results of efforts by the authors of the respective state constitutions to replicate the national Congress. We can understand Congress better by briefly describing American state legislatures, just as we have discussed foreign legislatures. Two perspectives are particularly helpful in summarizing information about the state legislatures: first, a review of their constitutional functions and powers, and second, discussion of a recent systematic evaluation of their relative effectiveness in their respective state political systems.

Constitutional Powers of State Legislatures

Just as America's national legislature is severely limited by restrictions placed on it in the Constitution, so are legislative powers limited by most state constitutions. Except for Nebraska, all states have a bicameral legislature, which is generally considered a weaker policy-making structure than the unicameral form. In many states there are a large number of constitutional agencies and election officials that perform some functions and tend to interfere with the legislature's freedom of action. For example, if the state's constitution decrees that there shall be a board of regents to govern the state's public institutions of higher education, to that extent the legislature's control over an important policy area is circumscribed. Many state constitutions contain highly specific material that might have been better included in laws and also impose fiscal restraints that severely limit the legislature's power to raise and spend money. Perhaps the ultimate constitutional restriction on the state legislature is the provision for the initiative and referendum, which has been adopted by several states. Under the initiative, the people may propose and adopt laws by their own vote. Under the referendum, the people can challenge a law passed by the legislature and reject that law in the upcoming election. In several states, recent constitutional amendments or the adoption of entirely new legislative articles have reduced or removed some of these traditional constitutional restraints. But the people seem to remain dubious about an unfettered state legislature that could embark on doubtful, expensive, or controversial programs. The recent experience in South Dakota is an illuminating example. The voters of that state in 1972 approved sweeping new executive and judicial articles that "modernized" both branches and generally made them more efficient and effective. But when given the opportunity to approve a new legislative article submitted by the Constitutional Revision Commission in 1974, the people turned it down by a vote of 138,590 to 86,293. People are often willing to let the administrative and adjudicative branches be rearranged but are more dubious about allowing their legislature to change. And while governors and judges generally seem to approve of and even encourage changes in the organization and operation of their respective branches, many leading legislators have worked strenuously to defeat reform proposals that would drastically change the legislative structure with which they are familiar. Further, interest groups, accustomed to the state legislature as it is, are often in the forefront of efforts to resist constitutional changes pertaining to the legislature.

Evaluating State Legislatures

Almost every state legislature has made some changes in recent decades. Among the more prevalent reforms have been improved budgeting systems, better information systems with respect to public policy problems and to the progress of bills through the legislative system, prefiling of bills before the session begins to facilitate legislative work, better salaries and perquisites for legislators, larger staffs for leaders and committees, and professional and permanent research organizations.

State legislatures, particularly the "unreconstructed" ones, are subject to much criticism (Ivians 1975; Broder 1983). A thorough and systematic evaluation of our state legislatures was conducted several years ago by the Citizens Conference on State Legislatures (CCSL). The study identified five critical factors and then carefully evaluated each state legislature on these factors, a process that produced a ranking based on quantified scores. Basically, the CCSL study asked five questions of each state legislature: Is it functional? Is it accountable? Is it informed? Is it independent? Is it representative?

Functional.   Legislatures were favorably rated on this factor if they had annual rather than biennial sessions, if the length of the session was unlimited rather than restricted to a specified number of days, if they had established uniform rules of procedure, if they made use of interim (between-session) study committees to prepare legislation or other recommendations for the following year, if they had a legislative research council, if adequate space was available in the legislative chambers and committee rooms, and if joint committees (ones containing members from both chambers of the legislature) and committees with large, clear-cut, and parallel jurisdictions were provided.

Accountable.   Legislatures were favorably rated if elections were democratic (that is, open, accessible, and equitable), if legislative meetings were open rather than secret, and if there were good facilities for observation of legislative business by press and public.

Informed.   The question here was whether the legislatures had provided themselves with ready information as to the status and potential impact of current legislative proposals: Was there a legislative fiscal director corresponding to the budget officer in the executive branch? Were "fiscal notes" attached to bills so that everyone could have immediate information about the estimated cost of prospective government programs? Were bills fully explained to members, and could bills be located quickly as they passed through the legislative system?

Independent.   Legislatures were given higher positive marks if they had the power to call themselves into special session to confront unexpected or emergency problems not handled in the regular session, if they had adequate staff to audit and review the work of agencies in the executive branch, and if there were sufficient restrictions on lobbying activities by special interest groups. In other words, was the legislature in charge of the legislative environment, or was it too often at the mercy of external forces?

Representative.   Legislatures were favorably rated if their members were elected from single-member districts rather than from multimember districts; if the salaries and perquisites were generous enough to make it economically feasible for most citizens to consider running for the legislature; and if members had adequate staff, equipment, and office space. As to salary, one long-time complaint about the representativeness of many state legislatures was that the salaries and allowances were so low that only well-to-do citizens could afford to serve without severe financial hardship. Salaries were kept low, so the argument went, because vested interests in the state wanted to restrict the opportunity to serve to the affluent. A more generous salary and allowance program encourages a broader reservoir of potential candidates for legislative office.

It is worth noting that the original CCSL rankings of the fifty state legislatures, published in 1971, named California, New York, Illinois, Florida, and Wisconsin in order as the five best legislatures, and Arkansas, North Carolina, Delaware, Wyoming, and Alabama as numbers 46 through 50 (see table 2-4). As a general rule, urban or midwestern and western states had more favorable rankings, while southern and northeastern states were on the lower end of the quality scales.

The following list comments on how Congress measures up to the five standards of the CCSL system. (Later chapters will consider many of these topics in detail; here we mean merely to compare Congress with the fifty state legislatures.)

1. *Functional.* Congress would get good marks on this measure because of Congress's annual and unlimited sessions, its research support, and its committee system with generally parallel jurisdictions in House and Senate, but poor marks for the limited space available for member and committee staffs and for the limited utilization of joint legislative committees.

2. *Accountable.* Congress would rate satisfactorily for its democratic elections, though many would object on the basis of the unequal distribution of campaign resources that give incumbents such an advantage. Congress has opened up its committee meetings to a considerable degree in the past decade or so, and televised House and Senate floor debates also help the accountability of Congress. Opportunities for press and public to observe congressional proceedings are about as good as they can be for a building of the age and size of the Capitol; the construction of House and Senate office buildings in this century has not directly helped press and public access.

3. *Informed.* Congress has provided itself with the staff, documents, and technology necessary to track legislation and to understand the budgetary

Table 2-4. "Best" and "worst" state legislatures according to CCSL analysis

	Functional	Accountable	Informed	Independent	Representative	Overall
Best Five[a]	California	Nebraska	New York	Florida	New York	California
	Hawaii	Kentucky	California	Illinois	California	New York
	New Mexico	California	Wisconsin	California	Michigan	Illinois
	New York	Illinois	Florida	Wisconsin	New Mexico	Florida
	Florida	Utah	Iowa	Pennsylvania	Missouri	Wisconsin
Worst Five[b]	Mississippi	Rhode Island	Arkansas	Montana	South Carolina	Arkansas
	Louisiana	Arizona	Delaware	North Carolina	Vermont	North Carolina
	Alabama	Delaware	Kentucky	Wyoming	Virginia	Delaware
	Kentucky	Georgia	Alabama	Missouri	Montana	Wyoming
	South Carolina	Alabama	Wyoming	Alabama	Arizona	Alabama

[a]States ranked first to fifth, top to bottom.
[b]States ranked forty-sixth through fiftieth, top to bottom.
Source: Burns, The Sometime Governments, 1971, pp. 52–53.

implications of legislation. The relatively new Congressional Budget Office greatly improves the ability of Congress to correlate spending and taxing laws. 4. *Independent*. The most negative aspect here is the question of regulating special interest groups, though it is probably true that such groups in state legislatures are a greater danger to the general public interest than they are in Washington. Congress would rank high on the criteria of schedule and agenda. 5. *Representative*. The salaries of members are far above the national average (but many could probably earn higher incomes in other occupations), and Congress certainly has provided itself with a generous list of perquisites. These financial compensations have not guaranteed a broadened reservoir of congressional candidates, however. Members are well educated and wealthy compared to most Americans, and higher percentages of them are male and white. Thus while it is openly and democratically elected, Congress is not even an approximate representation of a cross section of American citizens.

SUMMARY

The original specifications for Congress were written by founders who were familiar with the British and colonial legislative bodies. Congress has evolved on its own, with little attempt to copy developments in legislatures elsewhere. Rather, many other legislative bodies have followed or adapted U. S. congressional organization or practice. Congress has frequently adjusted its relationship to the executive branch. In this process of adjustment and accommodation, the critical factor is usually the personality and style of the president. Theodore Roosevelt, Woodrow Wilson, Franklin D. Roosevelt, and Lyndon Johnson were particularly notable for their efforts to dominate the policy-making process. Over the years, Congress has become more democratic, more responsive to parochial rather than national influences, and more visible to the public, partly because of advances in media technology and partly because of internal rules changes. To study Congress in historical and comparative contexts provides Americans with a better understanding of Congress's unique characteristics and thereby enhances our ability to evaluate its performance.

REFERENCES

ADAMS, HENRY. *Democracy: An American Novel*. New York: Farrar, Straus, and Young, 1952. (Originally published 1882)

ADAMS, JOHN CLARKE. *The Quest for Democratic Law: The Role of Parliament in the Legislative Process*. New York: Crowell, 1970.

BERMAN, HAROLD J. *Law and Revolution: The Formation of the Western Legal Tradition*. Cambridge: Harvard University Press, 1985.

BEARD, CHARLES A., and LEWIS, JOHN P. "Representative Government in Evolution." *American Political Science Review* (April 1932): 223–240.

BRODER, DAVID. "Congress and the Legislatures: Do They Deserve Our Confidence?" *Today Journal* (27 January 1983): 14.

BURNS, JOHN. *The Sometime Governments: A Critical Study of the Fifty American Legislatures by the Citizens Conference on State Legislatures*. New York: Bantam Books, 1971.

CRANE, JR., WILDER, and WATTS, JR., MEREDITH W. *State Legislative Systems*. Englewood Cliffs, N.J.: Prentice-Hall, 1968.

DAHL, ROBERT A. *Political Oppositions in Western Democracies*. New Haven, Conn.: Yale University Press, 1966.

GALLOWAY, GEORGE B. *History of the House of Representatives*. New York: Crowell, 1961.

IVIANS, MOLLY. "Inside the Austin Fun House: 'My God, You Mean There Are Twelve Worse Than This?' " *Atlantic Monthly* 235, no. 3 (March 1975).

JOSEPHY, JR., ALVIN M. *On The Hill: A History of the American Congress*. New York: Simon & Schuster, 1980.

KEEFE, WILLIAM J. *Congress and the American People*. 2nd ed. Englewood Cliffs, N.J.: Prentice-Hall, 1984.

LARSEN, J. A. O. *Representative Government in Greek and Roman History*. Berkeley: University of California Press, 1955.

LOEWENBERG, GERHARD, and PATTERSON, SAMUEL C. *Comparing Legislatures*. Boston: Little, Brown, 1979.

MACKENZIE, KENNETH. *The English Parliament*. New York: Penguin Books, 1950.

MANN, THOMAS E., and ORNSTEIN, NORMAN J., (eds). *The New Congress*. Washington, D. C.: American Enterprise Institute, 1981.

MONAHAN, ARTHUR P. *Consent, Coercion, and Limit: The Medieval Origins of Parliamentary Democracy*. Cheektowaga, N.Y.: University of Toronto Press, 1987.

MUIR, JR., WILLIAM K. *Legislature: California's School for Politics*. Chicago: University of Chicago Press, 1982.

NEALE, J. E. *The Elizabethan House of Commons*. New York: Peregrine Books, 1963.

OLSON, DAVID M. *The Legislative Process: A Comparative Approach*. New York: Harper & Row, 1980.

ORNSTEIN, NORMAN J., MANN, THOMAS E., MALBIN, MICHAEL J., SCHICK, ALLEN, and BIBBY, JOHN F. *Vital Statistics on Congress, 1984–1985*. Washington D. C.: American Enterprise Institute, 1984.

PAXTON, JOHN (ed.). *The Statesman's Year-Book, 1985–1986*. 122nd ed. New York: St. Martin's Press, 1985.

POLE, F. R. *Political Representation in England and the Origins of the American Republic*. Berkeley: University of California Press, 1966.

POUNDS, NORMAN J. G. *Political Geography*. 2nd ed. New York: McGraw-Hill, 1972.

ROSENTHAL, LAWRENCE. "Comrades No More: Decline of the Italian Left." *The Nation* 244 (27 June 1987): 878–881.

SAYLES, GEORGE O. *The King's Parliament of England*. New York: Norton, 1974.

SCHWARZ, JOHN E., and SHAW, L. EARL. *The United States Congress in Comparative Perspective*. Hinsdale, IL: Dryden Press, 1976.

SMITH, LACEY BALDWIN. *This Realm of England, 1399–1688*. 2nd ed. Lexington, Mass.: Heath, 1971.

GORDON, STRATHEARN. *Our Parliament*. London: Hansard, 1953.

U. S. Bureau of the Census. *Historical Statistics of the United States: Colonial Times to 1970*. Washington, D. C.: U. S. Census Bureau, 1975.

WILSON, WOODROW. *Congressional Government: A Study in American Politics*. New York: Meridian Books, 1956. (Originally published 1885)

WHEARE, K. C. *Legislatures*. Oxford, England: Oxford University Press, 1963.

III REPRESENTATION AND APPORTIONMENT

Representative democracy as a style of government owes much to ideas of individual liberty and dignity that developed in the ancient world. But particularly in large and powerful nations, representative democracy is a relatively new form of government and is by no means dominant in the world today. As we have seen in the previous chapter, representative institutions with independent lawmaking authority evolved slowly and uncertainly in Western Europe. That evolution seems to have been facilitated in England, a nation possessing or producing such favorable characteristics as (1) a high degree of homogeneity, patriotism, and amity; (2) considerable interest in and knowledge about political affairs; (3) political parties and interest groups able to express and aggregate distinctive points of view on governmental affairs; (4) a reasonably widespread and fluid distribution of wealth and economic opportunity; and (5) reasonably secure borders and frontiers to reduce the threat of foreign invasion. Little wonder then that representative democracy became explicit and tangible in the Constitution of the United States, a nation favored with the same auspicious characteristics.

Representative democracy is a system in which the people have control over government through a system of elections: The people choose the decision makers, and the decision makers write the laws and oversee the execution of those laws. At intervals, the decision makers must run for reelection. Their reelection indicates that the people are satisfied with how well their interests and wishes have been represented. If the society has developed the communications media and the political and electoral structures that allow the general dissemination of information about public affairs and if most of the people are reasonably intelligent, public-spirited, tolerant, secure in their property and livelihoods, and willing to balance skepticism with a degree of trust, the representative system is likely to work.

We will first consider the general idea of representation as a mechanism for giving citizens a significant role in government and second the more specific techniques of the apportionment of legislative seats, the process of defining the areas particular members will represent. This chapter (1) summarizes the major views about the nature of representation; (2) investigates how the Constitution attempts to bring representative theories to life through application of apportionment principles and practices; (3) discusses the reasoning and implications of the

Supreme Court's series of reapportionment decisions; and (4) illustrates the continuing problem of gerrymandering by discussing current apportionment practices in particular states.

THEORIES OF REPRESENTATION

The idea of political representation is as complex as it is fundamental to modern government. The theoretical literature of representation, according to Hanna Pitkin (1969, 7), is full of "puzzling, seemingly irresoluble conflicts and controversies. There does not even seem to be any remotely satisfactory agreement on what representation is or means." This lack of consensus makes it all the more important to survey the major theories on the subject.

The term *representation* implies that one entity is standing for, or re-presenting, another entity. In the nineteenth century, John Stuart Mill ([1861] quoted in Pitkin 1969, 181) wrote:

> The meaning of representative government is that the whole people, or some numerous portion of them, exercise through deputies periodically elected by they themselves, the ultimate controlling power, which, in every constitution, must reside somewhere.

The 535 members of Congress are charged with representing more than 200 million citizens of the United States. A fundamental question to be asked about this process of representation is whether the *wishes* or the *needs* of the citizen are to be represented. To emphasize the wishes of the people would be to expect that Congress enact the laws people say they want enacted. To emphasize the needs of the people would be to expect Congress to concern itself about the results or impact of the laws on the nation and its citizens. In the first case, Congress would do what public opinion dictated, which seems to imply a rather powerless, subservient role for Congress. In the second case, Congress would do what it thought best, which would imply a discretionary role for Congress.

The Roman adage "Quod omnes tangit ab omnibus approbetur" (What touches all should be approved by all) expresses the proposition that laws should be approved by those who are touched or affected by them. As we have seen in the case of early England, the representative character of the House of Commons made it an appropriate body for legitimizing law, giving law the aspect of popular assent. An extract from the record of the Parliament held at Westminster in 1339 acknowledges the link between the attitudes of the citizens and the policy enacted by the government.

> The reasons for summoning this Parliament were set forth and explained to the Lords and to the Commons, so that in this matter their counsel and advice might be attained in the best way possible. . . . And after the explanation had been given, everybody, great and small, was of the opinion that in this necessity a large "aid" would have to be granted. But as the aid had to be large, the Commons did not

dare consent until they had been given the opportunity of consulting their constituents.

Conferring with constituents is only part of the process of linking popular ideas with authoritative laws. The other part of the linkage is what David Mayhew (1974) calls "the electoral connection"—the people choosing the lawmakers. *The Federalist* expressed the matter clearly (Hamilton et al., 291):

> Who are to be the electors of the Federal Representatives? Not the rich more than the poor, not the learned more than the ignorant, not the haughty heirs of distinguished names more than the humble sons of obscure and unpropitious fortune. The electors are to be the great body of the people of the United States.

(The modern reader should remember that the Founders were thinking in terms of a suffrage limited to adult white males.)

Ideas about the nature of representation have given birth to three important points of view, which are discussed in the following sections. Keep in mind that few if any pure examples of the following representational types are found in legislative assemblies and that most legislators employ combinations of the salient characteristics of the major pure types, adopting one representational style for some kinds of issues and another style for other issues. Legislators may even change representational style over the years.

The Delegate View

This view specifies that a very close connection should exist between public opinion and public policy. What the public wants should be what the public gets. The test of a representative legislative body is not how wise or successful its laws may be but rather how closely the laws mirror the public's preferences. Echoing Montesquieu, the French jurist and philosopher, and at the same time reminding us of how modern-day pollsters rely on randomly selected respondents to measure national public opinion, the French philosopher Jean Jacques Rousseau (*The Social Contract,* 1762, 155) believed that legislators should be chosen by lot rather than by election. Rousseau wrote that random selection of legislators "wounds no one, is unpredictable, and gives all an equal chance to serve" their nation. Of course, Rousseau believed that legislators would be guided by the General Will. This rather populist view that any adult is wise and honest enough to be a legislator approaches the notion of direct democracy, where every citizen has the opportunity to take part in lawmaking. The theory also resembles what is called the delegate theory of representation, which holds that the duty of legislators is to vote on legislation as constituents direct them to vote.

In our era of great advances in telecommunications technology, some mind-boggling, futuristic proposals about popular policy making have been advanced. Political scientist Ted Becker has written about the possibility of nationwide, instantaneous electronic referendums, with legislative proposals flashed on television screens in millions of homes and switches for citizens to vote yes or no. Becker

(Malbin 1982, 58) claims that "with the help of teledemocratic process, public opinion will become the law of the land." Another political scientist, Michael Malbin (1982, 59) criticizes Becker's view, stating that to the Founding Fathers, democracy was less basic than liberty. The founders did not want the tyranny of a majority to endanger individual liberties. Malbin points out that representative systems have a feature that does not belong to the referendum process, that is, the capacity for expressing different points of view and for revising the language of legislative proposals in the course of debate.

> The answers given by citizens isolated in their homes would add nothing worth-while to the deliberative process. Political deliberation is not a solitary activity. Opinions only become refined through the give and take of discussion with people whose backgrounds and opinions differ from one's own.

Malbin continues with some thoughts on public opinion in the American system.

> This is not meant as a slap at the American people. The question is not so much the people's ability as how people choose to use their time. The purpose of the Republic, after all, is not to make every citizen a public figure. The United States is not and was not meant to be another Switzerland. Rather, the purpose of our government is to use public action to secure the private rights to life, liberty, and the pursuit of happiness.
>
> If referendums and initiatives are dismissed, what about the increased use of issue polls for purely advisory purposes? I have no doubt that both electronic and nonelectronic issue polling will continue their steady rate of growth. The problem with them is that the opinions they solicit are, in The Federalist's terms, unrefined and unenlarged. They are raw pieces of data that deserve to be treated with extreme caution.

Whatever one might think of the Becker-Malbin debate, political leaders are often eager to use public opinion (or at least their version of it) to justify their actions. An example of this can be found in the dove hunting controversy in South Dakota. By an overwhelming popular vote in 1972, the people of South Dakota abolished the hunting of mourning doves in their state. Then in 1979, during his first year as governor, William Janklow signed a dove hunting bill that had been passed by the state legislature. Governor Janklow defended his action in approving a policy that the people had rejected seven years earlier with the following state-ment:

> People who ran for the legislature [in 1978] were examined by the people as to where they stood on the mourning dove issue. That was reflected in how people voted.
>
> When it was passed again by the legislature, I could only assume that they were doing so with the assent of their constituents.

The governor's case seems to rely on the assumptions that the mourning dove issue was the predominant issue in every legislative race across the state in 1978, that every candidate emphatically expressed a position on the mourning dove issue, and that every voter cast a vote in the legislative race on the sole basis of the candidates' stands on dove hunting.

An emphatic statement of the delegate point of view was made long ago in the Virginia Senate (see Commonwealth of Virginia 1812).

> The right of the constituent to instruct the representative, seems to result . . . from the very nature of the representative system. Through means of that noble institution, the largest nation may, almost as conveniently as the smallest, enjoy all the advantages of a government by the people, without any of the evils of democracy—precipitation, confusion, turbulence, distraction from the ordinary and useful pursuits of industry. And it is only to avoid those and the like mischiefs that representation is substituted for the direct suffrage of the people in the office of legislation. The representative, therefore, must, in the nature of things, represent his own particular constituents only.

Opponents of the delegate view argue that three conditions are necessary for the view to be valid: First, the public must be well informed on all issues to be decided in the course of the legislative sessions. Second, each legislator must accurately measure the preferences of a majority of his constituents on each issue to be decided. Finally, the preferences of a majority of the constituents must remain constant over time, not changing as conditions change or as new arguments or information are advanced on a particular policy question. Several months after an election, a constituency might change its opinion on a current issue, in which case a legislator elected to support a proposition would now be obliged to oppose it. Even change in attitude by a small number of people would be enough to transform a minority into a majority position.

The Trustee View

The trustee theory of representation was expressed two centuries ago by Edmund Burke, a member of the House of Commons for thirty years, in a message to the people of his parliamentary district. Burke felt it was the duty of legislators to vote on the basis of their own information, judgment, and conscience, rather than simply on the basis of constituents' preferences, and to represent the general national interest rather than the particular local interest. The Burkean view holds that democratic elections produce legislators who have special wisdom, fairness, and national spirit. Burke believed that a representative's work must have a foundation in elections and popular consultations. Richard Fenno, Jr. (1978, 233) reminds us of this interconnection by commenting that the processes of campaigning and of representing are inseparable. Here is how Burke (1907, 164–165) put the matter in his oft-quoted "Speech to the Electors of Bristol":

> To deliver an opinion is the right of all men; that of constituents is a weighty and respectable opinion, which a representative ought always to rejoice to hear, and which he ought always most seriously to consider. But authoritative instructions,

mandates issued, which the member is bound blindly and implicitly to obey, to vote, and to argue for, though contrary to the clearest conviction of his judgment and conscience—these are things utterly unknown to the laws of this land, and which arise from a fundamental mistake of the whole order and tenor of our Constitution.

Parliament is not a congress of ambassadors from different and hostile interests, which interests each must maintain, as an agent and advocate, against other agents and advocates; but parliament is a deliberative assembly of one nation, with one interest, that of the whole—where not local purposes, not local prejudices, ought to guide, but the general good, resulting from the general reason of the whole. You choose a member, indeed; but when you have chosen him, he is not a member of Bristol, but he is a member of Parliament. If the local constituent should have an interest or should form an hasty opinion evidently opposite to the real good of the rest of the community, the member for that place ought to be as far as any other from any endeavor to give it effect.

As to a representative's responsibilities, Burke wrote:

But his own unbiased opinion, his mature judgment, his enlightened conscience, he ought not to sacrifice to you, or to any set of men living. These he does not derive from your pleasure—no, nor from the law and the constitution. They are a trust from Providence, for the abuse of which he is deeply answerable. Your representative owes you, not his industry only, but his judgment; and he betrays, instead of serving you, if he sacrifices it to your opinion.

Three considerations are pertinent in a discussion of representational styles. First, there is a difference between perceived self-interest and enlightened self-interest; after all, how many people really know what is good for them? Second, one should be wary of assuming that the national interest is simply the sum of all the parochial interests that exist in the nation. It can be argued that the achievement of the national interest requires the submersion of all parochial interests. Third, adoption of the Burkean, or trustee, style of representation may be feasible on one issue, even a very salient one, but becomes increasingly difficult as more and more issues are brought to the floor for resolution; the sheer volume may cause a member to retreat from sole reliance on personal judgment and conscience and heed instead the preferences expressed by influential groups in the constituency.

Hanna Pitkin (1969, 20–21) summarizes her discussion of the concept of representation by identifying two fundamental positions, which she associates with Edmund Burke and John Stuart Mill. Those who agree with Burke see representatives "as superior in wisdom and expertise to their constituents," as sensing the true interests of the nation, and as representing not individual people "but the great, stable, major interests which together make up the national interest." Right answers will emerge from the careful deliberations of wise statesmen. Those who agree with Mill, on the other hand, see the need to protect personal or local interests from a "threatening central power" and believe that the function of a representative body is more critical than constructive, defensive rather than deliberative.

Those who habitually yearn for middle-of-the-road solutions to human dilemmas may be inclined to accept the response of Marilyn vos Savant (1987, 15) to the question: "Which kind of political representative is more befitting a democracy: a delegate-type representative who votes as the constituents demand or a trustee-type who votes out of his or her own free will?" Vos Savant answers, "What about the best of both? I believe the best representative of the people will vote his conscience but that this will correspond to what he expects his constituents would demand if they were as well-informed as he is."

The Marxist View

In addition to the delegate and trustee views of representation, there is the view that open and competitive elections are only a sham, deluding the naive citizen into believing that voting will actually affect what the government does. Marx and others encouraged an attitude that relates to nonelective, or virtual, representation, which holds that the common people are incapable of knowing their own best interests and of asserting effective power to protect those interests. According to Marx, the people need the protection of a powerful organization—namely the Communist party—to care for them and their interests. In this view, only the Communist party can be trusted to understand society and to make proper policy decisions.

APPORTIONMENT OF HOUSE SEATS

The method by which members of a legislature are chosen has much to do with the legislature's approach to representing constituents. How to apportion, or distribute, the seats in Congress among the various states was one of the critical problems addressed by the Founding Fathers at the constitutional convention in 1787. The Connecticut Compromise was the solution that virtually ensured that the convention would be able to draft a Constitution that could be accepted. The compromise specified that each state would be allotted two senators; therefore, the less populated states would have as much power in at least one chamber as would the heavily populated states. In the House of Representatives, however, the more populous states would be represented more generously. But how were the proper proportions of representatives for each state to be worked out? The Founding Fathers spent considerable time on this question, as have conscientious legislators and adept statisticians since the Constitution was adopted. Each new census has produced a new apportionment of House seats among the states.

The original Constitution, using the best available figures for the populations of the thirteen states and keeping in mind the stricture that "the number of representatives shall not exceed one for every thirty thousand inhabitants," arbitrarily assigned a specific number of representatives to the various states, as follows: Virginia, ten; Pennsylvania and Massachusetts, eight; New York and Maryland, six; Connecticut, North Carolina, and South Carolina, five; New Jersey, four; New

Hampshire and Georgia, three; and Rhode Island and Delaware, one. The first national census in 1790 reported state populations, as shown in table 3-1.

Congress worked out a new apportionment of seats in the House based on the 1790 census information. But because of mathematical inconsistencies in the proposed apportionment bill, Secretary of State Thomas Jefferson and others advised President Washington not to sign the bill. Washington's veto of the apportionment act on April 5, 1791, was the first presidential veto exercised. Just a few days later, a new apportionment bill, known as the Jefferson Plan, was approved; this gave each state one representative for every 33,000 inhabitants (disregarding fractions). By this system, states with 71,000 and 90,000 inhabitants would each receive two representatives (two times 33,000 equals 66,000), and the remaining fractional populations (5,000 and 24,000, respectively) would be ignored for representation purposes. The 1791 act resulted in an increase in the size of the House from the constitutionally specified 65 seats to 106 seats, including seats for the three states (Vermont, Kentucky, and Tennessee) as they were admitted during the 1790s. Virginia gained nine seats, Massachusetts, six; North Carolina and Pennsylvania, five; and New York, four. Meanwhile, Delaware failed to gain a seat, and Georgia lost one of its three seats.

The Jefferson Plan was also used for the next several decennial censuses, with the divisor of 33,000 increased to reflect the general increase in the nation's population. In the 1830 apportionment, New York had by far the largest House

Table 3-1. Populations of states (1790 census) and apportionment of House seats for Fourth Congress, 1795–1797

State	1790 Population (thousands)	1795–1797 Apportionment
Virginia	748	19
Massachusetts[a]	476	14
Pennsylvania	434	13
North Carolina	394	10
New York	340	10
Maryland	320	8
South Carolina	249	6
Connecticut	238	7
New Jersey	184	5
New Hampshire	142	4
Vermont[b]	85	2
Georgia	83	2
Rhode Island	69	2
Kentucky[b]	—	2
Delaware	59	1
Tennessee[b]	—	1

[a]Includes present area of Maine, which was not admitted to statehood until 1820.
[b]Admitted to statehood after 1790.
Note: These are total counts of inhabitants, including blacks and Indians, and therefore not the counts for apportionment purposes as specified under the original Article I.
Source: U. S. Census of 1790.

delegation (40). Kentucky, Tennessee, and North Carolina, with 13 representatives apiece, had by this time overtaken Massachusetts, which had 12. The size of the House was 242 in the 1830s; as the number of states and the national population increased, the congressional apportionment acts tended to keep the seats assigned for the smaller states constant while awarding larger and larger delegations to the more populous states.

Daniel Webster and others argued that continued use of the Jefferson Plan was working against the smaller states in that disregarding the remaining population of a state after calculating the multiple of the quota meant that a larger proportion of the small states' populations would be unrepresented than would the large states' populations. This is what Webster had in mind: Take a situation where the quota for one seat was 70,000, one of the larger states had a population of 1.6 million, and one of the smaller states had a population of 200,000. The larger state under the Jefferson Plan would qualify for 22 seats, with 60,000 inhabitants left over as a remainder. These 60,000 would comprise less than 4 percent of that state's population (3.75 percent, to be exact). The smaller state would qualify for two seats and would also have an unrepresented remainder of 60,000 inhabitants. But the smaller state's remainder would comprise 30 percent of the state's population. Because of Webster's persistent arguments on the point, the congressional apportionment of 1842 provided that a state would receive an additional member if the remainder was over half of the quota.

But now a new apportionment problem became the focus. Both the Jefferson and Webster systems were criticized because the ultimate size of the House of Representatives could not be predetermined. The older plans based the calculation of seats on a predetermined quota, (for instance, one seat for every 100,000 inhabitants); therefore the exact number of seats to be apportioned was arrived at only after establishing the quota. If the ratio of representatives to inhabitants remained constant while the population continued to grow, the House would soon outgrow its chambers and, no doubt, the entire Capitol building. In fifty years the House had already grown from 65 to 242 members, a nearly fourfold increase. Therefore, for the six censuses of the remainder of the nineteenth century, the so-called Vinton Plan was used to apportion House seats among the states. The first step of this plan was to establish the total number of seats, after which the seats per state were calculated. But then the so-called Alabama Paradox was discovered. The Vinton method when applied to the 1880 census figures produced an absurd result: If the size of the House were to increase by one seat more than the predetermined size, the state of Alabama would lose one of its seats! This paradox troubled politicians and scholars from the time it was discovered until a more perfect formula was devised, and it serves as a reminder that "scientific" policies and formulas are not always as consistent and sensible as we may be led to believe.

Following the 1910 census, W. F. Willcox, a professor at Cornell University, showed that an endless priority list could be drawn up that would show in order, seat by seat, which state was most deserving of each seat to be added to the size of the House. Whether the House would have one hundred members or one thousand, the same priority list would be operative. At that time there were forty-eight states. Each state would have one seat to begin with. The forty-ninth seat would go to the state with the largest population, and the fiftieth seat, to the next largest state. The priority list would determine at what point the largest state would get its third seat, probably long before several states would be entitled to their second seats. Willcox's method was known as the "formula of major fractions."

In 1921 E. V. Huntington, a professor at Harvard University, developed the "method of equal proportions" and also worked out formulas and tables for the other known, constitutionally consistent methods of congressional apportionment: major fractions, harmonic mean, smallest divisors, and greatest divisors. In 1929 a committee of the National Academy of Sciences concluded that Huntington's equal proportions method was the most satisfactory. When 1930 census returns were used in the major fractions and equal proportions formulas, the distribution of seats among the forty-eight states was identical. But using the 1940 census configurations, the results were different. With the major fractions formula, Michigan would gain a seat at the expense of Arkansas, whereas with the equal porportions method, the seats of both states would remain unchanged. Because of this, Congress adopted equal proportions as the apportionment method to be used after the 1950 census. There are still arguments after each census and the ensuing reapportionment, generally coming from states that have either lost a seat or that are just a few notches below the priority list's cutoff line. Following the 1980 census, Congressman Floyd Fithian (D.–Ind.) tried without success to get Congress to return to the Vinton Plan. To date the equal proportions method has withstood the arguments of its opponents and is accepted as the soundest mathematical solution to the constitutional principle that representatives "shall be apportioned among the several states . . . according to their respective numbers." (It may also be noted that Congress in 1967 passed a law requiring representatives to be elected from single-member districts, as had long been the general practice.)

The 1980 census caused 17 of the 435 seats in the House to be shifted from one state to another. States losing seats were New York (five), Pennsylvania, Ohio, and Illinois (two each), and Michigan, Indiana, Missouri, South Dakota, Massachusetts, and New Jersey (one each). Florida gained four seats, Texas, three; California, two; and Washington, Oregon, Nevada, Utah, Colorado, Arizona, New Mexico, and Tennessee, one each. The last six seats on the equal proportions priority list went in order to Kansas, Pennsylvania, Colorado, Ohio, Florida, and New York. On the wrong side of the cutoff line (after number 435) were Indiana, Georgia, California, Alabama, and Missouri. The average population of the congressional districts after 1980 came to 519,328.

Projections have already been made about the 1990 census. A study by the American Federation of State, County, and Municipal Employees (*Political Report*

1985) reported that after 1990, California and Texas would gain five seats; Florida, three; and Arizona, Georgia, and Virginia, one; while New York and Michigan would lose three; Pennsylvania, Ohio, and Illinois, two; and Massachusetts, Iowa, West Virginia, and Kansas, one.

The Mathematics of Congressional Apportionment

The essence of the process of working out the method of equal proportions is as follows: Multipliers are determined for each seat a state may be awarded above the automatic first seat assigned to every state. The multiplier for a second seat is 0.707, for a third seat, 0.408, for a fourth seat, 0.289, and so on to the multiplier for a sixtieth seat of 0.017. The multiplier for each seat is the reciprocal of the geometric mean.

$$\text{for the second seat} \quad \frac{1}{\sqrt{2(2-1)}} = \frac{1}{\sqrt{2}} = .707$$

$$\text{for the third seat} \quad \frac{1}{\sqrt{3(3-1)}} = \frac{1}{\sqrt{6}} = .408$$

and so on.

All of these multipliers are applied to each state's population. The second seat for a small state with a population of 650,000 would have a priority value of 459,550 (0.707 × 650,000). The forty-second seat for a large state with a population of 20 million would have a priority value of 480,000 (0.024 × 20 million). Thus the larger state would receive its forty-second representative before the smaller state received its second.

THE REAPPORTIONMENT REVOLUTION

Apportioning seats is only half of the process of developing a system of representation. The second half of the process is to divide each state into a number of districts equal to the number of seats allotted to the state. This involves defining geographical boundaries, which is performed by the state legislature rather than by Congress. The rule of political equality requires that all districts in a state have substantially equal populations; otherwise, some residents (those living in districts with populations far above the average population per district) would be underrepresented, and others (those living in districts with populations far below the average) would be overrepresented. Even when districts are of substantially equal population, there is the possibility that the arrangement of their boundaries may increase the chances of one party winning more seats than the party is entitled to. This result is called a partisan gerrymander, which will be discussed in the next section.

Until the 1960s many states from time to time established congressional districting systems that were inequitable from a population standpoint. The courts generally stayed aloof from controversies about the apportionment of congressional or legislative seats and the drawing of district boundaries. In the 1940s certain citizens in Illinois filed suit against the apportionment system in their state legislature, claiming that the legislative districts in which they lived contained far more people than did other legislative districts, thus depriving them of a fair share of political influence. A lower court agreed, deciding that, since the Illinois state legislature had failed to establish equitable districts, all district boundaries in the state were to be dissolved and new elections conducted on a statewide, at-large basis. The Supreme Court, following precedent, overturned the lower court's decision, expressing the traditional "hands-off" view (*Colegrove* v. *Green,* 328 U. S. 549, 1946).

> We are of opinion that the appellants ask of this court what is beyond its competence to grant. This is one of those demands on judicial power which cannot be met by verbal fencing about "jurisdiction." It must be resolved by considerations on the basis of which this court, from time to time, has refused to intervene in controversies. It has refused to do so because due regard for the effective working of our government revealed this issue to be of a peculiarly political nature and therefore not meet for judicial determination.

Later in the decision, the court said that "due regard for the Constitution as a viable system precludes judicial correction. Authority for dealing with such problems resides elsewhere." Finally, the court admonished that "courts ought not to enter this political thicket."

Justice Hugo Black disagreed with the majority of his colleagues in the Colegrove decision and in effect set the precedent for the Court's reversal of its historic position sixteen years later.

> It is my judgment that the district court had jurisdiction; that the complaint presented a justifiable case and controversy; and that appellants had standing to sue, since the facts alleged show that they have been injured as individuals. . . . Under the circumstances, and since there is no adequate legal remedy for depriving a citizen of his right to vote, equity can and should grant relief.
>
>   It is said that it would be inconvenient for the state to conduct the election in this manner. But it has an element of virtue that the more convenient method does not have—namely, it does not discriminate against some groups to favor others, it gives all the people an equally effective voice in electing their representative as is essential under a free government, and it is constitutional.

The Tennessee state legislative districting system contained many examples of over- and underrepresentation, and in spite of the Court's decision in the Illinois case, a suit challenging the apportionment system was entered on behalf of residents of underrepresented districts. The Supreme Court in 1962 used this situation as the basis of its precedent-shattering decision in *Baker* v. *Carr* (369 U. S. 186, 1962), reversing the Colegrove decision by declaring legislative malapportionment to be a problem appropriate for judicial remedy. The Baker decision recognized the statistical evidence for the inequitability of the apportionment system of the Tennessee state legislature. A series of decisions in subsequent years applied the principles of *Baker* v. *Carr* to almost every kind of elective public policy-making body.

In *Gray* v. *Sanders* (372 U. S. 368, 1963), the Supreme Court declared the Georgia county unit system of electing the governor to be unconstitutional. Under Georgia's system, a candidate for governor had to carry a majority of the counties of the state to be elected, irrespective of the relative population of the counties or of the statewide popular voting result. The idea behind this system was to essentially eliminate the votes from heavily populated Fulton county, where the city of Atlanta is located. This system was struck down by the Court because votes were weighted differently depending on the county in which people lived. That is, the voters in very large counties had no more influence than the voters in the smallest county.

In *Wesberry* v. *Sanders* (376 U. S. 1, 1964), the Court applied the Baker principle to congressional districting, requiring that state legislatures draw the boundaries of congressional districts to produce districts with substantially equal populations. The extent of inequity in the size of congressional districts before the reapportionment revolution, along with the current district sizes, are shown in table 3-2. The congressional districts of 1964, not including the seven seats that were at that time filled on a statewide basis, ranged in size from the fifth district of Texas,

Table 3-2. Population of congressional districts in 1964, prior to the reapportionment revolution, and in 1985

Population range	1964 Percentage of districts[a]	1985 Percentage of districts[a]
Over 700,000	0.7	—
600,000 to 699,999	2.6	—
500,000 to 599,999	9.6	90.9
450,000 to 499,999	12.4	6.3
400,000 to 449,999	29.8	2.3
350,000 to 399,999	29.6	0.5
300,000 to 349,999	7.3	—
250,000 to 299,999	4.9	—
200,000 to 249,999	2.6	—
Under 200,000	0.5	—
Total	100.0	100.0

[a]Excludes seven at-large districts (two each in Hawaii and New Mexico, one each in Maryland, Ohio, and Texas) in 1964 and six at-large districts (one each in Alaska, Delaware, North Dakota, South Dakota, Vermont, and Wyoming) in 1985.
Source: Calculated by the author from data in *Congressional Directory,* 89th Cong., 1st sess., 1965, pp. 2–183 and *Congressional Directory,* 99th Cong., 1985–1986, pp. 4–209.

which covered Dallas county and had a population of 951,527, to the second district of South Dakota, which covered the western half of the state and had a population of only 182,845. The Texas district was more than twice as populous as the national median (a little over 400,000), while the South Dakota district was less than half as populous. That is, the Texas district was more than five times more populous than the South Dakota district. Again, the inequity did not arise because of an improper apportionment of congressional seats to Texas and South Dakota but because of inequitable districts established by the state legislatures. (Texas, it might be noted, had another congressional district, the fourth, with a population (216,371) almost as sparse as South Dakota's second district.)

In 1964 three states—South Dakota, Arizona, and Maryland—had remarkably inequitable districts. South Dakota's first congressional district had a population of 497,669, almost three times larger than its second district. Arizona's three districts had populations of 663,510, 440,415, and 198,236. Maryland's system was even worse; one Maryland congressman was elected at large, three were elected by districts that had more than 600,000 residents, three were elected by districts that had less than 300,000 residents, and one was elected by a district of roughly standard size (373,327). On the other hand, two states—Michigan and Wisconsin—had notably equitable congressional districts. All of Michigan's nineteen districts had populations of between 400,000 and 420,000. Wisconsin's districts all fell inside a limited range of 380,000 to 420,000. Disparities in the size of congressional districts almost totally disappeared in post-1980 reapportionments. Again, excluding the few statewide at-large districts from consideration, in 1985 over 90 percent of the nation's districts were in the 500,000 to 599,999 range, with the great bulk of these being under 550,000. The most populous of these districts was the fourth district of Alabama, represented by Democrat Tom Bevill of Jasper. The district stretches across the state north of Birmingham, touching Mississippi on the west and Georgia on the east. South Dakota's one and only congressional district is the nation's most populous, having 690,768 inhabitants. Democrat Tim Johnson of Vermillion is the state's lone U. S. representative. Touching South Dakota on its western border is the congressional district with the lowest population, Montana's second district, which covers the central and eastern thirds of Montana and is represented by Republican Ronald Marlenee of Scobey.

In many states the legislature's adherence to mathematical equality has been so precise as to be slavish. For instance, none of California's 45 districts had a 1980 population higher than 527,999 or lower than 524,000. In spite of the closeness of district populations, the congressional districting system in California has been challenged in the courts because the boundaries have been drawn to maximize the number of Democratic candidates likely to be elected (see further discussion in the next section of this chapter).

The case of *Reynolds* v. *Sims* (377 U. S. 533, 1964) concerned bicameral state legislatures and held that both chambers of a state legislature must be apportioned equitably.

Legislators represent people, not trees or acres. Legislators are elected by voters, not farms or cities or economic interests. As long as ours is a representative form of government and our legislatures are those instruments of government elected directly by and directly representative of the people, the right to elect legislators in a free and unimpaired fashion is a bedrock of our political system. . . . We hold that, as a basic constitutional standard, the equal protection clause requires that the seats in both houses of a bicameral state legislature must be apportioned on a population basis.

The decision in *Davis* v. *Mann* (377 U. S. 678, 1964) involved whether or not to include military personnel as citizens in legislative districts; by extension this decision involved any kind of transient or impermanent population in a district. The decision held that, under the equal protection clause, variances in legislative districts less than the extreme variances found in the electoral college are not sufficient to provide a constitutional case for sustaining a state apportionment scheme.

In *Roman* v. *Sincock* (377 U. S. 695, 1964), the Court sidestepped an invitation to specify precise mathematical requirements for district populations.

In our view the problem does not lend itself to any such uniform formula, and it is neither practical nor desirable to establish rigid mathematical standards for evaluating the constitutional validity of a state legislative scheme under the equal protection clause. Rather, the proper judicial approach is to ascertain whether, under the particular circumstances existing in the individual state when legislative apportionment is at issue, there has been a faithful adherence to a plan of population-based representation, with such minor deviations only as may occur in recognizing certain factors that are free from any taint of arbitrariness or discrimination.

A few years later, the Supreme Court became more specific as to allowable population deviations involving congressional districts in Missouri (*Kirkpatrick* v. *Preisler* [394 U. S. 526, 1969]) and in New York (*Wells* v. *Rockefeller* [394 U. S. 542, 1969]). The Missouri decision held that a deviation of 3.1 percent between the populations of the most and least populous districts was not allowable unless the deviation was justified by some rational factor or shown to result in spite of a "good faith" effort. In 1983 the Supreme Court ruled that New Jersey's congressional apportionment was unconstitutional because of a deviation of 0.698 percent in the sizes of the most and least populous districts (*Karcher* v. *Daggett* 462, U. S. 725, 1983).

In *Lucas* v. *Forty-Fourth General Assembly of Colorado* (377 U. S. 713, 1964) the Supreme Court went so far as to strike down a legislative apportionment scheme that had been approved by a statewide vote of the people. The apportionment worked out by the legislature and submitted to the people for their approval had given fewer legislative seats to the city of Denver than it was entitled to by its share of the state's population, a fairly typical instance of urban versus rural power in a state legislature. The Lucas decision included these pronouncements:

1. The individual's right to cast a vote cannot be denied even by a vote of a majority of the state's electorate.
2. The fact that a referendum has adopted an apportionment plan is insufficient to sustain its constitutionality or to induce a court of equity to refuse to act.
3. One's right to life, liberty, and property and other fundamental rights may not be submitted to a vote—they depend on the outcome of no election.
4. No plebiscite can legalize an unjust discrimination.
5. A citizen's constitutional rights cannot be infringed on simply because the majority of all the people choose to do so.

Legislative apportionment was thus the focus of the major constitutional revolution of the 1960s as far as legislative institutions were concerned. Reapportionment is by no means a closed matter. There will always be the problem of allowable deviations in the population of districts, as well as the even more debatable question of the shape of the districts. These problems are inherent in a system of single-member districts.

THE FINE ART OF GERRYMANDERING

Gerrymandering is the process of arranging district boundaries in such a way as to increase or decrease the political influence of particular parties, classes, or interests. Before discussing specific aspects and mechanics of the gerrymander, two recent developments in the area of congressional districting merit at least brief attention.

Members of Congress, as well as many other observers, have been aware of the problem of congressional district gerrymandering by state legislatures. Since the House is composed of men and women who have successfully sought election by their districts, it may be thought that the House is not very sensitive to the problem of gerrymandering. But representatives have been quite concerned about the shape and size of their districts, particularly in the months following publication of the decennial federal census figures, when state legislatures are charged with considering the mathematical equality and political reality of their state's districts. The concern about state legislative machinations is evident in H. R. 2349, cosponsored in 1981 by Rep. Robert Kastenmeier (D.–Wis.) and Rep. Jim Leach (R.–Iowa) and forty other representatives. To reduce what its authors referred to as "the chronic problem of gerrymandering," the bipartisan proposal offers the following redistricting standards to be imposed on state legislatures:

1. District boundaries should not be drawn to favor any political party, incumbent, or any other individual.
2. District boundaries should not deny effective voting representation to any language or racial minority group.
3. District boundaries should be drawn with due regard to significant natural geographic barriers so as to contain only contiguous (touching) territory.

4. District boundaries, to the extent possible in keeping with the contiguity requirement, should coincide with local political subdivision boundaries, such as counties, municipalities, and wards.
5. District boundaries, to the extent consistent with the two previous requirements, should be drawn so as to produce districts of compact shape (the most compact geometric shape is the circle, whereas elongated or angled shapes would reduce compactness).
6. Districts should have populations falling within 2 percent of the average population for congressional districts in that state.
7. State legislatures should enact congressional redistricting laws within three years of the decennial federal census.
8. Any eligible voter should be allowed to challenge a state's congressional redistricting law in a federal district court (and attorneys' fees may be awarded at the discretion of the court to the prevailing party).

In the 1983 case cited earlier (*Karcher* v. *Daggett*), the Supreme Court in a five to four decision threw out the congressional districting plan enacted by the New Jersey legislature following the publication of 1980 census figures. In a concurring opinion to that decision, Justice Stevens said that the dilution of the voting strength of a political party might be just as unconstitutional as the dilution of the strength of a racial bloc. He wrote: "A finding that the majority deliberately sought to make it difficult for the minority group to elect representatives may provide a sufficient basis for holding that an objectively neutral electoral plan is unconstitutional" (*Karcher* v. *Daggett*, 462 U. S. 725, 1983). In a dissenting opinion, Justice Powell wrote: "I believe that the injuries that result from gerrymandering may rise to constitutional dimensions." The New Jersey case involved a districting plan drawn up by a Democratic state legislature. In 1984 a federal court struck down a new state legislative districting law passed by the Republican-controlled Indiana state legislature. In the summer of 1986, the Supreme Court ruled that such political gerrymanders are indeed subject to constitutional challenge but stopped short of invalidating congressional apportionments in Indiana (which favored the Republican party) and California (which favored the Democratic party). The Court said that "relying on a single election to prove unconstitutional discrimination" was not a satisfactory way to determine whether a political gerrymander had been perpetrated (*Davis* v. *Bandemer*, 106 S. Ct. 2797, 1986). However, the decision was expected to reduce gerrymandering in the long run and generally to work in favor of the Republican party, since Democrats were in control of the redistricting process in far more states than were Republicans (see *Congressional Quarterly Weekly Report,* 1986, 1523–ff.).

The general problem involved in these and several other circumstances is that there is often a great disparity between a group's share of the votes cast and its share of the seats won in an election. A state with a Democratic registration of 40 percent may win only two of ten congressional seats. A state with a Democratic registration margin of 53 percent may win all six of that state's seats. The national congressional situation following the 1984 election is worth noting. In the nation as a whole, there was a virtual tie in the number of votes cast for Republican and Democratic candidates for the House of Representatives, but with the Democratic party in control of most state legislatures and thereby dominating the redistricting process, Democratic candidates won 253 House seats, Republican candidates only 182. The disparities may be the result of a carefully devised central strategy, or they may result accidentally. The single-member district system is more likely than other systems to produce disparities between vote ratios and seat ratios. The question is whether the advantages of the single-member district system, notably the presumed closer relationship between representatives and constituents, outweigh the disadvantages produced by questionable districting practices of a few state legislatures.

Every ten years, whenever the census data reflect state population shifts that make redrawing district boundaries necessary, incumbent congressional members may find their political careers at the mercy of their respective state legislatures. It is of some advantage if an incumbent's party is in control of the state legislature, for then the redistricting is likely to be more favorable than otherwise. But even in this case the incumbent is not guaranteed advantageous treatment, particularly if a member of the state legislature has ambitions for the congressional seat.

Our reliance on single-member districts to elect members of the U. S. House of Representatives, while having some obvious advantages in terms of directness and simplicity, has opened the door for a number of dubious and devious practices. Geographical areas, political parties, and ethnic and economic groups have all sought to gain advantage through influencing legislatures in shaping congressional districts. District lines can be arranged to help or hurt particular interests, a fact known since at least the beginning of our republic. In 1802 the *Salem Gazette* (quoted in Born, 1985, 305) commented on the situation in Pennsylvania.

> The people of Pennsylvania are about one-third Federalist, yet all their new members of Congress are Democrats. The legislature took great care, in laying out the districts, to make the elections as sure for the Democrats as if they had voted by a ticket at large.

Congressional Districting in South Carolina

Gerrymandering is not a lost art. Some of the opportunities and possibilities of gerrymandering can be illustrated by referring to the demographic circumstances in the state of South Carolina. The 1987 arrangement of the state's six congressional districts is shown in Map 3-1. Only one county, Berkeley, is divided between two districts; otherwise, county lines have been followed in establishing the districts. The population deviation among the districts is quite low, the second district being the most populous, with 520,776 inhabitants, and the sixth being the least populous, with 519,243 inhabitants.

In the 99th Congress (1985–1986), South Carolina was represented in the House by three Republicans (Thomas Hartnett of the first district, Floyd Spence of the second, and Carroll Campbell of the fourth) and three Democrats (Butler Derrick of the third, John Spratt of the fifth, and Robert Tallon of the sixth). The Democratic party picked up one of these seats in the 100th Congress (1987–1988), as a consequence of the fact that Hartnett ran unsuccessfully for lieutenant governor and Campbell was elected governor. (Hartnett's decision to leave the House to run for state lieutenant governor contradicts the general feeling that congressional office is more advantageous than state positions other than governor.) Arthur Ravenel, Jr., also a Republican, succeeded Hartnett in the first district seat, while Campbell was replaced by Democrat Elizabeth Patterson in the fourth district.

Map 3-2 shows the population of each county (in thousands) and by symbols indicates the margin (in thousands of votes) by which Republican

MAP 3-1. South Carolina's six congressional districts in 1987

Ronald Reagan or Democrat Jimmy Carter carried that county in the 1980 general election. Reagan carried the first, second, and fourth districts, while Carter won in the other three, thus making presidential and congressional outcomes by district identical. To establish the underlying partisan disposition of the counties of South Carolina, presidential election returns are used as a convenient and consistent base measure, but it should be understood that presidential party support may not be distributed in exactly the same pattern as support for a party's candidates for congressional, gubernatorial, or state legislative office. These data are the basic building blocks in the formation of districts. Gerrymandering arises when those who draw the boundaries do so in such a way as to help—or hurt—the electoral chances of a particular party or candidate. The basis of a Republican gerrymander would be to use the urban counties where the GOP commands significant margins in such a way as to build at least four districts with Republican majorities. One way to do this would be to form a district including Greenville county (with its sizable Republican advantage), running from Oconee county in the northwestern

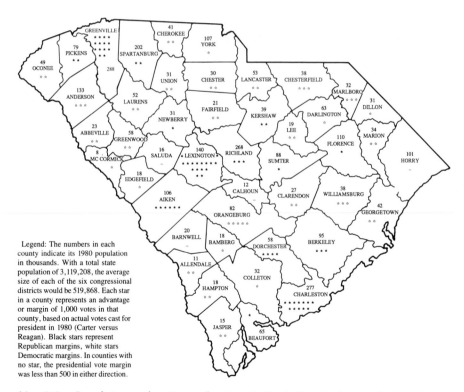

Map 3-2. Population and partisan advantage in South Carolina's counties (1980 data)

corner of the state to Fairfield county, another district running from Richland to Berkeley counties and including part of Lexington county, another district along the southwestern border from Anderson to Hampton counties and including the remainder of Lexington county, and a fourth district covering six counties around the city of Charleston (Charleston, Colleton, Beaufort, Jasper, Dorchester, and Orangeburg). The plan just described involves the breaching of just one county boundary, that of Lexington; if more county lines were to be breached, it might be possible for Republicans to form five districts with Republican majorities. This would require considerable cunning, imagination, and gall. Another problem, from the Republican point of view, would be that the Republican margins would be very narrow.

A Democratic gerrymander effort would attempt to use the Democratic margins in the many smaller counties in such a way as to dissipate the three formidable Republican bastions centering on Greenville, Lexington, and Charleston counties. Again, this could be done more easily if county lines were to be breached extensively. If the Democrats could find a way to offset the Republican concentration in just one of the three counties just mentioned, then they would secure a four to two edge among the state's representatives.

Many states could be used as examples of potential partisan gerrymanders. A state such as Tennessee, with four large population concentrations around Memphis, Nashville, Chattanooga, and Knoxville and the traditionally Republican counties in the Appalachian ridges to the east offers a good example as does the state of Washington, with its several distinct climatic areas and its widely separated population centers of Seattle and Tacoma in the west and Spokane in the east.[1]

Gerrymandering can involve one of two approaches: first, spreading supportive regions in order to assert dominance in the largest possible number of districts, albeit with fairly narrow margins; and second, concentrating supportive regions in order to increase the number of sure seats. The other side of the coin is that the gerrymander artist is either spreading the opposition so widely that it can win few seats or concentrating the opposition's areas in the smallest number of sure seats. (Other factors not considered in these hypothetical districting strategies include type of economic activity in a given area, surface transportation routes, residence locations of the current congressional incumbents, ethnic or racial makeup of the counties, and rates of in- or out-migration.)

SUMMARY

The electoral process makes Congress a representative body, but there are several different styles and emphases of representation that individual members may adopt.

The apportionment of seats to the states is mathematically equitable, but in determining the precise shape of each representative's district, state legislatures can still increase an individual incumbent's chances of being reelected or enhance a political party's chances of winning most of the state's congressional seats. The system of electing U. S. representatives from single-member districts tends to discourage the formation of third parties to run against Democrats and Republicans and also encourages a parochial, as opposed to a national, representational style. The most obvious and pervasive tensions with which this chapter has dealt involve two representational questions: First, does the member emphasize the national or the constituency point of view? Second, does the member rely on personal judgment or on constituents' expressed preferences in voting on legislation?

NOTE

1. For some details of sectionalism and congressional district gerrymandering by the South Carolina legislature, see the material in Barone and Ujifusa (1985), 1217, 1221–1234; (for Tennessee) 1245, 1249–1250, 1257–1258, 1260; (for Washington), 1408, 1411–1427.

REFERENCES

BAKER, GORDON. *The Reapportionment Revolution*. New York: Random House, 1966.

BARONE, MICHAEL, and UJIFUSA, GRANT. *The Almanac of American Politics 1986*. Washington D.C.: National Journal, 1985.

BORN, RICHARD. "Partisan Intentions and Election Day Reality in the Congressional Districting Process." *American Political Science Review* 79, no. 2 (June 1985):305.

BURKE, EDMUND. Speech to the electors of Bristol, on his being declared by the sheriffs, duly elected one of the representatives in Parliament for that city, on Thursday, the 3rd of November, 1774. In *The Works of Edmund Burke, Vol. II*. New York: Oxford University Press, 1907.

Commonwealth of Virginia. *Journal of the Senate* (1812): 82*ff.*

Congressional Quarterly Weekly Report (5 July 1986): 1523*ff.*

DIXON, JR., ROBERT G. *Democratic Representation*. New York: Oxford University Press, 1968.

FENNO, JR., RICHARD F. *Home Style: House Members in Their Districts*. Boston: Little, Brown, 1978.

HACKER, ANDREW. *Congressional Districting*. Washington, D. C.: Brookings, 1963.

HAMILTON, ALEXANDER, MADISON, JAMES, and JAY, JOHN. *The Federalist* or *The New Constitution*. Everyman's Library ed. New York: E. P. Dutton and Company, 1911. (Originally published 1787–1788)

LAKEMAN, ENID. *How Democracies Vote: A Study of Majority and Proportional Electoral Systems*. 3rd ed. London: Faber & Faber, 1970.

MCKAY, ROBERT B. *Reapportionment: The Law and Politics of Equal Representation*. New York: Twentieth Century Fund, 1965.

MALBIN, MICHAEL. "Teledemocracy and Its Discontents." *Public Opinion* (June/July 1982): 58–59.

MAYHEW, DAVID. *The Electoral Connection*. New Haven, Conn.: Yale University Press, 1974.

MILL, JOHN STUART. *Representative Government* [1861] in Hannah F. Pitkin, *The Concept of Representation*. Berkeley: University of California Press, 1967.

PITKIN, HANNA F. *Representation*. New York: Atherton, 1969.

RAE, DOUGLAS W. *The Political Consequences of Electoral Law*. rev. ed. New Haven, Conn.: Yale University Press, 1971.

ROUSSEAU, JEAN JACQUES. *The Social Contract*. New York: Penguin Classics, 1968. (Originally published 1762)

SCHMECKEBIER, LAWRENCE F. *Congressional Apportionment*. Washington, D. C.: Brookings, 1941.

SCHUBERT, GLENDON. *Reapportionment*. New York: Scribner's, 1965.

SPITZ, ELAINE. *Majority Rule*. Chatham, New Jersey: Chatham House, 1984.

U. S. CONGRESS, HOUSE. *Report of the Dicennial Population Census and Congressional Apportionment*. Subcommittee on Census and Statistics of the House Committee on Post Office and Civil Service, 1970, 91st Cong., 2nd sess., H. Doc. 91-1314.

VOS SAVANT, MARILYN. "Ask Marilyn." *Parade Magazine* (19 April 1987): 15.

IV CONSTITUENCIES AND THE ELECTORAL SETTING

The fundamental condition of representative government is the free and open election of representatives by the people. Each of our one hundred senators is elected by a statewide electorate, and there is great variation from state to state in the number of people who take part in senatorial voting. Seven million citizens voted in the 1986 California Senate contest between Democratic incumbent Alan Cranston and Republican challenger Ed Zschau, whereas in Alaska only 150,000 citizens voted in the Senate contest between Republican incumbent Frank Murkowski and Democratic challenger Glenn Olds. There were 50 California voters for every Alaska voter. Each of our 435 representatives is elected from a particular district, each containing about a half million inhabitants.

This chapter is concerned with the relationships between members of Congress and their constituents, the investment members have in their congressional careers, the recruitment of candidates, and important factors associated with electoral success in past congressional elections. (The campaign itself is the subject of chapter 5.)

MEMBER-CONSTITUENT RELATIONSHIPS

A member of Congress, as Roger Davidson and Walter Oleszek (1985, 109) noted, inhabits two spheres.

> All members of Congress move back and forth between two worlds. The Congress that labors on Capitol Hill is one of these worlds. . . . The polished corridors of the Rayburn House Office Building seem far removed from the Muncie senior citizens' basement bingo game. Yet these two worlds—the two Congresses—are tightly interlocked.

The most evident part of a member's public life takes place in Washington, but just as important to the member—and even likely to be more critical to prospects of keeping the seat—is the member's political life in the district. The reelection campaign itself takes up only a part of the member's time in the district. A member typically travels to the district several times each year; the frequency and duration of such trips depends to some extent on how far the district lies from Washington and the expectations of the constituents. The trip home is a time for work rather than for rest or attention to family concerns. There is much to be done—meeting with constituent groups, traveling to various parts of the district, conferring with close personal associates and political allies, contacting newsmen—few things are more important to a member than staying in touch with the people back home.

The work of Richard Fenno has in recent years focused attention on the various ways members of Congress relate to and approach their constituents. He has recently reminded his fellow political scientists of how little we know about these constituencies. In his presidential address to the American Political Science Association, Fenno (1986, 6) said that "students of politics must be students of context and of sequence." Regretfully, he added, "We love our constituencies, but we do not study them—not up close, in detail, and over time." Fenno also (1978, 4, 8) identifies and describes different levels of closeness that members establish in dealing with various elements in their constituencies. He begins with the largest circle, which constitutes the "most encompassing view" of the constituency. This circle includes the entire district and its people, institutions, and groups. According to Fenno, the internal characteristic that "best illuminates subsequent member perception and behavior" is the district's degree of homogeneity or heterogeneity. In this "outermost perceptual circle," the member thinks in terms of the entire district. The emphasis is on the whole, a consequence of the member's perception that the vote of the caretaker of the municipal swimming pool is as significant as the vote of the president of the largest bank in town and that there are more voters like the caretaker than there are like the banker.

The next circle is the "reelection constituency," the supporters whose work and votes allow the member to serve in Congress. At this level, the member perceives the constituents and communities in terms of whether or not they are supportive. According to Fenno (1978, 8, 17–18), "Members of Congress do have an idea of who votes for them and who does not." But "they do so with a good deal less certainty in their minds than we might previously have guessed." And they "do not take their reelection constituency for granted."

The third circle contains "the primary constituency," the strongest supporters who support the member through thick and thin, year after year. Fenno notes that highly subjective feelings of rapport and personal comfort are involved here. In one case, a member felt better on the flatlands of his district than in the mountains because he had been raised on the flatlands. Another member felt more at home in a labor union meeting than in a businessman's luncheon even though he realized that he had equal sized circles of labor and business supporters. A member may fashion "a highly subjective at-homeness index" to help differentiate between two locales (Fenno, 1978, 22–24).

Finally at the center exists the smallest of the concentric circles, the "personal constituency," or intimates. This circle encompasses those whose relationship with the member is "so personal and so intimate that their relevance cannot be captured" by such a description as "very strongest supporters." Some of these are close advisers with whom the member is in daily contact; others may be seen less frequently but are important for emotional sustenance (Fenno 1978, 24: see also Davidson and Oleszek 1985, 124–129)

Fenno also develops the idea that stages occur in the district career of a member that reflect the way members perceive and relate to their constituents. Fenno identifies two principal stages; expansionist and protectionist. In the first, the member builds a reliable reelection constituency. This stage begins before the member's first election. The second stage involves reaching out for new support areas or groups to cultivate a broader reelection constituency. The pace of movement from expansionist to protectionist varies for each member (Fenno, 1978, 171–178).

Just as members perceive and categorize their constituents, so do constituents develop images of the representative. Much of the member's work in the district is devoted to projecting a favorable image, particularly one of accessibility, sensitivity, trustworthiness, and effectiveness. Gary Jacobson (1983) concludes that members "achieve this aim to a remarkable degree." The member and staff devote much time to "casework" on behalf of constituents who have brought some problem to the member's attention, usually one involving a government program (such as veteran's or Social Security benefits, postal service, or help with a passport). Further, Jacobson (1983, 114) notes the widespread use by representatives of "the strategy of discouraging opposition before the campaign begins." Typically, according to Jacobson, congressional challengers are relatively obscure people who lack information or sufficient contact with the media to be able to use information against the incumbent or on behalf of themselves.

The member becomes a careful student of constituents, having a vested interest, of course, in such study. All contacts at home, and particularly the contacts that occur during reelection campaigns, enhance the member's opportunity to learn about the people of the district. As Marjorie Randon Hershey (1984, 268) notes, "The campaign learning environment affects the quality of the campaigners' understanding of people's wants and needs." One problem with this learning process, however, is that campaigners hear much more frequently and pointedly from special interest activists and organized groups and this can lead the campaigner to ignore or misunderstand the desires of the less vocal general public. The campaign, at best, is a two-way communication process; the public tells politicians what is wanted and campaigners tell the public what they intend to do if elected. The quality of campaign learning affects not only how campaigns are carried on but how (and which) public affairs and problems will be debated, discussed, and finally resolved. These points all reiterate and emphasize Fenno's basic point that the processes of campaigning and representing are inseparable.

The slavish attentiveness of members to the issues that concern their constituents is frequently noted, seldom more forcefully than in Congress's override of President Reagan's veto of an $88 billion highway and mass transit bill in the spring of 1987. The act provided over one hundred construction projects in various districts across the nation and also permitted states to raise the speed limit to 65 miles per hour on rural stretches of the interstate highway system. House Republican Leader Robert Michel of Illinois, beneficiary of a highway broadening project in his district, admitted that for the first time he was faced with a "very difficult, agonizing decision" to oppose his president on a major bill. Rep. Arthur Ravenel, Jr. (R.–S.C.) told his House colleagues in justifying his vote against the president: "You can bet your spring petunias this Congress will override the veto. President Reagan, he ain't going to be running in 1988, but I am." Speaker Jim Wright (D.–Tex.) interpreted the vote as a victory for conscience, congratulating his colleagues for standing up for "their own convictions" and for "standing up to blandishments and pressure from the White House." The override vote was a reflection of antipresidential, pro-constituency solidarity. In the House, Democrats divided 248 to override the veto, one to sustain; Republicans voted 102 to override, 72 to sustain. In the Senate, Democrats voted 54 to override, none to sustain, while the Republicans divided 13 to 33.

The characteristics of one particular congressional district may provide a more immediate example of the strong connections between the nature of the district and the priorities and behavior of the member who represents it. Much of what a member does is conditioned by perceptions of how each deed will "play" back home. Each district is, of course, unique. We've chosen a particularly scenic one to describe.

California's Sixteenth Congressional District

California's sixteenth congressional district is a beautiful district—so attractive and interesting, in fact, that it is a wonder that the people of the area can find a person willing to spend most of his time representing them in Washington. The district stretches along the California coast from Santa Cruz in the north to San Luis Obispo in the south and includes the spectacular scenery of the Monterey peninsula, Carmel, Big Sur, Morro Bay, and William Randolph Hearst's magnificent estate at San Simeon.

The district's population is concentrated in coastal cities such as Santa Cruz, Seaside, Monterey, and in other cities just a few miles inland such as Salinas, Watsonville, and San Luis Obispo. Several of these cities are notably attractive and have preserved a charming cultural heritage. Inland there are only a few sizable towns: Hollister, along the San Benito river and Gonzales, Soledad, and King City in the "long valley" of the Salinas river. Much of the district's interior consists of rugged ranges of hills and low mountains.

The district consists of all of Monterey and San Benito counties, the coastal part of Santa Cruz county, and the north coast of San Luis Obispo county.

Monterey county claims about 60 percent of the district's population, San Benito only about 5 percent, with the rest divided almost evenly between the counties of Santa Cruz and San Luis Obispo. The district population is 18 percent Hispanic, 5 percent Asian, 4 percent black, and 1 percent American Indian. The major economic activities of the district are tourism and agriculture, particularly the cultivation of vegetables in the northern valleys and coastal flatlands.

Rep. Leon Panetta, a Democrat who has represented the district since 1977, feels quite paternal about the people and the beautiful landscapes of the sixteenth district where he was born and raised. He works strenuously to protect the beauty, economy, and culture of his district.

In contrast to California's sixteenth congressional district and Rep. Panetta's protective care of it, consider other districts in the United States. For instance, Charles Rangel's Harlem-based sixteenth district of New York includes the Puerto Rican neighborhoods of East Harlem and Washington Heights and the Irish neighborhood of Inwood at the north end of Manhattan island. Or consider the remote first district of Tennessee, tucked into the northeastern corner of the state between the Blue Ridge and the main Appalachian ridge, represented by Jimmy Quillen. The seventh district of Minnesota, with its German and Norwegian farmers of sugar beets and wheat requires Rep. Arlan Stangeland's attention to its share of rural unrest. And the seventh district of Louisiana, where Cajun French is the mother tongue of nearly half the people and where oil has become the backbone of the economy, is represented by Rep. Jimmy Hayes. These are only a few examples, but they provide an idea of the enormous differences that exist among 435 districts in the United States.

MEMBERS' ORIGINS, RECORDS, AND AMBITIONS

A fuller understanding of the behavior of congressional members can be gained by studying their backgrounds, the political routes by which they reached Congress, and their political goals.

The money and time spent to get elected to Congress and the tenacity with which most members hold on to their seats suggest that congressional service is a very desirable occupation. The pay and perquisites, the special treatment bestowed by the Washington community, and the feeling of political influence combine to make Capitol Hill a particularly attractive place to work.

Congress, in short, is regarded as a career by members as well as by professional and clerical aides. Only a few members leave Capitol Hill voluntarily. Election to the House or the Senate is the capstone of the careers of most members. In a few cases, a senator may seriously entertain thoughts of becoming president, but representatives rarely aspire to the presidency. (Counterexamples can be found in the 1988 interests of Congressmen Jack Kemp of New York and Richard Gephardt of Missouri in the presidency.) A number of representatives become senators; one-third of the senators serving in 1985 previously served in the House. The reverse path, from Senate to House, is seldom taken. Four former representatives—Albert Gore, Jr., of Tennessee, Tom Harkin of Iowa, Paul Simon of Illinois, and Phil Gramm of Texas—all successfully ran for the Senate in 1984. Seven more new senators—John McCain of Arizona, Timothy Wirth of Colorado, Wyche Fowler of Georgia, John Breaux of Louisiana, Barbara Mikulski of Maryland, Harry Reid of Nevada, and Thomas Daschle of South Dakota—followed the same House-to-Senate path in the 1986 elections.

As of 1985 only one representative had previously served in the Senate, Congressman Claude Pepper (D.–Fla.). Pepper served as a senator from Florida from 1936 to 1951. After taking up his House career, Pepper was able to build sufficient seniority to become chairman of the House Rules Committee. Occasionally a representative will leave the House to run for governor of his state, as when in 1987 three representatives ran in Louisiana's unique unitary primary, seeking the office of governor. (Because Louisiana's gubernatorial elections are held in odd-numbered years, it is not necessary to retire from Congress to run for governor.) Another example is Rep. Bill Boner (D.–Tenn.) of the fifth congressional district, who was elected mayor of Nashville in 1987. Occasionally a member will give up a seat to accept a judicial appointment or an appointment to the president's cabinet, as when President Jimmy Carter induced Rep. Bob Berglund of Minnesota to become his secretary of agriculture and Sen. Edmund Muskie of Maine to become his secretary of state. But voluntary departures from Congress in favor of another elective office are rare. Being a member of Congress is clearly considered to be one of the best jobs around.

Origins

Most members of Congress are "home grown." Therefore they rightly feel that they are products of their family and community environments, which increases their efforts to reflect parochial values and positions. Of the 435 members of the House serving in 1985, 325 (or 74.7 percent) were born in the state they represented. Several large states had high "home-grown" rates: 22 of Texas's 24 representatives were born in Texas, 21 of Pennsylvania's 25 were born in Pennsylvania, 20 of Illinois's 23 were born in Illinois, and 21 of Ohio's 23 were born in Ohio. But only 26 of California's 45 representatives, only 7 of Florida's 15, and only 5 of Indiana's 11 were born in the state they served. While 17 of California's representatives were born outside California, 5 California natives were serving other states in the House.

What kinds of occupational origins are most prevalent among members of Congress? In the 98th Congress, according to information published in *Congressional Quarterly Weekly Report* (Jan. 8, 1983, 56–65) 261 of the 535 representatives and senators were lawyers, 167 came from business or banking, 55 had been in education, 35 in agriculture, and 29 in journalism. At least 2 but fewer than

10 members came from each of the following vocational areas: medicine, engineering, law enforcement, aeronautics, professional sports, the clergy, military service, and organized labor leadership. The preponderance of lawyers serving in Congress is striking and affects both the way Congress operates and the decisions it makes. This occupational configuration has remained fairly constant for the past thirty years, though the occupational backgrounds of members today are a little more diverse than they were a generation ago.

Means of Election

How do members first win election to Congress? This question was investigated for the 535 members serving in the 98th Congress (Ornstein et al. 1984, 55). The largest number of representatives, 183 (or 42 percent), originally ran for a seat where the retiring incumbent was of the same party as the successor. An additional 54 (12 percent) were elected to succeed a retiring incumbent of the opposite party, 108 (25 percent) defeated the incumbent in the November general election, and 30 (7 percent) defeated the incumbent in their party's primary election. Of the remaining representatives, 37 were elected from districts newly created following the 1980 census, 20 were originally elected to succeed deceased incumbents, and 3 were elected by defeating an opponent in November who had earlier defeated the incumbent representative in the primary election.

On the Senate side, a larger ratio of members than in the House was originally elected by defeating the incumbent: 36 in the general election, 8 in a party primary. Forty-three succeeded an incumbent who had voluntarily retired; 24 of the same party affiliation, 19 of the opposing party. Seven senators defeated a candidate in November who had earlier defeated the incumbent in a party primary, and the final 6 senators originally succeeded a deceased incumbent.

Special elections and appointments to fill vacancies in the Senate are irregular occurrences and show how chance occasionally plays a part in political careers. In these circumstances, friendships and factional or local concerns may be of paramount importance, submerging partisan and ideological considerations that are generally more significant in campaigns carried out in the regular election cycle. Under provisions of the Seventeenth Amendment (1913), the governor of the state may fill vacancies in the Senate on a temporary basis until the next general election. A number of senators began careers as appointees; six senators serving in 1987 originally came to the Senate by gubernatorial appointment (Ted Stevens of Alaska, George Mitchell of Maine, David Karnes of Nebraska, Howard Metzenbaum of Ohio, Robert Stafford of Vermont, and Dan Evans of Washington). Many appointive senators do not run for reelection, having announced this intention when originally appointed and some are defeated in the next Senate election, but some do succeed in being reelected (as have five of the above-named appointives). An instance of defeat for an appointee occurred in Minnesota in the late 1970s. Minnesota's Sen. Hubert Humphrey resigned his seat in 1964 to be sworn in as vice-president following his election on the Democratic ticket with Lyndon Johnson. The Governor of Minnesota, a Democrat, appointed Minnesota Attorney General Walter Mondale to assume the vacated seat. Mondale was subsequently elected to full six-year Senate terms in 1966 and 1972. Then in 1976 he was elected vice-president on the Democratic ticket with Jimmy Carter, and in late 1976, like Humphrey before him, resigned his Senate seat. Democratic Governor Wendell Anderson resigned as governor, and Lieutenant Governor Rudy Perpich, on succeeding to the gubernatorial chair, promptly appointed Anderson to take Mondale's Senate seat in January 1977. But Anderson did not fare as well as Mondale in the next Senate election, for in November 1978 Republican Rudy Boschwitz unseated Anderson. There was a further complication to an already complex series of political events. After his term as vice-president, Hubert Humphrey was elected to the Senate again in 1970 on the retirement of Democratic Senator Eugene McCarthy and then was reelected in 1976. When Humphrey died in office in January 1978, Governor Perpich appointed Humphrey's widow, Muriel, to replace him. She did not run as a candidate in the 1978 election and was succeeded by Republican David Durenberger. More recently, Durenberger and Boschwitz have been elected to full six-year Senate terms. Similar examples of multiple Senate vacancies in a short period of time occurred in Nebraska between 1951 and 1954 and in North Carolina between 1949 and 1954. Such aberrations have more impact on political trends and ambitions in the particular state where they occur than on the political or ideological complexion of the entire Senate, but on close roll-call votes, the Senate's decisions could rest on the votes of appointive, or at least inexperienced, members who have been suddenly raised to prominence.

Vacancies in the House of Representatives can be filled only by special election (such elections in England are called "by-elections"). Appointive representatives are not permitted under the Constitution. There have been two such special congressional elections in Texas in recent years. The first resulted when Phil Gramm resigned his seat after the Democratic leadership of the House stripped him of his committee seniority as punishment for supporting President Reagan's economic policies. Gramm changed his party affiliation from Democrat to Republican and was reelected to the House by the same district in a January 1983 special election. The second example occurred in the summer of 1985 in Texas's first congressional district in the northeastern corner of the state. The first district has a strong Democratic tradition, as indicated by the fact that no Republican has been elected to any elective office in any of the district's nineteen counties for more than a century. Another indication of the area's Democratic tradition is that the incumbent Democratic congressman was first elected to the House in 1976, received 98 percent of the vote in 1982, and had no opposition at all in his reelection bids of 1980 and 1984. The first district is also a rural and relatively poor district, only two districts in Texas having a lower average annual income. The occasion of the vacancy was the resignation of Congressman Sam B. Hall, Jr., to accept a federal judicial appointment from President Reagan. The White House reportedly made the appointment of Hall on the basis of a recommendation by Gramm, who saw an opportunity to improve the Republican party's status in Texas by winning another congressional seat.

Republican hopes centered on Edd Hargett, a rancher and engineer well known in Texas as a former star quarterback for the Texas A & M football team. Six Democrats also filed nominating papers, as did a candidate of the Christian Contenders Party.

Under Texas law, in such circumstances there is no provision for a primary election, and so a single special election involving candidates of all parties is held. If one candidate receives a majority of all the votes cast, he or she is declared elected. If no one receives such a majority, then a runoff election is held a few weeks later between the top two candidates in the first contest. Hargett won the most votes in the original election on June 29, but his total of nearly 30,000 votes amounted to only 42 percent of all the votes. In second place, with over 21,000 votes, or 30 percent of the total, was a Democratic attorney, Jim Chapman. All together, the six Democratic candidates attracted 57 percent of the vote, so the question was whether the Republican Hargett could attract enough Democratic votes to win the August 3 runoff. The Republican party threw more than one million dollars into the race, picturing the contest as a sort of popular referendum on President Reagan's economic policies. The Democrats, on the other hand, emphasized poor local economic conditions and the area's strong Democratic traditions. Chapman effectively criticized the Republican proposal to freeze Social Security benefits and blamed the Reagan administration's trade policy for an increase in steel imports, which were said to have resulted in layoffs in a local steel plant. In a very close race, Democratic efforts were successful, 51 to 49 percent. Republicans were left with the cold comfort that a popular candidate with national backing at least came very close to taking a seat away from the Democrats.

Margin of Election

Congressional districts are categorized as marginal, competitive, or safe on the basis of the margin of victory in percentile terms. Such categorizations can be extended to cover an entire series of elections; thus, a district could be classified as continuously, frequently, occasionally, or rarely marginal. Although many congressional elections are decided by razor-thin margins, most of them result in lopsided victories for the incumbent..A study by Albert Cover and David Mayhew (cited in Ornstein et al. 1984, 53) showed that in House contests from 1956 through 1982, an average of about 390 of the 435 representatives ran for reelection and that on far more than half of these attempts the incumbents were reelected with more than 60 percent of the two-party vote. In fact, in 1964, the poorest year for incumbents in this respect, 58 percent of incumbents won with more than 60 percent of the vote. In the best year, 1978, 78 percent of incumbents exceeded that 60 percent figure.

Stephen Salmore and Barbara Salmore (1985, 168) have identified three strategic situations in congressional campaigns that illuminate the election margin factor and how it affects the conduct of the campaign. In the first case, a candidate perceived to be far ahead of the opponent "will refuse to be drawn into debate," or to respond to opposition charges. In the second case, a candidate who has been perceived to be far ahead has somehow been placed on the defensive; the front runner has lost the early momentum and is in danger of "losing control of the dialogue." In the third case, both candidates "have advanced persuasive themes capable of mobilizing a winning coalition." The second and third cases, according to the Salmores, "take on the quality of an electronic debate—a volley of charges and countercharges on TV and radio and via direct mail."

Of all the 435 House campaigns of 1984, only 58 were won by a candidate who received less than 55 percent of the vote (see table 4-1, which includes results from both 1984 and 1986 elections). Another 56 candidates received between 55 and 60 percent of the votes. Democratic winners outnumbered Republicans in these marginal contests, 72 to 42. Republican winners outnumbered Democrats, 119 to 114, among those receiving from 60 to 80 percent of the vote. In contests that were least competitive, Democratic winners were far more numerous: 68 to 20. What was particularly interesting about the 1984 congressional races was that in the nation as a whole, the total votes cast for Democratic and Republican candidates were about even. Nationally speaking, party balance in Congress can be considered at least potentially marginal. But most persons elected to Congress won by a comfortable margin. In fact, 187 of them received more than 70 percent of the votes cast in their district. The 1986 results in table 4-1 show a similar pattern, with somewhat larger proportions of winners receiving more than 70 percent of the vote. Again, larger percentages of Democrats than of Republicans won their seats by very wide margins or were unopposed.

To probe relationships among important political variables, I have analyzed the 435 House contests of 1984 on the basis of three factors: (1) party affiliation of the

Table 4-1. Percentage of votes received by winning candidates for U. S. House of Representatives, 1984 and 1986 general elections

Percentage of votes received	1984						1986					
	Democrats		*Republicans*		*Total*		*Democrats*		*Republicans*		*Total*	
	n	*%*	*n*	*%*	*n*	*%*	*n*	*%*	*n*	*%*	*n*	*%*
Less than 55	32	13	26	14	58	13	22	9	24	13	46	11
55 to 59.9	39	15	17	9	56	13	18	7	24	13	42	10
60 to 69.9	77	30	57	31	134	31	65	25	59	33	124	29
70 to 79.9	37	15	62	34	99	23	76	30	50	28	126	29
Over 80, or unopposed	68	27	20	11	88	20	76	30	21	12	97	22
Totals	253	100	182	99[a]	435	100	257	101[a]	178	99[a]	435	101[a]

[a]Rounding error.

Source: 1984 data adapted and compiled by the author from "The '84 Vote," ABC News report, no date, (Table 4-2, pp. 434–451); 1986 data adapted by the author from *Congressional Quarterly Weekly Report*, March 14, 1987, pp. 486–493.

winning candidate, (2) the winning candidate's margin (in percentage points) over the closest opponent, and (3) the population density of the constituency. The third factor was measured by counting the number of counties covered by a congressional district. The most urbanized districts were those covering no more than one county, the high urban districts were those encompassing from two to five counties, the low urban districts were those with from six to nineteen counties, and the least urban districts were the remainder, including Nebraska's third district with sixty-two counties, Kansas's first district with fifty-eight counties, and the six one-district states.

Table 4-2 shows the relationship between winner's party and winner's margin, controlling for population density. It can be seen that the Democratic majority in House seats came largely from its success in the most urban districts, where it carried 106 seats and lost only 44—a margin of 62 compared to its overall House

Table 4-2. Winning party and margin of victory, controlled for population density, 1984 house elections

Margins	Democratic Winners		Republican Winners		Total
	number	percent	number	percent	
1. Most urban districts:					
Won by 20 percentiles or more, or unopposed	86	71	35	29	121
Won by 10 to 19 percentiles	13	81	3	19	16
Won by 5 to 9 percentiles	4	57	3	43	7
Won by 0 to 4 percentiles	3	50	3	50	6
Total	106	71	44	29	150
2. High urban districts:					
Won by 20 percentiles or more, or unopposed	37	49	39	51	76
Won by 10 to 19 percentiles	8	57	6	43	14
Won by 5 to 9 percentiles	7	70	3	30	10
Won by 0 to 4 percentiles	1	20	4	80	5
Total	53	50	52	50	105
3. Low urban districts:					
Won by 20 percentiles or more, or unopposed	49	49	50	51	99
Won by 10 to 19 percentiles	12	60	8	40	20
Won by 5 to 9 percentiles	7	78	2	22	9
Won by 0 to 4 percentiles	7	50	7	50	14
Total	75	53	67	47	142
4. Least urban districts:					
Won by 20 percentiles or more, or unopposed	15	56	12	44	27
Won by 10 to 19 percentiles	2	29	5	71	7
Won by 5 to 9 percentiles	1	50	1	50	2
Won by 0 to 4 percentiles	1	50	1	50	2
Total	19	50	19	50	38

Source: Calculated by author from election data appearing in the *Congressional Directory* 1985–1986 concerning the 1984 general elections.

margin of 71 seats. Particularly striking was the Democratic lead of 86 to 35 in contests where the margin of victory was 20 percentage points or more. In the least urban and most urban districts, Democratic wins tended to be associated with large margins of victory. In the two middle population density categories, however, Democratic victories tended to be associated with relatively low margins of victory.

A final note concerns those 1984 elections that produced new members. Republicans won thirty of these contests; Democrats, only thirteen. For both Republican and Democratic winners, as table 4-3 shows, the margin of victory tended to be lower than the winning margins in the races won by incumbent members. In fact, twenty-five of the forty-three new members won their seats with margins of less than ten percentage points.

The low turnover rate, the low number of close congressional election contests, and the low variation in seats controlled by a given party over the years produce a picture of a Congress that changes slowly and incrementally over time. This reduces the likelihood that Congress, especially the House, would often institute dramatic changes in policy direction and may explain in part the reputation of the executive branch for being the major source of policy initiatives.

It should be noted that in a presidential election year such as 1984, voter turnout is a little higher than in nonpresidential election years and that the personalities of the presidential candidates to some degree affect voter choices in other races on the ballot. In 1984 Republican congressional fortunes were raised somewhat by the widespread popularity of President Reagan as compared to his Democratic opponent, Walter Mondale.

Senatorial contests are usually more closely contested than House contests, as illustrated in table 4-4. The Democratic successes in 1986 Senate races were most notable in the closest contests, where Democrats won eleven races while losing only four.

Using and Defending a Record

Perhaps the most remarkable aspect of congressional elections over at least the past generation has been the persistent success of House incumbents who seek reelection. Incumbent members have obvious advantages over their challengers, including experience, staff, knowledge of the district and its problems, money from

Table 4-3. Margins of victory for new members, by party, 1984 congressional elections

Margin	New Democrats	New Republicans	Margin in seats
Won by 20 percentiles or more, or unopposed	5	5	0
Won by 10 to 19 percentiles	1	7	6 (Republican)
Won by 5 to 9 percentiles	4	6	2 (Republican)
Won by 0 to 4 percentiles	3	12	9 (Republican)
Totals	13	30	17 (Republican)

Table 4-4.   Percentage of votes received by winning senate candidates, 1986 general election

Percentage of votes received	Democrats	Republicans	Total
Less than 55	11	4	15
55 to 59.9	0	3	3
60 to 69.9	7	5	12
70 to 79.9	2	2	4
Over 80, or unopposed	0	0	0
Totals	20	14	34

Source: Compiled by the author from election data in *Congressional Quarterly Weekly Report,* March 14, 1987, pp. 486–493.

political action committees and other sources with whom the incumbent has developed cordial relations, media contacts, and name recognition. Seldom have fewer than 90 percent of incumbent representatives been successful in running for reelection. The lowest postwar success rate for incumbent representatives came in 1948, when "only" 79.3 percent of incumbents running for reelection were successful. Each of the six biennial elections from 1976 through 1986 showed an impressive success rate (see table 4-5). Since about 90 percent of incumbent representatives usually run for reelection, turnover in House seats has seldom reached as high as 20 percent since World War II. For example, 354 representatives (81 percent) serving in 1983 had been members of the House in the previous Congress. Forty incumbent members retired, 10 were defeated in primary elections, and 29 were defeated in November.

But as successful as House incumbents have generally been in seeking reelection, previous service can also be a detriment. Incumbents can be embarrassed by careless or ill-advised actions, statements, or votes, and the embarrassment is made more acute because it can often be verified in official government records. As *Congressional Quarterly Weekly Report* (December 7, 1985, 2565) notes, several incumbents "discovered in 1984 that obscure and seemingly inconsequential votes

Table 4-5.   Reelection rate for U. S. representatives running to retain their seats, 1976–1986

Election year	Percentage of successful incumbent candidates
1976	96
1978	94
1980	91
1982	91
1984	95
1986	98

Source: Calmes 1986, 2891–2892.

. . . would prove damaging to them when made the basis of oversimplified thirty-second commercials by the opponents." A problem for incumbents is that they are susceptible to falling into traps. An example of this occurred in late 1985 to Congressman Bill Alexander (D.–Ark.) when it was publicized that he had been the lone passenger on an Air Force flight to Brazil that cost $56,364. Originally, several other representatives were to have joined Alexander on the trip to Brazil, the purpose of which was to study alcohol fuel production. Alexander was also criticized for voting to produce a braille version of *Playboy* magazine, for making a statement that was allegedly derogatory to blacks, and for being photographed with Fidel Castro while on a trip to Cuba. Alexander was reelected in the 1986 election, but subsequently his hopes for promotion on the Democratic party ladder were dashed when the Democratic caucus made leadership decisions for the 100th Congress. In spite of the many advantages incumbents have, their records can be exploited by alert challengers.

Incumbent senators have not been as successful as representatives when seeking new terms. Only in 1960 and 1982 did Senate incumbents reach the 90 percent success rate. In 1946, the first postwar election, and 1980, the year of Reagan's first presidential victory, 60 percent of senators seeking reelection won. There are several explanations for the greater vulnerability of incumbent senators. For one thing, Senate contests generally have far greater visibility than House contests. For another, party control of the Senate is tighter, and both national parties are more likely to regard every contest as worthy of their best efforts and candidates. The quality of the challenging candidate is therefore likely to be higher than it is in House contests. Table 4-6 summarizes the fate of Senate incumbents by decade in the period 1946 to 1984.

Over the years a sizable number of senators and representatives have left Congress by voluntary retirement rather than by electoral defeat (see table 4-7), with a particularly sharp rise in the rate of congressional retirements since 1970. In some election years, in fact, turnover from retirement has exceeded turnover from electoral defeat. Some members retire if they believe their party is in a period of

Table 4-6. Senate incumbents and the elections of 1946–1984

Period	Retired	Defeated in primaries	Defeated in general election	Won reelection	Total seeking reelection	Incumbents' success rate (percent)[a]
1946–1954	31	17	35	98	150	65
1956–1964	23	2	24	128	154	83
1966–1974	26	12	18	115	145	79
1976–1984	30	7	30	101	138	73

[a]Excludes retirees
Source: Adapted and calculated by the author from data in Table 2-8 in Ornstein et al. 1984, 51, with the addition of data for 1984 election results.

Table 4-7.   Retirements from Congress, 1930–1984

Twelve-year period	House of Representatives			Senate			Total		
	Dem.	Rep.	Total	Dem.	Rep.	Total	Dem.	Rep.	Total
1930–1942	139	73	212	14	12	26	153	85	238
1944–1956	106	92	198	20	13	33	126	105	231
1958–1970	81	109	190	13	16	29	94	125	219
1972–1984	154	122	276	20	23	43	174	145	319

Source: Adapted by the author from Table 2-9 in Ornstein et al. 1984, 52, with additional data for 1984 from *Congressional Quarterly Weekly Report,* November 10, 1984, p. 2900. The original sources for data through 1978 are Lehmann, 1978, *Congressional Quarterly Weekly Report* (8 November 1980) 3302, 3320–3321; and *National Journal* (6 November 1982) 1881.

relative decline or is not likely to win control of the chamber; this would decrease a member's chances of heading an important committee or subcommittee. Members also retire because of ill health, personal dissatisfaction with political life, higher pay opportunities elsewhere, or a growing sense of frustration with the congressional job.

Seniority

An important long-run consequence of contests for congressional office is the degree of experience gained. When so many members seek reelection and are successful, there is a resultant high degree of seniority.

In the first centuries of the American republic, members of Congress were not as likely to devote a substantial part of their career to Congress. It was more likely that service in Washington represented for them an interruption of careers and family life-styles. Travel difficulties alone made Washington service unattractive. But late in the nineteenth century (for reasons that will be discussed in chapter 7), seniority became a particularly important factor in determining a member's power and visibility. Among other things, this made extended service more attractive and reduced the rate of voluntary retirement. By the middle of this century, Congress had in a number of ways added to congressional perquisites of staff, equipment, and allowances, making it more and more easy and desirable to stay in office.

These considerations produced a postwar Congress that exhibited a steady and high level of experience. Table 4-8 shows the proportions in recent decades of representatives and senators with various levels of seniority. This pattern can be compared with the situation in the 58th Congress (1903–1904) when only 13 percent of the representatives had served six terms or more (Witmer 1964, 538). In the past decade there has been a marked increase in the ratio of newcomers to veteran members. Still, as noted earlier in this chapter, Congress is an incremental body with a low turnover rate.

Table 4-8. Seniority of members of the House and Senate in four postwar congresses

Congress (years)	House of Representatives			Senate		
	Percent serving:			Percent serving:		
	1–3 terms	4–6 terms	7 + terms	1–6 years	7–12 years	13 + years
83rd (1953–1954)	44	29	26	38	43	15
88th (1963–1964)	41	24	36	44	27	29
93rd (1973–1974)	37	30	34	40	23	37
98th (1983–1984)	49	28	24	43	30	27

Source: Calculated by the author from various editions of the *Congressional Directory* 1953–1983. For more detailed data, see Ornstein et al. 1984, 18–19 (for the House), 20 (for the Senate).

SUMMARY

Members of Congress do not closely reflect the sex, race, income, or educational attainments of the people they represent. Every day members confront a number of tensions in their congressional work: how to balance the demands of family and of job; how to balance time spent on committee work (helping to write laws) and casework for constituents (working to get reelected); and whether to concentrate on improving conditions for all the people of the district or for specific groups of constituents such as farmers, steelworkers, nurses, or lumberjacks. Members take their representational duties very seriously, because such activities discourage the emergence of threatening challenges back home and thus help to assure the incumbent's reelection.

REFERENCES

CALMES, JACQUELINE. "Safe Seats, Hard Work, No National Discontent: House Incumbents Achieve Record Success Rate in 1986." *Congressional Quarterly Weekly Report* (15 November 1986): 2891–2892.

DAVIDSON, ROGER H., and OLESZEK, WALTER J. *Congress and Its Members.* 2nd ed. Washington, D.C.: Congressional Quarterly Press, 1985.

DEXTER, LEWIS A. *The Sociology and Politics of Congress.* Skokie, Ill.: Rand McNally, 1960.

FENNO, JR., RICHARD F. *Home Style: House Members in Their Districts.* Boston: Little, Brown, 1978.

FENNO, JR., RICHARD F. "Observation, Context, and Sequence in the Study of Politics." *American Political Science Review,* 80 (March 1986): 6.

FIORINA, MORRIS P. *Representatives, Roll Calls, and Constituencies.* Lexington, Mass: Lexington Books, 1974.

FROMAN, JR., LEWIS. *Congressmen and Their Constituencies.* Skokie, Ill.: Rand McNally, 1963.

HERSHEY, MARJORIE RANDON. *Running for Office: The Political Education of Campaigners.* Chatham, N. J.: Chatham House, 1984.

JACOBSON, GARY C. *The Politics of Congressional Elections.* Boston: Little, Brown, 1983.

LEHMANN, MILDRED. "Members of Congress Who Choose Not to Run for Reelection to the Seats They Occupy, 1930–1978." *Congressional Research Service* (18 May 1978).

MAYHEW, DAVID R. *Congress: The Electoral Connection*. New Haven, Conn.: Yale University Press, 1974.

ORNSTEIN, NORMAN J., MANN, THOMAS E., MALBIN, MICHAEL J., SCHICK, ALLEN, and BIBBY, JOHN. *Vital Statistics on Congress, 1984–1985*. Washington, D. C.: American Enterprise Institute, 1984.

PARKER, GLENN. *Homeward Bound: Explaining Changes in Congressional Behavior*. Pittsburgh: University of Pittsburgh Press, 1986.

SALMORE, STEPHEN A., and SALMORE, BARBARA G. *Candidates, Parties, and Campaigns: Electoral Politics in America*. Washington, D. C.: Congressional Quarterly Press, 1985.

WITMER, T. RICHARD. "The Aging of the House." *Political Science Quarterly* 58 (December 1964): 538.

V CONGRESSIONAL CAMPAIGNS

Because the selection of members of Congress is at the heart of the American system of representative government and because in congressional elections the stakes are so important, it is not surprising that these campaigns are often arduous, exhausting, expensive, and vitriolic.

Competitive elections should produce members whose attitudes and actions are in accord with the majority of voters. Those who believe in representative government trust that when voters cast their votes, they know what candidates stand for, how they differ, and whether they can be trusted to act in office as they have promised during the campaign.

This chapter identifies the major elements, the major players, and the critical factors for success in congressional campaigns. It will conclude with a case study of a 1986 congressional contest in Indiana.

ELEMENTS OF THE CONGRESSIONAL CAMPAIGN

Owing to the two basic constitutional principles of federalism and separation of powers, American voters are confronted with a complex set of election contests. Every four years candidates campaign for president, and in most states, governors are also elected every four years. The terms of members of the fifty state legislatures are such that most states have legislative elections every two years. County and municipal elections present an even busier schedule of elections, occurring in many areas on an annual basis.

Senate and House Campaigns

Elections for all members of the House of Representatives take place in November of each even-numbered year. Since one-third of the Senate is elected every two years, two-thirds of the states will have a Senate contest in any given even-numbered year, even apart from the possibility of special elections to fill out terms of incumbents who have resigned or died in office.

Senate elections are statewide and therefore must compete for attention and resources with presidential or gubernatorial contests taking place in the same year. Senators are more visible and thus more vulnerable than representatives. Accordingly, the organization and planning of Senate campaigns proceeds differently in some ways than House races. National and statewide issues tend to be played up to a greater degree in senatorial campaigns. The difference in the number of seats held by the two parties is smaller in the Senate than in the House, so the president is likely to be more interested in Senate contests than in House contests. Also, in many cases the state's governor will aspire to a Senate seat at some time in the future, and as a result senatorial and gubernatorial campaign operations and appeals may merge. Contests for House seats are generally not as involved; district problems and personalities are the dominant matters. Congressional, as opposed to senatorial, campaigns spend less money, stress local issues, and involve smaller organizations and more local media. Ordinarily, House contests are less competitive than Senate contests, and House challengers have less credibility and visibility.

Election Timing

Incumbent representatives and senators are always campaigning, although the reelection campaign itself may actually begin in the early spring of the election year, when candidacies are announced in advance of filing deadlines established by state law. Some primary elections occur fairly early in the year, some are in the spring, and others are at the very end of summer. In 1986 eleven states held primaries in May, twelve in June, ten in August, and sixteen in September. Illinois was earliest, holding its primary on March 18, and Hawaii and Louisiana were last, having theirs on September 20 and 27, respectively. Nine southern or border states provide for a runoff to be held from two to four weeks later if no candidate receives a majority of votes in the primary. (Presidential candidate Jesse Jackson complained in 1984 that runoffs in southern states were established years ago to reduce the likelihood that candidates supported by black voters would be elected.) By the end of September at the latest, the nomination stage is completed, the major and minor parties have named their respective candidates, and the general election campaign is underway. Media advertising, speeches, and the travels of candidates bring the campaign more and more forcefully—and at times irritatingly—to the attention of the public. The campaign effort culminates in rallies, pronouncements, and get-out-the-vote drives on the last preelection weekend.

It is the campaign that brings American politics together. The election campaign process brings all the political actors, institutions, issues, ideas, and movements into concentrated focus. Party organizations, candidates and their staffs, media professionals, polling consultants, and interest groups interrelate for a brief and hectic period of time. Where many aspects of government and politics may seem tame, routine, even dull, the campaign is characteristically full of excitement, passion, uncertainty, and anxiety.

Close observers of political campaigns have been struck by how rapidly campaign situations change and at the same time by how regularly campaigns take on a standard pattern. Fenno (1986, 5–6) puts it this way:

The campaign you see on the day you arrive is often not the campaign you see on the day you leave. And that is exactly the way the campaigners themselves perceive it. They talk to you about the campaign in the language of time, and of change and of sequence. They speak of stages and phases, or rhythms and flows, of plans and turning points, of gains and losses, of momentum and pace, of beginning games and end games. Campaigns, for all their improvisation, exhibit a good deal of sequential regularity.

Major Players

A fuller notion of what campaigning really involves can be gained by considering the major roles played by members of a typical campaign organization. Campaigns are increasingly dominated by specialists, whose skills have become virtually indispensible in the operation of a major campaign, and less involved with local political party organizations. In addition to specific campaign organizations for individual candidates, there are also political party organizations and interest groups (notably political action committees and single-interest groups) that work for or against specific candidates. In recent decades there has been a marked shift away from party-centered campaigns toward candidate-centered campaigns.

The roles of major players in a congressional campaign and the problems and tasks each player deals with follow:

1. Campaign manager

   - directs all campaign operations, relieving candidate of necessity of working closely and frequently with other campaign elements
   - hires staff for headquarters and field operations
   - arranges for office space and equipment
   - hires professional experts or consultants for such functions as media, publicity, polling, speech-writing, legal counsel, and accounting
   - directs overall campaign planning
   - schedules the candidate's time and travel
   - coordinates all campaign activities, including contact with political party and allied groups

2. Fund-raiser

   - plans and conducts special events and other efforts to raise money from likely major contributors
   - contacts political party organizations, political action committees, and other groups to solicit contributions
   - plans and carries out direct mail and print advertising appeals for contributions from the general public
   - helps plan campaign expenditures

3. Media buyer

   - evaluates the cost-benefit utility of all available media
   - helps formulate the campaign's advertising budget

- purchases space in newspapers and other periodicals and buys time on radio and television for campaign advertisements

4. Direct mail expert

- finds or builds mailing lists for the general public and for particular significant groups (such as physicians, pro-abortionists, pilots, livestock farmers, labor union members, plumbers, and so on)
- prepares special messages and appeals for each mailing
- oversees mailing operations and supervises handling of any returns and responses

5. Issues expert

- checks recent articles, speeches, polls, books, reports, and so forth on issues likely to be important in the campaign, especially potentially embarrassing issues
- develops messages and speeches on all relevant issues
- confers with others in the organization on how, where, when, and with whom the campaign's issue positions can best be developed

6. Public relations expert

- develops a coordinated advertising and publicity program
- develops positive contacts with newspaper, television, and radio personnel
- writes and distributes speeches, news releases, and so forth to the press and public
- helps plan and advertise the candidate's itinerary

7. Public opinion expert

- conducts or arranges for scientific public opinion studies of the electorate
- confers with others in the organization about information to be sought in public opinion polls and how results are to be incorporated into the campaign

8. Accountant and treasurer (the roles could be separated)

- sets up a system to monitor all campaign receipts and expenditures
- makes prompt and accurate reports to federal and state election offices on campaign receipts and expenditures, as required by federal and state law
- keeps campaign manager informed on a day-to-day basis of financial conditions

9. Legal adviser

- provides legal advice to the candidate, campaign manager, and others in the organization, with special attention to election administration arrangements, financial disclosure, conflict-of-interest questions, libel, and slander

- reviews any doubtful transaction, statement, or activity of the candidate or the opposition.

FACTORS AFFECTING CAMPAIGN SUCCESS

In her study of congressional elections, Barbara Hinckley (1981, 4) notes that there are several dimensions of electoral activity: "An election implies both individual choice and a collective event." The individual must first decide whether to vote and then which candidate to vote for. The campaign involves many processes, most notably the recruitment of candidates, the planning of strategies, and the distribution of information to the public through speeches, news releases, special events, and newspaper and television advertising. As Hinckley comments, "Elections, then, both aggregate and translate activity at one point and on one level to another" (4).

In their study, Goldenberg and Traugott (1984) were especially concerned about whether campaigns made much difference. They were concerned about "the development of campaign strategies and tactics, the allocation of a candidate's resources, the information about the campaign that becomes available to potential voters, and the consequence of campaigns for electoral outcomes" (2). They note that academic studies have attributed "minimal significance" to campaigns, while "candidates, political consultants, and members of the media" have felt that campaign strategies and messages have exerted great influence on the voting outcome (3–10). Their research demonstrates that amount of advertising, editorial endorsements, news coverage, and name recognition generally have considerable impact on electoral outcomes—at least in terms of producing significant degrees of change from the "normal vote" if not in terms of actually winning or losing a contest. Many observers, in assessing the effectiveness of particular campaign efforts, seem to think only about whether a candidate won or lost rather than about whether that candidate did better or worse than might have been expected from the pattern of recent elections (152–159).

Marjorie Randon Hershey's study of 1980 campaigns led her to conclude that voters provide only a small amount of direct feedback to candidates during campaigns and that consultants and journalists reach conclusions about the real meaning of a campaign only after the votes have been counted. Hershey (1984, 269) believes that campaigns do not sensitize candidates to the true feelings of the mass public, but instead the process "systematically amplifies the voices of organized groups, other office holders, party leaders, and media figures" while the voices of the ordinary public are muted.

My study of congressional campaigns of 1974, undertaken with several associates (Clem et al., 1976), was predicated on the assumption that several explicit variables were sufficiently interesting to merit scholarly attention. From these and other studies, several factors (discussed below) can be identified that are, or are thought to be, especially important in determining the outcome of congressional and senatorial campaigns.

Party Balance

The relative strength of the two major parties in each electoral district is the most important factor affecting the campaign. In some states and districts, the division between Democrats and Republicans is about even. In some areas, one party has been predominant over the years, but the minority party has been able occasionally to win a contest. In the remaining areas, the dominant party has won every major election in at least the past generation.

In senatorial contests during 1960 to 1986, for example, there is considerable variation in terms of the number of Democratic party victories. Table 5-1 shows that, on the basis of senatorial contests, Arkansas and Louisiana are the most Democratic states, and Kansas and Pennsylvania are the most Republican. (States would be classified differently if presidential, congressional district, gubernatorial, or state legislative district elections were used as a measure.)

Some states and congressional districts have uncontested elections, although this apparent lack of competition is belied by the fierce factional contests for the party nomination in the primary. In 1984, for example, there were sixty-eight uncontested elections for the House of Representatives. Fifty-four Democratic members of the House were reelected without Republican opposition (more than half of them from the South), while fourteen Republicans were reelected without Democratic opponents (most of them also from the South). On the other hand are districts (in some cases, entire states) that have a large number of very close contests (see chapter 4, "Margin of Election").

Who Holds the Office

Just as the most dependable way to become a millionaire is to have a millionaire for a parent, so the most dependable way to be elected to the House of Representatives

Table 5-1.   Victories for Democratic candidates, by state, for the U. S. Senate, 1960–1986.

Number of Democratic victories	States
10	Arkansas, Louisiana
9	Alabama, Georgia, Montana, West Virginia
8	Washington
7	Florida, Hawaii, Michigan, Mississippi, Ohio, Rhode Island, Wisconsin
6	Connecticut, Massachusetts, Minnesota, Missouri, Nevada, New Jersey, North Carolina
5	Alaska, California, Illinois, Indiana, Kentucky, New Mexico, North Dakota, Oklahoma, South Carolina, South Dakota, Tennessee, Texas, Virginia
4	Colorado, Iowa, Maine, Maryland, Nebraska
3	Arizona, Delaware, Idaho, New Hampshire, New York, Vermont
2	Oregon, Utah, Wyoming
1	Pennsylvania
0	Kansas

Note: In the period covered by this table, some states had a total of ten Senate races and other states had only nine, depending on the classes of their senators. Only elections for full six-year Senate terms are included.

Source: Calculated by the author.

is to be an incumbent. "Not all congressional candidates are created equal," Goldenberg and Traugott (1984, 181) note, and the most clear-cut advantage in a congressional campaign belongs to the incumbent. Incumbents, by definition, have run (and won) before in the district, so they are conversant with the district's interests and influentials. By cultivating individual constituents, incumbents (and their staffs) have broadened support throughout the district. Incumbents are highly visible: They make speeches, are interviewed on television, send newsletters to thousands of constituents at public expense, and do countless minor favors, such as sending flags to schools or infant care booklets to new mothers. Perhaps more important, incumbents know from experience where the money to fuel their reelection efforts can be obtained. Incumbents are likely to be offered campaign contributions by national and local interest groups that want to exploit congressional connections to secure more favorable legislation. This effort to woo support is particularly affected by a member's committee assignment. Political action committees (PACs) contribute much money to members of those standing committees with jurisdiction over policy areas of concern to them. Committee members on the majority side can expect greater PAC generosity than those from the minority party. For instance, PAC contributions to Republican members of the Senate Finance Committee in the first six months of 1985 averaged $161,000, compared to an average of $32,000 for Democratic members. In the House, Democratic members of the tax-writing Ways and Means Committee received an average of $54,000 in PAC contributions, while Republican members on average attracted $40,000.

This is not to say that challengers cannot win, only that fewer than 10 percent of them do. Some interest group effort and PAC money are aimed at defeating certain incumbents. This is particularly true if a member has taken a key role in opposing the legislative objectives of the group. For this reason, incumbents prefer to steer clear of such highly emotional and visible issues as gun control, school prayer, and abortion. Challengers can, by strenuous and persistent district efforts, build up large campaign treasuries; the resultant advertising effort made possible by a deep treasury will certainly help the challenger's chances of winning on election day.

In 1984, 411 of the members of the House of Representatives ran for reelection; an additional 2 incumbents sought reelection but died before the general election date. Of the 411, 3 were defeated in the primary, and 16 more were defeated in November, leaving 392 successful incumbents, a winning ratio of 95 percent. There was little difference in success rate by party; 95 percent of Democratic incumbents and 98 percent of Republican incumbents who ran for a new term were successful. House incumbents did even better in 1986 (as noted in chapter 4).

Money

The cost of campaigning has risen greatly in recent years, and so has the number of finance reports to be filed by candidates with the Federal Election Commission. (See table 5-2 for data on the increased costs of campaigns.) The rise of political

Table 5-2.   Campaign costs for Congress in recent nonpresidential election years

	1974	1978	1982
HOUSE CAMPAIGNS			
Total expenditures	$44,051,125	$86,129,169	$174,921,844
Average expenditures by			
Democrats	53,994	108,986	213,369
Republicans	54,835	109,995	245,020
Incumbents	56,539	111,159	265,001
Challengers	40,015	74,802	151,717
Open seat candidates	90,426	201,049	284,476
SENATE CAMPAIGNS			
Total expenditures	28,436,308	64,695,510	114,036,379
Average expenditures by			
Democrats	487,775	762,831	1,881,379
Republicans	382,343	1,151,407	1,682,252
Incumbents	555,714	1,341,942	1,858,140
Challengers	332,579	697,766	1,217,034
Open seat candidates	401,484	820,787	4,142,687

Source: Ornstein et al. 1984, 65, 66, 69, 70, Tables 3-1 and 3-4, which were compiled from reports issued by Common Cause (1974) and the Federal Election Commission (1978, 1982).

action committees has increased the number of sources of campaign money. These factors increase the strain on both incumbent and challenger.

Before elaborating on the influence of money in congressional elections, it is well to recall Gary Jacobson's (1980) conclusion that money is less important than party and incumbency in deciding the outcomes of campaigns. As long as both candidates have enough money to reach a threshold in terms of getting their messages to the public, the money factor is not likely to determine the outcome and very high spending will pass the point of diminishing returns. Over the eight-year period from 1974 to 1982, total campaign spending quadrupled for both House and Senate races. The progression for the House was from total spending of $44 million to $175 million, with the average rising from $53,000 to $228,000 per candidate. In 1974 only 10 House candidates reported spending more than $200,000; in 1982, 353 House candidates exceeded this figure. For the Senate, with far fewer races in a given year, a similar pattern is evident. Senate campaign spending was at $28 million in 1974, an average of $437,000 per contest, and by 1982 the figure had reached $114 million, or $1,782,000 per contest (Ornstein et al. 1984, 65–67, 69). Over the past decade, political parties and political action committees have both greatly increased dollar contributions to congressional and senatorial candidates.

According to Federal Election Commission reports, $375 million was spent by congressional and senatorial candidates in the two-year period from 1983 to 1984. Slightly more than half of that amount ($204 million) was spent in House races, with Democrats outspending Republicans $111 million to $92 million. (A total of about $700,000 was spent by candidates of other parties.) While the number of Senate contests was less than 10 percent of the number of House contests, $170 million was spent on Senate races, $88 million by Republicans and $82 million by Democrats. (A total of $214,000 was spent by candidates of other parties.) Table 5-3 shows the share of funding provided by various sources for House and Senate candidates in the 1983–1984 period.

Though political action committees give a lot of money to incumbents, particularly representatives, PAC money is also a major source of campaign funds for challengers and for candidates running for an open seat. For this reason, congressional candidates increasingly look to Washington consultants and organizations when planning campaigns. This tendency has the effect of reducing the candidate's ties to the district and, conversely, tightening the ties between candidates and national PACs (Watson, 1986). PAC contributions are especially influential because they show dedication to the candidate's cause and because they are often made early in the campaign, when the beneficiary can make best use of the money in planning and placing advertisements.

Currently, there is great concern over rising campaign costs and the potentially inappropriate influence of money and PACs on office holders. The 1970s witnessed a great effort to publicize and regulate the use of money in political campaigns. Federal laws were written to limit contributions and spending, to require that campaigns make complete and timely financial reports, and to provide administrative mechanisms to ensure that the new finance rules were followed. The federal legislation of the 1970s provided for

1. public funding of presidential campaigns, including primary campaigns and support for the national party conventions that nominate presidential candidates

Table 5-3.   Sources of 1984 campaign contributions

Contributor category	Open seats (percent)	Incumbents (percent)	Challengers (percent)
HOUSE OF REPRESENTATIVES			
Individuals	46	46	46
Political action committees	26	42	21
Political parties	10	3	14
Candidate	15	1	14
Loans, interest, etc.	4	7	4
SENATE			
Individuals	48	65	64
Political action committees	9	23	16
Political parties	8	6	12
Candidate	32	1	3
Loans, interest, etc.	3	6	4

Note: Columns may not add to 100 because of rounding.
Source: Adapted by the author from *FEC Record,* July, 1985, 9.

2. tax credits for political contributions
3. a check-off system whereby individual taxpayers are invited to place one dollar of their tax liability in their party's presidential campaign treasury
4. limits on the amount of money that can be contributed to political campaigns by individuals, political parties, and nonparty political action committees
5. limits on the amount of money a candidate can spend in campaigning for federal office
6. full reporting and disclosure of contributions to and spending by candidates
7. establishment of the Federal Elections Commission (FEC) to administer and enforce political finance regulations

The Supreme Court's decision in *Buckley* v. *Valeo* reduced some of the new regulatory apparatus, declaring that limiting candidates' rights to contribute their own money limited their freedom of speech and access to the political process guaranteed in the First Amendment. The decision further pointed up constitutional deficiencies in the methods of naming the FEC commissioners, a problem corrected by subsequent legislation.

Although Congress has provided the opportunity for public financing of presidential campaigns, it has not done so for congressional campaigns, evidently because of incumbent members' fears that such changes would tend to equalize campaign resources and thereby increase chances that challengers could unseat incumbents.

In April 1987, a bill was introduced by Sen. David Boren (D.–Okla.) to establish a partial public financing system for Senate campaigns. Boren's proposal was approved by the Senate Rules and Administration Committee, with some amendments suggested by Committee Chairman Sen. Wendell Ford (D.–Ky.), who in the past had not been a strong supporter of finance reform. The bill proposed a spending limit for each state, determined by the state's voting age population. Candidates would qualify for federal money by raising $250,000 or 20 percent of their state's limit, whichever was lower, in small contributions from individuals. Eighty percent of this amount had to come from in-state sources. Another provision of Boren's bill would lower PAC contributions from $5,000 to $3,000 and limit the total amount a candidate could accept from PACs in a two-year election cycle.

Candidate Characteristics

Several things about a candidate appear of special importance for the outcome of a campaign. Candidates' educational and occupational backgrounds influence their perspectives on and understanding of current issues and problems. Candidates' ideological and philosophical orientations help determine which issues are considered important and how many problems they believe can be alleviated by governmental action. Candidates who have had direct political experience, especially in holding office, are likely to know how the political system works, how decisions are made, and how other political figures can be influenced to work toward the policy objectives of the constituency. Candidates with little experience or information may have erroneous, irrational, and distorted ideas about what people want, the nature of current problems, and the efficacy of governmental action. A candidate who is open to new ideas and candid in discussing them tends to generate a positive and honest image. Some candidates, however, seem to prefer a negative or secretive approach, basing campaigns on suspicion and distortion. A warm, engaging, outgoing personality is more likely to attract votes than one that is cold, gloomy, or withdrawn.

Candidates can be classified on the basis of their relative experience, insight, and personality. If both candidates are perceived as similar, these measures are not likely to affect the outcome of the race. Candidate characteristics assume campaign significance when the public perceives sharp differences between the antagonists. Seldom do congressional campaigns hinge on such sharp personality differences as characterized the presidential contests of Harry Truman and Thomas Dewey (1948), Dwight Eisenhower and Adlai Stevenson (1952, 1956), John Kennedy and Richard Nixon (1960), and Ronald Reagan and Jimmy Carter (1980). Nonetheless, candidate personalities are occasionally crucial in congressional elections.

Issues

The theory of representative democracy holds that one of the basic functions of a campaign is to present issues so that citizens know how rival candidates stand on vital questions and consequently can vote for the candidate with the most proximate policy orientations. This notion has been challenged, the arguments being (1) that candidates avoid discussion of many difficult and critical issues, and (2) that few citizens are willing to listen to detailed debates about issues. Candidates have better and more vote-productive campaign activities than discussing and debating issues, and citizens are often distracted from the issues by such aspects of the campaign as partisanship, ideology, or personality. Making the matter even more problematic, many issues are presented in oversimplified and therefore unrealistic terms.

Four characteristics of political issues determine the relative importance of this factor in a campaign. First, how salient is the issue to the public? That is, what percentage of potential voters feels vitally affected by the issue? Some issues are highly salient to a large percentage of the public; others affect only a small number.

Second, how intensely does the public feel about the issue? An issue such as gun control or abortion may generate a lot of intense feelings, whereas another more salient issue, such as foreign aid or economic policy, might generate less intensity.

Third, on a given issue proposal, how does the public divide? In some cases, most people are predominantly on one side. The precise division of the public may be ninety to ten or sixty to forty. The really tough political questions, from the standpoint of candidates running for Congress, are those questions where the public is divided fifty–fifty. To take a strong public stand on such an issue will likely alienate half the electorate.

Finally, how polarized is the issue? That is, does the issue tend to be regarded in sharply different ways by different segments of the population, one group pitted against another group? Some examples of polarized issues are those concerning men versus women, whites versus blacks, older people versus younger people, the well-to-do versus the poor, and city residents versus small-town and rural residents. Of course, if voters believe that both candidates are taking essentially the same position on a given issue, that issue will not have much impact on voters' decisions.

Each campaign has its own degree of issue prominence; sometimes campaign outcomes depend largely on issues, and sometimes other factors appear more critical. In some races, national or general issues are emphasized; in other contests, local or special issues receive more attention. National issues often become more prominent in presidential election years. Different campaigns emphasize different economic, moral, security, or welfare questions. Government price support for wheat or tobacco is not likely to attract much attention in Massachusetts or Arizona, nor will U. S.-Canadian lumber trade negotiations be of "front-burner" interest in Kansas or Florida.

The choice and position taken on each issue raised is one of the basic strategic calculations a candidate for Congress must make early in the campaign. The process is reminiscent of the opening moves in chess: What issue (piece) do I raise (move)? How does my opponent respond? I will then have to respond to my opponent's response. Will my actions and reactions impress the groups and individuals counted on for support in the campaign?

Ideology

Partisan considerations determine how some people vote; many Americans vote consistently with their Democratic or Republican party identification. For other voters, issue considerations are critical factors in voting decisions. Falling somewhere between general partisan factors and more specific issue factors is ideology. That is, many voters respond to campaign appeals largely based on their own identification with what they consider liberalism or conservatism. What is critical is which candidate exhibits the most consistent attachment to an ideological point of view. For these voters there is an ideological dimension in most policy controversies, such as aid to Central America, U. S. policy toward South Africa, a national speed limit, universal military training, federal budget deficits, national defense, pollution controls, urban housing, health insurance, and scores of other perennial issues. These voters seek a candidate whose ideological consistency—liberal or conservative—they feel they can trust. Such voters can be a great help to a candidate who has adopted a clear-cut ideological stance, but they can also become a severe irritation when the candidate is in office. Issues become more complex and ambiguous when discussed in congressional committee hearings. Sharp differences in position gradually shade into gray as amendments and adjustments are suggested and as new data and arguments are presented. Solutions that sounded so logical and clear when speaking before the Rotarians in Shreveport or the League of Women

Voters in Spokane are challenged by a bewildering array of contrary authorities on Capitol Hill. To remain an ideological representative or senator requires a good deal of resolve and strength of character—or perhaps a finely selective ability to filter out information and arguments threatening to one's position. Most members of Congress, even those known for ideological consistency, find it necessary in the give and take of Washington politics to compromise and cooperate with the other side if they hope to operate effectively.

ANALYZING CAMPAIGNS

The campaigns that are likely to reveal something important are those in which the unexpected happens—that is, where an incumbent member is replaced involuntarily or where a seat moves from one party to another. Therefore it seems worthwhile to concentrate analytic attention on the small percentage of congressional campaigns resulting in such upsets.

An interesting methodological question arises: Would more be learned about congressional campaigns by emphasizing the norms and regularities than by concentrating on the few peculiarities and special circumstances? Most recent campaign research is of the former type, but the latter approach is of greater interest to some. Perhaps by looking at a few cases—cases involving involuntary replacement of an incumbent—we might be better able to identify, define, refine, and measure the really critical variables in the most interesting contests. Efforts to understand the conditions of campaign success can be frustrating, unsatisfying, and unrewarding, but such efforts are important and, it is to be hoped, will continue.

The following case describes the vigorously contested 1986 campaign in the eighth congressional district of Indiana.

Running for Congress: Indiana's 1986 "McRace"

Indiana's eighth congressional district encompasses twelve counties and parts of three others in the southwestern corner of the state and runs from Bloomington in the northeast to the confluence of the Wabash and Ohio rivers in the southwest. Evansville is the district's largest city; Indianapolis and Louisville, Kentucky, are close by.

In a state generally thought of as the core of the midwestern Republican heartland, southern Indiana has since the Civil War exhibited considerable Democratic strength. German Catholics are the most notable ethnic group, and the district's black population is only 2 percent of the total. The eighth district is, according to Barone and Ujifusa (1985, 468), "one of the nation's premier marginal congressional districts." The district's marginal status could hardly be more emphatically demonstrated than in the bitter backwash of the 1984 contest between incumbent Democrat Frank McCloskey, who had taken the seat two years before by defeating a one-term Republican incumbent with 51 percent of the vote, and his Republican challenger, Rick McIntyre.

The 1984 Recount Controversy

McCloskey, on election night 1984, appeared to have won by 72 votes, but a ballot recount in one county resulted in a 34-vote margin for McIntyre, which was subsequently certified by Indiana's secretary of state, a Republican. When the 99th Congress convened on January 3, 1985, the House voted along party lines (238 to 177) to leave the seat vacant and refer the matter to the Committee on House Administration because of the uncertainty and continuing controversy over the outcome. (Under the Constitution, each chamber of Congress is the final authority on seating its own members.) A complete ballot recount in the counties of the district put McIntyre ahead by 418 votes. Accordingly, in early February, House Republican Leader Robert Michel of Illinois moved that McIntyre be seated, pending a report from the House Administration Committee. This motion was successfully countered, 221 to 180, by a Democratic motion to refer Michel's resolution to the same committee. Five Democrats— three from Texas and one each from Ohio and Kentucky—at this point supported the Republican position. Rep. Bill Frenzel (R.–Minn.) referred to the action as murder and rape, to which Democratic Leader Jim Wright replied that Frenzel had gone beyond the bounds of decent debate. The House at the same time appointed a task force consisting of Leon Panetta (D.–Calif.), William Clay (D.–Mo.), and William Thomas (R.–Calif.) to look into the Indiana election. The task force sent officials from the General Accounting Office to Indiana to count the ballots. In April the task force concluded that McCloskey had won by four votes: 116,645 to 116,641. But Republican Thomas charged that his Democratic colleagues refused to count additional ballots once they had McCloskey in the lead, and at task force meetings in Evansville on April 18 and in Washington four days later, Thomas and Panetta (the task force chairman) engaged in heated shouting matches. The House Administration Committee, after receiving the task force report, concluded on April 23 that McCloskey had won by the four-vote margin. Republicans in the House charged that the Democrats were thieves who had stolen the election, and displayed buttons reading "Thou shalt not steal." On May 1, after attempts by Republicans to declare the seat vacant and call for a new election and after suggestions by some Democrats that McCloskey resign the seat and run again in a special election, the House finally voted 236 to 190 to approve a resolution seating McCloskey. Ten Democrats voted against the resolution. Four excerpts from the floor debate (Wright, Cheney, Panetta, Roberts, 1985) give a sense of the ongoing acrimony:

Jim Wright (D.–Tex.): It is not pleasant, it is not comfortable, it is indeed quite painful to hear the allegations that have been made through this chamber in the last four months. In the years I have served in Congress I have never known anything to have created such a degree of emotionalism. I deeply regret that. . . .

Please gentlemen, do you not understand, we are not so hard up for an extra seat in the House that we would want to deprive someone of it by theft. I really think it is beneath our dignity to engage in that kind of aspersion or that kind of allegation or that kind of consideration.

Dick Cheney (R.–Wyo.): I ask my friends and colleagues on the Democratic side of the aisle to put yourselves in our place for just a minute. Ask yourselves how you would feel were our positions reversed. What would you think if we Republicans on nearly straight party-line votes had twice voted to deny a seat to the duly certified winner of the race, had then established a task force which set aside Indiana law and imposed its own rules for counting the ballots. And finally stopped, thirty-two ballots short, when our man had pulled ahead by four votes. I believe your sense of outrage would be every bit as great as ours.

Leon Panetta (D.–Calif.): Yes there were judgments made here. Let us make no question about it. Every time you deal with an election, there are judgments that have to be made on a variety of issues, and we did that over nine weeks. The GAO auditors went to 233,000 ballots. They had to make judgments. The teams had to make judgments. We on the task force had to make judgments.

Some of the ballots were counted, some were not, based on those judgments. The question you have to ask as members of this House is: Were those judgments justified, reasonable, and supported by House precedent? . . .

The decisions were justified. They were supported, and they were right, and Mr. McCloskey ought to be seated.

Pat Roberts (R.–Kan.): . . . the special fabric that binds this institution in purpose and achievement is bipartisan. I am the first to admit that no political party has an exclusive patent on common sense or can lay claim to what is right. And, personally, I try very hard to work with my good Democrat friends. . . .

But I know this: On this issue you have torn that special fabric that holds us together as a House of Representatives. . . .

Yesterday, I stood to underscore my belief that Leon Panetta is a honorable man, only to be lectured by the majority leader that somehow my additional expression of frustration, anger, and outrage was beneath the dignity of this body. I say this to the majority leader—you folks dish it out daily, but you sure can't take it.

Republicans staged a brief walkout from the House after the May 1 vote, and the bitter aftertaste continued in the House for the remainder of the 99th Congress. The final formal action on the seating dispute occurred when the U. S. Supreme Court on May 28 unanimously denied Indiana permission to sue the House of Representatives in the Supreme Court.[1]

Back in the district, the bitterness was reflected in an editorial cartoon in the *Evansville Press* showing a hog wallowing in the mud near two roadsigns pointing to the homes of Hatfield and McCoy, the famous feuding hillbillies. Across the names had been written "McCloskey" and "McIntyre."

There was some speculation, in the wake of the 1984 campaign, that neither McCloskey nor McIntyre would seek the eighth district seat in 1986. McCloskey was interested in seeking the Democratic nomination to run against Republican Senator Dan Quayle. McIntyre was invited to consider running for secretary of state of Indiana. But by early 1986, both antagonists had decided to run for the same office again.

Spring Beginnings: The Primary Campaign

On February 19, 1986, Congressman McCloskey issued a statement announcing his intention to run again but made no overt reference to the 1984 outcome. His statement adopted a positive approach.

> We need a congressman who will continue to fight on the side of family farmers; on the side of the workers whose jobs are being exported overseas; on the side of the veterans who have served and suffered for their country; on the side of the elderly who need and deserve Social Security and Medicare benefits; on the side of the coal miners who fuel our country; on the side of the taxpayer who sees his and her tax monies siphoned off by sloppy and incompetent defense procurement; and finally, on the side of a world free from both tyranny and a nuclear holocost [sic].

He subsequently announced selection of his campaign staff, complete with treasurer, controller, Evansville office manager, volunteer coordinator, field coordinators, and "driver and aide." The campaign manager was Chris Sautter, managing attorney for the Bloomington office of the Legal Services Organization, who had worked on past McCloskey campaigns. McIntyre's campaign was managed by Joe Corcoran of Seymour, a member of the Indiana Senate.

McIntyre was unopposed in the Republican congressional primary, but McCloskey had an opponent, John W. Taylor, an Evansville sales manager. McCloskey pointed to efforts by "fanatic disciples of the bizarre ideologue Lyndon LaRouche" to infiltrate the Indiana Democratic party. (LaRouche has been a "far-out" presidential aspirant for several years, whose disruptive presence was especially notable in several Illinois contests in 1986.) McCloskey won the primary over Taylor by capturing 89 percent of the votes.

One of McCloskey's primary activities was to sponsor a March 15 presentation of "Eleanor: In Her Own Words" at the Shawnee theater. His newsletter gave directions to those interested in attending; the newsletter informed readers that McCloskey would be glad to have them join him for dinner at the Landing restaurant next to the theater at 6 P.M.

Meanwhile the unopposed McIntyre was busily gathering county Republican endorsements and making "Lincoln Day" dinner speeches at Washington and Linton.

The substantive issue receiving the most publicity during the primary season was McCloskey's opposition to U. S. support for the Contra rebels in Nicaragua. McCloskey was excoriated by McIntyre as well as the National Conservative Political Action Committee (NCPAC) in several newspaper and television ads that attacked the Democrat's voting record. The television ads (which asked, "Congressman McCloskey, why are you letting the Communists take over Central America?") were taken off the air after two days, and McCloskey was given the opportunity to respond.

Summer Fun: Goats and Catfish

With the primary out of the way, the election campaign moved into its early, fairly relaxed, summer stage. The Indiana Homesteaders and Dairy Goat Breeders Association invited both candidates to take part in a goat-milking contest at the Bloomington Community Farmers Market on Saturday, June 21. McIntyre was declared the winner for extracting 1.5 pounds of milk from his goat in the allotted 60 seconds, compared to the 1.4 pounds extracted by McCloskey. The event gave the *Bedford Herald-Times* (Higgs, 1986) an opportunity to remind its readers of the close 1984 election and the recount procedure by commenting that McIntyre's goat-milking victory "is not subject to state or federal review."

On July 4 a Catfish Festival was held in Shoals (population 1,039) to raise money to enable the Shoals park board to build a tennis court. There was to be a canoe race, country and popular music, fireworks, a softball tournament, a five-kilometer run, and a flea market. The banner event was to be a no-holds-barred debate, which one newspaper hailed as the "Great McBate." The *Shoals News* and radio station WKMD of Loogootee sponsored the debate portion of the festivities and invited each candidate to submit questions for the other to answer; the sponsors then narrowed the number of questions to twelve. A front-page article in the *Loogootee Tribune* (Johnson, 1986) described the scene: "The two political adversaries stepped onto the flatbed platform stacked with hay bales, dressed rather casually, for the debate/issues forum, one in short sleeves, the other with sleeves rolled up; both hoping perhaps to give the appearance of being one of the 'good ole boys.' " Both sides were well represented, with enthusiastic supporters in the crowd, easily identified by their green (McCloskey) or red (McIntyre) T-shirts and campaign buttons. The questions concerned women's right to abortion, proposed budget cuts in federal social programs, the proposed balanced budget amendment, federal farm policies, support for small businesses, a cancelled study at the Crane Naval Ammunition Depot in Martin county, removing the Hoosier National Forest from the jurisdiction of the U. S. Forest Service, federal highway funding cuts, continuation of cooperative extension services, federal tax reform, government funding of research on AIDs, and two fundamental questions: "Who is more capable of representing the district?" and "Who will win in November?" Each candidate, not surprisingly, felt that he would be more representative of the district. McIntyre said he hoped the results would not be close. McCloskey said he thought he was leading "right now" but declined to predict the November outcome. The *Bedford Herald-Times* (Van der Dusseau, 1986) summed up "McBate" with this statement: "The debate clearly was more substantive and spirited than anyone had expected. Both candidates held their own well, and both clearly enjoyed it, saying afterward it had been a lot of fun." The debate at the Catfish Festival was only the beginning; both candidates were looking forward to televised debates in Bloomington and Evansville in late September, and challenger McIntyre was hoping for additional debates at Vincennes and Oakland City.

As the race heated up, well-known politicians made appearances on behalf of McCloskey or McIntyre. Prominent Republican visitors included Transportation Secretary Elizabeth Dole, former President Gerald Ford, Congressman Guy Vander Jagt of Michigan, and Governor Robert Orr of Indiana. Vander Jagt, chairman of the Republican Congressional Campaign Committee, told a news conference in Evansville in October that the eighth district race "is our number 1 House race in history." Vice-President George Bush came to Evansville on Wednesday, October 15, to campaign for McIntyre at a $50-a-plate luncheon attended by about 660 persons. Also in attendance were Governor Orr and Health and Human Services Secretary Otis R. Bowen, a former governor of Indiana. Congressman Richard Gephardt of Missouri came to help his Democratic colleague.

Autumn Intensity: Debates, Charges, Polls

In late July, McCloskey and McIntyre formally agreed to take part in televised debates in Bloomington on Sunday, September 21, and in Evansville one week later. The first debate was sponsored and arranged by the Monroe county League of Women Voters, the Evansville debate, by the Vanderburgh county League of Women Voters and Sigma Delta Chi, the journalism society. Both debates were held before auditorium audiences and televised over public television stations.

The red-versus-green color competition continued in the Bloomington debate. Red-shirted McIntyre supporters and green-shirted McCloskey fans occupied sections near the stage, and there was frequent cheering and booing despite pleas from the moderator. The first debate produced few sharp disagreements on major issues; both candidates favored the present NATO defense treaty and the NASA space program. There was some mutual sniping about stands on drug enforcement policy, permitting off-road vehicles in the Hoosier National Forest, and U. S. intervention in foreign countries. Responses to questions about legalizing marijuana and abortions drew both lusty cheers and boos from the crowd. Though the two candidates managed enough civility to shake hands on stage at the conclusion of the debate proper, they continued to verbally slash and hack at each other in a postdebate news conference.

The Evansville debate, at which the protagonists sat elbow to elbow at a table, seemed to probe somewhat deeper into substantive issues. Discussion focused particularly on provisions of the huge spending authorization bill, (which amounted to $563 billion) that had just passed in the House by a vote of 201 to 200. This close result made McCloskey's vote in favor of the spending bill the target of several questions from McIntyre, which centered on inclusion of a congressional pay raise and numerous expensive "pork barrel" items. McCloskey was able to counter McIntyre's earlier assertion that he (McCloskey) was soft on drugs by noting that the antidrug campaign was included in the spending bill.

Charges made in the formal debates were but a prelude to a running battle of charges and countercharges that dominated district headlines in October. McIntyre continued to castigate McCloskey with what McCloskey called old, worn-out, and irrelevant charges about his opposition to U. S. involvement in Vietnam in the 1960s and his experimentation with drugs. McIntyre said that McCloskey, as mayor of Bloomington, had failed to urge prosecution of city staff personnel charged with drug dealing and had himself used hard drugs. McCloskey admitted only that he had experimented with marijuana and said he had not been soft on drug traffickers. Within a few days, two men who had served on the Bloomington police force during McCloskey's term as mayor came to McIntyre's office to offer evidence supporting McIntyre's charges against McCloskey and volunteered to take polygraph tests to verify the truth of their charges. Two subsequent news conferences at which these charges were publicized seemed to have a devastating effect on McCloskey. There were reports that his standing in tracking polls declined sharply for a few days. Then McCloskey launched a counterattack, via advertisements and news releases, in which he charged McIntyre with dirty politics and negative advertising. He claimed that McIntyre's campaign was "bordering on absurdity." Editorial response, especially in Evansville, was generally more supportive of McCloskey's defense than of McIntyre's attack; as one observer put it, McCloskey was able to "get his spin on the story."

Seated next to McIntyre at a medicine and health forum at the University of Evansville on Friday evening, October 10, McCloskey (Sanders, 1986) stood when his turn to speak came and told the audience:

You're witnesses to an historic event, the last time you're ever going to see me in the same room with Rick McIntyre. Mr. McIntyre has spent the last two days slandering me personally and my record as mayor of Bloomington. If you elect this gentleman, you'll be electing a slanderer.

Later, McIntyre shrugged off McCloskey's pledge to avoid personal contact, saying, "That's anyone's option."

An Indiana University (IU) poll in late September indicated a virtual dead heat, with 37 percent of the respondents favoring McCloskey, 36 percent favoring McIntyre, 21 percent undecided, and 16 percent refusing to answer. *Newsweek* magazine ("McRace, Again") noting the IU poll, described the eighth district campaign as being "short on issues but long on acrimony." In its final preelection assessment, *Congressional Quarterly Weekly Report* (11 October 1986: 2487), while noting that no incumbent in recent years seemed to have been safe in the district, concluded that the district "leans Democratic."

Congressional Quarterly Weekly Report's assessment referred to several real and potential issues. First, that McIntyre decided early on not to attempt to replay or emphasize the disputed 1984 outcome. Second, that McCloskey's chances in 1986 would depend less on the exchange of personal charges between the two antagonists than on "the old-fashioned incumbency" politics McCloskey had been practicing throughout his second term. Particularly noteworthy in this connection were his defense of the naval weapons support center at Crane (the district's largest employer) against Defense Department suggestions that part of the center be turned over to private control and his investigation of possible PCB contamination from a Union Carbide plant near the district.

Neither candidate had a significant monetary advantage. McIntyre's campaign manager, Joe Corcoran, estimated in mid-October that the Republican campaign would cost close to $500,000, while McCloskey's campaign manager, Chris Sautter, estimated that the incumbent would spend about $425,000.

Climax and Denouement

The eighth district race from the beginning was one of the most closely watched House races of 1986. National attention increased on Wednesday morning, October 29, when President Reagan, making a sidetrip from his energetic eight-state effort to protect Republican control of the U. S. Senate in the closing days of the campaign, flew to Evansville to correct "the great injustice" House Democrats had done to the people of the eighth district when they seated McCloskey rather than McIntyre in May 1985. Reagan spoke to a roaring crowd of 9,000 in Roberts Stadium. McIntyre rode in the presidential motorcade through Evansville and introduced Reagan as "the greatest leader of the Western world." Reagan spoke of the improved economy and of the need for his space-based antimissile defense system, funds for which he said McCloskey had voted against "not one but seven times." Noting that his own name would never appear on a ballot again, Reagan (Van der Dusseau, Oct. 1986) told the audience, "If you'd like to vote for me one more time, you can do so by voting for Rick McIntyre."

The final day of campaigning found both campaigners in an upbeat mood and as busy as ever, though McIntyre might have been taken aback by news of a poll conducted by Indiana and Purdue universities showing his Democratic opponent ahead by seventeen percentage points. McIntyre started the day in Bloomington and Ellettsville, shaking hands and urging people to go to the polls. "I didn't run into a soul in Bloomington who didn't say they were going to vote for me," he said. He joined Senator Quayle at an Evansville rally and then made an appearance in a media class at Pike Central high school near Petersburg.

Meanwhile McCloskey said, "I'm feeling good," and "there's something pleasant in the air," in spite of a grilled cheese sandwich with pickles for lunch in Orleans and a chili dinner at Vincennes University, which was also attended by McIntyre. Driving between Shoals and Montgomery, McCloskey's car was delayed behind a slow-moving car plastered with McIntyre stickers. Symbolically, the driver thought later, the McCloskey car was finally able to pull around the car on a straight stretch of road.

McIntyre, also partaking of the chili dinner in Vincennes, was reminded of McCloskey's earlier declaration that he would never be in the same room with McIntyre again. "That's another broken promise," McIntyre quipped. McIntyre made it a point to shake hands with everyone except McCloskey. As the two men were talking with voters on opposite sides of the same table, McCloskey stopped and looked at McIntyre. McIntyre didn't return the glance.

Finally the campaigning was over and the voting began. The results, to everyone's relief, did not depend on a handful of votes. McCloskey won a clear-cut victory, with 53 percent of the vote, 106,662 to 93,586. Most of McCloskey's margin came in Vanderburgh county (Evansville), which he carried by about 10,000 votes; Vanderburgh accounted for 30 percent of the votes cast in the eighth district. McCloskey carried the six southernmost counties, the traditional Democratic strongholds of the area. He also carried, by closer margins, three of the more northern counties. McIntyre ran ahead in six northern counties, including Monroe (Bloomington), Knox (Vincennes), and Lawrence (Bedford). The turnout in this nonpresidential year was about 86 percent of the turnout in 1984. McCloskey received about 10,000 votes less in 1986 than he had in 1984, but McIntyre suffered a loss of more than 20,000 votes.

On reflection, there were several reasons why McCloskey was sanguine about his chances. Though McIntyre had run a strong race against him in 1984, 1986 was the year of the "six-year itch" in which the president's party traditionally loses many seats in Congress. McCloskey had worked hard in the campaign and had made good use of the perquisites of congressional office.

McIntyre's campaign was not very specific, dramatic, or positive; especially toward the end, observers said, McIntyre appeared to be harping on the same old points.

Looking back at the contested 1984 election, while a neutral observer might have thought the election system would have been better served if the seat had been declared vacant and a new election had been called, one can at the same time understand McCloskey's insistence on being declared the winner and his refusal to resign the seat after being installed in it. His party had the votes to back up his claim to victory. It was unlikely that a true count of 1984 votes could ever have been determined to the satisfaction of both sides and of the public. Races such as the 1984 contest leave a sour taste in everyone's mouth. Confidence in our election system and in our Congress would be heightened if Congress would adopt more judicious and neutral—and less partisan—procedures in settling such election disputes in the future. Perhaps the model of the two committees where each party has an equal number of members—the House Standards of Official Conduct Committee and the Senate Ethics Committee—would be useful in such settlements.[2]

SUMMARY

The conduct of congressional campaigns has become much more visible, sophisticated, and expensive in the past few decades. Members of Congress are plagued by the constant tension between attending to their congressional work in Washington and maintaining their political contacts and popularity back home. Many recent laws, written ostensibly to reform or streamline the political system, have had the effect of helping ensure the reelection of incumbents, which reduces the likelihood that congressional elections will produce much change either in congressional personnel or in the shape of policy. For this reason, there is a certain amount of conflict in our biennial elections between stability and change.

Incumbents and challengers must decide whether to emphasize substantive issues when campaigning or to stress superficial, personal, or image factors. The question becomes whether one prefers representation by a member who agrees with the views of a majority of constituents or by a candidate with a more appealing appearance and personality.

NOTES

1. This summary of the recount battle was based on articles by Cook (1986), Bragdon (1986), Plattner (1985, 1986), and Witt (1985). The following articles "General Accounting Office Auditors to Count Indiana's 8th District Votes," (1985) "House Task Force to Propose Rules for Counting Ballots in Disputed Indiana 8th District Race," (1985) and "Indiana 8: A Score to Settle" (1986) were also used as sources.

2. This account of the 1986 campaign was based on descriptions of the eighth congressional district of Indiana in Barone and Ujifusa (1985, 442–443, 447, 467–470) and in articles from *Congressional Quarterly Weekly Report, The Political Report, Newsweek,* and several area newspapers, namely the *Bedford Times-Mail,* the *Bloomington Herald-Telephone,* the *Sunday Herald-Times* of Bedford and Bloomington, the *Evansville Courier,* the *Evansville Press,* the *Indianapolis Star,* the *Linton Daily Citizen,* the *Loogootee Tribune,* the *Paoli News,* the *Salem Democrat,* the *Vincennes Sun-Commercial,* and the *Washington* (Ind.) *Times-Herald;* also various campaign materials were supplied by Melinda Plaisier of McCloskey's staff and information was supplied by Margaret Ford and Steve Nix, who were associated with the Republican campaign.

REFERENCES

BARONE, MICHAEL, and UJIFUSA, GRANT. *The Almanac of American Politics 1986.* Washington, D. C.: National Journal, 1985.

BRAGDON, PETER. "House Again Refuses to Seat McIntyre." *Congressional Quarterly Weekly Report* (9 February 1986): 282.

Buckley v. *Valeo,* 424 U. S. 1, 1976.

CHENEY, RICHARD. *Congressional Record,* 99th Cong., 1st sess., 1985, 131:9809.

CLEM, ALAN L., et al. *The Making of Congressmen: Seven Campaigns of 1974.* Boston: Duxbury Press, 1976.

COOK, TIMOTHY E. "The Electoral Connection in the 99th Congress." *PS* 19 (Winter 1986): 16–22.

FENNO, JR., RICHARD F. "Observation, Context, and Sequence in the Study of Politics." *American Political Science Review* 80 (March 1986).

GAUNT, JEREMY. "Senate Rules Committee OKs Major Campaign Finance Bill." *Congressional Quarterly Weekly Report* (2 May 1987): 832–833.

"General Accounting Office Auditors to Count Indiana's 8th District Votes." *Election Administration Reports* 15 (18 March 1985): 1–2.

GOLDENBERG, EDIE N., and TRAUGOTT, MICHAEL W. *Campaigning for Congress.* Washington, D. C.: Congressional Quarterly Press, 1984.

HERSHEY, MARJORIE RANDON. *Running for Office: The Political Education of Campaigners.* Chatham, New Jersey: Chatham House, 1984:1–10, 151–160.

HIGGS, STEVEN. "McIntyre Bests McCloskey during Goat-milking Contest." *Bedford Herald-Times* (22 June 1986):A-10.

HINCKLEY, BARBARA. *Congressional Elections.* Washington, D. C.: Congressional Quarterly Press, 1981.

"House Task Force to Propose Rules for Counting Ballots in Disputed Indiana 8th District Race." *Election Administration Reports* 15 (4 March 1985): 3–4.

"Indiana 8: A Score to Settle." *The Political Report* (26 July 1986): 6–9.

JACOBSON, GARY C. *Money in Congressional Elections.* New Haven, Conn.: Yale University Press, 1980.

JACOBSON, GARY C. *The Politics of Congressional Elections.* 2nd ed. Boston: Little, Brown, 1987.

JOHNSON, MICKEY. "The McIntyre-McCloskey McBattle." *The Loogootee Tribune* (10 July 1986): 1.

MANN, THOMAS E., and ORNSTEIN, NORMAN J. (eds.). *The New Congress*. Washington, D. C.: American Enterprise Institute, 1981.

"McRace Again." *Newsweek* (27 October 1986): 5.

ORNSTEIN, NORMAN J., MANN, THOMAS E., MALBIN, MICHAEL J., SCHICK, ALLEN, and BIBBY, JOHN F. *Vital Statistics on Congress, 1984–1985*. Washington, D. C.: American Enterprise Institute, 1984.

PANETTA, LEON. *Congressional Record*, 99th Cong., 1st sess., 1985, 131: 10017–10018.

PLATTNER, ANDY. "Republicans Seethe over Indiana 8th Decision." *Congressional Quarterly Weekly Report* (27 April 1985): 773–775.

PLATTNER, ANDY. "Republicans Walk Out in Protest After House Seats McCloskey." *Congressional Quarterly Weekly Report* (4 May 1985): 821–825.

ROBERTS, PAT. *Congressional Record*, 99th Cong., 1st sess., 1985, 131:10009–10010.

SALMORE, STEPHEN A., and SALMORE, BARBARA G. *Candidates, Parties, and Campaigns: Electoral Politics in America*. Washington, D. C.: Congressional Quarterly Press, 1985.

SANDERS, CRAIG. "McCloskey's Opium Accusation Is Slander." *Bloomington* (Ind.) *Herald-Telephone* (11 October 1986): 1.

VAN DER DUSSEAU, KURT. "Lively Debate Marks Start of 'McRace II': Shoals Holds Campaign's First McCloskey-McIntyre Meeting." *Bedford* (Ind.) *Sunday Herald-Times* (6 July 1986): A-1, A-12.

VAN DER DUSSEAU, KURT. "Reagan Urges Voters to 'Make Up for 1984.' " *Bloomington* (Ind.) *Herald-Telephone* (30 October 1986): A-1, A-6.

WATSON, TOM. "PAC Pilgrimage Becomes Candidates' Ritual." *Congressional Quarterly Weekly Report* (22 March 1986): 655–659.

WATSON, TOM. "Business PACs Wary of Campaign Finance Bill." *Congressional Quarterly Weekly Report* (25 April 1987): 782–784.

WITT, ELDER. "Court Refuses to Consider Disputed Indiana Election." *Congressional Quarterly Weekly Report* (1 June 1985): 1062.

WRIGHT, JAMES. *Congressional Record*, 99th Cong., 1st sess., 1985, 131:9818.

VI CONGRESSIONAL LIFE

A legislator's life is not an easy one. There are persistent pressures, frequent frustrations, and endless demands: A member must attend party caucuses; scurry to committee and subcommittee meetings; confer with lobbyists and executive branch officials about pending legislation; greet constituents in the office (and take them to lunch); take part in the essential legislative work of debating and voting on bills on the floor; and scan memoranda, documents, staff reports, newspapers, and opinion journals, often into the wee hours of the night.

Fortunately, members of Congress have the power to solve or reduce some of their worst problems. They have voted to enlarge their own staffs, build new buildings, and install new equipment on Capitol Hill. Members are free to fire as well as hire their own assistants. Members control their own work environment. On a more informal level, members of Congress over the years have developed habits, conventions, courtesies, and ceremonial rituals that help mitigate internal conflict and reduce ill will; these ways of compensating make the hectic life on Capitol Hill more bearable.

This chapter describes certain major aspects of congressional life: the physical environment of Capitol Hill and the city of Washington, the professional and clerical assistants employed by members and committees, and the frustrations and challenges that face members in their daily activities.

CAPITOL HILL AND THE CITY

The rise of land rimming the eastern reaches of the picturesque Mall, running eastward from the Potomac river and the Tidal Basin, is known today as Capitol Hill, but its original name was more prosaic: Jenkins's Hill. Whatever the beauties of unspoiled nature, the view today from Capitol Hill is probably more impressive and inspiring than the pristine view of two hundred years ago. In the early days of Washington, what is now the Mall was a malarial swamp. The hills of Virginia could be seen across the Potomac river to the west, and the White House would have been visible to the northwest, toward the old settlement of Georgetown. Today, from the western face of the Capitol along the ridge about ninety feet above the level of the Mall, one can see broad avenues, lovely lawns, trees and flowers, a reflecting pool, and several notable structures: the Jefferson Memorial to the southwest, the Smithsonian buildings, the National Gallery of Art, the Museum of Natural History, the Museum of Amerian History and Technology, the National Air and Space Museum, and, most dramatic, the Washington and Lincoln monuments directly west. Constitution and Independence avenues run along the north and south sides of the Mall, respectively, and flanking these broad avenues are the buildings of the Departments of Agriculture, Health and Human Services, Commerce, Labor, and Justice.

Traditionally, presidents have been inaugurated in ceremonies on the east front of the Capitol, facing away from the Mall and most of the nation. President Reagan broke precedent when he was sworn in on the west front in January 1981, standing at the top of the rise of old Jenkins's Hill, looking out over the Mall and the nation beyond to the west.

The Capitol is easily the most prominent building in a city full of majestic public and private edifices (see figure 6-1). Its central section was sufficiently completed in 1800 to accommodate the two houses of Congress and the Supreme Court. The Capitol was damaged by the British in 1814 and subsequently completed in its original design in 1829. Large wings were added for the House of Representatives (the southern wing) in 1857 and the Senate (the northern wing) in 1859. A new dome, made necessary to give architectural balance to the enlarged building, was completed in 1865. The distance from the base line on the east front of the Capitol to the top of the Statue of Freedom is 287 feet. The House and Senate chambers are, of course, the centers of legislative activity. The grand rotunda under the dome, Statuary Hall between the rotunda and the House chamber, and the old Supreme Court chamber on the Senate (northern) side of the Capitol are the areas most frequented by tourists. In addition, the Capitol houses several committee rooms, conference rooms, restaurants, the Senate library, and offices for clerks, sergeants-at-arms, parliamentarians, policemen, and journalists. At the lower levels, subways enter the Capitol, linking it to the three House office buildings across Independence Avenue to the south and the Senate office buildings across Constitution Avenue to the north. The famous Senate subway train offers a quick ride from the Senate office buildings. Visitors may use the railway, but are in danger of being "bumped" by senators hurrying to answer a quorum call.

The Capitol grounds contain driveways, sidewalks, gardens, and a wide variety of trees and shrubbery that help reduce the noise and pollution of a modern city. Other imposing buildings surround the Capitol: the Cannon, Longworth, and Rayburn House office buildings; three buildings of the Library of Congress; the beautiful white Supreme Court building; and the Russell, Dirksen, and Hart Senate office buildings. Not all of these buildings are regarded as architectural or aesthetic successes; Nelson Polsby (Mann and Ornstein 1981, 23) uses the terms *monstrous* and *grotesque* to describe the Rayburn building and also decries the Kennedy Center built on the once beautiful Potomac river parkland as a "leaky behemoth" and an "enormously undistinguished building." Down the gentle slopes to the north of the Capitol may be seen the memorial to Senator Robert Taft of Ohio and, beyond that, the old Union Station, which until the middle of this century was Washing-

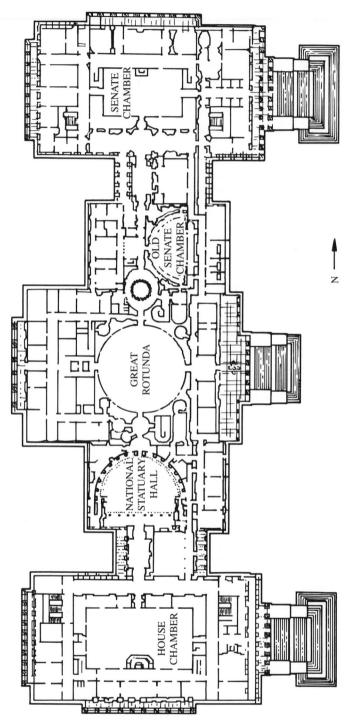

Figure 6-1 The United States Capitol: Plan of the second (or principal) floor

N →

ton's transportation hub. Pennsylvania Avenue is the well-known route of inaugural parades and connects Capitol Hill with the Treasury Building and the White House to the northwest. To the southeast, Pennsylvania Avenue is a tree-lined boulevard of churches, restaurants, grocery stores, shops, small financial institutions, and residences—the revitalized marketing center for residents of old southeastern Washington. To the east toward Robert F. Kennedy Stadium runs East Capitol Avenue, beginning at the Supreme Court and Library of Congress buildings and proceeding past the Folger Shakespeare Library and becoming another broad, quiet, tree-lined residential street.

A few words about the District of Columbia will complete the description of the geographical environment in which Congress operates. There is no real central business district. Before the advent of suburban shopping malls after World War II, a central shopping area existed east of the Treasury Building and north of Pennsylvania Avenue. This area has fallen on hard times, particularly north of New York Avenue, where one walks at some peril. Connecticut Avenue, running north-northwest from the general area of the White House, remains a central thoroughfare of high-quality hotels, offices, restaurants, and shops. Massachusetts Avenue N. W. is a favored location of embassies, churches, and research enterprises.

Inside the District of Columbia's boundaries are such old, self-contained communities as Georgetown to the northwest and Anacostia to the southeast. There are slums as well as beautiful residential areas. Many areas of the older parts of the district are badly deteriorated, but in many sections, especially near Capitol Hill, older sections have been elegantly refurbished and present a pleasing environment for living and working. Much of the district's real estate is devoted to religious, charitable, and educational institutions: Georgetown, George Washington, American, Catholic, and Howard universities; St. Elizabeth's Hospital; the Shrine of the Immaculate Conception; and the Cathedral of Saints Peter and Paul (popularly known as the National Cathedral). Government installations of various kinds are scattered around the city: the Soldiers' Home, the Walter Reed Army Medical Center, the Naval Observatory, the Washington Navy Yard, Fort Leslie McNair, and Bolling Air Force Base. The district contains a number of parks: beautiful Rock Creek Park and the zoological gardens, the National Arboretum, East Potomac Park, Fort Dupont Park, and the Glover Archbold Parkway are prime examples.

THE PEOPLE OF CAPITOL HILL

Thousands of people spend their working hours on Capitol Hill; many are employed by the legislative branch, and many are privately employed. These denizens of Capitol Hill can be grouped into three general categories.

Institutional Staff

Each chamber of Congress has its own administrative, clerical, and support offices. On the Senate side are a chaplain; a secretary of the Senate, heading an office force of about fifty people, including the parliamentarian and the historian; a sergeant-at-arms; the office of the legislative counsel; and the office of Senate legal counsel. These top Senate officials are chosen by the caucus of the majority party. There are also special offices and assistants for senators occupying leadership positions such as president pro tempore, majority leader, assistant majority leader, minority leader, and majority party and minority party secretaries. Not to be forgotten in this detailed listing is the vice-president of the United States, who is the president of the Senate and has a ceremonial office in the Capitol as well as offices in the Dirksen Senate Office Building, the Old Executive Office Building next to the White House, and the White House itself.

In the House of Representatives, in addition to the representatives who lead their parties (the speaker, the majority leader and whip, and the minority leader and whip), there are the following institutional officers: parliamentarian, chaplain, clerk, sergeant-at-arms, doorkeeper, postmaster, law revision counsel, legislative counsel, and architect of the Capitol (who is also acting director of the United States Botanic Gardens located at the bottom of Capitol Hill on Independence Avenue).

Miscellaneous officials and agencies connected with Congress as a whole are the Capitol police force, the Capitol page school, the office of the attending physician, the telecommunications officer, a Western Union office, and airline and railroad ticket offices.

Perhaps the most important and tangible products of institutional support are the official records of Congress's activity. Most notable are the daily *Congressional Record,* produced by the Government Printing Office located a few blocks north of the Capitol. The *Record* is based on notes taken by small armies of clerks in each chamber. It is something short of a miracle that each member, and many others, has a printed copy of the past day's Senate and House activities early each morning. Perhaps the most helpful part of the *Record* is the "Daily Digest" section, which summarizes what has happened and what is scheduled to happen on the floor of the House and Senate and in the standing committees and subcommittees. The bulk of the *Record* is divided into separate parts, which purport to be verbatim accounts of what is said. In actuality, members are given the opportunity to edit their remarks before the *Record* is published; thus, sloppy syntax, errors of fact, heated and indecorous political quarreling, and insulting personal references are generally not to be seen in the *Record.* "By consent of the body," extended remarks—paragraphs and even pages of material that were never spoken on the floor—may be printed.

Barbers, guards, cooks, waitresses, dishwashers, shoeshine boys, and custodians further enlarge the corps of people who work each day on Capitol Hill.

Staff of Ancillary Agencies

Over the years, Congress has authorized the establishment of specialized agencies to provide particular important services. The Library of Congress was established by statute in 1800 to "collect such books as may be necessary for the use of Congress." This library ranks today as one of the greatest in the world in terms of the number, variety, and quality of holdings and may be considered the national library of the United States. Particularly important to Congress is the Congressional Research Service, which conducts research and issues reports for committees and individual members on request. It employs some of the best-known scholars and writers to carry out this research effort. The three large Library of Congress buildings are directly across the street from the Capitol.

The General Accounting Office (GAO) was created by the Budget and Accounting Act of 1921 to take over auditing functions previously assigned to other agencies by the original Treasury Act of 1789. Headed by the comptroller general of the United States, the GAO assists Congress in its oversight activities; performs accounting, auditing, and claims settlement functions; and makes recommendations for more efficient and effective government programs. GAO headquarters are located a few blocks northwest of the Capitol.

The Office of Technology Assessment (OTA) was authorized by Congress in 1972 to help Congress stay abreast of the consequences of modern technology. The OTA informs Congress about the beneficial and adverse effects of technological applications and suggests policy alternatives for related issues. The OTA is located a few blocks southeast of the Capitol on Pennsylvania Avenue.

The Congressional Budget Act of 1974 revised the annual budget process in the federal government and established the Congressional Budget Office (CBO), which advises Congress on priorities for national resource allocation and helps establish basic fiscal policy for the nation. The CBO headquarters are located a few blocks southwest of the Capitol.

The Library of Congress and the GAO each employ about 5,000 workers; the CBO, 200; and the OTA, somewhat over 100.

Other People of the Hill

In addition to congressional employees, there are two very important working groups: reporters representing the news media and lobbyists representing a multitude of interest groups. (These groups will be discussed in chapter 10).

There are also two groups that contribute to the air of drama and intensity on the Hill but not to legislative activity: (1) the thousands of tourists that visit the Capitol and (2) the bevy of hangers-on who beseige offices looking for jobs or for someone (perhaps even a member of Congress) who will listen to their ideas for saving the world, the republic, the budget, the farmers, the party, and so on. Some of these hangers-on hang on so long—making their daily circuit from one sympathetic, tolerant office to another—that they come to be regarded as employees conducting essential congressional business. Sometimes such a person can even acquire a sort of squatter's right to a chair in the member's reception room and use part of a shelf to temporarily store an impressive pile of books and papers.

CONGRESSIONAL STAFFS

There are two major categories of congressional staffs: those who work for committees and those who work for individual members. These staffs have undergone the most change in the past generation. Committee staffs have grown considerably; personal staffs, even more dramatically. These enlargements have put progressively greater pressure on limited office space. Even before the turn of the century, the Capitol and nearby boarding houses were becoming very crowded. To address this circumstance, the Senate in 1891 purchased a four-year-old five-story apartment house at New Jersey Avenue and B Street (now Constitution Avenue) near the Senate wing of the Capitol. The former Maltby House thus became the first congressional office building, to the consternation of the even-more crowded House of Representatives. Several construction and maintenance problems developed, but the Senate continued to use the Maltby Building until the Russell Senate Office Building was occupied in 1909.[1]

Committee Staffs

Most professional and clerical employees of the standing committees of the Senate and House are appointed by the party having the majority of seats in the chamber, but some of the committee staff positions are reserved for appointment by the minority party.

There is some variation in the size of committee staffs. The smallest committee staffs had about two dozen members in 1983, the largest well over one hundred. The size of the committee staff is not a real reflection of the relative power or importance of the committee; other factors that enter into the size of committee staffs are the amount and complexity of proposed legislation in the policy area under the committee's jurisdiction and the personal ambitions and goals of the committee chairman. The total number of employees on committee staffs has grown from 103 in 1891 to 275 in 1930, 910 in 1960, and 3,108 in 1980 (Ornstein *et al*. 1984, 126).

Only a few of the standing committees are located in the Capitol building. These favored committees are (for the Senate) the Appropriations Committee and (for the House) the Appropriations, House Administration, and Rules committees. Ten of the Senate standing committees are housed in the Dirksen Building, and four are in the older Russell Building (as of 1986). The Rayburn Building is home to eleven House committees; the Longworth Building, to five; the Cannon Building, to two; and the Budget Committee is located in a nearby annex building. The committee suites contain general reception and work areas, small private offices for a few of the top professional staff, and a large hearing room. The hearing rooms have seating for the committee members themselves, the committee's professional and clerical staff, witnesses giving testimony, and the general public.

The heads of the committee staffs have a variety of titles: staff director, chief counsel, chief clerk, executive director, and general counsel. Samuel Patterson (Davidson and Oleszek 1985, 248–250) has identified three main types of committee staff organization. In type 1, a distinctly hierarchical arrangement, the chain of command runs from the committee chairman to the staff director to the remainder of the staff. In type 2, a looser system often associated with smaller staffs, the committee chairman may deal with the staff directly, without going through the staff director. In such situations, everyone has direct access to the committee chairman, and vice versa. In type 3, the staff director is the link between the committee chairman and the professional staff, while the chief clerk is the link between the chairman and the clerical staff.

Member Staffs

Around the turn of the century, no more than about 100 people served as assistants to members of Congress. By 1930 the number of member employees had increased to 1,150 (870 in the House, 280 in the Senate). The figure jumped to 2,030 in 1947, 3,556 in 1957, 5,804 in 1967, 10,496 in 1977, and 11,665 in 1983 (Ornstein, et al. 1984, 121).

More than a generation ago, Donald Matthews (1960, 82–84) held member staffs to be among the fastest-growing bureaucracies in Washington. Matthews found great variation in terms of staff organization in 1958, but did identify two types: the "bureaucratic" type in which the senator delegates many responsibilities and establishes a clear-cut chain of command; and the "individualistic" type in which the senator delegates very little authority and where the staff has "little influence and less authority." The administrative assistant's job "is reduced to that of a 'paper-shuffler.' " Matthews wrote of the lack of job security, the need for staff loyalty and confidentiality, and the downright terror on the part of some staffers that they would be fired if they in any way irritated or offended "the boss." Matthews noted that the way a senator organizes an office "tells a great deal about him as a man, what his problems and preoccupations are, and how he defines his role."

A more recent study applies managerial perspectives to the analysis of congressional staffing. Harrison Fox and Susan Hammond (1977) have enlarged on several factors that characterize staff organization and work. Three of these factors are of particular concern.

First, Fox and Hammond (179) define three categories of staff administrative organization. In the hierarchical pattern, the member works closely with one of the staff, who in turn assigns functions and responsibilities to the remainder of the staff and coordinates and evaluates their work. In the coordinative pattern, the member works closely with two staff members. In the individualistic pattern, there is no discernible concentration of member-staff contact; the member relates directly with every staffer. The authors found that the individualistic pattern was most prevalent in the Senate; the hierarchical, in House offices and committee offices.

Second, the authors identified five basic professional roles performed by professional (as opposed to clerical) staff members in the Senate. The "interactor" is involved in meeting with lobbyist and special interest groups, handling constituency problems (both community projects and casework for individual constituents), visiting with constituents in Washington, and answering pressure and opinion mail. The "supporter" accompanies the member to committee meetings; writes floor remarks and speeches; drafts and analyzes bills; and writes articles, books, and speeches other than those for floor use. The "corresponder" writes letters of congratulation and condolence to constituents (generally based on local newspaper accounts of births, weddings, graduations, deaths, and so on); writes other correspondence; answers requests for information; handles opinion ballots; and mails government publications. The "advertiser" advertises the member through the media and often works on reelection campaigns. The "investigator" is responsible for overseeing activities in the executive and judicial branches of government that are of special interest to the member (92–95).

Third, these researchers found that there were essentially three ways of dividing labor among a congressional member's staff. In the system of division by subject area, one person (or, in some cases, a specific team) handles all aspects of a particular subject, including speech writing, gathering information, answering mail, issuing news releases, and arranging meetings and programs. In the system of division by committee, staff work is divided on the basis of whether or not the work is related to the member's committee assignments. In the system of division by function, which was the most prevalent form in Fox and Hammond's classification, the basic categories are office administration and management; press relations; legislative analysis; constituent casework; and "back-ups," including typists, computer technicians, receptionists, and mail clerks.

In my study (Clem 1981, 68–71) of congressional staffs of one midwestern state in 1980, I categorized the basic functions performed by staff members in 1980 and then counted the full-time equivalent positions devoted to each function. Table 6-1 shows the functional breakdown.

Finding and keeping good staff members is a demanding task for members and their administrative assistants. When staffing, there is a question of whether to hire people from back home or people who live in Washington and have experience on the Hill. One administrative assistant (Clem, 1981, 4) said that a severe problem

is balancing a preference for employees from the state with the need to thoroughly interview employees and ensure they are fully competent for the job being offered. . . . While seemingly mundane and easily overcome, it in fact is a problem

Table 6-1.   Staff work assignments in four congressional offices in a midwestern state, 1980

Function	Full-time equivalent staff (percent)
Supervisory	8
Member appointments, personal correspondence, etc.	6
Legislative assistants	24
Press, public relations	7
Casework for constituents	25
Receptionists, typists, mail clerks	15
Special assignments, miscellaneous	16
Total:	101

Note: Column does not add to 100 because of rounding; n = 88.
Source: Clem 1981, 3.

mentioned often by many Hill administrators. The problem is one which would not often occur in business . . .

While the standard management problems in any organization, motivation, communication, and the like, are not terribly different in a congressional office than in other organizations, this problem of separation between the major office and the preferred potential employee pool is unique. In the more standard areas of organizational problems, the leader is probably communication between Washington and state staff. Washington needs full and frequent feedback from the state on both specific problems and general reaction to congressional actions and issues of the day. The field needs both specific information from D. C. and a general sense of what the congressman is doing and what the office is doing legislatively to avoid feeling they are a second-fiddle adjunct to the D. C. office . . .

While working hours are extremely long, close to sixty hours per week being the average, general motivation in offices I have worked in has only been a minor, infrequent problem. Close association with the member, belief in his objectives, and knowledge that he puts in an even longer work week than most staff provides ample motivation to keep staff on course.

Another administrative assistant (Clem, 1981, 4) comments:

Unless you personally know the skills of the individual concerned, it is hard to bring state people to Washington. If they don't work out, then you feel responsible for finding them another employment opportunity.

Many people use congressional jobs as stepping stones to careers elsewhere in government or into the private sector. The staffs are not large and you have to make sure that all the legislative and administrative bases are covered at all times, even with the anticipated turnover. This becomes a special problem when a key professional legislative assistant moves out. You have to find someone who can "hit the ground running" on both the substance and the procedures of the position involved.

It is always a challenge to not only be responsive to state correspondence and project concerns while, at the same time, going forward on legislative and administrative matters in which the state has a special interest. There are never enough hours in the day to do both at a high-performance level, so frequently there has to be some trade-off on one over the other.

In addition to the basic qualifications of each staff person, it is important that the entire staff be able to get along together and function as a working unit. This is easier said than done.

There is value having continuity on a staff, as it saves a good deal of time and effort . . .

The above comments clash with some rather cynical comments about congressional staffing recorded by Michael Malbin, writing in a collection of essays about the contemporary Congress (Mann and Ornstein 1981, 149). Several members told Malbin that their policy is to "hire them young, burn them out, and send them on." Malbin also notes a fairly common feeling on the part of young professional staffers that they do not have a "real job" and that they are being left behind by others in their generation who are moving up in their law firms or business concerns, while the congressional aide is marooned on a sort of island that has little potential for promotion and that might be inundated at any time by an adverse electoral tidal wave.

To be a member of a congressional staff is to be in a peculiar situation. Hill offices are reminiscent of medieval fiefdoms, where staffers are part of an entourage loyal to and dependent on one elected suzerain. There are rewards—such as the excitement of being at the center of important work and reasonably good financial incentives—but there is no job protection. The staffer is just a handful of votes away from unemployment.

My 1981 study of midwestern congressional staffs cited earlier concludes that the staffs were hard working, highly motivated, loyal to their employers, young, excited, ambitious, intelligent, and helpful. On the other hand, staff members were thought to be (1) not always well integrated and organized, (2) seldom carefully trained except in terms of the very specific assignments they are given (so that many of them do not have any kind of general viewpoint), and (3) in some cases not really monitored. Each staff studied had several experts who knew as much or more about a specific issue area or problem than the member or the administrative assistant, and this situation sometimes led to real communications problems.

The personal staffs of senators and representatives have increased dramatically in size, creating in many offices too much information and too many people, a situation that overloads the communications network. Malbin (Mann and Ornstein 1981, 135, 142) reports that one former representative, Abner Mikva of Illinois, related that he often dealt with this problem by going to a hideaway office where his staff could not find him.

Another facet of congressional staffing is the high turnover on both committee and member staffs. In his study of communication networks among staff dealing with health issues, David Whiteman (1987) constructed rosters of committee and member staffers handling such issues. Whiteman reports that on both Senate committees involved, the committee staff members with primary responsibility for the issue being studied changed three times during the 99th Congress (1985–1986). This was also true of the House Ways and Means Committee. The staff of the House Energy and Commerce Committee remained stable. As to the members' staffs, "fewer than half of the members had the same staff person covering the same issue for the entire two-year period, and a few members even had three different staff covering the issue" (223).

Do larger staffs mean that members can provide better representation and efficiency for constituents? No answer to that general question will be attempted here. But it does seem useful to summarize the conclusions of Malbin's study of congressional staffs. He notes that staffers did a creditable job of representing district interests in meetings with other government officials. Further, congressional staffers were effective in protecting members from incursions on their time. These advantages were thought by Malbin to be offset by (1) the administrative burden that a staff of ten or twenty puts on the member, (2) the lessening of direct contact among the elected legislators themselves, and (3) the fact that many professional staffers come from intellectual backgrounds that lead them to become ideologues committed to radical views on current problems rather than pragmatists able to find the middle ground of necessary compromise. The process, wrote Malbin (Mann and Ornstein 1981, 177),

> no longer forces members to talk to each other to resolve the tough issues; the agenda keeps them busy with other things. . . . If Congress is to play its crucial representative role . . . it must find some way to limit its agenda and reinforce the role of direct deliberation.

Increased staffing has not only failed to solve these problems, it has made them worse. Polsby (Mann and Ornstein 1981, 13) comments that the recent growth in the "enormous, ambitious, and not terribly accountable" congressional staff is a major reason for the growing unmanageability of Congress. The theme of staff irresponsibility was echoed in James Ceaser's (1987, 55) comments on the Iran-Contra hearings: that few observers "could fail to remark on the spectacle of nonelected committee lawyers dressing down the nonelected lieutenant colonel [Oliver North] while lecturing the American public on the authoritative meaning of the Constitution." Furthermore, the growing number of staff workers has changed the Capitol environment, producing a situation of less personal communication between members.

The argument for a substantial staff to aid members of Congress nevertheless remains strong. Staffers help the member gather information and exert influence on other decision makers, thereby adding to the member's clout in dealing with lobbyists, executive agencies, and party and committee leaders on Capitol Hill. Congressional staffs, similar to White House and top executive staffs, add leaven to the nonpolitical civil service, producing a necessary turnover after every election that brings in employees with fresh points of view closely attuned to public opinion.

The following description of the organization and operation of the staff of former Rep. Tom Loeffler of Texas is a concrete illustration of the general principles of congressional staffing. How the staff of a given member works is affected less by the member's party, ideology, region, seniority, and political ambitions than by the member's personal style of work and management.

The Staff of Congressman Tom Loeffler of Texas

Tom Loeffler was a young man of thirty-two when he was first elected in 1978 to represent the vast twenty-first congressional district, which stretches across west central Texas from the Big Bend country along the Rio Grande River to

San Antonio. A native of the "German country" north of San Antonio, Loeffler was an attorney who had served on the staff of Sen. John Tower and as special assistant for legislative affairs to President Gerald Ford. Having won reelection by better than three-to-one margins in both 1982 and 1984 and having advanced to the position of chief deputy Republican whip, Loeffler seemed to be politically secure, but his ambitions drove him to enter the Texas gubernatorial contest in 1986.

The twenty-first district is by far the largest in area in the state. *The Almanac of American Politics, 1986* (Barone and Ujifusa 1985, 1334) describes it as "a collection of five rather different constituencies," including (1) the Big Bend territory along the Rio Grande river west of the Pecos, a virtually uninhabited and rugged territory with peaks reaching 7,000 feet; (2) the small city of Midland, "headquarters of the people who run the Permian Basin," with one of the highest income levels of the nation; (3) the older city of San Angelo, where cattle and oil constitute the economic base; (4) the Texas German country in the hills in the eastern part of the district, settled before the Civil War by antislavery Germans who became and remained Republicans; and (5) the northern part of the city of San Antonio, which is generally well-to-do, Anglo, and Republican.

Congressman Loeffler's office was located in Room 1212 of the Longworth House Office Building. His staff in 1985, before the maturation of his plans to leave the House and run for governor in 1986, consisted of ten permanent full-time employees in Washington and seven persons located in four district offices (four individuals in San Antonio, including a district director, and office managers in Kerrville, Midland, and San Angelo). The Longworth suite contained three main rooms. One room was reserved for Congressman Loeffler. The central room housed a receptionist, the congressman's personal secretary, the office manager, the chief of staff, and a legislative assistant. The third room contained stations for the legislative director, three legislative assistants, the press secretary, and the system operator, plus a meeting area. Thirty years ago, a typical congressman's suite in Longworth included one room for the member and a second room for three or four staff members (usually an administrative assistant or senior secretary, a press secretary, and one or two clerk-typist/receptionists).

The Loeffler staff did not appear to have a very rigid hierarchical arrangement. Each staffer had easy access to the congressman and to each other, as duties directed. There were no formal channels for internal communication. The following listing suggests the general distribution of influence from top to bottom: chief of staff, legislative director, personal secretary, office manager, press secretary, three legislative assistants, receptionist, and system operator.

Only two members of the Loeffler staff were over fifty years of age, the others being in their twenties, thirties, and forties. The median salary reported was just under $30,000. The prior residence of ten of the staffers was Texas. Six staffers had bachelor's degrees, one had an MBA. Four persons reported working directly with Loeffler more than ten hours in the typical week, while five reported no hours of personal working contact; the rest of the staff said they spent from one to five hours per week working with the congressman. As to total years of working experience on Capitol Hill (including 1985), one Washington staffer reported fifteen years of service, two reported seven, one reported five, and the others reported less. Three of the district office workers had been with Congressman Loeffler for seven years (his entire congressional service); the others, less.

As a general rule, district staff members were somewhat older than the Washington staffers, received lower salaries, and were more likely to have originally come from the district. Table 6-2 shows the office functions performed by fifteen of the seventeen staffers. Constituent casework and policy-legislative research were the functions named by the largest number of staffers.

Table 6-2.   Staff functions performed by members of Congressman Loeffler's Washington and district staffs

Functions	Washington staff									District staff					
	A	B	C	D	E	F	G	H	I	J	K	L	M	N	O
Constituent casework			x	x	x				x	x	x	x	x	x	x
Clerical	x		x							x		x	x		
Publicity							x				x	x			
Managerial		x									x	x			
Policy research			x	x	x	x	x	x		x	x				
Committee work								x							
Political work		x				x									

Source: Based on questionnaire responses received from nine of ten Washington staff members and six of seven district staff members. Each letter designates a staff member.

THE MEMBER'S PERSPECTIVE

A member's experience of congressional service can often seem fragmented and hectic. A family crisis can occur on the morning a member is scheduled to join three colleagues for brunch with the president at the White House or the day the member is expected to take the leading role in a committee hearing on the costs of a new space surveillance system. Everything seems to happen at once. The mayor of the biggest city in the district is on the phone inquiring about federal funds for a waste treatment plant, one of the clerks in the office wants approval for the fourth draft of a form letter to be sent to all high school principals in the district, bells are ringing to indicate an important vote is about to be taken on the floor, a lobbyist and a White House liaison official are waiting in the corridor outside to offer final arguments to sway the member's vote, and one of the children calls to say that Aunt Mildred's flight will have to be met at the National Airport at 6:30 P.M. The need to respond almost simultaneously to so many critical situations can be bewildering, but it is also part of a challenging lifestyle that is stimulating for many and even addictive for some.

In his classic study three decades ago, Matthews (1960, 75–81) reported that "most senators find (congressional life) powerfully attractive" and noted the haste, frenzy, uncertainty, and lack of a fixed schedule of work on the Hill.

Congressman Jim Wright (1976, 197–198) quotes a fellow member of the House: "There is hardly ever a time in which [a member] may pause to reflect, ponder, contemplate, or 'think consecutively' in any depth unless he simply secludes himself for a period of time."

John Bibby and Roger Davidson (1972, 120–121) make a similar point in their summary of a day in the life of Sen. Abe Ribicoff (D.–Conn.).

> The day had been a memorable one but in one respect quite typical: the wide range of topics thrown at the senator had required unflagging mental agility. In contrast to bureaucrats and scholars, legislators cannot afford the luxury of prolonged concentration on single problems.

Charles Clapp (1963, 30–31) suggested to new members that they not irritate or alienate their colleagues. But congressional apprenticeships today do not seem to be as long or as restrictive as they used to be. Andy Plattner (1985, 1626–1630) analyzed different behavior patterns of freshmen representatives. Rep. Peter Visclosky (D.–Ind.), assuming a traditionally modest role, "concentrates on district problems, taking a low-key, behind-the-scenes approach to finding federal publicworks dollars for Indiana. He has yet to introduce a bill, offer a floor amendment, or take a substantive part in floor debate." But Rep. Jim Kolbe (R.–Ariz.) "represents a new generation of members who plunge into a range of House activities immediately upon arrival, often taking an aggressive role on issues that are not before their own committees."

The late Congressman Clem Miller (1962, 93) of California described the basic "aura of friendliness that surrounds the life of a congressman." The socialization process begins with the ceremonies opening each Congress.

> Opening day is a time of great excitement and ferment. During the off-season, Capitol Hill simmers along, hardly a ripple breaking the empty stillness of the long halls and passageways. Opening day is moving day. A vast game of musical chairs takes place as some congressmen move out of their offices and newcomers move in. . . .
>
> When the buzzers sound for the opening call of the House, the corridors begin to seethe, people emerge from everywhere. . . . Everyone moves a bit faster. You feel good. You feel friendly toward everyone. It's like the first day of school; it seems brand new and hopeful. . . .
>
> This may appear to outsiders as part of the ordinary political spectacle, the general overfriendliness of the trade, but it is much more than that. The emotions

are real. The affection is a heartfelt display. It is the camaraderie of the shared experience. These people, these congressmen, have all been through the mill. They have returned from the indifferent cruelties of the political wars. . . . So, the freshly painted office, the familiar furniture, the trusted staff, their fellow ambulants constitute a refuge, warm, friendly, understanding. (80–81)

In the cloakroom near the floor of the House, according to Miller,

weighty policy seems seldom a topic. . . . It is . . . a place of escape from the ceaseless press of business; a place of refuge from the insistent and the importunate. Talk among the leather couches is general banter, idle trivia of the most ordinary sort. . . . To some it is an accustomed station, where they will repair with friends to talk endlessly of remembrances past. (78–79)

Former Rep. G. William Whitehurst (R.–Va.) describes (Whitehurst, 1985, 4) the House with these words: "In many respects it is like a college fraternity in its camaraderie and factionalism. There is also exclusivity born not of pretense but of the experience of political survival. . . ."

On the other hand, Eric Uslaner (1987) has written of a growing impersonalization of daily life in Congress, and John Bibby (1983) likewise notes the decline of collegiality. Norman Ornstein (Mann and Ornstein 1981, 370) observes that the Senate is less "clubby" than it used to be, its members less likely to be close to many colleagues than in former times.

The decline in congressional civility was further illustrated in late February, 1988, during the course of Senate debate on campaign finance legislation. Majority Leader Robert Byrd (D.-W.Va.) called on Senate Sergeant-at-Arms Henry Guigni to *arrest* several Republican senators, who had been taking part in a filibuster against the bill, and bring them to the floor in order to maintain the necessary quorum to conduct business. Guigni used a passkey to unlock the office of Sen. Robert Packwood (R.-Ore.) and, with the help of three Capitol policemen, brought Packwood to the floor. This led to further acrimonious debate on the Senate floor, led by Sens. Arlen Specter (R.-Pa.) and Dale Bumpers (D.-Ark.).

New members may feel overwhelmed by the new responsibilities, somewhat like a little fish in a large pond, but "may expect to be a full partner in the day-to-day operations" of Congress (Clapp, 1963, 10) and as such to have an "everyday brush with the facts of American life" (490).

One of the changes in Hill life in the past decade or so has been the increasing sensitivity of the old guard to the ambitions of junior members. This may be a consequence of the larger proportion of new members in recent years and of the awareness on the part of veterans that junior members may be in a better position to understand changes in societal attitudes. Bibby's (1983, 7–9, 21) interviews with members newly elected in 1978 showed considerable satisfaction on the part of new members of both parties with the way their committee assignment requests were handled. House Republicans made a significant change in the procedures of their committee-on-committees by reducing the voting power of Republican members from such strongholds as California and Ohio. New members were also given guidance in setting up their Washington and district offices and quickly learned that behind the seemingly dull and ritualistic House sessions lay the opportunity to talk with many colleagues: The House floor was seen as an important "communications mechanism."

Members of Congress are each different—in outlook, personality, and politics. The idiosyncracies of district, personality and ambition make each member a fascinating study. *The Almanac of American Politics* (Barone and Ujifusa 1987) and *Politics in America* (Ehrenhalt 1986) are essential compendia of the details of political life. A promotional flyer for the 1988 edition of *Politics in America* evaluated political personalities on the basis of three questions. The comments and information in the publication are sufficient to guide term papers, master's theses, doctoral dissertations, and scholarly articles for many years to come: (1) "Is this member a grandstander who gets you in the media, or an insider who gets you the votes?" Patricia Schroeder (D.–Colo.) is described as "outrageous and outspoken . . . a political gadfly with a sharp irreverence and a sense of humor that some find refreshing and others find annoying." (2) "Is this member's focus on local or national interests?" Frank Wolf (R.–Va.) is described as a person who "pursues local causes with a zeal bordering on fanaticism. Listening to his speeches or reading his literature, it is hard to tell whether he is running for Congress or the Arlington County Board." (3) "What does this new member's background tell you about his sympathy to your problem?" Mike Espy (D.–Miss.) is described as "a sophisticated politician whose credentials are safely mainstream and whose manner is low-key and businesslike".

Many roles are open to members of Congress—maverick or team player, realist or idealist, bipartisan statesman or highly partisan politician, national spokesperson or district delegate espousing parochial appeals, advocate for special groups or supporter of broad causes, peacemaker or combative in-fighter.

In Washington, a member of Congress must deal with the immediate family, office staff, colleagues (especially those serving on the same committees or sub-committees, those whose offices happen to be located in the same corridor, and members from the same state), constituents, and interest group representatives.

In the district, a member may retain business interests or property holdings that must be attended to with some regularity. Inevitably, though, many members begin to spend more time in their Washington residences than in their home district, especially if it is a long way from Washington. Distance between district and Washington also affects the frequency and duration of trips home. Congressional duties continue at home, where most members have at least a skeletal staff. At the least, there are interest groups and political party officials to maintain contact with and luncheons and banquets and other special events to attend.

Several writers have described the daily schedules of particular senators or representatives (see Miller 1962, Wright 1976, Bibby and Davidson 1972, Jones 1982). The general pattern is as follows: Mornings are devoted to office work, committee meetings, and appointments on the Hill or downtown; noon and early afternoon are spent on or near the floor, with a quick lunch at one of the Capitol restaurants; in late afternoon the member returns to the office to clean up and look over what the staff has been busy with all day; evenings are generally spent attending political or social functions or doing "homework," particularly reading documents and reports from the staff or drafting correspondence or memoranda. One "official" survey (U. S. Congress 1977, 18–19) found that, on average, representatives spend 2 hours and 53 minutes in the House chamber, 1 hour and 24 minutes on committee or subcommittee work, 3 hours and 19 minutes in the office, 2 hours and 2 minutes in other places on the Hill or in the city of Washington, and 1 hour and 40 minutes in "other" places (including work at home or on the telephone).

This chapter closes with a description of the background and daily schedule of Rep. Leon Panetta (D.–Calif.). The schedule reflects the broad range of contacts and issues to which a member must respond.

Two Days in the Congressional Life of Representative Leon Panetta

Leon Panetta was born in Monterey in 1938. After law school (Santa Clara) and army service, he became, as a young Republican, legislative assistant to Sen. Tom Kuchel (R.–Calif.) in the late 1960s. Then he became director of the Office of Civil Rights in the Department of Health, Education, and Welfare (1969–1970) and executive assistant to the mayor of New York (1970–1971). He practiced law for several years before being elected to Congress in 1976 as a Democrat, defeating a veteran Republican, Burt Talcott. Panetta has been reelected in every campaign since.

Panetta quickly became noticeable in the House and, though holding "no high-ranking position, has been one of the most influential and powerful members of the House" (Barone and Ujifusa 1985, 135). He figured prominently as a member of the Budget Committee in the first Reagan term, though the three-term limit rule caused him to be removed from that committee after 1984. He was a member of the Agriculture Committee, ranking tenth of twenty-six Democratic members in 1985–1986, and he chaired the subcommittee on domestic markets, consumer relations, and nutrition. Because he has no major crop subsidies to defend, he is in a good position to work out compromises among major farm commodity interests. Panetta also served on the three-member task force involved in the controversy over the seating of Congressman Frank McCloskey from Indiana's eighth congressional district in 1985. (See chapter 5.)

Representative Panetta maintains district offices in Monterey, Hollister,

Salinas, San Luis Obispo, and Santa Cruz. He returns to his district almost every weekend. His working schedule for two days in the spring of 1986 is as follows.[2]

Tuesday, April 29

8:00A.M. Met with Democratic Budget Group and Budget Chairman William Gray of Pennsylvania in 210 Cannon. (Though no longer a committee member, Panetta continued to be regarded as very knowledgeable in the budget area.)

9:00A.M. Addressed Natural Resources Council at the American Forestry Association, 1319 18th Street, N. W.

9:30A.M. Attended joint hearings of the Agriculture Department Operations Subcommittee in 2318 Rayburn. (Panetta is the fourth-ranking Democrat on the subcommittee on department operations, research, and foreign agriculture.)

10:30A.M. Presided over office meeting (339 Cannon) on the subject of waste treatment in Watsonville.

12:00P.M. Attended immigration policy meeting in Rayburn room. (House goes into session at noon.)

1:30P.M. Met in office (339 Cannon) with several other members concerned about off-shore oil drilling on outer continental shelf.

2:00P.M. Met in office (339 Cannon) with Roses, Inc., a nursery industry group concerned about foreign trade legislation. (About 40 percent of the nation's commercial roses are grown in the sixteenth district.)

3:00P.M. Met at 600 17th Street, N. W., with Ambassador Clayton Yeutter, the U. S. trade representative, on the subject of trade legislation.

4:00P.M. Met with Sen. Pete Wilson (R.–Calif.) in 720 Hart Senate Office building for continuing discussions to preserve the Big Sur area.

5:30P.M. Met with representatives of the Florida Sugar Cane League in 1300 Longworth House Office Building.

Evening. Choice of attending one of four receptions on the Hill or a round-table on U. S./Soviet relations in H-130 Capitol.

Wednesday, April 30

7:35A.M. Interviewed in office (339 Cannon) by *Wall Street Journal* reporter.

8:00A.M. Met with the California congressional delegation in the speaker's dining room in the Capitol.

9:00A.M. Democratic caucus on the House floor.

10:00A.M. Attended hearings of the Select Committee on Hunger and International Nutrition in Raybun 2212.

11:30A.M. Met in office on outer continental shelf oil drilling.

12:30P.M. Attended meeting with fellow Democrats on party effectiveness in H-324 Capitol.

1:00P.M. Met in office with a visiting constituent from San Luis Obispo.

1:30P.M. Met in office with an Agriculture Committee counsel to discuss drafting of legislation.

2:30P.M. Met in office with representatives of the California Bankers As-

sociation. (There was a conflicting meeting with the bipartisan Nicaraguan Task Force in H-324 Capitol.)

3:00P.M. Met in office on outer continental shelf oil drilling. (Met for the
third time in two days. House goes into session at 3:00 P.M.)

4:00P.M. Met with constituents of Rep. Berkley Bedell (D.–Iowa) in Rayburn
2359.

4:30P.M. Met with other members on the page program in H-326 Capitol.

5:00P.M. Met with other members on immigration policy in Rayburn Room.

6:00P.M. Attended unveiling of portrait of Sen. Alan Cranston in the Hart
Senate Office Building.

6:30P.M. Attended the Sioux City steak dinner, hosted by Congressman
Bedell, in the Rayburn House Office Building. (The California Bankers
Association was also holding an evening reception at 144 Constitution
Avenue on Capitol Hill.)

SUMMARY

Members' political lifestyles and priorities are reflected by the people they hire, the
way they manage and evaluate these staff members, and the functions to which
members devote the greatest share of personal time. In the case of many staff
positions, there is a choice to be made between hiring assistants who are familiar
with Washington and Capitol Hill and those who are from the district. Should
members hire on the basis of staff knowledge of substantive policy fields (especially
those related to the member's committee assignments and legislative interests) or of
staff familiarity with groups and influentials from the district? Does the member try
to dominate the work of the staff, or is major authority over the staff delegated to an
administrative assistant? How much of the member's time is spent in committee
meetings, on the floor, meeting with constituents, attending social and political
functions? The member's daily existence involves the constant balancing of demands and tensions.

NOTES

1. More information on the Maltby House can be found in "The First Senate Office
   Building" (1986) in *Senate History,* a periodical published by the historical office in the
   Office of the Secretary, U. S. Senate.
2. These schedules were derived from conversations and correspondence with Diana Marino, administrative assistant to Congressman Panetta.

REFERENCES

BARONE, MICHAEL, and UJIFUSA, GRANT. *The Almanac of American Politics, 1986.*
Washington, D. C.: National Journal, 1985.

BARONE, MICHAEL and UJIFUSA, GRANT. *The Almanac of American Politics, 1988*. Washington, D.C.: National Journal, 1987.

BIBBY, JOHN F. (ed.). *Congress Off the Record: The Candid Analysis of Seven Members*. Washington, D.C.: American Enterprise Institute, 1983.

BIBBY, JOHN F., and DAVIDSON, ROGER H. *On Capitol Hill: Studies in the Legislative Process*. 2nd ed. Hinsdale, Ill.: Dryden, 1972.

CEASER, JAMES. "Saying Good-Bye to a Nice Affair: Thoughts on the Iran-Contra Hearings." *Public Opinion* 10 (September/October 1987): 55.

CLAPP, CHARLES L. *The Congressman: His Work as He Sees It*. Washington, D.C.: Brookings Institution, 1963.

CLEM, ALAN L. "South Dakota's Congressional Staffs." *Public Affairs* 81 (June 1981).

DAVIDSON, ROGER H., and OLESZEK, WALTER J. *Congress and Its Members*. 2nd ed. Washington, DC: Congressional Quarterly Press, 1985.

EHRENHALT, ALAN. *Politics in America*. Washington, D.C.: Congressional Quarterly Press, 1985.

"The First Senate Office Building." *Senate History* 11(February 1986): 1, 9–10.

FOX, JR., HARRISON J., and HAMMOND, SUSAN W. *Congressional Staffs: The Invisible Force in American Lawmaking*. New York: Free Press, 1977.

JOHANNES, JOHN R. *To Serve the People: Congress and Constituency Service*. Lincoln, Neb.: University of Nebraska Press, 1984.

JONES, CHARLES O. *The United States Congress*. Homewood, Ill.: Dorsey Press, 1982.

JONES, ROCHELLE, and WOLL, PETER. *The Private World of Congress*. New York: Free Press, 1979.

MALBIN, MICHAEL J. *Unelected Representatives: Congressional Staff and the Future of Representative Government*. New York: Basic Books, 1980.

MANN, THOMAS E., and ORNSTEIN, NORMAN J. (eds.). *The New Congress*. Washington, D C: American Enterprise Institute, 1981.

MATTHEWS, DONALD R. *U. S. Senators and Their World*. Chapel Hill, N.C.: University of North Carolina Press, 1960.

MILLER, CLEM. *Member of the House: Letters of a Congressman*, (ed.) John Baker. New York: Scribner's, 1962.

ORNSTEIN, NORMAN J., MANN, THOMAS E., MALBIN, MICHAEL J., SCHICK, ALLEN, and BIBBY, JOHN F. *Vital Statistics on Congress, 1984–1985*. Washington, D. C.: American Enterprise Institute, 1984.

PLATTNER, ANDY. "Freshmen Adopt Varied Styles of Legislating." *Congressional Quarterly Weekly Report* (17 August 1985): 1626–1630.

U. S. CONGRESS, HOUSE. *Administrative Reorganization and Legislative Management*. Vol. 2. 95th Cong., 1st sess., 29 September 1977. H. Doc. 95-232.

USLANER, ERIC. "The Decline of Comity in Congress." Paper presented at the 1987 annual meeting of the Midwest Political Science Association, 10 April 1987, Chicago, Illinois.

WHITEHURST, G. WILLIAM. *Diary of a Congressman: Abscam and Beyond*. Norfolk, Va.: The Donning Company, 1985.

WHITEMAN, DAVID. "What Do They Know and When Do They Know It? Health Staff on the Hill." *PS* 20 (Spring 1987): 221–225.

WILSON, WOODROW. *Congressional Government*. New York: Meridian, 1956. [1885]

WRIGHT, JIM. *You and Your Congressman*. rev. ed. New York: Capricorn, 1976.

VII CONGRESSIONAL LEADERSHIP

Congress has no single, perennial leader. Abraham Lincoln's comment that "you can fool all of the people some of the time, and some of the people all of the time, but you cannot fool all the people all of the time" can be rephrased to describe congressional leadership: "You can lead some of the members all of the time, and you can lead all of the members some of the time, but no one can lead all of the members all of the time." Congress's divided structure makes quick, decisive action difficult. Congress often seems to be a large and uncoordinated body whose movements are sluggish, uncertain, and irregular.

Recently, House leaders have made impressive attempts to centralize powers, but such efforts face immense structural obstacles.

In this chapter, attention is devoted to the various external elements that attempt to provide direction for Congress and to the internal processes that determine its leadership: how and by whom the leaders are chosen, under what conditions they are replaced, and how they operate.

WHO LEADS?

Various modes of directing the lawmaking process might have been contemplated by the founders of the republic: direction by a single leader, direction by a small group of wealthy and strategically placed influentials, or direction by public referenda, among others. From experience and reason, the Founding Fathers may have realized that these modes seldom if ever are permanent, wise, just, and effective. Leadership by too small a group can be dictatorial, harsh, rigid, discriminatory, and insensitive to the interests of the common people. Leadership by too large a group can be chaotic, rash, unpredictable, unstable, and insensitive to the judgments of wiser minds.

With these considerations in mind, and with an abhorrence of the remote and unlimited power exemplified by the British government of their time, the Founding Fathers based the new constitutional system on a representative elective body that had limited lawmaking power and no single leader.

Congress, of course, has leaders; among these are the speaker of the House, the party leaders for both parties in the two chambers, the chairs of the various

121

House and Senate standing committees, and policy specialists whose views in their respective areas of expertise have great weight among their colleagues. The speaker is probably the most visible and powerful single leader on Capitol Hill (especially in such circumstances as the first six years of the Reagan presidency when the Senate was under the control of the president's party). No one of these leaders, however, can presume to speak for the entire legislative branch.

If Congress has no single external spokesman or internal leader, how is Congress's policy agenda determined? Congress is sensitive to many interests and forces. External forces include the president, national or regional public opinion, interest groups, political parties, and the courts. Internal forces include party leaders, committee chairs, and members with reputations as spokespersons for particular regional, economic, or ideological interests. Can this list of putative leaders be simplified? Four models of congressional leadership suggest themselves.

The Presidential Model

In this model, policy direction comes from the president. The Constitution instructs the president to report to Congress on the "state of the Union" and to suggest solutions for the national problems identified. Several presidents were notably free in publicly giving advice to Congress, especially Woodrow Wilson, Franklin Roosevelt, and Lyndon Johnson. A leading exponent of this view of presidential initiation was Alexander Hamilton, President George Washington's secretary of the treasury, who regarded it as the president's prerogative to present Congress with major legislative proposals and to push vigorously for their enactment. Theodore Roosevelt later made this view the basis of his stewardship theory of aggressive presidential leadership.

The Political Party Model

This model holds that Congress should be led by the political party enjoying majority status. This view is associated with Thomas Jefferson and his congressional followers, who saw party allegiance as a bond cementing cooperation between the president and Congress. This was in contrast to the Hamiltonian model of presidential leadership, which was predicated on a situation in which the White House and Congress were controlled by different parties. In the early decades of the republic, national political parties were based in and controlled by their congressional members, but later, national parties developed power bases and nomination processes that existed outside of Congress. Several party instruments evolved, such as national nominating conventions, the party platform, national party committees and chairs, and the presidential candidate, not to mention the party leaders in each state. As a result, consideration of the political party model raises the question of which party instrument would be the means to lead a party-directed Congress. The platform approved by the most recent national convention of the majority party could be a possible basis by which that party could direct its congressional agenda. Congress would, in this case, be directed by an outside agency. Such a system would run counter to American practice, certainly, although the system would adhere to the principle of responsible party government as practiced in most modern western democracies. In such systems, the election of a socialist or a conservative party to majority status in the national legislature largely determines which programs and policies will be debated and enacted by the legislature. Two characteristics of the American system reduce the viability of this model. First, Americans do not think in terms of "party government" because party control of the executive and legislative branches is so often divided. Second, American political parties are fragmented, being more responsive to parochial concerns than to national ones. There is also a problem with this model in a bicameral legislature such as Congress when the two chambers are not controlled by the same party. An alternative to control by external party elements would be policy direction by the internal majority party caucus, but here again arises the problem of how to coordinate the two chambers.

The Public Opinion Model

In this model, the opinions of the general public are the major source of policy leadership. In this view, it is the function of Congress to enact the popular will. If a majority of the public wants to increase Social Security benefits or to stiffen the penalities for violent crimes, then Congress's duty is to pass such laws. Public opinion should become policy. Several states use the initiative and referendum devices by which the people can propose and approve laws or reject laws passed by the state's legislature. There is no such mechanism on the national level, but in this era of sophisticated public opinion measurement techniques and electronic communication devices, as noted in chapter 3, it is easy to imagine some sort of national television arrangement by which legislative proposals could be signalled to television sets and viewers could cast yes or no votes.

Ideas of adopting national policy polls have intrigued more than one observer. Among the more serious problems with "teledemocracy" are: (1) how the agenda (the identity and sequence of the proposals to be decided) would be determined, and (2) how it would be possible to amend a particular proposal or to present and discuss favorable and unfavorable arguments. There are a number of technical problems with government by referendum, but philosophically the idea of a Congress whose direction comes from the directly expressed will of the majority of the people is interesting and worthy of discussion.

In this connection, it is worth noting that many members of Congress conduct public opinion polls of their constituents and use the results to guide their own behavior.

The Polyarchal Model

The final model is based on the premise that Congress should be directed by its own internal majority, or dominant coalition. This view seems closest to the expectations of the Founding Fathers, particularly James Madison, whose notes remain the best evidence of the Founders' thoughts as they worked out the structure of the American system. The logic of this view is as follows: The voters are (or should be) aware of the past performance of the political parties and of the candidates for Congress. Each district or state elects its representatives and senators. These members then meet and, on the basis of their preferences and through such internal institutions as party caucuses and legislative committees, establish the legislative agenda and shape the final form of laws through debate and compromise. Members may, of course, consider political party platforms, presidential requests, or the presumed preferences of the majority of the public, but none of these external forces is to be dominant or determinate. Congress is to be guided in its policy deliberations by shifting coalitions of its own members rather than by the national majority party, the president, or public opinion. Each member can be expected to promote the economic and other interests of the district, and the national interest emerges from the resulting compromises among competing local interests.

Thus, the question "Who should be in charge?" can be answered in at least four ways. At one time or another, each of the four models has been an accurate assessment of congressional leadership, but no one model has dominated Congress for an extended period of time.

Incremental Policy Making and Real Power

Two considerations qualify what has been said about national leadership in policy making. First, contemporary policy making is incremental in character. That is, the policies that Congress enacts today are, for the most part, merely modifications or extensions of policies that have been in effect for several years, even decades. Seldom does Congress take new directions in making policy. A period such as the New Deal, when many dazzling new solutions to problems were enacted under Franklin Roosevelt's dynamic presidential leadership, represents an exception to this rule of incrementalism in policy making. This incremental character was evident, at least until very recently, in the annual federal budget process. A program that received, say, $10 billion last year could expect to receive about the same amount the following year, unless some dramatic development indicated either that there was a heightened need for extension of the program or that the program had failed and should be scrapped. Even given such developments, the likelihood was that budget additions or reductions would not exceed 10 percent. Generally speaking, neither the substance of policy nor the size of budget allocations changed very much from one year to the next.

Second, there is a difference between formal power and real power. The Constitution establishes the ground rules, that laws are to be written only by Congress. But Congress is a large and diverse body and is affected by many outside forces. To determine who really leads, then, one must first identify which member, or group of members, exerts the greatest amount of influence over Congress as a whole and second, determine the outside groups that might influence congressional decisions through possession and manipulation of valuable political resources such as campaign money, political information, access to large voting blocs, or influence over nominating entities such as state or national party conventions. The concern is whether we are governed by the political institutions shaped by the Constitution or by hidden power brokers who have a critical impact on policy decisions. Such external influence, if it does exist, might occur on all issues all of the time, on all issues some of the time, or on some issues some of the time. The naive reader may assume that Congress has the power the Constitution says it has, while the more skeptical reader may be convinced that real policy-making power generally, or at least frequently, lies outside Congress.

PARTY CONTROL

Party control of Congress is at issue in the November elections of every even-numbered year, when all of the representatives and one-third of the senators must face the voters again or retire. The party in each chamber that wins the majority of seats will play the dominant role in writing legislation. It will control all the leadership positions, all the standing committees, the agenda, and floor procedures and decisions. These areas will be explored in subsequent chapters; suffice it to say here that the stakes of party control of Congress are high.

As a general rule, one party controls both chambers. In only sixteen of the first ninety-nine congressional bienniums have different parties controlled the two chambers. In this century, there has been split control of the House and the Senate in five different Congresses: in 1911–1912 when William Howard Taft was president; in 1931–1932 when Herbert Hoover was president; and in 1981–1986 during Ronald Reagan's term of office. Generally, split party control makes it more difficult for legislation that divides the parties to get through Congress. These circumstances tend to strengthen the position of the president as a final arbiter in shaping the specifics of legislation.

While a margin of just one vote is sufficient to allow one party to control a chamber, it is, of course, preferable to work with a larger margin. Two considerations are important in the matter of party balance. First, American political parties are not particularly homogeneous or cohesive. Both Democratic and Republican congressional ranks have substantial numbers of members who do not agree with many of the policy goals of the majority of their fellow party members and who consequently vote against their party majority almost as often as they vote with it. As all recent congressional leaders can attest, it is not easy to maintain control of a majority throughout a congressional session. A party's majority can win the leadership positions at the beginning of each biennial Congress, but it may not hold together on many of the key legislative decisions that will be made over the ensuing twenty-four months. Party majorities in Congress fall apart as frequently as they hang together. Thus, groupings other than the fundamental party majority—such as the "conservative coalition," the ideological majority formed by Republicans and conservative Democrats—often control legislative action on given bills or at given times (see chapter 10).

Second, it is important in certain circumstances to have control of far more than just a majority of votes. Three examples illustrate this point. To stop a filibuster in the Senate requires the assent of sixty of the one hundred senators. To propose an amendment to the U. S. Constitution requires a two-thirds majority in each chamber. Similarly, to override a presidential veto of legislation requires the support of two-thirds of the members of each chamber. Thus there is sometimes talk of a "veto-proof" Congress, as in the 89th Congress under President Lyndon Johnson (1965–1966) when the Democrats outnumbered the Republicans better than two-to-one in both the Senate and the House. In the years of Johnson's presidency and the overwhelming congressional control by the Democratic party— years of sweeping civil rights and antipoverty legislation, the Great Society, and the escalation of the war in Vietnam—the minority Republicans were hard put to amend, delay, or even question the initiatives of the majority party. Even so, in attempting to understand and explain American congressional activity, one must constantly resist the temptation to think of either Democrats or Republicans as members of monolithic organizations whose votes may be taken for granted. Whether he needs 51 percent or 67 percent of the vote, a congressional leader must know more about his colleagues than their party label.

While one-party control of both houses of Congress is generally the rule, this is not true between the legislative and executive branches. Consider the period since World War I. (Table 7-1 gives data on party strength in Congress at selected times.) The Republican party controlled the White House from 1921 through 1932 (under Presidents Harding, Coolidge, and Hoover) and both chambers of Congress through 1930. In the last two years of Hoover's term Congress was under split control. The next fourteen years (1933–1946) saw the Democrats in control of the White House

Table 7-1. Party strength in the House and Senate, selected congresses, 1917–1988

Congress (years)	House			Senate		
	Democrats	Republicans	Other	Democrats	Republicans	Others
65th (1917–1919)	210	216	9	53	42	1
70th (1927–1929)	195	237	3	47	48	1
75th (1937–1938)	333	89	12	75	17	4
80th (1947–1948)	188	246	1	45	51	0
85th (1957–1958)	234	201	0	49	47	0
90th (1967–1968)	248	187	0	64	36	0
95th (1977–1978)	292	143	0	61	38	1
96th (1979–1980)	277	158	0	58	41	1
97th (1981–1982)	243	192	0	46	53	1
98th (1983–1984)	268	167	0	46	54	0
99th (1985–1986)	253	182	0	47	53	0
100th (1987–1988)	258	177	0	55	45	0

(Franklin Roosevelt or Harry Truman) and Congress. The Republicans won control of both the House and Senate for the 1947–1948 biennium. The Democrats returned to full control for four more years (1949–1952) under Truman. President Eisenhower's election in 1952 also gave the Republican party narrow but effective control over the House and Senate in 1953–1954, but Democrats took control of both chambers in the 1954 election and remained in charge through 1980 regardless of which party occupied the White House (Republican Eisenhower through 1960, Democrats John F. Kennedy and Lyndon Johnson from 1961–1968, Republicans Richard Nixon and Gerald Ford from 1969–1976, and Democrat Jimmy Carter from 1977–1980). A recent essay by Thomas E. Mann (1988) comments on the implications of various patterns of party control over the legislative and executive branches.

Since World War II Democratic strength in the Senate has varied from a high of sixty-eight seats in 1965–1966 to a low of forty-six seats in 1953–1954, 1981–1982, and 1983–1984. Republicans in the postwar era hit their high in 1983–1984 with fifty-four senators, and their low in 1965–1966, with only thirty-two senators. In 1948, 41 percent of the Democratic senators were from the South, and 22 percent were from the Rocky Mountain area. By 1982 Democratic senators were more evenly distributed across the nation, with 24 percent of them from the South, 15 percent from border states, 13 percent each from New England and the Midwest, and 11 percent from the Rocky Mountain states. In 1948 the largest groups of Republican senators came from the Plains states (24 percent), New England (21 percent), and the Midwest (19 percent). By 1982 the Republican Senate base had shifted considerably: The South and Rocky Mountain areas lead, with 20 percent, followed by the Plains, with 17 percent, and New England and the Pacific Coast, with 11 percent each.

For the House in the post–World War II era, the number of Democrats reached a high of 295 in 1965–1966 and nearly matched that level with 292 in 1977–1978 and 291 in 1975–1976; lows occurred in 1947–1948 (188) and in 1953–1954 (213). Republicans have not held as many as 200 House seats since 1957–1958.

Southern predominance among House Democrats remained about as strong in 1982 as it had been in 1948 in terms of members. The largest Democratic contingents in 1982 came from the South (30 percent), the Midwest (16 percent), the Mid-Atlantic states (16 percent), and the Pacific Coast states (14 percent). The largest Republican contingents came from the Midwest (22 percent), the South (21 percent, compared to only 1 percent in 1948), the Mid-Atlantic area (17 percent), and the Pacific Coast (14 percent).

Of particular importance is the comparison between the ratios of popular votes received and House seats won for each party. The Democratic party, which has generally been the majority party since 1932, almost invariably wins a higher percentage of seats than would be indicated by the share of the nationwide vote its House candidates receive. Only in the elections of 1946 and 1952, when Republicans won control of the House, did the Democratic seat-to-vote ratio suffer.

Otherwise, Democrats' ratio of seats was usually from five to eleven percentage points above its share of votes received across the nation. (For detailed data for 1946 through 1982, see Ornstein et al. 1984, 41–42.)

OBSTACLES TO LEADERSHIP

Leadership does not come easily on Capitol Hill. In fact, the setting is not conducive to strong and centralized leadership. Congress is a large body of ambitious, intelligent, experienced individuals who have adopted national politics as their career. Its members are at least as concerned about district and personal goals as they are about national goals. They represent a highly diverse nation and respond to different economic, social, and cultural forces. And they have different attitudes about their place in the congressional system. Some may take a traditional view of organizational power, expecting to be led by one congressional leader or another and perhaps hoping one day to become a leader. Other members, however, may take a dim view of attempts to influence their legislative behavior. This group includes members who consider themselves self-appointed representatives of important issues such as peace, civil rights, or fiscal responsibility as well as members who are psychologically independent—legislative mavericks who go their own way and march to their own drummer.

Christopher Deering (1986, 37) has shown how competing forces make the life of a legislative leader difficult, using the example of Senate Republican Leader Robert Dole of Kansas:

> As majority leader, Dole must play to at least five closely related constituencies and overcome numerous obstacles to succeed. He must represent [President] Reagan. He must represent his Republican party colleagues. He must protect the interests of the twenty-two Republican Senate seats at risk in the 1986 election— including his own. He must represent and to some extent promote the interests of the entire Senate. And, of course, he must represent the people of Kansas. It need hardly be added that the interests of these constituencies frequently conflict.

Attempts by external elements to lead Congress are frequent, as has been noted, but successes have been intermittent at best. A new president who is in public favor can be a powerful motivating force for Congress. Examples of such leadership include Franklin Roosevelt's New Deal of the 1930s, Lyndon Johnson's active sponsorship of the Great Society and civil rights legislation of 1964 and 1965, and Ronald Reagan's tax and economic initiatives of 1981 and 1982. These periods are thought of as political honeymoons. At other times, interest groups and alliances, party platforms, and national celebrities or spokespersons have taken central roles in setting the congressional agenda. But usually Congress is able to settle policy disputes within its own chambers and committee rooms. Thus, it is not so much a question of whether Congress responds to or rejects the proposals of the president or some other outside figure but rather a question of which of several policy options Congress will arrive at through its internal deliberations. Others may propose, but Congress disposes.

Internal leadership of Congress is a different matter. Any member would agree that if someone must lead Congress, better that it be a colleague than an outsider. Two of Congress's basic structural conditions—its bicameral form and its system of standing committees—work against unity of action and purpose, but at the same time there is present a countervailing force of party loyalty.

LEADERSHIP FUNDAMENTALS

In much of its activity—listening to lobbyists, responding to constituents, working toward the next reelection campaign—Congress is highly individualistic. But in the fundamental activity of lawmaking, Congress can act positively only if there are central officers to enter bills onto the agenda and guide them through the shoals of floor debate. What coherent leadership there is in Congress comes from the party caucuses that elect most of the formal leaders.

The relative importance of the various top party figures in Congress might follow this order: the speaker of the House, the majority leader of the Senate, the majority leader of the House, the minority leader of the Senate (because this member is so often consulted by the majority leader as to the sequence of pending business), and the minority leader of the House. These rankings could vary, depending on personality differences or the distribution of party control in the two chambers and the White House. A party leader of the Senate or House whose party does not control the White House has a more independent, and more visible, position. In the Reagan years, this situation enhanced the relative importance of House Speaker Tip O'Neill, a Democrat, compared to that of Senate Majority Leaders Howard Baker (1981–1984) and Robert Dole (1985–1986). Two decades earlier, Senate Minority Leader Everett Dirksen's importance was thought to have been greater (because a Democrat occupied the White House during his leadership) than that of his successor, Hugh Scott, during the Republican administration of Richard Nixon.

Among the more tangible powers of party leaders in Congress are their influence in organizing their own party's caucus committees, in organizing the chamber and its staff, in distributing patronage, and in establishing the chamber's legislative agenda. All these functions give these leaders multiple opportunities to educate their party followers, especially in terms of supporting the party's legislative goals. Party leaders also have easy access to the media, which may be used to appeal to the public or to the president in order to advance the congressional party's particular causes.

PARTY CAUCUSES AND THEIR COMMITTEES

There are four party caucuses, or conferences, and these caucuses form the basis of party control of congressional organization and activity. The more important caucus in each chamber is that of the majority party. In addition to choosing its own leaders, the majority caucus authenticates committee assignments and names the clerks, parliamentarian, and other personnel who record the business conducted by the chamber. Party caucuses meet at the beginning of each biennial Congress to make leadership and staff selections. The caucus is all powerful while it meets, but it does not meet frequently. Generally, once the caucus has elected the party leaders and whips, authenticated assignments to standing committees, and named members to a few party committees, it meets no more during the biennium. Over the years, attempts to call caucus meetings and thereby to require members to exhibit loyalty to the party in their voting have frequently proved embarrassing to the party.

The most interesting and significant of the four party caucuses is the Democratic caucus in the House of Representatives. This caucus has instituted several important changes in the past two decades. The secret ballot has been adopted, which has tended to lessen the power of the party establishment. If the leadership does not know for sure how a junior member has voted on a key caucus issue, it cannot discipline that member for an antiestablishment vote; a member's independence and individuality can be more safely expressed when secret ballots are used.

Another change directly resulting from the secret ballot is the authority of the caucus to remove the chair of a standing committee or to deprive a member of committee seniority. Traditionally, a majority party member became chair of a committee strictly by means of seniority, that is, by having the longest continuous service on the committee. The chair retained this position as long as the Democratic party controlled the House and the seat was maintained. The Democratic caucus removed three chairs of committees in 1975, replacing them with more junior colleagues whose policy preferences, personal styles, or approaches were more in line with the preferences of the caucus majority. Barbara Salmore and Stephen Salmore (1987) suggest that these infrequent caucus actions against committee chairs have not been part of a systematic, positive program to reform party leadership; rather, the actions have been essentially negative, having the intention of removing aging or ailing chairs or chastising unreliable members. Leon Epstein's (1986, 51) conclusion that "seniority prevails as the working principle in both houses" of Congress supports the Salmores' point. Still, the ouster of a few committee chairs acts as a warning to all.

It is difficult to generalize about why the caucus selects one colleague rather than another for critical party leadership positions. Without doubt, sectional and ideological considerations play a role. Moderate leaders who can unify the party inside the chamber and who can cooperate effectively with other party leaders outside the chamber are generally preferred to colleagues who take extreme or controversial positions on political issues. A member's reputation inside the chamber is likely to be more important in leadership contests than visibility and popularity outside the chamber. A warm and helpful personal style is likely to be more useful than an aloof, superior attitude. Knowledge of the rules governing procedure in the chamber is certainly important, for the majority party expects to be in control and to use its control to advance the party's policy goals and, not incidentally, to advance the political careers of its members. Many of these generalizations about party leadership selection are drawn from Nelson Polsby's study of the selection of Carl Albert of Oklahoma to succeed John McCormack of Massachusetts as Democratic leader (Peabody and Polsby 1977, 324–354). Albert's defeat of Richard Bolling of Missouri was characterized by Polsby as a victory of an "inside" strategy over an "outside" strategy. Albert, the party whip and a well-liked member, was already a central part of the party's power structure; he was trusted by his colleagues and had strong personal friendships with and mutual obligations to many of them. Bolling, on the other hand, was a more "public" member, whose liberal positions were well known to the press and to other political influentials. Albert personally called on members to solicit their support, while the "pleasant but reticent" Bolling adopted an aloof posture, counting on support from the younger, more liberal colleagues. Bolling withdrew from the contest when it was clear he could not come near the necessary 130 votes in the caucus.

Each of the four caucuses has several committees that perform specified functions that continue throughout the congressional biennium.

The House Democratic caucus has (1) a campaign committee, which is committed to helping elect more Democrats to the House; (2) a personnel committee, which distributes patronage appointments among Democratic members; and (3) a steering and policy committee, which assigns Democratic members to House committees (a function formerly performed by Democratic members of the Ways and Means Committee), argues policy, plans strategy, and acts as an executive committee for the caucus. The steering and policy committee contains thirty-one members, eight of whom are chosen by the speaker, eleven of whom hold their position ex officio, and twelve of whom are chosen to represent geographical areas of the nation. A particularly significant example of a decision by the steering and policy committee took place in 1981 when Rep. Phil Gramm (D.–Tex.) was given a place on the Budget Committee. His subsequent support of President Reagan's fiscal proposals enraged many Democrats so much that two years later the Democratic caucus denied Gramm's reappointment to the Budget Committee. In consequence, Gramm resigned his House seat and filed as the Republican party's candidate in the subsequent special election, which he won (see chapter 4).

House Republicans have a policy committee to plot party strategy on current bills, a research committee, a campaign committee, and a committee on committees to assign Republican members to House standing committees.

In the Senate, the Republican party has a policy committee, a campaign committee, and a committee on committees.

Senate Democrats have the same three committees as their Republican rivals but refer to their committee on committees as the steering committee.

The following is a list of the chairs of the party caucuses and of selected important caucus committees for the 100th Congress (1987–1988):

1. House Democrats: caucus chair, Richard Gephardt of Missouri; steering and policy committee, Jim Wright of Texas; congressional campaign committee, Beryl Anthony of Arkansas.
2. House Republicans: conference chair, Jack Kemp of New York; policy committee, Richard Cheney of Wyoming; campaign committee, Guy Vander Jagt of Michigan; committee on committees, Robert Michel of Illinois.
3. Senate Democrats: conference chair, Robert Byrd of West Virginia; policy committee, Robert Byrd of West Virginia; steering committee, Robert Byrd of West Virginia; campaign committee, John Kerry of Massachusetts.
4. Senate Republicans: conference chair, John Chafee of Rhode Island; policy committee, William Armstrong of Colorado; campaign committee, Rudy Boschwitz of Minnesota; committee on committees, Paul Trible of Virginia.

American political parties exist as national party organizations, as mass-membership associations with which individual citizens identify, and as party members occupying public office. Although congressional parties are just one manifestation of national parties, Leon Epstein (1986, 41) notes that "the congressional parties are the most continuously organized, the most regularly important, and the most nearly similar to their counterparts in other Western democratic nations." Alan Ehrenhalt ("Interview" 1987) makes a related point about the growing importance of the party in its congressional manifestation when he notes that congressional campaign committees today perform several important functions of a national party: recruiting candidates, giving them money to finance their campaigns, and training them to be effective campaigners.[1] Salmore and Salmore (1987) compare today's party caucuses to the situation in the pre-Jacksonian period when the congressional leadership cadre known as King Caucus dominated national policy and presidential candidate decisions.

Two recent comments further accentuate Congress's growing sense of self-importance. First, Charles O. Jones made the point that "not for a long time has so much policy initiative and integration been expected of Congress." Second, Walter Oleszek has expressed the belief that congressional leadership, as exerted in recent years by Tip O'Neill, Jim Wright, and Robert Byrd, has become stronger, more visible, and more assertive especially vis-a-vis the executive branch.[2]

PRESIDING OFFICERS

The Constitution in Article I specifies the officers who are to preside over the two chambers of Congress. The vice-president is designated the president (that is, the presiding officer) of the Senate. The House of Representatives is to select its speaker by vote. This means that the speaker, a far more powerful and partisan figure than his Senate counterpart, is in effect chosen by the marjority party caucus in the House.

The parliamentary powers of the vice-president as presiding officer of the Senate are just that: to preside over Senate sessions and to cast a tie-breaking vote in cases where senators have divided evenly on a question. In the absence of the vice-president, the president pro tempore presides; by tradition, this is the member of the majority party with the longest service, but junior senators also preside with increasing frequency. The succession of presidents pro tempore in recent decades is as follows: Styles Bridges (R.–N. H., 1953–1954), Walter George (D.–Ga., 1955–1956), Carl Hayden (D.–Ariz., 1957–1968), Richard Russell (D.–Ga., 1969–1970), Allen Ellender (D.–La., 1971–1972), James Eastland (D.–Miss., 1972–1978), Warren Magnuson (D.–Wash, 1979–1980), Strom Thurmond (R.–S. C., 1981–1986), and John Stennis (D.–Miss., 1987–1988).

The powers of the speaker of the House of Representatives are a good deal more significant than those of the vice-president. The speaker is the most powerful member of the majority party and, as we have seen, has a good deal of influence over the caucus and the party committees that are established by the caucus. The speaker presides over the House, is the central figure in the day-to-day arrangement of the chamber's agenda, and is the chief spokesperson for the party in the House. When the Senate is controlled by the other party, the speaker must be considered the party's chief spokesperson for Congress as a whole. This was the situation that applied under President Reagan when the House was under Democratic control and the Senate under Republican control. Speaker O'Neill inevitably and effectively assumed the role of chief critic of the president's statements and actions. Because a representative becomes speaker only after long service in the House, he or she is seldom considered to be a likely future candidate for the presidency, but the speaker is nonetheless a nationally recognized figure whose voice gives expression to party frustrations and policy aspirations. The power of the speaker was at its greatest around the turn of the century, and though sharply reduced in the wake of the revolt against Speaker Joe Cannon in 1910–1911, the speaker is still the most powerful, visible, and significant member of Congress.

Since World War II only death, resignation, retirement, or change in party control has caused a new speaker to be chosen. The vote for speaker is, of course, along party lines, and the result is a foregone conclusion once the results of the November elections are known. There have been no caucus contests for speaker in this period, because whenever a vacancy has occurred in the office, the Democratic caucus has promoted the majority leader into the speakership. There have been several hotly contested caucus votes for the party leadership position, as will be discussed in the next section of this chapter. The speakers since 1953 are as follows: Joseph Martin (R.–Mass., 1953–1954), Sam Rayburn (D.–Tex., 1955–1961), John McCormack (D.–Mass., 1962–1970), Carl Albert (D.–Okla., 1971–1976), Thomas O'Neill (D.–Mass., 1977–1986), and Jim Wright (D.–Tex., 1987–1988). Martin lost the speakership when the Democrats returned to power following the 1954 elections; Rayburn died in office; and McCormack, Albert, and O'Neill retired from Congress.

FLOOR LEADERS AND WHIPS

The legislative leader of the Senate is the majority leader. As with the speaker of the House, recent tradition is that the member is not removed as party leader by the caucus. Successful efforts to change party leadership in the Senate occur at the whip level, not at the top.

Alben Barkley (D.–Ky.) served as majority leader of the Senate from 1937 until the end of 1946, when the postwar election brought the Republican party to power and placed Wallace White (R.–Maine) in the majority leadership. Barkley was elected vice-president in 1948, so when the Democratic party took control again of the Senate in 1949, Scott Lucas of Illinois became majority leader. A strange thing happened in 1950: The majority leader of the Senate was defeated in his reelection bid by Republican Everett Dirksen. So the Democrats had to choose a new leader, and the mantle fell to Ernest McFarland of Arizona. Then another strange thing happened: McFarland was defeated in his 1952 reelection effort by Barry Goldwater. In that election, the Republicans came back to power, and though Styles Bridges of New Hampshire had been their party leader through 1952 when they were in the minority, the Republican conference named Robert Taft of Ohio to lead the party. Taft died in the summer of 1953 and was replaced as majority leader by William Knowland of California. (Even though Taft's seat was filled by a Democrat, giving the Democrats forty-eight seats, the Republicans forty-seven, with one Independent, Knowland continued as majority leader until the end of the 83rd Congress.)

After this series of sudden changes, stability returned to the majority leadership following the 1954 elections, when the Democratic party took clear control of the Senate and installed Lyndon Johnson of Texas as their leader, a position he held for six years until his election as vice-president in 1960. Johnson was an ambitious, energetic, and persuasive majority leader. Democrats chose the mild-mannered and popular Mike Mansfield of Montana to take Johnson's place, and Mansfield remained the Senate majority leader through 1976, when he decided not to seek reelection. Democratic Whip Robert Byrd of West Virginia succeeded to the majority leadership and remained there for the four years of the Carter administration. When the Republicans gained control in 1981, Howard Baker of Tennessee became majority leader, and when he retired four years later, his place was taken by Robert Dole of Kansas. After 1986 Byrd returned.

On the minority side, Barkley served as Democratic leader in the 80th Congress and was followed by Republicans Kenneth Wherry of Nebraska and Styles Bridges (1949–1952); Democrat Lyndon Johnson (1953–1954); Republicans William Knowland (1955–1958), Everett Dirksen (1959–1969), Hugh Scott of Pennsylvania (1969–1976), and Howard Baker (1977–1980); and Democrat Robert Byrd (1981–1986).

The number two person to the party leader is the whip. This succession is important because ordinarily the whip moves up when a vacancy occurs in the party leadership. On several occasions in recent years, the whip has been ousted by the party caucus in favor of an ambitious challenger. Such caucus contests can produce lasting scars. Following the 1968 elections, Edward Kennedy of Massachusetts defeated the previous whip, Russell Long of Louisiana. After holding the office of Democratic whip for only two years, Kennedy was ousted in favor of Robert Byrd, and Byrd held the whip position for six years until he succeeded Mike Mansfield as party leader on the latter's retirement. When Byrd moved up, the Democratic caucus chose Alan Cranston of California to be the new whip. The Republicans demoted Robert Griffin of Michigan from the whip position following the 1976 elections, replacing him with Ted Stevens of Alaska, an ignominious development that contributed to Griffin's defeat by Democrat Carl Levin in 1978. Stevens continued as Republican whip until he was defeated by Robert Dole in the 1984 struggle to succeed Majority Leader Howard Baker; the Republican caucus picked Alan Simpson of Wyoming to be the new whip.

As we have seen, the speakership in the House passed from Sam Rayburn to John McCormack to Carl Albert to Tip O'Neill to Jim Wright. At each transition there was a leadership contest in the party caucus. We have seen how Albert became majority leader when McCormack replaced Rayburn as speaker. When Albert in turn subsequently succeeded McCormack as speaker in 1971, the Democratic caucus promoted Hale Boggs of Louisiana to the position of majority leader; opposing candidates for the promotion were Morris Udall of Arizona, James O'Hara of Michigan, Wayne Hays of Ohio, and B. F. Sisk of California. Boggs was killed in a plane crash in Alaska in 1972 and was succeeded by Tip O'Neill, who had been serving as whip. Following O'Neill's elevation to the speakership in 1977, Jim Wright of Texas was chosen by the caucus over Philip Burton of California, John McFall of California, and Richard Bolling of Missouri.[3] Democratic whips are the number three members in their party; the most recent have been John Brademas of Indiana, Thomas Foley of Washington, and Tony Coelho of California.

House Republicans have been harder on their party leaders, perhaps out of frustration at being so long out of power. Joseph Martin of Massachusetts had served as speaker of the House in 1947–1948 and 1953–1954 and otherwise as minority leader through World War II and the postwar years. Restive Republicans were successful in removing him following the disastrous 1958 elections, choosing Charles Halleck of Indiana in his place. But Halleck's days as minority leader were numbered. The Republicans removed him after the 1964 elections and replaced him with Gerald Ford of Michigan. Ford continued as party leader until he was chosen vice-president by President Nixon in 1973 following Spiro Agnew's resignation. Ford's place was taken by John Rhodes of Arizona. When Rhodes retired from the House, Robert Michel of Illinois succeeded to the position, moving up from the whip position he had held for six years. Trent Lott of Mississippi became the new whip.

Challenges developed for the party leadership in the Senate caucuses of both parties following the elections of 1984. On the Democratic side, Sen. Lawton

Chiles of Florida failed in his bid to unseat the veteran Democratic leader Robert Byrd. The vote was thirty-two to ten in Byrd's favor. The Republican contest was to fill the vacancy in the party leader's position caused by the retirement of Sen. Howard Baker of Tennessee. There were five contenders for Baker's position: Robert Dole of Kansas, Ted Stevens of Alaska, James McClure of Idaho, Pete Domenici of New Mexico, and Richard Lugar of Indiana. The last three were successively eliminated on the first three ballots, and on the fourth ballot, Dole defeated Stevens, twenty-eight to twenty-five.[4]

Similarly, House Democrats filled vacancies at the top following Speaker Tip O'Neill's retirement at the end of the 99th Congress. What often happens in such cases is referred to by Robert Peabody (1976) as the "automatic escalator" of promotion in the House: the majority leader becomes speaker, the whip becomes majority leader, and a new whip is chosen. This process reduces competition and expedites party business. Rivalries are muted but not finally resolved. Though he failed to stop Wright's promotion to the speakership, Ways and Means Committee Chairman Dan Rostenkowski of Illinois still harbors the ambition of becoming speaker and bypassing the ritualistic game of musical chairs. Rostenkowski's comments at the time reflect the general view of the primacy of the speaker's position: "I can't conceive of any member . . . not wanting to be speaker (quoted in Calmes 1987, 7). Such indications of restiveness on the part of some members give further credence to Norman Ornstein's contention that in the 1980s there are fewer incentives for members to bide their time, patiently waiting for seniority to provide a place in the top leadership echelons (Mann and Ornstein 1981, 369).

Recent history provides at least one example of the five ways in which a leadership position can change hands: (1) by the death of the incumbent (Boggs); (2) by retirement of the incumbent (Rhodes); (3) by change in party control of the chamber (Martin); (4) by the incumbent's movement to a different office (Ford); and (5) by defeat of the incumbent in the party caucus (Halleck).

SENIORITY AND COMMITTEE LEADERSHIP

Party caucuses have traditionally exerted little control over one kind of major congressional position: the chair of a standing committee. We have already noted one change in the 1970s by the House Democrats, whereby their caucus has removed committee chairs on a few occasions. The growing number and power of subcommittees also has changed the situation, particularly with the Democrats' reliance on voting rather than strict seniority for determining subcommittee chairs. Departure from strict adherence to the seniority rule is an unsettling and destabilizing action. There is no sign that House Republicans would similarly repudiate the seniority rule, even to a limited extent, however; it must be admitted that there are few signs that House Republicans will ever achieve majority status where they might adopt an alternative nonseniority-based system.

Neither party in the Senate has acted contrary to the traditional seniority system. The situation is different in the Senate. First, committees are not as significant in the Senate as they are in the House. Second, each senator typically has several committee assignments, and occasionally a particular senator will qualify under the seniority system as chair of two standing committees. In such a case, the senator must decide which committee to chair, a decision that also affects the chairing of the other committee. This happened after the 1984 elections when Jesse Helms (R.–N. C.) became the senior Republican on both the Agriculture and Foreign Relations committees. Helms was ultimately prevailed on to keep the Agriculture Committee chair, as he had pledged he would do to the people of his state. This allowed Richard Lugar of Indiana to assume the prestigious Foreign Relations mantle, succeeding Charles Percy of Illinois who had been defeated in his bid for reelection.

There are three aspects of seniority. The most important aspect, which has just been discussed, is a member's ranking on a standing committee. (The mechanics and impact of the seniority system will be further discussed in chapter 8.) The other two aspects are the matter of seniority among all colleagues in the same chamber and among all colleagues of the same party in the same chamber. A member's overall seniority may result in a better office suite or parking place, but little else of importance.

Seniority can be calculated on the basis of interrupted or uninterrupted service. If two members are sworn in on the same day, then other factors are taken into account—previous service in the same chamber, in the other chamber of Congress, and as governor of the home state.

Reliance on seniority to establish the rank of each member on the standing committees is a major factor in limiting the power of the congressional party caucuses and leaders. Committee leadership is an important counterpoise to strict party control, because chairs of committees have considerable control (although less than they formerly had) over several critical phases of the legislative process, namely, (1) choosing which bills under their committee's jurisdiction will be expedited and which will be pigeonholed and thereby forgotten, (2) scheduling hearings and mark-up sessions, (3) inviting witnesses to testify at committee hearings, (4) appointing committee members to its subcommittees, (5) presiding over committee meetings, and (6) reporting committee recommendations to the floor of the chamber.

A number of cases of significant leadership change in Congress have been thoroughly described by journalists or scholars, notably the promotion of Carl Albert to the Democratic floor leadership in 1961, the selection of Gerald Ford to replace Charles Halleck as House Republican leader, the replacement of Edward Kennedy by Robert Byrd as Democratic whip in the Senate, and the selection of Jim Wright to succeed Tip O'Neill as House leader when the latter became speaker. The case to be used here to illustrate leadership change is the elevation of Les Aspin of

Wisconsin to chair the House Armed Services Committee. This example is important for a number of reasons, chiefly in its relationship to resolving a basic and continuing national security policy question.

The Selection of Les Aspin to Chair the House Armed Services Committee

Democratic members of the House who wanted a more emphatic voice on defense policy matters against President Reagan and against a Republican Senate replaced the aging chair of the House Armed Services Committee, Melvin Price of Illinois, with Les Aspin of Wisconsin in January of 1985.[5]

Aspin, aged forty-six at the time of his elevation, had earned a master's degree from Oxford and a Ph.D. in economics at MIT. He had served an Army tour in the Pentagon and was a staff assistant to Walter Heller on the Council of Economic Advisors. Elected to Congress from Wisconsin's first congressional district in 1970, he was assigned to the House Armed Services Committee. He advanced with typical slowness through the seniority ranking on that committee, from twenty-fifth of twenty-five Democrats in his first term, to fifteenth of twenty-six by 1977–1978, to seventh of twenty-eight in 1983–1984.

For several years there had been talk of removing Price from the Armed Services chair, which he had obtained in 1975 as a consequence of the ouster by the Democratic caucus of three aging committee chairs. Aspin and Rep. Dave McCurdy (D.–Okla.) led the dissident chorus in 1984, although there were no overt signs of rebellion. Over the Christmas holidays of 1984, however, Aspin, McCurdy, and several colleagues undertook a telephone campaign to attempt to oust Price.

When members returned to Washington on January 3, 1985, to convene the 99th Congress, the anti-Price movement was visible, and party leaders moved to quash it. The Democratic steering and policy committee voted to nominate Price for reelection as chair; there were no negative votes on the committee, but there was one abstention. The Democratic caucus met behind closed doors on January 4, with one hour allotted to debate Price's nomination. Speaker Tip O'Neill led several members in defending Price, and only McCurdy spoke against him. According to Rep. Mel Levine of California, O'Neill's speech was very emotional and effective and had the effect of turning a landslide (against Price) into a cliff-hanger. The Democratic caucus voted 121 to 118 to remove Price from the chair.

The steering and policy committee then met and decided, by a seventeen to five vote, to nominate the second-ranking committee member, Charles E.

Bennett of Florida, for the chair. The caucus reconvened to hear that nomination and to receive Aspin's nomination from the floor. Two other members of the Armed Services Committee who ranked above Aspin—Samuel Stratton of New York and Bill Nichols of Alabama—were thought to have been interested in the position but were not nominated. The subsequent secret ballot vote was 125 to 103 in favor of Aspin. Bennett's candidacy was evidently hampered by his aged appearance. Rep. Bob Edgar of Pennsylvania said that many Democrats favored Aspin because they felt he could do a better job of articulating defense issues, especially on radio and television. Another Democratic representative, Barney Frank of Massachusetts, stressed that the caucus decision was based on policy rather than personal considerations.

Aspin's elevation did not markedly change defense policy. Within a couple of months, Aspin was supporting House passage of the MX missile program promoted by the Reagan administration (as will be described in chapter 9). Speculation continued through 1986 that there might be a serious effort at the beginning of the 100th Congress in 1987 to challenge Aspin's continuance as chair. Bennett and Rep. Marvin Leath of Texas both announced during the summer that they were running for Aspin's job.

The House Democratic caucus took up the question of the Armed Services chair at the beginning of the 100th Congress. On January 7, 1987, the caucus voted 124 to 130 against Aspin remaining chair. Fifteen days later, the caucus reconsidered the question, with three alternative members—Bennett, Leath, and Nicholas Mavroules of Massachusetts—on the ballot with Aspin. On the first ballot, the count was Aspin 96, Leath 69, Bennett 44, and Mavroules 35. The liberal Mavroules, who had only been campaigning for the position for a few days, was dropped from the second ballot as the trailing candidate on the first ballot. Thus the liberals, who had been most anxious to pick a chair who would oppose President Reagan on weapons buildup and intervention in Nicaragua, lost their favorite candidate. The voting on the second ballot was as follows: Aspin 108, Leath 91, and Bennett 47. The moderate Bennett, whose selection would have best accorded with the seniority principle, thus fell by the wayside, leaving the decision to a third ballot in which Aspin was left with a single conservative antagonist. Aspin and Leath each picked up 25 votes on the third and final ballot (Aspin 133, Leath 116), giving Aspin a second term as chair (see Calmes 1987). Liberal votes had evidently been crucial in the negative vote on Aspin in early January, but liberals were probably not very keen on supporting Leath, Aspin's strongest opponent. Still, Aspin was humbled by the challenge in the Democratic caucus. The result for the 100th Congress was expected to be a reduction of tension within the Democratic party and the evolution of a more unified Democratic posture in Congress on defense issues vis-a-vis the administration.

SUMMARY

Tension is built into the basic structure of Congress: tension between the chambers, between the parties, and among the committees. These tensions are most evident at top leadership levels, which are occupied by members having the greatest amount of control over the structural elements of Congress. Within each party caucus, continuing tensions exist, as ambitious members set their sights on leadership positions held by others. Maintaining leadership status is not automatic or easy, and it is particularly difficult for leaders of the minority party to hold their positions. Intraparty democracy and competition often discourage current congressional leaders from providing coherent and consistent leadership. These leaders are often understandably more concerned about what is going on among their party colleagues, on whose support their own continuance as leaders depends, than about choosing the correct path for the nation to follow. As for Congress in the aggregate, tensions assume more public and complex dimensions when influence from the White House, pressure from external national party organs or powerful lobby alliances, or evidence of strong public opinion are involved.

NOTES

1. Ehrenhalt is a political writer for the *Congressional Quarterly Weekly Report*.
2. The comments by Jones and Oleszek were made at a panel meeting on "The Changing Congress," at the annual meeting of the Midwest Political Science Association in Chicago on April 10, 1987. At the same conference, Eric Uslaner (1987, 1–2) emphasized the increasing congressional contentiousness. Uslaner contrasted the usually "remarkably restrained" tone of debate in Congress with the more tumultuous and virulent style of debate in the British House of Commons. Among the evidences of growing acrimony in Congress, Uslaner cited the disputed 1984 congressional campaign in Indiana's eighth district (discussed in chapter 5), a "strike" on the Energy and Commerce Committee to protest party ratios on the subcommittees, accusations by a California representative that many Democrats were "weak" on national defense, procedures for debating legislation that would impose sanctions on South Africa, and transition rules in the tax reform bill of 1986.
3. The story of Wright's selection is told by Thomas Southwick (1976).
4. For a description of Dole as a majority leader that is full of insights about the expectations and ambitions of senators and Senate leaders, see Ornstein (1985).
5. The principal source for this case is information contained in Cohodas and Granat (1985, 7–9).

REFERENCES

BAILEY, STEPHEN K. *Congress in the Seventies*. 2nd ed. New York: St. Martin's Press, 1970.

CALMES, JACQUELINE. "The Hill Leaders: Their Places on the Ladder." *Congressional Quarterly Weekly Report* (3 January 1987): 5–10.

CALMES, JACQUELINE. "Aspin Makes Comeback at Armed Services." *Congressional Quarterly Weekly Report* (24 January 1987): 139–142.

COHODAS, NADINE, and GRANAT, DIANE. "House Seniority System Jolted: Price Dumped, Aspin Elected." *Congressional Quarterly Weekly Report* (5 January 1985): 7–9.

DAVIDSON, ROGER H., and OLESZEK, WALTER J. *Congress and Its Members.* 2nd ed. Washington, D. C.: Congressional Quarterly Press, 1985.

DEERING, CHRISTOPHER J. "Leadership in the Slow Lane." *PS* 19(Winter 1986): 37.

EPSTEIN, LEON D. *Political Parties in the American Mold.* Madison: University of Wisconsin Press, 1986.

"Interview with Alan Ehrenhalt." In Stuart Rothenberg (ed.), *The Political Report.* Washington, D. C.: Institute for Government Politics, 1987.

JONES, CHARLES O. *Minority Party Leadership in Congress.* Boston: Little, Brown, 1970.

MACKAMAN, FRANK H. *Understanding Congressional Leadership.* Pekin, Ill.: The Dirksen Congressional Center, 1981.

MANN, THOMAS E. "Rebublicans [sic]: The Permanent Minority Party." *The Christian Science Monitor* (7 March 1988): 14.

MANN, THOMAS E., and ORNSTEIN, NORMAN J. (eds.). *The New Congress.* Washington, D. C.: American Enterprise Institute, 1981.

ORNSTEIN, NORMAN J. "Dole as Majority Leader: An Early Assessment." In *Report.* Pekin, Illinois: Dirksen Congressional Center, 1985.

ORNSTEIN, NORMAN J., MANN, THOMAS E., MALBIN, MICHAEL J., SCHICK, ALLEN, and BIBBY, JOHN F. *Vital Statistics on Congress, 1984–1985.* Washington, D. C.: American Enterprise Institute, 1984.

PEABODY, ROBERT L. *Leadership in Congress: Stability, Succession, and Change.* Boston: Little, Brown, 1976.

PEABODY, ROBERT L., and POLSBY, NELSON (eds.). *New Perspectives on the House of Representatives.* 3rd ed. Skokie, Ill.: Rand McNally, 1977.

RIPLEY, RANDALL B. *Party Leaders in the House of Representatives.* Washington, D. C.: Brookings Institution, 1967.

RIPLEY, RANDALL B. *Majority Party Leadership in Congress.* Boston: Little, Bown, 1969a.

RIPLEY, RANDALL B. *Power in the Senate.* New York: St. Martin's Press, 1969b.

SALMORE, BARBARA G., and SALMORE, STEPHAN A. "Back to Basics: Party as Legislative Caucus." Paper presented at the annual meeting of the Midwest Political Science Association, 11 April 1987, Chicago.

SCHLAES, JOHN B., and LICHT, ERICK. *Movers and Shakers: Congressional Leaders in the 1980s.* Washington, D. C.: Institute for Government and Politics, 1985.

SINCLAIR, BARBARA. *Majority Leadership in the U. S. House.* Baltimore, Md.: Johns Hopkins University Press, 1983.

SOUTHWICK, THOMAS P. "House Democrats Elect Leaders, Slow Reforms." *Congressional Quarterly Weekly Report* (11 December 1976): 3291–3295.

TOBIN, MAURICE. *Hidden Power: The Seniority System and Other Customs of Congress.* Westport, Conn.: Greenwood Press, 1986.

USLANER, ERIC. "The Decline of Comity in Congress." Paper presented at the annual meeting of the Midwest Political Science Association, 10 April 1987, Chicago.

VIII CONGRESSIONAL COMMITTEES

Most of Congress's legislative decisions are made in its standing committees rather than on the floor of the House or Senate, which is in keeping with John Stuart Mill's (1958, 76–77) belief that large groups are no better fitted for writing laws than for administering them:

> There is hardly any kind of intellectual work which so much needs to be done, not only by experienced and exercised minds, but by minds trained to the task through long and laborious study, as the business of making laws. This is a sufficient reason, were there no other, why they can never be well made but by a committee of very few persons.

The committees of Congress are highly selective in their work. Only a small percentage of bills introduced in the House and Senate in a given year have hearings conducted on their merits. Many bills are forgotten, for all practical purposes, after they are referred to committee. The more fortunate bills are given hearings, with testimony from proponents and opponents, and then are sent to the floor with a favorable report. The bill then must get on the chamber's agenda, be called up, debated and perhaps amended on the floor, and finally voted for or against. Some critical decisions are made in the course of floor debate, to be sure, but generally policy decision making is a decentralized process in which the standing committee, or subcommittee, having jurisdiction over the policy field makes the essential determinations. Committees dominate the flow of business in Congress and generally work as independent entities.

In comparing bill handling in Congress and in the California state legislature, William Muir, Jr. (1982) points out that the size of the U. S. House of Representatives and the volume of bills introduced make it imperative to segregate bill consideration among committees having jurisdiction over particular policy areas and to give those committees virtually complete control over the fate of legislation. This procedure contrasts with the "author system" of California, where the individual member controls "his or her bills, from inception to the governor's desk" (57–58). The member is expected to arrange for committee witnesses, seek publicity, guide the bill through committee mark-up, and lead debate on the floor.

Congressional committees are notably more significant in the American legislative process than are the committees in the British House of Commons. In London, legislative committees are more transient and short lived. Bills are referred to committees only after the House has voted its general agreement with their major features, and the work of the committee is merely to write the perfecting details. The central cabinet arranges the parliamentary agenda in the British system, a process that in the United States involves the positive input of committee chairs as well as of party leaders.

EVOLUTION OF THE COMMITTEE SYSTEM

For several reasons, we will consider the House of Representatives in more detail than the Senate. Most of the interesting committee developments occur in the House, and House committees are more significant in the policy-making process than committees are in the Senate. For one thing, a representative's committee assignment is likely to be more politically important than is a senator's. For another, it is easier to amend legislation on the Senate floor than on the House floor, a circumstance that tends to enhance the authority of House committees. Finally, most fiscal legislation begins in the House—the Constitution so provides with respect to revenue bills, and this principle of House origination has been extended by tradition to appropriations bills as well.

Originally, there were no standing committees in Congress. Since there was not a large volume of bills, each bill could be debated on the floor of the House and approved or rejected almost at once. Most bills, though, were approved (see Skladony 1985). Gradually, however, larger and larger bills came before Congress. Skladony notes that by the end of the 10th Congress (1807–1809), a large number of the bills introduced were still pending, indicating that more and more bills were being pigeonholed. Ad hoc or special committees were formed and eventually these coalesced into permanent committees made up of members with special knowledge, experience, or interest in the subject matter. According to Skladony (1985, 18–20), a few favored members were assigned and reassigned to select committees, while many received no committee assignments whatsoever. A member would move to have a select committee formed to deal with particular legislation, and then that member would be appointed to chair that committee. These committees quickly took on one of the basic functions of congressional committees: to review the work of the executive branch in carrying out laws. Through such expertise born of early committee experience, members became more aware of the potentialities of Congress vis-a-vis the president. This new awareness made Congress more independent than it had been under Washington and Jefferson and caused some congressional leaders to see themselves as true national leaders.

The House had established more than two dozen standing committees by 1825, the chief of which was the Committee on Ways and Means, through which revenue measures passed. A Rules Committee was developed to write the rules under which each bill would come to the floor and be debated. By 1880 this committee had become a major tool of House central control. The Rules Committee was then composed of five members: the speaker and the chairs of the Ways and Means and Appropriations committees from the majority party and two minority members, referred to as mere ornamental barnacles.

After a succession of strong speakers, in 1910 progressive insurgents in the House under Rep. George Norris (R.–Neb.) were successful in ousting Speaker Joe Cannon (R.–Ill.); as a consequence, the speaker lost the power to appoint party members to committees. The Rules Committee also lost some of its powers. One result of the revolt against Speaker Cannon was that House committees became more independent of party leadership; that is, committees emerged as power centers no longer dependent on the commands of the party leader. The growth of the seniority system contributed to committee independence, since members' advancement in committees now depended on relative years of service. Seniority meant that the longer members remained in Congress, the greater their power and independence. Finally becoming chair of a committee meant that a member was free of the influences of the speaker and the majority leader to a considerable degree.

After World War II the Legislative Reorganization Act of 1946 reduced the number of House committees by half, producing a situation in which the number and jurisdictions of House and Senate committees were at least roughly equalized and correlated with executive branch departments. With minor changes, the system of congressional committees established by the 1946 act continues today.

In recent years two new types of committees have emerged. Budget committees have been established in each chamber as part of a broadly revised annual budget process, and ethics committees act as a means of monitoring ethically questionable activities of members. Ethics committees (such as the Standards of Official Conduct Committee in the House and the Ethics Committee in the Senate) are different from the other standing committees in that there is an equal number of members from majority and minority parties. Few if any members wish to serve on ethics committees.

In 1961, after several decades during which the House Rules Committee under Southern Democratic domination had delayed or weakened civil rights legislation, Speaker Sam Rayburn and President John Kennedy, in an unusual display of forceful leadership, expanded the size of the Rules Committee and thereby gave it a liberal majority. It required floor approval on a close 217–212 roll-call vote to approve the addition of John Young (D.–Tex.), Claude Pepper (D.–Fla.), and James Quillen (R.–Tenn.) This brought the composite ideology of the Rules Committee into closer alignment with the Democratic leadership and in that sense weakened the committee's independence.

As noted in the previous chapter, the House Democratic caucus brought about several reforms during the 1970s. The important change from the standpoint of the committee system is that the party caucus now reviews each chair at the beginning of each Congress and may replace the senior member with a chair whose thinking is more in tune with the issue preferences and goals of the caucus majority.

Another recent development in the congressional committee system is the growth in the number of subcommittees. Committees generally approve, with little or no change, the decisions of their subcommittees, which means a further decentralization of congressional authority.[1]

The growing number of subcommittees has also meant that more members can gain attention, publicity, and power by being in charge of a significant element of the total legislative machine.

In his study of congressional committees, Richard Fenno (1973) notes six fundamental ways in which committees differ from one another: (1) in the amount of power they have, (2) in their success in getting their legislation through Congress, (3) in their degree of expertise with respect to their subject matter, (4) in the amount of control over committee actions exercised by the committee chair, (5) in the degree of domination by the executive branch agency dealing with the same policy area, and (6) in the ideological profile or shape of the committee. To summarize Fenno's findings:

1. Some committees are powerful; others are not.
2. Some committees get most or all of their bills through the chamber; others are successful with only a few bills.
3. Some committees know as much about the subject matter of their legislation as anyone; others seem to know less about their legislation than do executive agency or interest group experts.
4. Some committees are dominated by the chairs; others have several members with considerable influence over committee decisions.
5. Some committees follow the lead of executive agencies that they (supposedly) "oversee"; other committees are more likely to exert real direction over their agency.
6. Some committees are composed of hard-line ideologues or single-interest spokespersons and are characterized by sharp, polarized confrontations; other committees are composed of a higher percentage of centrist and moderate members who collectively and effectively strive for internal committee consensus.

Fenno also identifies five variables that he uses to analyze and classify committees: the goals of the members, environmental constraints, strategic premises, decision-making processes, and output.

In addition to the standing committees dealt with in this chapter, there are also other kinds of committees in Congress. Special and select committees are occasionally established for particular purposes. Joint committees are permanent committees composed of members from both chambers, such as the Joint Economic Committee and the Joint Committee on Taxation. Conference committees are a form of joint committee and are set up to work out differences in House and Senate versions of legislation on the same subject; these committees have an equal number of representatives and senators and generally complete work in a few hours and are then dissolved.

Though conference committees have a very short life and limited jurisdiction, they have considerable influence. Kenneth Shepsle and Barry Weingast (1987, 86) argue that the conference committee's "ex post adjustment" power—the power of taking action after the original House and Senate committees have prepared the bills and the bills themselves have been thoroughly debated on the floor of the two chambers—provides the conference committee "with subtle yet powerful means to affect the voting and proposing power of other members on the floor during the earlier legislative stages." Shepsle and Weingast show that from 1981 to 1983, almost every senator and representative appointed to serve on a conference committee was a member of the original committees of jurisdiction (98). Conference committees are generally composed of the leading members of the House and Senate committees that prepared the legislation in the first place. If Congress did not have conference committees, Shepsle and Weingast conclude, "we doubt committees would play the consequential roles they do in the U. S. Congress" (102).

THE KEY COMMITTEES IN EACH CHAMBER

Table 8-1 shows the names, party ratios, ranking members, and number of subcommittees of the standing committees of Congress as of 1987. All committees, as Fenno has noted, are not equal. Scholars have classified committees on the basis of their relative power and attractiveness. This discussion will be limited to describing the jurisdiction and organization of seven particularly important committees, four in the House and three in the Senate.

1. The House Ways and Means Committee is important because of its control over the nation's tax system. It shares this control with the Senate's Finance Committee, but the fact that revenue bills must originate in the House of Representatives augments the importance of the Ways and Means Committee. The revenue power means that this committee plays a critical role in international trade and social welfare policy, inasmuch as both policies depend on revenue laws—tariffs in the case of trade, the Social Security tax in the case of social welfare and unemployment compensation. The Ways and Means Committee is chaired by Rep. Dan Rostenkowski (D.–Ill.). The attractiveness of this committee to members is suggested by the fact that Reps. Cecil Heftel (D.–Hawaii) and Wyche Fowler (D.–Ga.), who began their House service a decade earlier, were in 1986 still only about halfway up the seniority list on the Democratic side. Nor was either of them closer than three positions from the chair of the two subcommittees on which they were serving.

Ways and Means has six subcommittees: Trade, Oversight, Select Revenue Measures, Health, Social Security, and Public Assistance and Unemployment Compensation.

Until the Democratic caucus began making use of its steering and policy committee to assign Democratic representatives to committees, the Democratic members of the Ways and Means Committee also performed that function, making service on the committee even more significant.

2. The House Appropriations Committee is another traditionally powerful panel. This is the largest standing committee in Congress and is chaired by Rep. Jamie Whitten (D.–Miss.). Its thirteen subcommittees roughly parallel the organization of the president's cabinet. Its function is to appropriate money for the programs that have been previously authorized by its sister standing committees.

3. The new House Budget Committee, chaired by Rep. William Gray (D.–Pa.) has eight task forces that reconcile authorizations and appropriations with the annual federal budget. The president presents budget proposals to Congress early in the year, and the Budget Committee develops these proposals into resolutions passed in May and September and into last-minute reconciliation measures.

4. The House Rules Committee is one of the smallest of the standing committees. Though not as central as it has been historically, it still is the major control for the flow of House legislation from the standing committees to the floor. It controls the several calendars and determines the amount of floor time devoted to each measure (as discussed in chapter 9). The speaker names the majority party's members on this committee. The committee is chaired by Rep. Claude Pepper (D.–Fla.) and has only two subcommittees, Legislative Process and Rules of the House.

5. The Senate Budget Committee is the counterpart of the House committee of the same name and does not require further discussion. It does not have subcommittees.

6. The Senate Foreign Relations Committee, chaired by Sen. Claiborne Pell (D.–R.I.) is most prestigious because of its role in the approval of treaties and diplomatic appointments made by the president. Its changing membership and ideological composition will be discussed in further detail elsewhere in this chapter. It has six subcommittees: Western Hemisphere Affairs; International Economic Policy, Oceans, and Environment; African Affairs; European Affairs; Near Eastern and South Asian Affairs; and East Asian and Pacific Affairs.

7. The Senate Judiciary Committee is included here because of its role in the approval of judicial nominations as well as its jurisdiction over constitutional amendments and the judicial and election systems. This committee is chaired by Sen. Joseph Biden (D.–Del.). Its subcommittees are Patents, Copyrights and Trademarks; Criminal Law; Constitution; Immigration and Refugee Policy; Courts; Administrative Practice and Procedure; Security and Terrorism; and Juvenile Justice.

In the vignette that follows, the Senate Foreign Relations Committee will be used as an example of the composition and operations of an important congressional committee. Standing committees are the prime shapers of legislation in their respective areas of policy expertise. The composition of a committee, especially its ideological balance, is a powerful determinant not only of how issues will be debated and resolved but of which issues will even be considered by the chamber as a whole.

The Senate Foreign Relations Committee

With the election defeat of Sen. Charles Percy of Illinois in November of 1984, and given Sen. Jesse Helm's decision to keep the position of chair of the Agriculture Committee in preference to that of Foreign Relations (to which his

Table 8-1. Congressional committees, party ratios, and leaders, 100th Congress, 1987–1988

Committee	Democrats to Republicans	Chair	Year entered chamber	Year became chair	Ranking Republican
HOUSE OF REPRESENTATIVES					
Agriculture	26/17	de la Garza (TX)	1965	1983	Madigan (IL)
Appropriations	35/22	Whitten (MS)	1941	1979	Conte (MA)
Armed Services	31/20	Aspin (WI)	1971	1985	Dickinson (AL)
Banking, Finance, and Urban Affairs	30/20	St. Germain (RI)	1961	1981	Wylie (OH)
Budget	21/14	Gray (PA)	1979	1985	Latta (OH)
District of Columbia	7/4	Dellums (CA)	1971	1979	McKinney (CT)
Education and Labor	21/13	Hawkins (CA)	1963	1985	Jeffords (VT)
Energy and Commerce	25/17	Dingell (MI)	1955	1981	Lent (NY)
Foreign Affairs	25/17	Fascell (FL)	1955	1985	Broomfield (MI)
Government Operations	24/15	Brooks (TX)	1953	1975	Horton (NY)
House Administration	12/7	Annunzio (IL)	1965	1985	Frenzel (MN)
Interior and Insular Affairs	23/14	Udall (AZ)	1961	1977	Young (AK)
Judiciary	21/14	Rodino (NJ)	1949	1973	Fish (NY)
Merchant Marine and Fisheries	25/17	Jones (NC)	1966	1981	Davis (MI)
Post Office and Civil Service	13/8	Ford (MI)	1965	1981	Taylor (MO)
Public Works and Transportation	30/20	Howard (NJ)	1965	1981	Hammerschmidt (AR)
Rules	9/4	Pepper (FL)	1963	1983	Quillen (TN)
Science and Technology	27/18	Roe (NJ)	1969	1987	Lujan (NM)
Small Business	27/17	LaFalce (NY)	1975	1987	McDade (PA)
Standards of Official Conduct	6/6	Dixon (CA)	1979	1985	Spence (SC)
Veterans' Affairs	21/13	Montgomery (MS)	1967	1981	Solomon (NY)
Ways and Means	23/13	Rostenkowski (IL)	1959	1981	Duncan (TN)

Table 8-1. *(continued)*

Committee	Democrats to Republicans	Chair	Year entered chamber	Year became chair	Ranking republican
SENATE					
Agriculture	10/8	Leahy (VT)	1975	1987	Helms (NC)
Appropriations	16/13	Stennis (MS)	1947	1987	Hatfield (OR)
Armed Services	11/9	Nunn (GA)	1973	1987	Thurmond (SC)
Banking, Housing, and Urban Affairs	10/8	Proxmire (WI)	1957	1975	Garn (UT)
Budget	12/10	Chiles (FL)	1971	1987	Domenici (NM)
Commerce, Science, and Transportation	11/9	Hollings (SC)	1966	1987	Danforth (MO)
Energy and Natural Resources	10/9	Johnston (LA)	1973	1987	McClure (ID)
Environment and Public Works	9/7	Burdick (ND)	1960	1987	Stafford (VT)
Finance	11/9	Bentsen (TX)	1971	1987	Packwood (OR)
Foreign Relations	11/9	Pell (RI)	1961	1987	Helms (NC)
Governmental Affairs	8/6	Glenn (OH)	1975	1987	Roth (DE)
Judiciary	8/6	Biden (DE)	1973	1987	Thurmond (SC)
Labor and Human Resources	9/7	Kennedy (MA)	1962	1987	Hatch (UT)
Rules and Administration	9/7	Ford (KY)	1975	1987	Stevens (AK)
Small Business	10/8	Bumpers (AR)	1975	1987	Weicker (CT)
Aging	10/9	Melcher (MT)	1977	1987	Heinz (PA)
Veterans' Affairs	6/5	Cranston (CA)	1969	1977	Murkowski (AK)
Select Ethics	3/3	Heflin (AL)	1979	1987	Rudman (NH)
Select Intelligence	8/7	Boren (OK)	1979	1987	Cohen (ME)

seniority also entitled him), Sen. Richard Lugar of Indiana became chair of the Foreign Relations Committee at the beginning of the 99th Congress in January 1985. Except for Helms, the Republican contingent was composed mainly of moderate and liberal Republicans. These members were not known for their foreign policy competence nor were they very experienced. The most senior Republican members, Lugar and Helms, had only joined the committee in 1979.

On the Democratic side, the ranking member was Claiborne Pell of Rhode Island, who had joined the committee in 1965. Three other Democrats, Joseph Biden of Delaware, John Glenn of Ohio, and Paul Sarbanes of Maryland, had served on the committee longer than any Republican, and Edward Zorinsky of Nebraska came on in the same year as Lugar and Helms. Zorinsky was the only Democrat who could be described as other than a liberal.

Table 8-2 shows the composition of the Foreign Relations Committee for a succession of recent Congresses. Of particular importance are the progress of

Table 8-2. Membership on the Senate Foreign Relations Committee, with reasons for departure from committee, 1967–1988

90th Congress (1967–1968)	91st Congress (1969–1970)	92nd Congress (1971–1972)	93rd Congress (1973–1974)	94th Congress (1975–1976)
DEMOCRATS				
Fulbright	Fulbright	Fulbright	Fulbright[2]	Sparkman
Sparkman	Sparkman	Sparkman	Sparkman	Mansfield[1]
Mansfield	Mansfield	Mansfield	Mansfield	Church
Morse[2]	Gore[2]	Church	Church	Symington[1]
Gore	Church	Symington	Symington	Pell
Lausche[2]	Symington	Pell	Pell	McGee[2]
Church	Dodd[2]	McGee	McGee	McGovern
Symington	Pell	Muskie	Muskie[4]	Humphrey
Dodd	McGee	Spong[2]	McGovern	Clark
Clark[2]			Humphrey	Biden
Pell				
McCarthy[4]				
Totals 12	9	9	10	10
REPUBLICANS				
Hickenlooper[1]	Aiken	Aiken	Aiken[1]	Case
Aiken	Mundt	Mundt[1]	Case	Javits
Carlson[1]	Case	Case	Javits	Scott[1]
Williams[6]	Cooper	Cooper[1]	Scott	Pearson
Mundt	Williams[1]	Javits	Pearson	Percy
Case	Javits	Scott	Percy	Griffin
Cooper		Pearson	Griffin	
Totals 7	6	7	7	6

95th Congress (1977–1978)	96th Congress (1979–1980)	97th Congress (1981–1982)	98th Congress (1983–1984)	99th Congress (1985–1986)
DEMOCRATS				
Sparkman[1]	Church[2]	Pell	Pell	Pell
Church	Pell	Biden	Biden	Biden

90th Congress (1967–1968)	91st Congress (1969–1970)	92nd Congress (1971–1972)	93rd Congress (1973–1974)	94th Congress (1975–1976)
Pell	McGovern[2]	Glenn	Glenn[4]	Sarbanes
McGovern	Biden	Sarbanes	Sarbanes	Zorinsky[3]
Humphrey[3]	Glenn	Zorinsky	Zorinsky	Cranston
Clark[2]	Stone[2]	Tsongas	Tsongas[1]	Dodd
Biden	Sarbanes	Cranston	Cranston	Eagleton[1]
Glenn	Muskie[8]	Dodd	Dodd	Kerry
Stone	Zorinsky			
Sarbanes				
Totals 10	9	8	8	8
REPUBLICANS				
Case[2]	Javits[2]	Percy	Percy[2]	Lugar
Javits	Percy	Baker	Baker[1]	Helms
Pearson[1]	Baker	Helms	Helms[7]	Mathias[1]
Percy	Helms	Hayakawa[1]	Lugar	Kassebaum
Griffin[2]	Hayakawa	Lugar	Mathias	Boschwitz
Baker	Lugar	Mathias	Kassebaum	Pressler
		Kassebaum	Boschwitz	Murkowski
		Boschwitz	Pressler	Trible
		Pressler	Murkowski	Evans
Totals 6	6	9	9	9

100th Congress (1987–1988)	
DEMOCRATS	REPUBLICANS
Pell	Helms
Biden	Lugar
Sarbanes	Kassebaum
Cranston	Boschwitz
Dodd	Pressler
Kerry	Murkowski
Simon	Trible
Sanford	Evans
Adams	McConnell
Moynihan	Totals 9
Total 10	

Key to reasons for departure from committee: 1 = retired at end of term; 2 = defeated for reelection; 3 = died in office; 4 = transferred voluntarily to another committee; 5 = dropped from committee owing to reduction in party seats on committee; 6 = waived committee seniority for next Congress; 7 = waived committee seniority for next Congress, allowing Lugar to become chair, but reinstated in ranking position for 100th Congress; 8 = resigned from Senate in 1980 to become secretary of state in President Carter's cabinet (his position was taken for the remainder of the 96th Congress by Tsongas).

Source: Compiled by the author from various editions of the *Congressional Directory.*

any individual member up the party seniority ladder over the years and, more generally, the causes for members leaving the committee and the resultant changes in committee ideological balance.

In 1985 and 1986 the Foreign Relations Committee operated with six subcommittees. Five of these subcommittees were concerned with particular areas of the globe: Western Hemisphere Affairs, chaired by Senator Helms of North Carolina; African Affairs, chaired by Senator Kassebaum of Kansas; Near Eastern and South Asian Affairs, chaired by Senator Boschwitz of Minnesota; European Affairs, chaired by Senator Pressler of South Dakota; and East Asian and Pacific Affairs, chaired by Senator Murkowski of Alaska. The other subcommittee, chaired by Senator Mathias of Maryland, was concerned with international economic policy, oceans, and the environment.

The activities of the Foreign Relations Committee in 1985 were undertaken with a new chair, Richard Lugar (R.–Ind.). Under the former chair, Charles Percy of Illinois, the Foreign Relations Committee had recently "lost much of its luster," according to an article in the *Congressional Quarterly Weekly Report* (Felton 1985a, 84). Lugar, it was thought, might be a more effective chair than Percy because Lugar was considered more conservative and thus closer to the ideology of the Senate majority. Lugar was expected to try to build a more cohesive Foreign Relations Committee by downplaying the role of subcommittees, with the full committee handling major issues such as arms control. Lugar also said he would not allow individual committee members who disliked particular nominees to delay ambassadorial nominations indefinitely.

Lugar planned a series of hearings early in 1985 on "the totality of American foreign policy." Among the early witnesses were Secretary of State George Shultz, Secretary of Defense Caspar Weinberger, and former Secretaries of State Henry Kissinger and Cyrus Vance. In discussions on arms control, Senators Biden, Kassebaum, Pressler, and Glenn expressed concern about the effectiveness of President Reagan's plan for space-based defense against intercontinental ballistics missiles. Senators Dodd and Pell argued with Shultz and Weinberger over U. S. policy toward Nicaragua. Shultz responded to Senator Helms's concern that South Africa might fall under the sway of the Soviet Union by emphasizing that the United States should not blindly accept whatever solution South Africa decided to make as to apartheid and that "we're very clear in our opposition to the nature of the society (as quoted in Felton 1985b, 198). Shultz stated, in the face of doubts expressed by Senators Pell and Dodd, that the Reagan administration would continue to support the treaty that established genocide as an international crime.

Lugar's effort to produce a more harmonious and effective Foreign Relations Committee appeared to be at least partially successful when in March 1985, the committee approved a $12.8 billion foreign aid authorization bill for fiscal year (F.Y.) 1986. Only Senator Helms voted against the bill. Lugar was able to reach compromises with the Democrats on the committee on the sensitive issues of sanctions against the government of South Africa and of freezing foreign aid funding levels to F.Y. 1985 amounts.

In its March deliberations, the Foreign Relations Committee voted on a number of critical motions (see Felton 1985c, 573–575):

1. The committee by an eight to eight tie vote rejected a Dodd amendment to bar foreign aid to any country that provided funding or material support to the Contras.
2. The committee voted nine to eight to restrict aid to the antigovernment Contras in Nicaragua, then disagreed on exactly what it had done; Democrat Pell insisted that the vote barred the administration from conspiring with foreign aid recipients to channel money to the guerrillas; Republican Lugar insisted that the vote only barred the use of U. S. foreign aid to support the Contras.
3. The committee rejected on a six to ten vote an amendment to bar foreign aid to the Contras; to impose conditions on aid to El Salvador and Guatemala; and to reduce aid to Costa Rica, El Salvador, Guatemala, and Honduras.
4. The committee rejected seven to ten an amendment to place conditions on military aid to El Salvador.
5. The committee rejected an amendment to place conditions on military aid to Guatemala by a vote of eight to nine.
6. The committee rejected an amendment by Senator Kassebaum to delete from the bill authorization in F.Y. 1987, 1988, and 1989 for economic and development aid to Central America.
7. The committee voted nine to four to impose a ratio on U. S. military aid to Greece ($500 million) and Turkey ($715 million), and individual committee members expressed criticism of recent actions by both governments.
8. The committee voted to include in the bill a requirement that the president certify to Congress that Saudi Arabia had met all the conditions imposed by President Reagan in 1981 in connection with the sale of five AWACS radar planes.
9. The committee by a nine to seven vote adopted Senator Kassebaum's amendment to change administration policy that was suspending U. S. funding for international population control programs.
10. The committee at the same time adopted by a thirteen to three vote Senator Helms's amendment aiming to bar further U. S. funding for the United Nations Fund for Population Activities.
11. The committee rejected by an eight to nine vote an amendment offered by Sen. John Kerry (D.–Mass.) to cut U. S. military aid to the Philippines from $100 million to $40 million.
12. The committee adopted an amendment by Sen. Larry Pressler (R.– S.D.) to stop foreign aid to any country attempting to obtain U. S.

material or technology to build a nuclear weapon and then also voted to require the president to suspend all aid to Pakistan if he determined that it had obtained a nuclear weapon.

The full committee met on ninety-nine days in 1985, including eight days in executive session. The latter were devoted to CIA reports on Soviet strategic and foreign policy (February 22), defense and intelligence reports on Nicaragua (March 19), a briefing on the Geneva arms control negotiations (May 6), an informal off-the-record briefing on the situation in the Philippines (June 5), embassy security (July 17), the nuclear agreement with China (October 8 and November 8), and Central America counterterrorism proposals (November 18). Other major topics discussed at several meetings were the genocide convention, the South African situation, and budget authorizations for the State Department and related programs. The committee also held joint meetings with the Judiciary Committee on May 13, 14, and 15 on international terrorism, insurgency, and drug trafficking. The committee's formal year began with a report on famine in Africa (January 17) and ended with preparations for the February 1986 Philippine presidential election (December 18).

The six subcommittees in 1985 met a total of twenty-three days, twice in executive session.

During the calendar year 1985, the Foreign Relations Committee issued eight executive reports, thirteen committee reports to accompany legislation to the Senate floor, and nine sets of committee hearings. Fifteen new public laws were passed in 1985 concerning matters under the jurisdiction of the committee. Among them were P.L. 99-8, to authorize appropriations for famine relief in Africa; P.L. 99-81, to appeal for the release of Soviet Jewry; P.L. 99-90, condemning the passage of Resolution 3379 in the United Nations; P.L. 99-162, relating to the proposed sales of arms to Jordan; and P.L. 99-183, relating to the approval and implementation of the proposed agreement for nuclear cooperation between the United States and the People's Republic of China.

Early in 1986, after nearly four decades of intermittent debate and following issuance in July 1985 by the Foreign Relations Committee of an executive report on the Genocide Convention, the Senate finally approved a treaty declaring genocide to be a crime. The genocide pact had been approved by the United Nations in 1948, and in the next year President Truman submitted it to the Senate for approval. Sen. William Proxmire of Wisconsin had spoken for approval of the treaty for years, and all presidents except Eisenhower had favored adoption, but the final successful push came from Majority Leader Dole. "We have waited long enough. As a nation which enshrines human dignity and freedom as God-given rights in its Constitution, we must correct our anomalous position on this basic rights issue." The vote for the treaty was eighty-three to eleven; all of the opponents were Republicans (see U. S. Congress 1985; Cohodas 1986).

The Iran-Contra hearings of 1987 focused world attention on the long-standing question of executive versus legislative control over U. S. foreign policy making. The president's role is strengthened by his control of information, of contact with foreign governments, of the diplomatic service, and of the armed forces. Congress, on the other hand, has the power to declare war, to severely restrict presidential options (as asserted by the War Powers Resolution and elsewhere), and to grant or withhold funds. In the discussion of these and related points in 1987, particularly in connection with the Iran-Contra hearings presided over by Sen. Daniel Inouye (D.–Hawaii) and Rep. Lee Hamilton (D.–Ind.), the Foreign Relations Committee as such was not a major factor. It is not likely that on such fundamental constitutional and political questions either chamber will allow a single committee, even one as prestigious as Foreign Relations, to determine the answers.

COMMITTEE ASSIGNMENTS

One of the critical steps in the organization of each biennial Congress is the assignment of representatives and senators to standing committees. Few congressional decisions have more influence on the course of an individual member's congressional career than the member's committee assignments.

Committee assignments are made by committees of each of the four party caucuses, the steering committees for the Democrats in the House and Senate, and the committees on committees for the Republicans. The party committee responsible makes up the slate of proposed assignments and submits the slate to the caucus; approval is usually routine. Most of the committee positions are filled by reappointing members to the same committees they served on in the previous Congress. But there are also many vacancies to be filled, either because some members have retired, been defeated for reelection, decided to transfer to a different committee, or because there has been a change in party control of the chamber and the former majority party must give up some of its committee seats to the new majority party.

To transfer from one committee to another midway in one's congressional career is a tricky step. Is it worthwhile to give up eight years of seniority on a committee of average prestige and power in order to take a junior position on a more prestigious committee, such as Ways and Means or Foreign Relations? Sometimes it is better to be a big fish in a little pond than to be a little fish in a big pond.

On a given committee of twenty-five members, perhaps eighteen of the positions will be filled by members carrying over from the previous Congress, many of whom will probably be moving up a notch or two on their party's seniority ranking. One party then may have four seats to fill on the committee; the other party, three seats. Members of the chamber inform party leaders as to their preferences of committee assignments. Members may stay with the present committee, if desired. Where several members are competing for a single vacant seat on a committee, preference will generally be given to members having the longest service in the chamber and to those with some particular expertise or interest in the committee's policy area. Other factors that might be taken into account in making committee assignments are the ideological and regional balances of the committee and how a particular appointee will affect those balances. Being friendly with party leaders has not been known to hurt a member's chances of receiving a choice committee assignment. Details of actual committee membership changes from one Congress to the next can be seen in the vignette concerning the Foreign Relations Committee.

The general rule is that each senator will be given two major assignments and one major or minor committee assignment, while each representative will have either one "exclusive" committee assignment (Ways and Means, Appropriations, or Rules), or one major and one minor committee assignment, or two minor committee assignments. The House Democratic caucus defines eight committees as "major" committees: Agriculture; Armed Services; Banking, Finance, and Urban Affairs; Education and Labor; Energy and Commerce; Foreign Affairs; Judiciary; and Public Works and Transportation.

Table 8-3 illustrates how committee assignments and ranks of veteran mem-

Table 8-3.   Career committee assignments and rank positions for eight veteran members of Congress

Year committees (member's rank/total party members on committee)

HOUSE OF REPRESENTATIVES
William Broomfield (R.–Mich.)
1957 Public Works (15/15)
1959 Public Works (9/12)
1961 Foreign Affairs (10/13)
1963 Foreign Affairs (5/13)
1965 Foreign Affairs (5/12)
1967 Foreign Affairs (5/15)
1969 Foreign Affairs (4/17)
1971 Foreign Affairs (3/17)
1973 Foreign Affairs (3/18)
1975 International Relations (1/12)
1977 International Relations (1/12); Small Business (4/12)
1979 Foreign Affairs (1/12); Small Business (4/14)
1981 Foreign Affairs (1/16); Small Business (4/17)
1983 Foreign Affairs (1/13); Small Business (3/14)
1985 Foreign Affairs (1/17); Small Business (3/17)
1987 Foreign Affairs (1/17); Small Business (3/17)

Silvio Conte (R.–Mass.)
1961 Appropriations (18/20)
1963 Appropriations (14/20)
1965 Appropriations (9/16)
1967 Appropriations (9/21)
1969 Appropriations (8/21)
1971 Appropriations (7/22)
1973 Appropriations (5/22)
1975 Appropriations (3/18); Small Business (1/12)
1977 Appropriations (3/18); Small Business (1/12)
1979 Appropriations (1/18); Small Business (2/14)
1981 Appropriations (1/22); Small Business (2/17)
1983 Appropriations (1/21); Small Business (2/14)
1985 Appropriations (1/22); Small Business (2/17)
1987 Appropriations (1/22); Small Business (2/17)

Table 8-3.   *(continued)*

Dante Fascell (D.–Fla.)
1955 Post Office and Civil Service (11/13); Government Operations (16/18)
1957 Foreign Affairs (14/17); Government Operations (13/17)
1959 Foreign Affairs (11/21); Government Operations (12/19)
1961 Foreign Affairs (10/20); Government Operations (12/19)
1963 Foreign Affairs (10/20); Government Operations (10/19)
1965 Foreign Affairs (9/24); Government Operations (10/23)
1967 Foreign Affairs (9/21); Government Operations (10/20)
1969 Foreign Affairs (5/21); Government Operations (9/20)
1971 Foreign Affairs (5/21); Government Operations (7/23)
1973 Foreign Affairs (5/22); Government Operations (6/23)
1975 International Relations (5/24); Government Operations (4/29)
1977 International Relations (3/25); Government Operations (4/29)
1979 Foreign Affairs (3/22); Government Operations (3/25)
1981 Foreign Affairs (3/21); Government Operations (3/23)
1983 Foreign Affairs (2/24); Government Operations (2/25)
1985 Foreign Affairs (1/25, chair)
1987 Foreign Affairs (1/25, chair)

Morris Udall (D.–Ariz.)
1961 Post Office and Civil Service (13/14)
1963 Post Office and Civil Service (6/14); Interior and Insular Affairs (12/20)
1965 Post Office and Civil Service (6/17); Interior and Insular Affairs (11/22)
1967 Post Office and Civil Service (4/15); Interior and Insular Affairs (8/19)
1969 Post Office and Civil Service (4/15); Interior and Insular Affairs (8/19)
1971 Post Office and Civil Service (3/15); Interior and Insular Affairs (7/22)
1973 Post Office and Civil Service (3/15); Interior and Insular Affairs (4/22)
1975 Post Office and Civil Service (2/19); Interior and Insular Affairs (4/29)
1977 Post Office and Civil Service (2/17); Interior and Insular Affairs (1/29, chair)
1979 Post Office and Civil Service (2/13); Interior and Insular Affairs (1/26, chair)
1981 Post Office and Civil Service (2/14); Interior and Insular Affairs (1/23, chair)
1983 Post Office and Civil Service (2/15); Interior and Insular Affairs (1/25, chair)
1985 Post Office and Civil Service (12/12); Interior and Insular Affairs (1/22, chair); Foreign
     Affairs (24/25)
1987 Post Office and Civil Service (13/13); Interior and Insular Affairs (1/23, chair); Foreign
     Affairs (21/25)

SENATE
Mark Hatfield (R.–Ore.)
1967 Agriculture (5/5); Interior and Insular Affairs (6/6)
1969 Aernonautics and Space Sciences (3/6); Interior and Insular Affairs (5/7)
1971 Commerce (7/8); Interior and Insular Affairs (5/7)
1973 Appropriations (7/11); Interior and Insular Affairs (4/6); Rules and Administration (4/4)
1975 Appropriations (6/10); Interior and Insular Affairs (3/5); Rules and Administration (1/3)
1977 Appropriations (4/9); Energy and Natural Resources (2/7); Rules and Administration (1/3)
1979 Appropriations (2/11); Energy and Natural Resources (1/7); Rules and Administration (1/4)
1981 Appropriations (1/15, chair); Energy and Natural Resources (2/11); Rules and Administration
     (2/7)
1983 Appropriations (1/15, chair); Energy and Natural Resources (2/11); Rules and Administration
     (2/7)
1985 Appropriations (1/15, chair); Energy and Natural Resources (2/10); Rules and Administration
     (2/8)
1987 Appropriations (1/13); Energy and Natural Resources (2/9); Rules and Administration (2/7)

Claiborne Pell (D.–R. I.)
1961 Rules and Administration (6/6); Labor and Public Welfare (10/10)
1963 Rules and Administration (4/6); Labor and Public Welfare (9/10); Government Operations
     (7/10)

Table 8-3. *(continued)*

1965 Rules and Administration (4/6); Labor and Public Welfare (8/11); Foreign Relations (13/13)
1967 Rules and Administration (4/6); Labor and Public Welfare (7/10); Foreign Relations (11/12)
1969 Rules and Administration (3/5); Labor and Public Welfare (4/10); Foreign Relations (8/9)
1971 Rules and Administration (3/5); Labor and Public Welfare (3/10); Foreign Relations (6/9)
1973 Rules and Administration (2/5); Labor and Public Welfare (3/10); Foreign Relations (6/10)
1975 Rules and Administration (2/6); Labor and Public Welfare (3/10); Foreign Relations (5/10)
1977 Rules and Administration (2/6); Human Resources (3/9); Foreign Relations (3/10)
1979 Rules and Administration (1/6, chair); Labor and Human Resources (3/9); Foreign Relations (2/9)
1981 Rules and Administration (3/5); Labor and Human Resources (4/7); Foreign Relations (1/8)
1983 Rules and Administration (2/5); Labor and Human Resources (3/8); Foreign Relations (1/8)
1985 Rules and Administration (2/7); Labor and Human Resources (2/7); Foreign Relations (1/8)
1987 Rules and Administration (2/9); Labor and Human Resources (2/9); Foreign Relations (1/11, chair)

William Proxmire (D.–Wis.)
1958 Banking and Currency (8/8); Post Office and Civil Service (7/7)
1959 Banking and Currency (7/10); Agriculture (8/11)
1961 Banking and Currency (5/10); Agriculture (6/11)
1963 Banking and Currency (5/10); Agriculture (6/11)
1965 Banking and Currency (4/10); Appropriations (17/18)
1967 Banking and Currency (2/9); Appropriations (16/17)
1969 Banking and Currency (2/9); Appropriations (12/14)
1971 Banking, Housing, and Urban Affairs (2/8); Appropriations (10/13)
1973 Banking, Housing, and Urban Affairs (2/9); Appropriations (9/15)
1975 Banking, Housing, and Urban Affairs (1/8, chair); Appropriations (8/16)
1977 Banking, Housing, and Urban Affairs (1/9, chair); Appropriations (5/16)
1979 Banking, Housing, and Urban Affairs (1/9, chair); Appropriations (4/17)
1981 Banking, Housing, and Urban Affairs (2/7); Appropriations (1/14)
1983 Banking, Housing, and Urban Affairs (1/8); Appropriations (3/14)
1985 Banking, Housing, and Urban Affairs (1/7); Appropriations (3/14)
1987 Banking, Housing, and Urban Affairs (1/10, chair); Appropriations (3/16)

Strom Thurmond (D. [1955–1964], R. [1965–1985] S. C.)
1955 Interstate and Foreign Commerce (IFC) (8/8); Government Operations (7/7); Public Works (5/7)
1957 Interstate and Foreign Commerce (6/8); Government Operations (6/7); Labor and Public Welfare (7/7)
1959 Interstate and Foreign Commerce (5/11); Armed Services (8/11)
1961 Interstate and Foreign Commerce (5/11); Armed Services (7/11)
1963 Commerce (4/12); Armed Services (7/12)
1965 Banking and Currency (3/4); Armed Services (3/5)
1967 Judiciary (5/5); Armed Services (2/6)
1969 Judiciary (5/7); Armed Services (2/8); Rules and Administration (4/4)
1971 Judiciary (4/7); Armed Services (2/7); Veterans (1/4)
1973 Judiciary (4/7); Armed Services (1/6); Veterans (2/4)
1975 Judiciary (4/6); Armed Services (1/6); Veterans (2/3)
1977 Judiciary (1/6); Armed Services (2/7); Veterans (2/3)
1979 Judiciary (1/7); Armed Services (2/7); Veterans (3/4)
1981 Judiciary (1/10, chair); Armed Services (2/9); Veterans (2/7)
1983 Judiciary (1/10, chair); Armed Services (2/10); Veterans (2/7)
1985 Judiciary (1/10, chair); Armed Services (2/10); Veterans (3/7); Labor and Human Resources (6/9)
1987 Judiciary (1/6); Armed Services (2/9); Veterans (3/7); Labor and Human Resources (4/7)

Note: In calculating rank positions and size of party contingents, territorial delegates have been omitted.
Source: Compiled by the author from various editions of the *Congressional Directory,* 1955 to 1987.

bers of Congress change—sometimes dramatically—over the years and also shows how the time required to reach high-ranking positions on a committee can vary by chamber, party, and committee.

All four of the senators in table 8-3 became committee chairs. It took both Proxmire and Pell eighteen years of service in the Senate to do so; Hatfield made the grade in just fourteen years. Thurmond, who first became a senator in 1955 and served as a Democrat until 1965, did not become a chair until 1981. All four senators also, at one time or another, qualified as their party's ranking member on another committee (in table 8-3 see Thurmond 1971, 1973, 1975; Proxmire 1981; Pell 1981, 1983, 1985; Hatfield 1975, 1977, two committees in 1979). When this happens, adjustments in seniority rankings are generally made so that the opportunity to chair a committee is made as widely available as possible in the majority party. For example, when Thurmond became the ranking Republican senator on the Judiciary Committee in 1977, he accepted a demotion from first to second position on the Republican side of the Armed Services Committee. This allowed John Tower to assume the Armed Services chair in 1981 when the Republican party assumed control of the Senate, while Thurmond became chair of the Judiciary Committee. When Tower retired, Thurmond allowed Barry Goldwater to replace him at the top of the Republican list and thereby to succeed Tower as Armed Services chair in 1985.

Both veteran Democratic representatives (see table 8-3) became chairs of a committee: Udall of Interior and Insular Affairs in 1977, sixteen years after his original election in a special election in May 1961; and Fascell of Foreign Affairs after thirty years of continuous House service. Fascell dropped his Government Operations Committee assignment when he became chair of the Foreign Affairs Committee, but Udall maintained his number 2 status on the Post Office and Civil Service Committee for nine years after becoming chair of Interior and Insular Affairs. In 1985, however, Udall gave up his number 2 position on Post Office and Civil Service and dropped all the way to the bottom on the Democratic list. Udall also in 1985 took the twenty-fourth position on the Foreign Affairs Committee. Udall gave up his seats on the Post Office and Civil Service and Foreign Affairs committees for the second session of the 99th Congress (1986).

The two Republicans listed in table 8-3 have for several Congresses been the ranking minority members of their respective House committees. William Broomfield of Michigan joined the House in 1957, received an appointment to the Foreign Affairs Committee in 1961 (after serving for two terms on the Public Works Committee), and worked his way up the seniority ladder until becoming the ranking Republican in 1975. Since becoming chair of this committee depends on surviving until the Republicans take control of the House, Broomfield will probably have a long wait before chairing Foreign Affairs. In roughly the same situation is Silvio Conte of Massachusetts, who was assigned to the Appropriations Committee in his first term (1961) and in 1979 reached the ranking Republican position after nine terms. Conte and Broomfield were also placed on the Small Business Committee later in their House careers, Conte in 1975 and Broomfield in 1977. Conte surrendered his ranking status on that committee in 1979 when he reached the Republican apex on Appropriations.

An interesting aspect of these fundamental committee arrangements occurs when one member qualifies at the same time for two chairs. As noted in an earlier chapter, this happened following the 1984 elections when Sen. Jesse Helms, already chair of the Agriculture Committee, became the senior Republican on the Foreign Relations Committee because of the retirement of Sen. Howard Baker and the defeat of Sen. Charles Percy. When Helms decided to keep the Agriculture chair, Richard Lugar became Foreign Relations chair, and Helms moved down one notch to the number 2 position on the Republican side of the committee. Helms reclaimed his ranking Republican status on the committee at the opening of the 100th Congress. A similar thing happened in the minority Democratic party following the 1982 election, when John Stennis of Mississippi became the ranking member on both the Armed Services and Appropriations committees. Stennis had previously served as chair of the Armed Services Committee from 1969 to 1981. In spite of that experience, the Mississippian chose to accept ranking minority status on the Appropriations Committee.

HOW COMMITTEES OPERATE

During the biennium that constitutes one Congress, scores or even hundreds of bills may be referred to a given committee. Most bills are referred to a particular committee, but a growing number are multiply referred. There are three types of multiple referrals: split referral—certain parts of a bill go to one committee and other parts to another committee; joint referral—a bill is referred to two different committees at the same time; and sequential referral—an entire bill is referred to one committee that acts on it, and the bill is then referred to a second committee. According to Roger Davidson and Walter Oleszek (1987, 7–8), about 11 percent of the bills introduced in the House in the 98th Congress (1983–1984) were referred to more than one committee. Almost all of these were of the joint referral type. Multiple referral, Davidson and Oleszek conclude, strengthens the power of House leaders vis-a-vis the committees and at the same time facilitates coordination among House committees.

Hearings on Proposed Legislation

The fundamental phase of committee work on a particular bill commences when the chair determines whether the bill is sufficiently important, interesting, timely, and promising to justify hearings. Most bills do not survive this test and are accordingly pigeonholed and forgotten.

The chair of the committee, in consultation with committee colleagues, determines which bills, or sets of related bills, will be the subjects of committee hearings. The dates of these hearings must be established and invitations issued to persons or groups who might have significant points of view on or facts concerning the proposed legislation. Considerable effort is made to ensure that opponents as well as proponents have an opportunity to present statements and respond to questions from committee members. Among the more likely types of experts giving testimony are members of Congress who are not members of the committee but have special interest or expertise in the legislation, representatives of executive agencies likely to be affected by the legislation, lobbyists from related interest groups, and scholars and writers who are informed on the issues and have opinions and recommendations to proffer.

A typical example of this initial stage of a bill's development was the June 1985 hearings on regulation of gambling on American Indian reservations. It had been reported that nearly one hundred Indian tribes in a total of eighteen states were conducting public gambling. Federal officials were frustrated by a provision in federal law that exempted tribal gambling from federal regulation. Three bills were introduced that put forth different methods of dealing with the problem. A bill introduced by Rep. Norman Shumway (R.–Calif.) would place reservation gambling under the laws of the state in which the reservation was located. Another bill, introduced by Rep. Morris Udall (D.–Ariz.), chair of the House Interior Committee, would place reservation gambling under the federal Department of the Interior. A third proposal, introduced by Sen. Dennis DeConcini (D.–Ariz.) would permit regional commissions organized by tribes to regulate gambling but would leave residual powers to the secretary of the interior. Among the questions raised about gambling on the reservations were whether the tribes realized enough profit to make its efforts and outlays worthwhile and whether organized crime was already or might soon be involved.

After hearings on a proposal have ended, the committee moves to what is called the mark-up stage. Here the committee meets, usually with some reporters and lobbyists observing, to consider the proposed legislation point by point, deleting one provision, amending another, and adding new provisions to the original version. In this stage the most conscious, focused effort is made to perfect every detail of the bill so that it says precisely what the committee wants it to say and so that it will go to the floor with the greatest chance of passing without further important amendments. Every member is given a chance to comment on each section of the bill.

In an effort to protect the work already done on the bill, committee leaders often reintroduce the amended bill as a clean bill with a new bill number when the bill goes to the floor. This means that the amendments made by the committee do not have to be considered and voted on by the entire chamber. It also serves to shelter amendments that might otherwise be considered nongermane, that is, unrelated to the basic purpose of the bill.

When mark-up on a bill is finished, the committee staff prepares a report to accompany the bill to the floor. Reports, of course, are almost invariably favorable; to issue an unfavorable report would mean that the committee had wasted time and energy on a bill that might better have been pigeonholed from the start. Reports generally describe the current problem the bill is meant to solve, the programs the bill would establish, the executive agencies that would be responsible for program administration and evaluation, and the important arguments raised in hearings on the bill. Also included in the report might be minority statements emphasizing contrary arguments or restating alternative policies that have not been accepted by the committee's majority. These reports, as well as the verbatim record of the hearings, are printed and available to the press and public.

Later, when the bill comes up on the floor, debate for and against the measure is likely to be led by the same committee members who have participated in hearings and in the mark-up and report stages. The floor managers for a bill—that is, the members from each side who are in charge of coordinating the presentation of the party's arguments in floor debate and assigning speaking time to party colleagues who wish to make speeches or rebut the opposition's arguments—are generally senior members of the majority and minority sides on the standing committee that reported the bill.

Overseeing Administrative Actions

Sometimes standing committees hold hearings to review the effectiveness of certain programs under the committee's jurisdiction or to investigate charges of wrong doing, ineptitude, or inefficiency in the administration of those programs. In this way Congress performs its vital function of legislative oversight. In some cases, these hearings may lead to new legislation designed to correct faults and abuses, but often corrections are made simply by conveying committee findings and wishes to the responsible administrators.

Committee hearings and statements clarify the positions of party leaders on and off the committee, of executive agencies, and of affected interest groups. Therefore, committee activities often take on symbolic significance above and beyond the formal decisions and reports they produce.

Scheduling Activities

As noted earlier, scheduling committee activities is a complex and important matter. Committees and subcommittees develop regular meeting times so that members, lobbyists, and journalists can plan their week's work with some degree of certainty. For senators, who have more committee assignments than do representatives, and for senatorial staff employees, it is particularly difficult to attend every committee and subcommittee meeting. The following are excerpts from the congressional committee schedule for Wednesday, February 26, 1986 and indicate whether the hearings will be open or closed to the public. (Also, the "Daily Digest" section of the *Congressional Record* includes announcements of upcoming committee and subcommittee meetings.)

> Senate Appropriations. 9:30 A.M. Open (to the public). Labor, HHS, Education, and related agencies subcommittee. Fiscal 1987 budget hearings for

the Bureau of Labor Statistics, Employment Standards Administration, Pension Benefits Guaranty Corporation, Mine Safety and Health Administration. 116 Dirksen Office Building.

Senate Armed Services. 2:30 P.M. Closed. Business meeting, to resume markup of staff proposal for defense reorganization. 232A Russell Office Building.

Senate Foreign Relations. 9:30 A.M. and 2:00 P.M. Open. European Affairs subcommittee. On the most favored nation status of Romania. 419 Dirksen Office Building.

House Interior and Insular Affairs. 9:45 A.M. Open. Mark up various Indian land bills. 1324 Longworth Office Building.

House Merchant Marine and Fisheries. 10 A.M. Open. Oceanography subcommittee. Mark up bills on deep sea-bed minerals and abandoned shipwrecks. 1334 Longworth Office Building.

House Ways and Means. 10 A.M. Open. Mark up extension of expiring tax provisions. 1100 Longworth Office Building.

COMMITTEE DECISION MAKING

Even though it is true that a large percentage of congressional decisions are made at the standing committee level, less attention is generally given by journalists and scholars to voting patterns on committees than to voting patterns on the floors of the House and Senate. One example of a critical and dramatic committee action was the series of motions and votes in the House Judiciary Committee in the summer of 1974, when the committee was considering the impeachment of President Nixon. On a series of nineteen motions, beginning July 26 and ending July 30, seven were passed and twelve rejected. The motions concerned a wide range of issues and details. The first, moved by Rep. Robert McClory (R.–Ill.) would have delayed committee deliberations "on the articles of impeachment for ten days if President Nixon agreed by noon July 27 to make available to the committee the tapes of the sixty-four presidential conversations which he had been ordered by the Supreme Court to turn over to Federal Judge John J. Sirica." The motion was defeated eleven to twenty-seven. The nineteenth, moved by Rep. Edward Mezvinksy (D.–Iowa), charged the president with "knowingly and fraudulently evading portions of his federal income taxes from 1969 through 1972 and violating his oath of office by receiving unconstitutional emoluments." This was rejected, twelve to twenty-six.[2]

A second example was the action by the Senate Foreign Relations Committee in the fall of 1979 recommending approval by the Senate of the strategic arms limitation treaty (SALT II) (see *Congressional Quarterly Weekly Report* 1979). The sequence of motions indicated interest of various members in three major points: (1) that the proposed arms reductions were too small (McGovern); (2) that treaty approval would affect the U.S. defense budget (Zorinsky wanted it to be higher); and (3) that verification problems were not solved (Glenn). In January 1980, after the Soviet invasion of Afghanistan, President Jimmy Carter asked the Senate to defer action on ratification of SALT II. A Republican motion on January 22, 1980, asking the president to withdraw the treaty was defeated, thirty-six to fifty.

In early March 1985 the Senate Budget Committee was wrestling with several important policy decisions having to do with spending plans for F.Y. 1986 and subsequent years. Four critical motions came up, as shown in table 8-4. On the first three motions, the majority Republican party was able to determine the outcome; on the first roll call, the Democrats agreed with the Republicans. But on the final motion, by Chair Pete Domenici, the majorities of the two parties took opposite sides and the Democratic side won.

Table 8-4. Voting by Senate Budget Committee members on four committee roll calls, March 1985

	Roll calls[a]					
Member	*First*	*Second*	*Third*	*Fourth*	*Agreement with party majority (percent)*	*Agreement with committee majority (percent)*
REPUBLICANS						
Domenici	yes	no	no	yes	100	75
Armstrong	yes	no	no	yes	100	75
Kassebaum	yes	no	no	yes	100	75
Boschwitz	yes	no	no	yes	100	75
Hatch	no	no	no	no	50	75
Andrews	yes	no	yes	no	50	75
Symms	no	[b]	[b]	[b]	0	0
Grassley	yes	no	no	no	75	100
Kasten	no	yes	no	no	25	50
Quayle	no	no	no	yes	75	50
Gorton	yes	no	no	yes	100	75
Danforth	yes	no	no	yes	100	75
DEMOCRATS						
Chiles	yes	no	no	no	75	100
Hollings	yes	no	yes	yes	25	50
Johnston	yes	yes	no	no	100	75
Sasser	yes	yes	no	no	100	75
Hart	yes	yes	no	no	100	75
Metzenbaum	yes	yes	no	no	100	75
Riegle	yes	yes	no	no	100	75
Moynihan	yes	yes	no	no	100	75
Exon	yes	no	yes	yes	25	50
Lautenberg	yes	yes	no	no	100	75

[a]First roll call: motion by Hollings and Andrews approving defense spending plan. Approved eighteen to four. Second roll call: Moynihan motion to allow a cost-of-living allowance for Social Security recipients for F.Y. 86. Rejected eight to thirteen. Third roll call: Hollings motion to freeze the Social Security cost-of-living allowance for one year, except for those with incomes at 110 percent of the poverty level or less. Rejected three to eighteen. Fourth roll call: Domenici motion to freeze the Social Security cost-of-living allowance across the board for one year. Rejected nine to twelve.
[b]Did not vote.
Source: Adapted and calculated by the author from *Congressional Quarterly Weekly Report,* March 9, 1985, p. 429.

Six of the twelve Republicans—Domenici, Armstrong, Kassebaum, Boschwitz, Gorton, and Danforth—always voted with the majority of their follow Republicans, while Hatch, Andrews, and Symms had lower party regularity scores. Seven of the ten Democrats always voted with their party's majority position; Hollings and Exon voted with the Republican majority more often than with their own party. Two members, Republican Grassley and Democrat Chiles, voted each time on the winning side.

A study by Richard Hall (1987, 105) investigated the participation of members in committee decision-making processes and was predicated on the notion that "truancy at committee meetings is severe." Nonparticipation in committee processes is a puzzling phenomenon, given the widespread belief that legislative decisions are made mostly in committee. If committee deliberations are so important to the legislative product, why would some members have low committee participation? Hall studied the House Education and Labor Committee during the 97th Congress (1981–1983) and measured individual participation in its deliberations on the basis of the following scale of activities:

engaged in no activities
attended
voted
spoke (minor participant in discussion)
spoke (major participant in discussion)
offered minor, technical, grammatical amendment
offered substantive amendment
played significant agenda-setting role

Hall compared participation rates with such other variables as member's goals, motivational intensities, and committee position (being in the majority or minority party, and being high or low on the seniority ladder). After noting that committees are not a cross section of the chamber but instead tend to be composed of members with deep interest in the committee's policy area, Hall concludes that participation "is selective and purposive." He feels these "behavioral patterns require greater attention if we are fully to understand the phenomenon of representation in a decentralized Congress" (122).

SUMMARY

The congressional committee system promotes tension in several ways. There is continuing tension between the major spending and agenda committees (the House Rules Committee and the House and Senate Appropriations committees) on one side and the larger number of committees dealing with specific policy areas, such as agriculture or welfare, on the other side. There is also tension between parallel House and Senate committees having jurisdiction over the same policy area, especially where different parties or ideological groups are in control of the two committees. There is tension between floor leaders chosen by the party caucus and committee chairs who, because of the traditional (but changing) seniority system, are somewhat independent of control by the caucus or party leaders. There is tension within a standing committee between the competing claims and interests of the subcommittees. Finally, as noted in earlier chapters, tension arises from the competing demands for members' attention from committee duties and policy-making considerations on the one hand and obligations to constituencies on the other. The committee system forces most members to become policy specialists, and committee meetings increase the pressures on members' time and staff.

NOTES

1. Ron Kirkwood (1985) makes the point that the more fragmented Congress has become in the addition of new subcommittee layers to the committee system, the easier it has been for interest groups to dominate, or at least affect, policy making in their special areas of policy concern.
2. For the complete lay-out of the committee voting on these 19 motions, see *Congressional Quarterly Weekly Report*, August 3, 1974, 2018–2019.

REFERENCES

BAZELON, DAVID T. (ed.). *Point of Order: A Documentary of the Army-McCarthy Hearings*. New York: Norton, 1964.

COHODAS, NADINE. "Decades-Old Genocide Treaty Finally Wins Senate Approval." *Congressional Quarterly Weekly Report* (22 February 1986): 458–459.

Congressional Quarterly Weekly Report (10 November 1979): 2515–2516.

COOPER, JOSEPH. *The Origins of the Standing Committees and the Development of the Modern House*. Houston, Texas: Rice University Studies, 1970.

DAVIDSON, ROGER H., and OLESZEK, WALTER J. *Congress and Its Members*. 2nd ed. Washington, D. C.: Congressional Quarterly Press, 1985.

DAVIDSON, ROGER H., and OLESZEK, WALTER J. "From Monopoly to Interaction: Changing Patterns in Committee Management of Legislation in the House." Paper presented at the annual meeting of the Midwest Political Science Association, 10 April 1987, Chicago.

FELTON, JOHN. "Lugar Moves to Put Stamp on Foreign Relations." *Congressional Quarterly Weekly Report* (12 January 1985a): 84–85.

FELTON, JOHN. " 'Consensus' on Foreign Policy Proves Elusive." *Congressional Quarterly Weekly Report* (2 February 1985b): 197–198.

FELTON, JOHN. "Sidestepping Most Controversies: Senate Panel, Moving Quickly, Marks Up $12.8 Billion Aid Bill." *Congressional Quarterly Weekly Report* (30 March 1985c): 572–575.

FENNO, RICHARD F. *Congressmen in Committees*. Boston: Little, Brown, 1973.

GOODWIN, JR., GEORGE. *The Little Legislatures: Committees of Congress*. Amherst, Mass.: University of Massachusetts Press, 1970.

HALL, RICHARD L. "Participation and Purpose in Committee Decision Making." *American Political Science Review* 81 (March 1987):105–127.

KEEFE, WILLIAM J., and OGUL, MORRIS S. *The American Legislative Process: Congress and the States.* 6th ed. Englewood Cliffs, N. J.: Prentice-Hall, 1985.

KIRKWOOD, RON. Comment during panel presentation at the convention of the Midwest Political Science Association, 20 April 1985, Chicago.

MANLEY, JOHN F. *The Politics of Finance: The House Committee on Ways and Means.* Boston: Little, Brown, 1970.

MILL, JOHN STUART. *Considerations on Representative Government.* Currin V. Shields (ed.). Indianapolis: Liberal Arts Press, 1958. (Originally published in London, 1861)

MORROW, WILLIAM L. *Congressional Committees.* New York: Scribner's, 1969.

MUIR, JR., WILLIAM K. *Legislature: California's School for Politics.* Chicago: University of Chicago Press, 1982.

SHEPSLE, KENNETH. *The Giant Jigsaw Puzzle: Democratic Committee Assignments in the Modern House.* Chicago: University of Chicago Press, 1978.

SHEPSLE, KENNETH, and WEINGAST, BARRY. "The Institutional Foundations of Committee Power." *American Political Science Review* 81 (March 1987):85–104.

SKLADONY, THOMAS W. "The House at Work: Select and Standing Committees in the U. S. House of Representatives, 1789–1818." Paper presented at the Midwest Political Science Association convention, April 1985, Chicago.

SMITH, STEVEN S., and DEERING, CHRISTOPHER J. *Committees in Congress.* Washington, D. C.: Congressional Quarterly Press, 1984.

U. S. CONGRESS, SENATE. Committee on Foreign Relations. *The Genocide Convention.* 99th Cong., 1st sess., 1985. S. Rept. 99-2.

IX CONGRESSIONAL PROCEDURE

Legislative procedure is not always an impressive or awe-inspiring activity; it is certainly complicated and often downright messy. As an old saying goes: "There are two things you don't want to see made—sausages and laws."

The processing of legislation—introducing, scheduling, debating, amending, and approving bills—is the fundamental activity of Congress. Each Congress disposes of thousands of bills, pigeonholing most of them but also giving considerable attention to hundreds. Congress has developed an intricate system of procedures for handling this massive work load, and this chapter describes this system.

VOLUME OF LEGISLATIVE BUSINESS

Before describing congressional bill procedures, some discussion of the volume of bills that comes before Congress is appropriate.

There are several ways of measuring legislative activity. One is to count all bills introduced in Congress. In recent years there has been a dramatic decline in bills introduced in the House and a moderate decline in Senate bills (see table 9-1). In the 1970s changes were made in rules governing cosponsorship that reduced the need for several members to introduce separate but identical bills to be able to claim credit for sponsorship. Introducing bills allows members to publicize their interest and activity in particular policy areas. The largest number of House bills (22,060) was introduced in the 90th Congress (1967–1968). Just 8,094 bills were introduced in the 97th Congress (1981–1982), which was about the same as the number (7,611) introduced in the 80th Congress (1947–1948). The Senate changes were less dramatic over the postwar decades: 3,186 bills in the 80th Congress, 4,400 in the 90th, and 3,396 in the 97th. (For more complete data, see Ornstein et al. 1984, 143–146.)

A more satisfactory measure of bill activity is the number of bills passed. Again, in recent Congresses, there has been a decline in activity: 1,739 bills were passed by the House in the 80th Congress, 2,482 in the 81st, 1,213 in the 90th, and only 704 in the 97th. In terms of percentage, the decline has been marked: 23 percent of the bills introduced in the 80th Congress were eventually passed, compared to 24 percent in the 81st Congress, 6 percent in the 90th, and 9 percent in

TABLE 9-1. Volume of bills introduced and rate of bills passed, selected recent congresses

Congress (years)	House		Senate	
	Bills[a] introduced	Bills[a] passed (percent)	Bills[a] introduced	Bills[a] passed (percent)
80th (1947–1948)	7,611	23	3,186	52
85th (1957–1958)	14,580	14	4,532	49
89th (1965–1966)	19,874	8	4,129	40
90th (1967–1968)	22,060	5	4,400	31
95th (1977–1978)	15,587	7	3,800	28
99th (1985–1986)	6,499	15	3,386	28

[a]Includes bills and joint resolutions.
Sources: Congressional Record Dec. 31, 1948, p. D537 (80th Cong.); Aug. 23, 1958 p. D610 (85th Cong.); Oct. 22, 1966, p. D604 (89th Cong.); Oct. 14, 1968, p. D483 (90th Cong.); Oct. 14, 1978, p. D925 (95th Cong.); and Jan. 6, 1987, p. D10 (99th Cong.). (Scott Henderson, a graduate student at the University of South Dakota, helped in the collection of this data.)

the 97th. The Senate passed 1,670 bills in the 80th Congress, a postwar high of 4,518 bills in the 84th Congress, and 803 bills in the 97th Congress. The percentage of Senate bills that were eventually passed in those three Congresses were, respectively, 52, 56, and 24, following the same trend as the House.

Volume of business may also be measured on the basis of laws' quality (or importance) as well as their quantity. In 1985 in the first session of the 99th Congress, 7,777 measures (bills and resolutions) were introduced in the House or Senate, and from these, 240 public laws were added to the statutes of the United States. Six bills were vetoed by President Reagan, and one of these vetoes was overridden, resulting in P. L. 99-158. By no means were all of these new laws significant. Very few of them authorized major new programs or major shifts in old programs. Some laws extended existing programs. Almost half (105) of the 240 laws (*Congressional Record,* Jan. 21, 1986) might be considered merely public relations gestures. Eighty-seven of these laws designated special days or weeks, such as National Independent Retail Grocers Week (P. L. 99-20) or National Asthma and Allergy Awareness Week (P. L. 99-32). Five laws designated the names of certain public buildings, such as the John W. Byrnes Post Office and Federal Building in Green Bay, Wisconsin (P. L. 99-210). Eight laws commemorated or recognized anniversaries, such as those of the first U. S. weather satellite, the Bay of Pigs invasion, and the Peace Corps. Four "authorized and requested" the president to issue a proclamation designating some observance, such as the National Organ Donation Awareness Week (P. L. 99-21). Another nine of these new laws did such things as authorizing the printing of a revised edition of "Senate Procedure," providing for the minting of a coin in commemoration of the centennial of the Statue of Liberty, recognizing the pause for the Pledge of Allegiance as part of National Flag Day activities, appealing for the release of Soviet Jewry, commending the people of Switzerland for their contributions to liberty, reaffirming our historic solidarity with the people of Mexico following the devastating earthquake there, reaffirming U. S. friendship with the people of Colombia following the devastating volcanic eruption there, and waiving the printing on parchment of Senate Joint Resolution (S. J. Res.) 372 increasing the statutory limit on the public debt (P. L. 99-176).

Recorded roll-call votes have increased in number in both chambers since the early 1970s. In the House, there were 159 in the 80th Congress, 1,540 in the 95th, and 812 in the 97th. In the Senate, there were 248 recorded votes in the 80th Congress, 1,290 (the postwar high) in the 94th Congress, and 952 in the 97th.

As to the number of hours in session, both chambers recorded their postwar highs in the 95th Congress (1977–1978)—1,898 hours for the House and 2,510 for the Senate. The low Congress in this respect was the 84th (1955–1956)—937 hours for the House and 1,362 for the Senate.

There has been a general decline in the number of public bills enacted in both chambers; from the 80th through 89th Congresses, the average was 833 per Congress, while from the 90th through the 98th Congresses, the average was 592. On the other hand, the length of the public bills enacted has increased from an average length of 2.6 pages per statute for the 80th through 89th Congresses to an average length of 6.3 pages per statute for the 90th through 98th Congresses (Ornstein et al. 1984, 150).

A final, though not very significant or praiseworthy, statistic on congressional work load is that 43.5 million pieces of congressional franked mail (at no cost to the member) were sent out in 1954, 110.5 million in 1964, 321 million in 1974, and 581.7 million in 1982 (Ornstein et al. 1984, 152).

PRINCIPLES OF LEGISLATIVE PROCEDURE

To the amateur observer who is perplexed and sometimes even outraged by the apparent confusion, slowness, and indecisiveness of congressional sessions, it may come as a surprise to learn that the purpose of the rules governing legislative procedure is to expedite rational and orderly decision making. Bringing order out of chaos, however, is not easy. Perhaps, given the multitude of cross pressures and cross purposes existing in Congress and the many different sets of chamber, party, and committee rules, it is a wonder anything gets done.

Two hundred years ago, the English Utilitarian philosopher Jeremy Bentham studied Parliamentary processes and in his *Essay on Political Tactics* (Gordon 1964, 89–95) enunciated six fundamental principles he felt ought to govern procedure in a national legislative assembly.

First, he wrote, there should be the fullest publicity, both inside and outside the assembly, for everything that has happened, is happening, or is scheduled to happen, unless such publication should "favor the projects of an enemy" or result in injustice to individuals. This would include such routine matters as prior publication of the hours of legislative or committee sessions, the topics on the agenda, and the major persons to be heard. Obviously, publicity does not work to everyone's advantage. Many procedures of Congress seem deliberately to be kept from public notice and discussion. In his study of congressional leadership selection, Nelson Polsby (1977, 324–354) pointed out that Congress took routine steps to insulate its decision making from certain kinds of outside influences (such as the president, the press, and interest groups). Committee mark-up of legislation ordinarily took place in executive session until recently. The House often met as the committee of the whole, a parliamentary device that relaxes many procedural restrictions and eliminates the need for exhaustive records of words and votes.

The second of Bentham's principles is the idea of equality, that all members have equal status, equal voting power, and equal opportunity to speak.

The third principle stresses the absolute impartiality of the presiding officer of the legislative chamber, whose function it was, Bentham believed, to serve as a judge in disputes between members and as an agent for the entire assembly in its relations with other government officials and institutions. This rule of Bentham's, while honored by the traditional neutrality of the speaker of the British House of Commons, is distinctly breached in the United States, where the speaker of the House of Representatives is clearly and definitely a partisan figure.

Bentham's fourth principle is that the majority shall rule. "How far so ever the will of the simple majority may be from the really universal will," he wrote, "it is nearer to it than the contrary will."

That there should be a logical order of the stages of legislative business was Bentham's fifth rule. Legislators should not mingle the processes of proposing, debating, and voting on bills, and only one question should be debated at a time. The body should decide each problem before proceeding to the next.

Finally, in order to protect the minority, there must be freedom of speech. Of course, speech must be controlled to some degree if the legislature is to reach final decisions, given that there are such problems as filibusters and other methods of conscious obstruction that legislators sometimes use to frustrate the majority. The freedom to speak, then, is necessarily qualified to some degree, but generally all members are affected equally by the rules and have equal access to the floor.

Briefly, the purpose of the rules is to facilitate the transaction of business and to promote cooperation and harmony. Every proposition presented for decision should be fully and freely discussed by the members. Every member has the right to know at all times what the question is and what its effect will be. Only one question is to be considered at a time.

A final point concludes this introduction to congressional procedure. There are several marked differences between the chambers of Congress, and these differences affect the chambers' respective approaches to procedural regulation. Proceedings in the House seem to be more impersonal and expeditious; the Senate, with its smaller size, usually acts at a slower pace and in a warmer atmosphere. As Lewis Froman, Jr. (1967, 8–10) notes, "The informal and more congenial Senate is able to function with quite lax and flexible rules," notably the unlimited debate rule and the weakly enforced rule of germaneness. More recent observers, however, as we have seen in chapter 6, notice signs of a reversal in these comparisons.

The remainder of this chapter is organized around three phases of bill procedure: (1) how a bill gets on the agenda for floor debate, (2) what stages a particular bill goes through from introduction to final approval, and (3) how a bill is debated and amended once it gets to the floor.

THE AGENDA: CONTROL AND PRIORITIES

After a bill is favorably reported by a standing committee, it joins the many other bills that have also been approved by standing committees and is placed in the order of bills to be brought to the floor.

In the more informal Senate, the scheduling of legislation is characteristically casual, at least in comparison with the House. The majority leader establishes the bill sequence after conferring with the minority leader and key members of his own party, including the chairs of the committees from which the bills emerged. From time to time, the majority leader will take the floor to advise members on the order of upcoming business. The following remarks by Majority Leader Robert Dole are illustrative (*Congressional Record* Apr. 11, 1986, S4099).

> Mr. President, under the standing order, the leaders will have ten minutes each. I do not think we intend to use that time as we have a rather tight schedule. That will be followed by special orders for Senator Hawkins, Senator Proxmire, Senator Quayle, Senator Cranston, and Senator Melcher. The remarks of Senator Hawkins will be delivered by Senator Hatch.
>
> Routine morning business will follow the execution of the special orders, not to extend beyond the hour of 9:30 A.M.
>
> Right at 9:30, we hope to resume S. 1017, the regional airports bill under a unanimous-consent agreement, providing for final passage no later than 12 noon.
>
> Mr. President, there could be as many as four votes between now and then, so I would advise my colleagues to be alert. Because of the time constraints—this is a rather tight agreement—we are going to limit the roll-call votes to as close to fifteen minutes as possible. I would urge staff who may be tuned in this morning to advise their senators that roll-call votes will be fifteen minutes. There could be some exceptions, but that is our present intention. . . .
>
> Following the regional airports bill, we will take up the hydro-relicensing bill. Hopefully, we can work that out, maybe, without a vote. I am not certain about that.
>
> That will hopefully be followed by the crime bill, S. 1236, which will be followed by S. 1774, the Hobbs Act. . . .
>
> Mr. President, we will be in session and there will be votes. Again, I am certain there will be votes. I do not want to mislead anyone by suggesting that perhaps there will not be votes. There will be votes, and they will probably start as early as 9:45 this morning. We could have votes up to around 2 or 2:30 this afternoon.

Near the end of a typical day's session, the majority leader (or, in the example that follows, his assistant) will announce various orders and arrangements concerning the next day's business, as does the Assistant Majority Leader Alan Simpson of Wyoming in the following remarks (*Congressional Record* Feb. 6, 1986, S1119, S1200):

> Mr. President, after conferring with the Democratic leader, I ask unanimous consent that once the Senate completes its business today, it stand in recess until the hour of 12 noon on Friday, February 7, 1986. . . .
>
> Mr. President, following the recognition of the two leaders under the standing order, I ask unanimous consent that the senator from Wisconsin [Mr. Proxmire] be recognized for not to exceed fifteen minutes under a special order. . . .
>
> Following the Proxmire special order, I ask unanimous consent that there be a period for the transaction of routine morning business, not to extend beyond the hour of 12:30 P.M., with senators permitted to speak therein for not more than five minutes each. . . .
>
> Mr. President, I must advise my colleagues that there are groups meeting with regard to technical corrections on the farm bill, S. 2067. Those are ongoing at this moment.
>
> We are also attempting to obtain a Genocide Treaty time agreement. That is going forward. Perhaps that will be completed tomorrow. We certainly hope so, so that we can begin that when we return from the recess.
>
> There will be appointment of conferees on the Superfund bill. The House has now completed the appointment of conferees. . . .
>
> Mr. President, there being no further business, in accordance with the previous order, I ask unanimous consent that the Senate recess until 12 noon tomorrow.
>
> There being no objection, the Senate, at 6:16 P.M., recessed until tomorrow, Friday, February 7, 1986, at 12 noon.

The daily calendar of business for the Senate lists the pending business. The Senate calendar for Wednesday, January 23, 1980, identified four items, Senate Concurrent Resolution (S. Con. Res.) 47 to approve the extension of nondiscriminatory treatment with respect to the products of China, S. 1648 to improve the nation's airport and airway system, H. R. 3236 to provide better work incentives and improved accountability in the disability insurance program, and H. R. 5168 to extend certain expiring provisions relating to personnel management of the armed forces. Accompanying the bills were provisions specifying the speaking time allotted to each side and the senators in charge of assigning that time. For example, the order under a unanimous consent agreement calling up H. R. 5168 specified:

> Ordered, That when the Senate proceeds to the consideration of H. R. 5168 (Order No. 454), an act to extend certain expiring provisions of law relating to personnel management of the Armed Forces, debate on any amendment (except an amendment to be offered by the Senator from Colorado (Mr. Armstrong), (Military Pay-Cap) on which there shall be four hours; and an amendment to be offered by the Senator from New Mexico (Mr. Schmitt) (on private negotiators at in-

ternational conferences) on which there shall be thirty minutes) shall be limited to thirty minutes, to be equally divided and controlled by the mover of such and the manager of the bill; and debate on any debatable motion, appeal, or point of order which is submitted or on which the chair entertains debate shall be limited to twenty minutes, to be equally divided and controlled by the mover of such and the manager of the bill: Provided, that in the event the manager of the bill is in favor of any such amendment or motion, the time in opposition thereto shall be controlled by the minority leader or his designee: Provided further, that no amendment that is not germane to the provisions of the said bill shall be received.

Ordered further, that on the question of final passage of the said bill, debate shall be limited to two hours, to be equally divided and controlled, respectively, by the Senator from Georgia (Mr. Nunn) and the Senator from Iowa (Mr. Jepsen): Provided, that the said Senators, or either of them, may, from the time under their control on the passage of the said bill, allot additional time to any senator during the consideration of any amendment, debatable motion, appeal, or point of order.

Since the Senate calendar on most days does not contain such orders, it is of limited help in predicting what the Senate will actually be debating on a given day. The Senate floor agenda is in a constant state of flux from hour to hour. If they are to have a sense of the Senate schedule, members, staffers, and observers must keep track of a bewildering array of calendars, whip notices, legislative notices from the party policy committees, leadership announcements (which are often given by the majority leader at the beginning and ending of each day's session), and even standing committee agendas. Agenda information is provided in printed form and by electronic means.

Agenda setting in the House is a good deal more complicated and formalized. The Rules Committee, one of the House's standing committees, has important powers in regulating the flow of bills from the other standing committees to the floor. Since the speaker of the House (when a Democrat) names the Democratic members of the Rules Committee, since the Rules Committee acts to protect the majority party's interests, and since the speaker is the House's presiding officer, the speaker has as much control over the House agenda as the majority leader does over the Senate agenda. The printed daily calendar for the House of Representatives commonly lists special orders and unfinished business at the beginning. For Thursday, February 7, 1980, for instance, there were special orders, all by unanimous consent, under which Representatives Vander Jagt, Gonzalez, Lundine, Payser, Cavanaugh, Gingrich, and Annunzio were given permission to address the House for various specified lengths of time (five minutes was the shortest period, sixty minutes the longest) at the conclusion of the day's legislative business. For that same day, there were three items of unfinished business: H. R. 4546, to amend the District of Columbia Redevelopment Act of 1945; H. R. 5461, to designate the birthday of Martin Luther King, Jr., a legal holiday; and H. R. 2551, concerning protection of agricultural land.

The House uses several special scheduling devices to sort out its agenda. Taxation and appropriations bills are placed on what is called the "union" calendar, while other major legislation authorizing programs is placed on the House calendar. These are the major calendars of the House and are generally used during the middle of the week when attendance is usually higher than it is on Monday or Friday. There are other calendars for bills. For the "consent" calendar, each party appoints one of its members to act as a "watchdog" to ensure that there is no bill on this calendar to which any member of the party is likely to object; with this method, one objection is sufficient to stop a bill. Bills from the consent calendar may be brought to the floor on the first and third Mondays of each month. Bills from the "private" calendar, which involve individual citizens, come to the floor on the first and third Tuesdays of each month, and again each party has a watchdog to keep the calendar clear of any bill to which a member might object. Bills relating to the District of Columbia come up on the second and fourth Mondays of each month. There are two seldom-used devices that can be employed to bring bills to the floor: the "discharge" calendar, which brings bills up on the second and fourth Mondays of each month except during the last six days of a session, and "Calendar Wednesday," which brings bills up on any Wednesday except during the last two weeks of a session. Finally, bills may come to the floor under suspension of the rules (a two-thirds vote is required) on any Monday or Tuesday and during the last six days of a session.

The rule under which a particular bill comes to the House floor specifies the amount of time to be made available to each side in debate. A closed rule means that only committee amendments may be considered. An open rule means that any member of the House may propose an amendment. A modified rule means that amendments may be made to some parts of the bill, but not to other parts.

STAGES OF THE BILL PROCESS

The general sequence of stages or steps through which a bill passes on its way to becoming a law can be quickly enumerated.

1. The bill is introduced in one chamber (House or Senate).
2. The bill is referred to the appropriate committee having jurisdiction over the subject matter.
3. The bill is the subject of committee hearings, where pro and con arguments are presented and discussed.
4. The bill is amended by committee members in mark-up sessions.
5. The bill is favorably reported by the committee to the floor of the chamber.
6. The bill is placed on the chamber's agenda of business for a particular day.
7. The bill is debated (and perhaps amended) on the floor of the chamber.
8. The bill is passed in the first chamber.
9. The bill is introduced in the second chamber.
10. The bill is referred to the appropriate committee.
11. The bill is the subject of committee hearings.

12. The bill is amended in committe mark-up sessions.
13. The bill is favorably reported by the committee.
14. The bill is placed on the chamber's agenda.
15. The bill is debated (and perhaps amended) on the floor.
16. The bill is passed in the second chamber.
17. If House and Senate versions of the bill differ, they are referred to a conference committee for resolution. The conference committee is composed of equal numbers of senators and representatives.[1]
18. The bill, now an act of Congress, goes to the president for his signature.
19. If the president vetoes the act, it returns to Congress as privileged business. If both houses vote by a two-thirds majority to override the president's veto, then the act becomes law.

These nineteen steps can be recombined into six major phases: introduction (steps 1, 2, 9, 10), committee (steps 3 through 5 and 11 through 13), schedule (steps 6 and 14), decision (steps 7 through 8 and 15 through 16), conference (step 17), and executive (steps 18 through 19).[2]

Each chamber has developed special procedural devices in the schedule and decision stages. The most important and interesting of these devices follow:

1. *Committee of the whole.* The House generally debates legislation in "committee of the whole," which allows debate to proceed under easier and more informal procedural controls. The number of members necessary to establish a quorum—that is, the required number to be present for the House to conduct business—is reduced from 218, which is a majority of all members, to 100. The speaker does not preside in committee of the whole and is thus freed to participate in debate if desired, and nonrecord votes are allowed to be taken. If the vote on a bill in committee of the whole is favorable, the committee dissolves and reports its action to the full House, the speaker again presiding. The full House then takes an official, recorded roll call. As noted earlier, revenue and appropriations bills are placed on the union calendar, which is formally the calendar of the Committee of the Whole House for the State of the Union. Other public bills are debated on the House calendar, which is formally the calendar for the Committee of the Whole House.

2. *Suspension of the rules.* This device, dating back to 1822, enables the House to take a variety of actions that would otherwise be in conflict with its standing rules. When suspension is moved, debate on the question to suspend the rules is limited to forty minutes. A two-thirds majority of members voting is needed to suspend the rules. Under suspension of the rules, amendments to the bill being debated are not in order; this is sometimes called the "take it or leave it" rule.

3. *Privileged matters.* Certain kinds of legislative business can be taken up at any time without regard to the regular schedules and calendars and are thus called "privileged." Included in this category are bills from the Appropriations and Ways and Means committees, bills from a conference committee, and bills that have been vetoed by the president. In the Senate, treaties and presidential nominations of

judges, ambassadors, and top executive branch officials are considered on a special executive calendar. (The Senate uses only two calendars: executive and regular.)

4. *Unanimous consent.* By unanimous consent—that is, where no member opposes the motion—almost anything can be done. Much of the Senate's agenda is arranged by means of unanimous consent agreements, as noted earlier. These unanimous consent agreements in the Senate are comparable to rules issued by the House Rules Committee for bills in that chamber.

5. *Quorum calls and ruinous amendments.* These are two devices that are available to a minority wanting, for some reason, to delay proceedings. When the question of the presence of a quorum is called, the presiding officer must determine if a sufficient number of members are indeed present to conduct business. Formerly, it usually took more than a half hour to read the roll of House members, and several of these calls could, obviously, take up most of a legislative day and wreak havoc with the leadership's legislative schedule. Electronic voting equipment has reduced the effectiveness of this delaying tactic in the House. Another way for the minority to delay is to submit contradictory amendments or amendments that would in effect negate the purpose of the bill.

6. *Nongermane amendments.* The rules of the House forbid amendments that are not germane (that is, unrelated) to the bill being debated. The House committee reporting the bill probably would not have considered the issues posed by such amendments. However, the Senate is not so persnickety about amendments. As a consequence, bills coming out of the Senate are sometimes strange creations. This often presents a problem at the conference stage, when bills with different language on the same subject must be reconciled.

7. *Filibuster and cloture.* Senate rules allow unlimited debate. Senators obtaining the floor may keep it as long as they (and other collaborating senators) are physically able to speak. The cloture rule, however, provides a device by which such a filibuster can eventually be halted. The cloture process begins with the filing of a petition containing the signatures of sixteen senators. This motion is then to be voted on within two days. If three-fifths of the entire membership of the Senate (sixty senators)[3] vote for cloture, then a final vote on the bill being debated must be taken after no more than one hundred additional hours of debate; all time spent on quorum calls, roll-call votes, and other parliamentary procedures are counted in computing the one-hundred-hour limit.

To reduce the chance of a filibuster occurring to delay the Senate's work, much of the business of the Senate is conducted with unanimous consent agreements that allow specified amounts of time to members wishing to speak for or against the pending legislation.

While congressional procedures may seem overly complex, technical, and ponderous, it must be remembered that these very characteristics encourage the achievement of consensus and compromise and also serve to protect the interests of minorities by giving them the means to regularly and significantly affect the course of legislative decision making.

To give an example of how Congress processes legislative proposals and to illustrate many of the procedural devices discussed in this chapter, a fairly extensive description of the 1985 debate on the MX missile question is presented. The issue was very controversial and the debate was one of the major topics for several days, appearing on the front pages of newspapers and on the evening network television programs. The MX missile case illustrates:

1. the complexity of many issues that come before Congress
2. the appeals to basic but often conflicting national goals, (in this case, the cost of armaments, the need for national security, and the impact of U. S. actions on world opinion)
3. the effectiveness of arguments on various sides of the issue
4. the conflicting pressures on members as they listen to arguments from the White House, their congressional party leaders, colleagues who serve on the Armed Services Committee and others recognized as defense specialists, prominent interest groups with a major stake in the outcome, spokespersons from the academic and religious worlds, and constituents back home
5. the inevitable compromises, especially from the side that eventually wins, made as a consequence of the exhaustive committee hearings and floor debates

The committee actions reported in the following vignette were most unusual in terms of public visibility and speed of action; to authorize a program and then appropriate money for it within two days is extraordinary.

The MX Missile Controversy (1985 Phase)

The MX missile controversy has been at the center of U. S. security policy debates for more than a decade. The MX, a missile seventy feet in length, was designed in the 1970s to have the capacity to shoot 10 powerful warheads a distance of 8,000 miles with an accuracy of inside a quarter of a mile from the target. Its designed purpose was to destroy armored underground missile launchers and other Soviet military targets in order to counteract the threat of Soviet weaponry already capable of such feats.

In the first Reagan administration, opposition to the MX grew from groups who believed American development of the missile would serve to escalate the nuclear arms race. Democrats in the House adopted the MX as its major target in attacking Reagan's large defense program. When Reagan in 1984 decided to put the new missiles in existing launchers that were considered to be highly vulnerable to Russian attack, opposition to the MX grew in the Senate. An effort to kill the MX in the June 1984 Senate debate on the defense authorization bill was rejected, fifty-five to forty-one. Then, when Sen. Lawton Chiles (D.–Fla.) moved to provide enough money to preserve the option of future MX production without buying the twenty-one additional missiles the president wanted in fiscal 1985, Vice-President George Bush's tie-breaking vote was required to stop the anti-MX effort.

The MX grew out of advanced intercontinental ballistic missile (ICBM) technology that had begun with funding of $7.9 million in fiscal 1973 during the Nixon administration and grew to $158 million in fiscal 1979 during the Carter administration. In the latter year, specific funding for development of the MX began, at $150 million. Funding for MX development quickly grew to $1.5 billion in fiscal 1981 and to $2.5 billion in fiscal 1983. Funding for MX procurement originated in fiscal 1984 at $2.2 billion.

The background to the legislative history of the authorization and appropriations legislation in 1985 can best be summarized by the opening paragraphs of Senate Report 99-14 (U. S. Congress. Senate. 1985, 2).

> Pursuant to provisions of the Department of Defense Appropriations Act, 1985, contained in Public Law 98-473, the continuing resolution for fiscal year 1985, S. J. Res. 75 is the Senate vehicle by which Congress may approve the obligation and expenditure of $1.5 billion of prior-year appropriations for procurement of twenty-one MX Peacekeeper missiles. By law, in order for such funds to be made available, Congress must first adopt a resolution referred to the Armed Services committees of each House, approving authorization for the release of such funds to continue the MX Peacekeeper procurement program and then adopt a second resolution approving the obligation and expenditure of the prior-year funds.
>
> On March 4, 1985, President Reagan transmitted to the Congress his formal report on the continued procurement of the MX Peacekeeper missile. On March 5, the authorization version of the required MX resolution (S. J. Res. 71), was introduced by Sen. Barry Goldwater, chairman of the Senate Armed Services Committee. The day following, March 6, Sen. Ted Stevens, chairman of the Subcommittee on Defense, introduced S. J. Res. 75, which was referred to the Committee on Appropriations. S. J. Res. 71 was reported to the Senate by the Armed Services Committee on March 18, 1985, and was adopted by the Senate on March 19, 1985, by a vote of fifty-five to forty-five.
>
> The provisions of S. J. Res. 75 were established by law, as were procedures for debate on the Senate floor. The resolution is not subject to amendment under these same provisions. The scope of formal consideration is limited to that of continued procurement of the MX missile in fiscal year 1985. The committee's action on S. J. Res. 75 should not, therefore, be construed to go beyond that.

The Senate Armed Services Committee, chaired by Sen. Barry Goldwater (R.–Ariz.), took its critical action approving the obligation of funds for the twenty-one missiles on March 18 by a vote of eleven to six (see table 9-2). Two

Table 9-2.   The MX missile vote in the Senate Armed Services Committee, March 18, 1985

	Republicans	Democrats	Totals
For	Goldwater AZ	Nunn GA	
	Thurmond SC	Stennis MS	
	Warner VA		11
	Cohen ME		
	Quayle IN		
	East NC		
	Wilson CA		
	Denton AL		
	Gramm TX		
Against	(none)	Hart CO	
		Exon NE	
		Levin MI	6
		Kennedy MA	
		Bingaman NM	
		Glenn OH	
Totals	9	8	17

Note: Republican Humphrey (NH) and Democrat Dixon (IL) did not vote. The phi coefficient is a statistic that measures the direction and degree of association between two dichotomous variables. It ranges from zero, indicating no relationships, to 1.00, indicating perfect relationship. The plus or minus sign indicates whether the relationship is direct or inverse. For this case, phi = + 0.78.

days later the Appropriations Committee chaired by Sen. Bob Packwood (R.–Ore.) voted to release the funds by a narrow fifteen-to-fourteen margin (see table 9-3). Among those giving testimony were Secretary of Defense Caspar Weinberger; General John Vessey, chair of the Joint Chiefs of Staff; General Bennie Davis, commander in chief of the Strategic Air Command; and Paul Nitze of the Arms Control and Disarmament Agency.

Senate floor debate took place on Monday and Tuesday, March 18 and 19. Senator Goldwater was in charge of the five hours of debate time allocated to proponents of the legislation. Minority Leader Robert Byrd (D.–W. Va.) asked Sen. Gary Hart (D.–Colo.) to take control of the five hours given to opponents of the legislation. Goldwater led off the proceedings, stressing two reasons he felt made favorable action on the MX missile both more important and more likely: first, Russia's decision to return to the arms reduction negotiating table in Geneva and, second, "the expanding pattern of Soviet violations of important arms control agreements" (*Congressional Record,* Mar. 18, 1985, S3026). Before debate concluded the next day, at least half of the senators had taken advantage of the opportunity to have their say on the MX issue. The MX debate resumed at the close of morning business on Tuesday. Sens. John Warner (R.–Va.) and Gary Hart (D.–Colo.) made the last remarks for and against the measure (*Congressional Record,* Mar. 19, 1985, S3164).

Table 9-3. The MX missile vote in the Senate Appropriations Committee, March 20, 1985

	Republicans	Democrats	Total
For	Stevens AK	Stennis MS	
	McClure ID	Byrd WV	
	Laxalt NV	DeConcini AZ	
	Garn UT		
	Cochran MS		15
	Abdnor SD		
	Kasten WI		
	D'Amato NY		
	Mattingly GA		
	Rudman NH		
	Specter PA		
	Domenici NM		
Against	Hatfield OR	Proxmire WI	
	Weicker CT	Inouye HI	
	Andrews ND	Hollings SC	
		Chiles FL	
		Johnston LA	14
		Burdick ND	
		Leahy VT	
		Sasser TN	
		Bumpers AR	
		Lautenberg NJ	
		Harkin IA	
Totals	15	14	29

Note: phi = + 0.59.

Mr. Warner. . . . As we look at the reasons for the Soviets coming back to the negotiating table, it is my judgment, first, they saw the forging and the strengthening of an alliance between the United States and our allies throughout the world, principally NATO.

This afternoon, the Senate leaves in a second alliance, namely, that of the Congress of the United States—because I believe certainly the House will follow the action we are about to take—an alliance between the Congress and the President in working at the negotiating table for a more peaceful world.

I thank the distinguished chairman of the Senate Armed Services Committee for the leadership he has given in this matter, and the distinguished senator from Georgia (Mr. Nunn). I yield to my colleague from Colorado.

. . .

Mr. Hart. Mr. President, I wish to return the kind words of the senator from Virginia and compliment him also on the manner in which he has conducted his side of this debate. I would like to reiterate once again the remarks that he has made, and the distinguished majority leader. This is not a partisan issue. There will be Democrats on both sides and Republicans on both sides, however the outcome comes out.

I regret that the consensus which we should have on a major issue such as this is not greater. But I fear that as long as this issue is before us it will continue to divide not only the Senate but the American people. I thank the senator from Virginia.

Mr. Warner. Mr. President, I see no other senator seeking recognition. I yield back all time under my control.

Mr. Hart. I yield back my time.

The Senate vote was fifty-five to forty-five in favor of building the additional twenty-one missiles. Table 9-4 shows, by party, the distribution of Senate support and opposition. Analysts for the *Congressional Quarterly Weekly Report* (Towell, Cohodas, and Pressman 1985, 515–523) noted that the voting decisions of nine senators were particularly critical: Democrats Byrd, Lloyd Bentsen of Texas, Russell Long of Louisiana, and David Boren of Oklahoma and Republicans Arlen Specter of Pennsylvania, Charles Mathias of Maryland, Bob Packwood of Oregon, and Gordon Humphrey of New Hampshire had at various times been opposed to the MX missile but voted for it, while Republican Nancy Kassebaum of Kansas changed from being an MX supporter to an opponent.

House action on the MX issue in 1985 was just as swift.[4] The House Armed Services Committee reported the bill favorably on March 20; table 9-5 shows the committee vote breakdown by party. But the House Appropriations Committee narrowly voted against the release of funds, twenty-eight to twenty-six (see table 9-6).

Floor debate in the House opened on Monday, March 25, and Rep. Les Aspin (D.–Wis.) took the floor (*Congressional Record* Mar. 25, 1985, H1390).

Table 9-4. The MX missile vote on the Senate floor, March 20, 1985

	Republicans	Democrats	Total
For	45	10	55
Against	8	37	45
Total	53	47	100

Note: phi = + 0.64.

Table 9-5. The MX missile vote in the House Armed Services Committee, March 20, 1985

	Republicans	Democrats	Total
For	20	17	37
Against	0	8	8
Total	20	25	45

Note: phi = + 0.42.
Democrat Lloyd of Tennessee did not vote.

Table 9-6.   The MX missile vote in the House Appropriations
Committee March 20, 1985

	Republicans	Democrats	Total
For	16	10	26
Against	4	24	28
Total	20	34	54

Note: phi = + 0.49.
Republicans Pursell of Michigan and Rogers of Kentucky and Democrat
Stokes of Ohio did not vote.

> Mr. Speaker, pursuant to Public Law 98-525, I move that the House resolve
> itself into the Committee of the Whole House on the State of the Union for the
> consideration of the House joint resolution (H. J. Res. 180) to approve the
> obligation of funds made available by Public Law 98-473 for the procurement
> of MX missiles, subject to the enactment of a second joint resolution.

The House accordingly resolved itself into committee of the whole status, with
Rep. William Natcher (D.–Ky.) in the chair replacing Speaker O'Neill. The first
speech of substance came from Rep. Samuel Stratton (D.–N. Y.), who reviewed the history of the MX missile. Debate continued from about 1:00 P.M.
until 6:20 P.M. Debate resumed the next day, Tuesday, March 26, at 12:20
P.M. Excerpts from the speeches of two representatives, one an opponent of the
MX resolution and one a supporter, are included here to summarize and
provide some of the flavor of the contrary points of view. Rep. Berkley Bedell
(D.–Iowa), an opponent, presents his view (*Congressional Record* Mar. 26,
1985, H1480).

> Advocates of this legislation contend the MX is necessary for several reasons.
> We are told the MX is a vital bargaining chip that strengthens President
> Reagan's hand in convincing the Soviets that the best way in which to have
> fewer nuclear weapons rests upon the production of more nuclear weapons.
> We are told approval of the MX represents a display of national resolve that
> induces the Soviets to reduce their deployment of heavy missiles. We are told
> deployment of the MX guarantees the United States long-term deterrent
> capacity over the Soviet Union. We are also told deployment of the MX
> represents the best way to keep the Soviets at the bargaining tables in
> Geneva. All in all, we are told approval of the MX is vital to the long-term
> national security interests of the United States. While it is certainly true that
> the proponents spent a great amount of time in putting these arguments
> together, I remain unconvinced.
>
> The expression goes, if you want to dance, you have got to pay the
> band. My trouble with the MX two-step though is that its advocates keep
> changing the tune. . . . So far, we've danced to just about every tune they've
> thrown out there including such greats as "the window of vulnerability

blues," "the come back to the bargaining table rag," and who can forget this year's hit, "how much is that MX in the silo? or was that window?" I always confuse the two. One can only guess as to which tune we shall be paying the piper for next year.

The point is, does the MX make any military sense? . . . In my view, the answer is no.

The military utility of the MX must be questioned. Deployed in fixed silos, the MX will become vulnerable to a first-strike attack as Soviet missile accuracies improve over the next decade. Today, we must evaluate whether it is necessary for the United States to mirror Soviet ICBM forces by deploying a first-strike weapon in a fixed silo, or whether our national security interests are best served by forgoing the MX and moving on a mobile ICBM force that is less vulnerable to Soviet attack. MX advocates contend that we cannot attain Soviet concessions on reducing their current inventories of heavy ICBMs unless we build the MX and that we cannot go mobile until we have the MX in fixed superhardened silos. This makes no military sense whatsoever. Regardless of silo hardening, fixed ICBM silos on both sides are, and will continue to become, increasingly more vulnerable to a first-strike attack as missile accuracies on both sides continue to improve. . . .

Mr. Chairman, the United States is currently engaged in the largest peacetime buildup of our military forces. Much of this investment falls into the categories of strategic modernization, including the Trident II, Stealth bomber, and advanced cruise missile systems which all serve to enhance U. S. deterrent capacity over the Soviet Union. MX does little to enhance this capacity. In fact, MX reduces it. For that reason, our path remains clear, we should reject the MX and send the band home, they're out of time and they're out of tune and they are out of step with the nation.

Next Rep. James Courter (R.–N. J.) voices his opinion (*Congressional Record* Mar. 26, 1985, H1481).

Many of those people who are arguing that $1.5 billion is too much for the defense of this country last year were tripping all over themselves to vote about $8.5 billion for the bailout of the International Monetary Fund. I think if you vote $8 billion for foreign loans, you can spend $1.5 billion for the security of America.

Also it has been mentioned by some of my colleagues that you can do two things, you can continue the production line of the MX missile and keep the fence on, in other words, keep the money from being spent, and also all those contractors and subcontractors will actually stay on the job. Nothing could be further from the truth. I have reams of paper to show the types of subcontractors that would leave, that would not be able to stay if the fence was kept on this money, if this money was not released. . . .

They [the Soviets] are about to deploy the new SS-X-24. . . . It is cold-launched, it is rail-mobile, it has ten warheads. . . .

. . . our planners will have the entire rail system of the Soviet Union to keep in mind, from one side of the Soviet Union to the other. So I would like to say that the Soviet Union is not resting, they are not stopping, they are continuing to modernize their land-based leg of the triad.

It has been argued here that if we deploy the MX system that our strength is destabilizing, that strength is provocative. I disagree. I think weakness is provocative. Weakness is destabilizing. It is absolutely essential that both the Soviet Union and the United States have parity, have equality when it comes to their strategic systems. We cannot permit the Soviet Union to have greater strategic capabilities than we. If we do not deploy MX, if we keep the fence on, they not only have the fourth generation of ICBMs, the 17s, the 18s, and the 19s, they will increase their capability manifold by the deployment of the SS-X-25 and SS-X-24.

I plead with you, please vote to unfence. Please vote yes on the resolution.

Finally, Rep. Les Aspin (D.–Wis.) makes the closing plea for MX funding (*Congressional Record* Mar. 26, 1985, H1512).

Mr. Chairman, this issue, the MX issue, we have debated not only for the ten hours that we have been debating it these last couple days, but for weeks, for many, many times over the years. We have gone into the issue of its cost. We have gone into the issue of its vulnerability. We have gone into the issue of whether it is or is not a first strike. We have gone into the issue of whether it is or is not a bargaining chip.

Mr. Chairman, the House is about as evenly divided on this issue as I guess it can possibly be, but I would like to address two issues that are relevant to this vote as opposed to any of the other votes that we have had on the MX. One is the issue of money. The money in this bill that we are unfencing by this vote is money that is in the fiscal year 1985 bill. It is money that is in the deficit that is in effect over the dam. We have passed that point. It is not a deficit reduction issue to deal with by voting against these twenty-one missiles. That is the 1985 bill. It is the 1985 deficit. . . .

Mr. Chairman, the role of Congress in this area of arms control and foreign policy is to support the president when he is right and oppose the president when he is wrong. On the beginning of these arms control talks, the president is right. . . .

Ladies and gentlemen of the Congress, I beg of you, the negotiations are there. The negotiators are in Geneva. They are at the table. Let us give these negotiators the tools so they can do the job.

The committee of the whole rose, Representative Natcher reported to the speaker, and the speaker called the question. "The question was taken," the *Congressional Record* tells us (Mar. 26, 1985, H1512), "and the speaker announced that the noes appeared to have it." But Representative Aspin demanded a record vote, and the electronic device came up with a narrow decision in favor of the MX program, 219 to 213 (see table 9-7).

TABLE 9-7. The MX missile vote on the House floor, March 26, 1985

	Republicans	Democrats	Total
For	158	61	219
Against	24	189	213
Total	182	250	432

Note: phi = + 0.62.
This is the vote on the MX authorization resolution. The vote on the accompanying MX appropriations resolution was 217 to 210. The appropriations roll call (on H. J. Res. 181) produced a phi score of + 0.62, showing the same magnitude and direction of association between political party affiliation and support for the MX missile system.

TELEVISING FLOOR DEBATE

Live television coverage began for the House of Representatives in 1979 and for the Senate in 1986. Many have worried about the effects of televising congressional proceedings, particularly in terms of the behavior of members on the floor and the quality of legislation. In the course of Senate debate in early 1986 as to the advisability of live coverage, an opponent, Sen. Bennett Johnston (D.–La.) expressed the view that the public would not be able to comprehend the special role played by the Senate and the unique rules and procedures it has adopted.

> The public will never understand why it's important to this institution and to the nation for the Senate to play the role of the saucer where the political passions of the nation are cooled.
>
> It doesn't work efficiently. It's a messy, untidy spectacle to watch. But I think it is vital to the nation.

But both Republican Leader Robert Dole of Kansas and Democratic Leader Robert Byrd of West Virginia favored the television experiment. Dole spoke of the beginning of a "new era" in the life of the Senate (*Congressional Record* March 12, 1986, S2464).

> For the first time, our proceedings will be heard by the people unedited: all the debates, the filibusters, the roll-call votes and, of course, all the bleeps, bloops, and blunders, and the delays. One thing I would hope that could come from live radio and TV coverage would be more orderly procedures, more discipline, and less wasted time. I hope the American people demand that of those of us who are honored to serve in the U. S. Senate.
>
> . . . The Senate is a whole different ballgame, and you cannot superimpose the two Houses. . . . There are rules and procedures here that most likely will baffle, confuse, and frustrate our radio and TV audiences. Believe me, they will have my sympathy. Nevertheless, these very rules of the game make the Senate a unique and important voice in the system of checks and balances that are the

foundation of our government. These special rules protect the rights of the minority and allow one man or one woman to make a difference. This is the essence of our democracy.

After one year of live televising of floor activities, the Senate did not seem to have changed much, according to a staff writer of the *Congressional Quarterly Weekly Report* (Nutting 1987). Majority Leader Robert Byrd reports that he believes senators are "making better speeches" and that debate "has improved from a substantive standpoint." Senator Johnston, an opponent of live television coverage, comments that televised coverage "seems to be an unalloyed success" and "our fears were unfounded." Sen. William Proxmire (D.–Wis.) expresses the view, however, that televised debates are boring and of little interest to most of the public, and concludes, "It is not performing any useful function for our country."[5]

PACE AND PROCEDURAL CONFUSION

Congress is not noted for fast action. Its pace seems to imply that there is plenty of time. But every session has its ending, and as the autumn advances and the elections or the holidays approach, a sense of urgency and haste generally is felt on Capitol Hill. In these times, decisions on legislation can be dangerously capricious. An example of hasty, harried congressional work occurred in December 1985. Lawmakers were anxious to leave Washington well before Christmas, so by December 19 they had resolved a mammoth spending bill debate that might have dragged on for weeks in another season. As Rep. John Edward Porter, (R.–Ill.) put it: "Time is a weapon. Everybody is tired and they want to go home" (Granat 1985, 2664). In a similar vein, Rep. Lynn Martin (R.–Ill.) said of late night sessions: "It's never wise to keep the House in after 11 [P.M.]. It's like managing a nursery school without a nap" (2664).

Most readers have heard about, if not watched or participated in, meetings of social, fraternal, professional, or other groups that become so bogged down by a bewildering sequence of parliamentary motions that no one seems sure just what question is being argued or how to get out of the procedural maze. If humble meetings of ordinary mortals can produce complex sequences of motions, it is no wonder that the most powerful legislative bodies spend so much time trying to extract themselves from procedural quagmires so that they can come to the point and make decisions. Helen Dewar, an award winning journalist, has made these comments about covering Congress ("1984 Dirksen", 2–4)

> I know a lot of reporters who cover normal activities who come up here and they can't understand it, and they don't like it, because it works in such a strange way. It seems like endless quorum calls and delays and stalls. . . .
>
> It can be very trying, particularly when you are used to fast-paced stories that have a beginning, a middle, and an end. The Senate is just an endless middle. . . .
>
> I think Congress is confusing. And it works in this messy fashion. Nothing

ever really begins and ends. People don't understand its role. They get turned off by the politicking that's going on and think that's just a bunch of politicians who don't accomplish anything anyway.

One example of procedural confusion in 1975 was cited by the *Wall Street Journal*. Amid a flurry of motions and points of order by Sen. James Allen (D.–Ala.), the Senate voted on

> a motion to table a motion to reconsider a vote to table an appeal of a ruling that a point of order was not in order against a motion to table another point of order against a motion to bring to a vote the motion to call up the resolution that would institute the rules change.

Procedural confusion is increased by some members' purposeful use of stalling or manipulative tactics. Many members of Congress use their knowledge of procedural rules as a major tactical weapon, and in many cases the fate or final shape of legislation has been determined by procedural tactics. Sen. James Allen (D.–Ala.) was particularly adept in his use of the rules to affect legislation. One of Senator Allen's greatest coups occurred in late 1973 when, as the holidays approached, he used the threat of a filibuster to derail the efforts of Sen. Edward Kennedy (D.–Mass.) to add a provision for federal financing of elections to a debt limit bill.

A more recent example of procedural confusion and partisan wrangling occurred in the House of Representatives on Thursday, October 29, 1987, when Speaker Jim Wright held a vote open for ten minutes until Rep. Jim Chapman (D.–Tex.) switched sides on the vote (Wehr 1987, 2653). Thus by a 206 to 205 margin, the speaker was able to secure passage of the so-called Guaranteed Deficit Reduction Act, involving $11.9 billion in new taxes and $3 billion in spending cuts, but also $14 billion in spending increases including a new $2700 pay increase for Congress to be tacked onto an earlier congressional pay raise. Republican floor leader Robert Michel (R.–Ill.), speaking for frustrated Republicans and a few disgruntled Democrats, said Speaker Wright was "getting right on the fringe where the speaker himself is getting mighty damned autocratic." Wright responded that he was enjoying the fight and that it was just another Republican attempt to contrive an issue.

THE SEQUENCE OF MOTIONS

Earlier in this chapter we saw how bills are reported by standing committees and then are placed on the chamber's agenda to be debated on the floor on a given day. That a bill gets this far means that there have been strong pressures for its passage. But floor acceptance of bills that have survived the early stages in the legislative gauntlet is by no means certain. Some bills are ultimately rejected, some are amended before passage, some pass without substantial floor amendment.

Several kinds of motions may be made by members, and the rules of the Senate and House, interpreted by the presiding officer on advice from the parliamentarian, determine which motions have precedence, that is, which are to be decided first. A motion to recommit a bill is less privileged than a motion to table a bill and would therefore be superseded; the vote would be taken first on the motion to table.

Motions to amend the pending legislation are particularly important in shaping laws. What motions are in order? Consider a bill on the floor stating that the Bureau of Labor Statistics of the Department of Labor is to calculate and publish each month a current commodity price index. A member thinking it would be more helpful to have an index calculated and published more frequently might move to amend the bill by striking the words "each month" and inserting instead the words "every two weeks." As debate continues, it becomes clear that many members believe every two weeks is not often enough. One of them moves to amend the pending amendment by changing the time period to every week. But before the amendment to the amendment is resolved, other members express a preference for less frequent calculation of the index. The proper parliamentary move at this point is to move a substitute amendment to change the basic wording "every two weeks" to read "every six months." It is still possible at this point in the parliamentary skirmishing to propose a final amendment to the substitute amendment, one that proposes that "every six months" be changed to "every three months." This is as far as amendments on a point in a bill may be carried; to put it another way, this is as far as "the amendment tree" can branch out (see figure 9-1). A decision must be

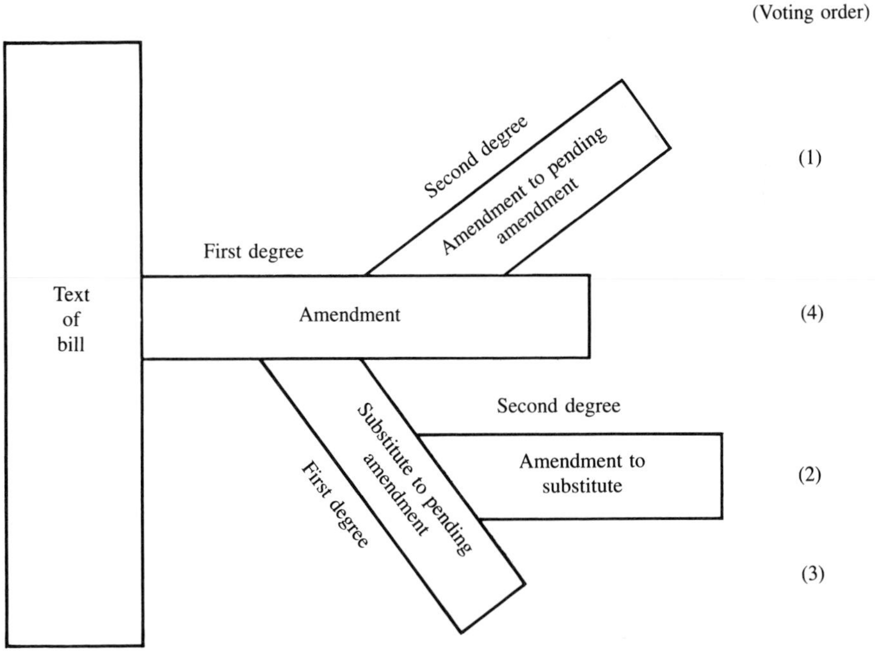

Figure 9-1. The basic amendment tree

reached, and the sequence of determination of the conflicting motions is determined by the standing rules. The idea is to "perfect" the two first-degree alternatives before the body chooses between them. The first question that is to be resolved is the amendment to the amendment (the "every week" proposal). Then comes the vote on the amendment to the substitute amendment (the "every three months" proposal), then the vote on the substitute ("every six months"), and finally the vote on the basic amendment.

There are several guidelines for making amendments. First, amendments should be timely. A bill should be worked through section by section. When the chamber is discussing the merits of section 3 of the bill in question, an amendment should not be offered pertaining to section 2. Second, only one amendment may be pending and discussed at a given time. Third, all amendments must be different; repetitious amendments are out of order. Fourth, under the principle called "the bigger bite," amendments should be moved in such a way that all parts of the bill affected by the amendment should be included in the motion. If a unifying idea is involved that would amend sections 2 and 3, then both sections should be included in one motion rather than having to move two separate amendments having the same effect on sections 2 and 3. Fifth, amendments must be germane, or related to the issue. Sixth, clearly dilatory (delaying) amendments should be ruled out of order, though in practice they seldom are. Seventh, once an amendment has been accepted, the specific point so amended may not be amended further. Finally, committee amendments are acted on before amendments from the floor.

The amendment tree fits into larger procedural regulations, such as a rule on a particular bill calling for no amendments or a rule calling for one hour of debate for each side. The amendment tree emphasizes that debate is a matter of progressively narrowing the legislature's choices—a sort of funnel effect. Sometimes this funneling, or focusing, effect can seem irrational or unfair, since the final decisions are affected by the sequence of amendments. The aim of the amendment tree, though, is wisdom and fairness in legislation through a neutral system of procedure.

Adoption of an amendment shuts off debate on that point. Theoretically, there can be an endless number of second-degree amendments in sequence, as long as each amendment is defeated. The text of the bill becomes unamendable only when all branches have been amended, that is, when the amendments have been accepted.

SUMMARY

The basic purposes of procedural rules are to promote timely, open, rational, and thorough discussion of issues. Congressional procedure has three aspects: (1) determining the order in which various bills are to be considered; (2) defining and regulating the stages through which a particular bill must pass if it is to become a law; and (3) determining the rules by which bills may be debated, amended, and approved on the floor of the legislative chamber. Maintaining a healthy and proper balance between complete freedom and perfect order is a constant source of tension for congressional leaders and strategists. Individual members are often torn between the need to know substantive information about specific policy proposals and the need to understand the general procedural rules. Certainly knowledge of the rules of procedure can help a member achieve important legislative goals, and ignorance of the same rules can prevent a member from having an impact on legislation being debated. Knowing the rules helps make a member more powerful and effective.

NOTES

1. Usually, the differences between House and Senate bills are resolved when the first chamber agrees to the changes that have been made by the second chamber. Sometimes, though, a new compromise version is worked out by the conference committee. The new version must then be returned to both chambers for approval. In a rare instance of postconference intransigence between House and Senate in late 1985 and early 1986, H. R. 3128 went to each chamber five times after the original conference action on December 19, as neither side could draft an adjustment that would please the other chamber. Finally, on March 20, 1986, the House accepted a Senate proposal made on March 14, and the bill was cleared for the president.
2. For what is still one of the best and clearest extended narratives of how a bill progresses through Congress, see Miller 1962, 143–160.
3. Until 1959, a vote of two-thirds of the entire Senate was needed to invoke cloture. This was relaxed to specify two-thirds of the senators present and voting. The present three-fifths rule was adopted 22 February, 1979, by a vote of seventy-eight to sixteen (see Cooper 1979, 319). For a comment on the filibuster's continuing frustration of Majority Leader Robert Dole's leadership efforts in recent years, see Malbin 1985, 2–4.
4. For the parallel story on House action, see Towell, Cohodas, and Pressman 1985, 563–571.
5. For a discussion of how congressional processes discourage adequate treatment by television network news, see Ornstein and Robinson, 1986.

REFERENCES

BAILEY, STEPHEN K. *Congress Makes a Law: The Story Behind the Employment Act of 1946.* New York: Columbia University Press, 1950.

BERMAN, DANIEL M. *A Bill Becomes a Law: The Civil Rights Act of 1960.* New York: Macmillan, 1962.

Congressional Record. "Daily Digest." Washington D. C., Dec. 31, 1948; Aug. 23, 1958; Oct. 22, 1966; Oct. 14, 1968; Oct. 14, 1978; Jan. 21, 1986; Jan. 6, 1987.

Congressional Record. Washington, D. C., Mar. 18, 1985; Mar. 19, 1985; Mar. 25, 1985; Mar. 26, 1985; Feb. 6, 1986; Mar. 12, 1986; Apr. 11, 1986.

COOPER, ANN. "Senate Limits Post-Cloture Filibusters." *Congressional Quarterly Weekly Report* (24 February 1979): 319–320.

EIDENBERG, EUGENE, and MOREY, ROY. *An Act of Congress: The Legislative Process and the Making of Education Policy.* New York: Norton, 1969.

FROMAN, JR., LEWIS A. *The Congressional Process: Strategies, Rules, and Procedures.* Boston: Little, Brown, 1967.

GORDON, STRATHEARN. *Our Parliament*. London: Hansard Society, 1964.

GRANAT, DIANE. "Historic Votes, Long Nights Cap Final Week of Congress." *Congressional Quarterly Weekly Report* (21 December 1985): 2663–2664.

HOOK, JANET. "Senators Look for New Ways to Increase Efficiency." *Congressional Quarterly Weekly Report* (5 December 1987): 3001–3002.

JONES, CHARLES O. *The United States Congress*. Homewood, Ill.: Dorsey Press, 1982.

MALBIN, MICHAEL. "Leading a Senate Filibuster." *Extensions* (Spring 1985): 2–4. Norman, Okla.: University of Oklahoma, Carl Albert Congressional Research and Studies Center.

MILLER, CLEM. *Member of the House*. New York: Scribner's, 1962.

"1984 Dirksen Award Winner Helen Dewar on the Budget Beat, Political Reform, and Bumping into Senators." *Report* (August 1985): 2–4.

NUTTING, BRIAN. "Cameras an Accepted Feature Now: After One Year of Television, Senate Is Basically Unchanged." *Congressional Quarterly Weekly Report* (30 May 1987): 1140.

OLESZEK, WALTER J. *Congressional Procedures and the Policy Process*. 2nd ed. Washington, D. C.: Congressional Quarterly Press, 1984.

OLSON, DAVID M. *The Politics of Legislation: A Congressional Simulation*. New York: Praeger, 1976.

ORNSTEIN, NORMAN J., MANN, THOMAS E., MALBIN, MICHAEL J., SCHICK, ALLEN, and BIBBY, JOHN F. *Vital Statistics on Congress, 1984–1985*. Washington, D. C.: American Enterprise Institute, 1984.

ORNSTEIN, NORMAN, and ROBINSON, MICHAEL. "Where's All the Coverage? The Case of Our Disappearing Congress." *TV Guide* (11–17 January 1986): 4–10.

POLSBY, NELSON W. "Two Strategies of Influence: Choosing a Majority Leader, 1962." In Robert L. Peabody and Nelson W. Polsby (eds.) *New Perspectives on the House of Representatives*. Chicago: Rand-McNally, 1977.

REDMAN, ERIC. *The Dance of Legislation*. New York: Simon & Schuster, 1973.

REID, T. R. *Congressional Odyssey: The Saga of a Senate Bill*. New York: W. H. Freeman, 1980.

SULLIVAN, TERRY. *Procedural Structure, Success, and Influence in Congress*. New York: Praeger, 1984.

TOWELL, PAT, COHODAS, NADINE, and PRESSMAN, STEVEN. "Senate Hands Reagan Victory on MX Missile." *Congressional Quarterly Weekly Report* (23 March 1985): 515–523.

U. S. CONGRESS, SENATE. Committee on Appropriations. 99th Cong., 1st sess., 1985. S. Rept. 99-14.

WEHR, ELIZABETH. "Republicans Cry 'Foul' Over Floor Tactics: Wright Finds a Vote to Pass Reconciliation Bill." *Congressional Quarterly Weekly Report* (31 October 1987): 2653–2655.

X CONGRESSIONAL VOTING BEHAVIOR

Several hundred times each year, members of Congress publicly cast votes that can lose them their seats in the next election. Even though, as noted in chapter 9, Congress does not pass a very impressive number of substantial laws in a given year, members do deal with procedural motions, amendments, amendments to amendments, and substitute amendments as well as final passage of bills. Since a number of bills pass in one chamber but do not get through the other chamber, the number of roll calls on which a member must take a public position is larger than the number of laws produced.

While a member's political fate does not hang on every issue, roll-call votes on any question may be used against a member in the next campaign, and thus most roll calls involve some political risk. These votes are tangible, recorded actions that reflect the individual member's beliefs, goals, and preferences. Partisan strategists study voting patterns for possible use in planning a campaign. Scholars and journalists study voting patterns to better understand the forces that affect congressional decision making.

There are many approaches to the study of congressional voting behavior. Most recent studies have used computer technology and multivariate modeling to develop complex explanations of voting decisions. Much attention has been devoted to "cue giving" and "cue givers" to show how members respond to one another's actions in deciding how to vote. Many voting studies have been concerned with the impact of pressure from the president, party leaders, and ideological or sectional interest groups on legislators' support for bills. Some studies have concentrated on pairwise voting, measuring how often a pair (dyad) of legislators vote the same way. Some studies expand on pairwise analysis, concentrating on the formation, composition, and influence of blocs, or groups of legislators who habitually vote the same way. The essential goal of roll-call research is to explain both aggregate voting outcomes and individual voting decisions.

This chapter (1) considers the importance of party, ideology, and the president in shaping aggregate voting outcomes; (2) classifies and analyzes 1985 roll-call votes with respect to the voting behavior of Democrats and Republicans in the House and Senate; and (3) discusses the voting decisions of individual members.

193

INFLUENCES ON ROLL-CALL VOTING

A few years ago, Rep. Lee Hamilton (D.–Ind.) undertook to identify for his constituents the major factors that seem to influence how a member of Congress votes on legislation. Hamilton believed that members have three goals when they vote on the floor: (1) to make good policy, (2) to gain respect within Congress, and (3) to get reelected. Hamilton lists the factors influencing voting in this order: constituents, colleagues, lobbies, the president, party leadership (party leaders inside Congress are far more important than national or district party leaders), the media, and the member's staff.

Hamilton's comments are based on his own experiences and observations. Scholars have adopted more objective and sophisticated methods for measuring the impact of various factors on congressional voting decisions. Advanced statistical methods make it possible to sort out which of several factors has the greatest impact on roll-call voting decisions as well as to compute the cumulative impact of several factors on voting. It is beyond our present purpose to describe or summarize these findings, which, in any case, are generally drawn from a limited range of issues, a short time span, and a single legislative body. In this section, we discuss the relative effects of political party affiliation, ideology, and the president's position on congressional roll-call voting outcomes.

Political Party

Not surprisingly, the characteristic that is the best predictor of how members will vote on roll calls is party affiliation. Party voting can be measured for individual members and for the aggregate of all party members. For individual members, the basic calculation is the percentage of roll calls where the member votes in agreement with the majority of party colleagues. For the aggregate party, the basic calculation is how often majorities of the two parties are opposed to one another.

Tables 10-1 and 10-2 show the distribution of 1985 senators and representatives who voted in agreement with the majority of their respective parties. Several easterners, many of them on the liberal side of the Republican spectrum, are located toward the bottom of the Republican party unity scale. On the Democratic side, many southerners are near the bottom of the scale.

Somewhat less than half of the congressional roll calls in the postwar period have resulted in the majority of one party voting in opposition to the majority of the other party (see table 8-3 in Ornstein et al. 1984, 182, which is based on calculations in the *Congressional Quarterly Weekly Report*). Annual figures from 1953 through 1983 show that in the House, party-line votes appeared on 59 percent of the roll calls (the high figure in the period) in 1957 and on only 27 percent of the roll calls (the low figure) in 1970 and 1972. In eight of these thirty-one years, party-line votes occurred at least half the time, while in thirteen of the same years party-line votes occurred less than 40 percent of the time. In the other ten years, the party-line percentage fell to between 40 and 49. As for the Senate in the same period, in only

Table 10-1. Party unity scores in the Senate, 1985

Score	Democrats	Republicans
90 to 100	0	2
80 to 89	6	11
70 to 79	13	8
60 to 69	11	10
50 to 59	2	6
40 to 49	2	2
30 to 39	3	5
20 to 29	1	2
10 to 19	7	4
0 to 9	0	1
−1 to −19	2	2
Totals	47	53

Note: Each senator's party unity score is the party agreement percentage minus the party disagreement percentage. A minus sign indicates the senator voted more frequently against than with the majority position of the party.
Source: Calculated by the author from data in *Congressional Quarterly Weekly Report,* Jan. 11, 1986, 89.

three years (1956, 1961, and 1966) did the party-line percentage ascend as high as 50. Ten times the percentage was between 30 to 39; the rest of the time it was between 40 to 49. Party-line voting in the Senate was lowest in 1955 (30 percent of the roll calls) and highest in 1961 (62 percent).

The percentage of party members voting in agreement with the majority of their party colleagues in the House and Senate has been remarkably consistent over the past three decades (see table 8-4 in Ornstein et al. 1984, 183–184). In fact, in

Table 10-2. Party unity scores in the House of Representatives, 1985

Score	Democrats	Republicans
90 to 100	23	6
80 to 89	72	27
70 to 79	51	32
60 to 69	33	32
50 to 59	26	25
40 to 49	19	20
30 to 39	6	12
20 to 29	4	7
10 to 19	8	9
0 to 9	6	0
−1 to −20	2	9
−21 to −100	2	3
Totals	252	182

Note: The score is calculated as in table 10-1.
Speaker O'Neill (Democrat) did not vote.
Source: Calculated by the author from data in *Congressional Quarterly Weekly Report,* Jan. 11, 1986, 90–91.

only two years did the party support score for any caucus group fall below 70 percent. Both cases involved Senate Republicans; in 1974 only 68 percent of the Republicans voted in agreement with a majority of their party on party-unity votes, and in 1978 this figure was only 66 percent. Otherwise, for Democrats and Republicans in the House and Senate from 1954 through 1983, the percentages varied between 70 and 85. The figure for southern Democrats as a group generally ran 10 or more percentage points below the figure for all Democrats.

Ideological Voting

The terms *liberal* and *conservative* are often used when discussing ideology in American politics. The general difference between liberals and conservatives can be simply stated as respective preferences for larger and stronger governmental activity, particularly in the protection of individual rights (the liberal approach) or for the reduction of the scope of government and reliance instead on private initiative and activity (the conservative approach). These basic definitions can be used as a first step in classifying roll-call issues and thereby measuring each legislator's liberal or conservative voting tendency.

However, we will use a more objective basis for ideological differentiation in our discussion. The best-known method for measuring ideological voting in Congress is based on the idea of the conservative coalition, a concept and term used by *Congressional Quarterly* analysts. *Congressional Quarterly* defines the conservative coalition as all Republicans and southern Democrats. A conservative coalition vote occurs whenever the majority of this coalition votes in opposition to the majority of nonsouthern Democrats. On the basis of these roll calls only, *Congressional Quarterly* calculates a conservative coalition support score and a conservative coalition opposition score for each member.

Over the years, the conservative coalition has appeared on about 20 percent of the roll calls in the House and Senate (see table 8-5, Ornstein et al. 1984, 185) and has been on the winning side of issues far more often than on the losing side. For example, in 1983 the conservative coalition appeared on 18 percent of the roll calls in the House and was victorious on 71 percent of those votes. In the Senate in 1983, the conservative coalition appeared on 12 percent of the roll calls and was successful on 89 percent of those votes. A notably "poor" year for the conservative coalition was 1965, the height of President Johnson's Great Society program, when the coalition appeared on 25 percent of House roll calls (with a success rate of only 25 percent) and 24 percent of the Senate roll calls (with a success rate of only 39 percent).[1] Obviously, large percentages of southern Democrats and Republicans vote in agreement with the conservative coalition. Over the years, northern Democrats in both chambers have voted in agreement with the conservative coalition on about one out of four coalition roll calls.

Tables 10-3 and 10-4 show the relationship between ideology and political party in 1985. The data in these tables can be simplified for the purpose of drawing some conclusions about the overall ideology of Congress and about the relationship

Table 10-3.   The relationship of party and ideology
in the 1985 Senate

Ideological score	Democrats	Republicans
70 to 100	2	29
30 to 69	11	16
0 to 29	7	5
−1 to −29	4	2
−30 to −69	18	1
−70 to −100	5	0
Totals	47	53

Note: Score was computed by subtracting the conservative
coalition opposition score from the conservative coalition
support score.
Source: Calculated and categorized by the author from data
in *Congressional Quarterly Weekly Report,* Jan. 11, 1986,
80.

between party and ideology. Let us begin by reducing the ideological categories
from six to three. We will consider those members who vote in support of the
conservative coalition on 70 percent or more of the roll calls to be "conservatives."
"Moderates" will be those who vote on the conservative side up to 69 percent of the
time. (Obviously, this means that these "moderates" are really more conservative
than liberal, but all we are concerned about here is keeping the members in order.)
The remaining members are "liberals," those who oppose the conservative coalition
more often than they vote with it.

This simplification of the data in tables 10-3 and 10-4 reveals a Senate that is
somewhat less liberal than the House. The Senate breakdown is 31 percent con-

Table 10-4.   The relationship of party and ideology
in the House of Representatives, 1985

Ideological score	Democrats	Republicans
70 to 100	20	107
30 to 69	35	58
0 to 29	23	13
−1 to −29	36	1
−30 to −69	69	3
−70 to −100	69	0
Totals	252	182

Note: Computed by subtracting the conservative coalition
opposition score from the conservative coalition support
score.
Speaker O'Neill (Democrat) did not vote.
Source: Calculated and categorized by the author from data
in *Congressional Quarterly Weekly Report,* Jan. 11, 1986,
78–79.

servative, 39 percent moderate, and 30 percent liberal; the House breakdown is 29 percent conservative, 30 percent moderate, and 41 percent liberal. No single category constitutes a majority in either chamber, so the moderates held the balance of voting power in both.

In both chambers, the larger number of conservatives were Republicans and the larger number of liberals were Democrats. Twenty-nine of 31 Senate conservatives (94 percent) and 197 of 127 House conservatives (84 percent) were Republicans. Twenty-seven of 30 Senate liberals (90 percent) and 174 of 178 House liberals (98 percent) were Democrats. Democrats comprised 46 percent of the 39 Senate moderates and 45 percent of the 129 House moderates.

Ideological voting data can also be used to describe the ideological orientation of the standing committees. Table 10-5 shows the composite ideological position of

Table 10-5. Mean conservative coalition support scores for members of House and Senate standing committees, 1983

Mean score	House committees	Senate committees
100		
75		Agriculture
74	Armed Services	
70		Armed Services
66		Appropriations
65	Veterans Affairs	
63		Budget, Finance
61		Judiciary
60	Agriculture	Environment and Public Works, Governmental Affairs, Rules and Administration
59		Banking, Housing, and Urban Affairs, Veterans Affairs
58		Commerce, Science, and Technology, Energy and Natural Resources
56	Public Works and Transportation	Labor and Human Resources
55	Science and Technology, Small Business, Standards of Official Conduct, Ways and Means	
54	Interior and Insular Affairs	
53	Government Operations, Merchant Marine and Fisheries	
52	Appropriations	Foreign Relations
50	Banking, Finance, and Urban Affairs, Budget, Energy and Commerce	
49	House Administration	
48	Rules	
47	Judiciary, Post Office and Civil Service	
42	Foreign Affairs	
40	District of Columbia	
39	Education and Labor	
0		

Note: 100 is the maximum conservative coalition support score; 0 is the minimum.
Source: Ornstein et al. 1984, 187–189, 193–195. The same source also gives data for the 1959, 1969, 1977, 1979, and 1981 sessions.

the House and Senate standing committees in 1983 voting. It may be noted that the Agriculture and Armed Services committees are notably conservative in both chambers, while the labor and foreign policy committees are on the liberal end of the scale in both House and Senate.

Table 10-5 is based on the mean ideological scores for all members of the various standing committees. Another dimension of the ideological division within committees is the percentile difference in the mean positions of the two party contingents on each committee. To illustrate this, table 10-6 shows how far apart the Republican and Democratic contingents on each committee are. On some committees there is considerable ideological distance between the two parties. This distance could result from conscious effort by the respective party leaders when making committee assignments to emphasize ideological differences between the parties on bills within that committee's jurisdiction, or this distance might also have something to do with the operations and decision-making processes of the committee. Whatever the case, there is no apparent consistency between chambers as to which policy areas have committees of relatively high or low ideological disparity.

Presidential Support

The position of the president on many congressional roll calls is announced and well known, and hence it is a simple matter to measure each president's success in

Table 10-6. Congressional committees categorized on the basis of the difference in mean ideological positions of their Democratic and Republican members, 1983

Size of difference	House committees	Senate committees
Considerable (50 or more percentiles)	Post Office and Civil Service District of Columbia Rules Judiciary Interior and Insular Affairs Budget Energy and Commerce Standards of Official Conduct House Administration	Labor and Human Resources Banking, Housing, and Urban Affairs Foreign Relations
Moderate (30 to 49 percentiles)	Foreign Affairs Ways and Means Education and Labor Public Works and Transportation Appropriations Banking, Finance, and Urban Affairs Government Operations Merchant Marine and Fisheries Veterans Affairs Science and Technology	Armed Services Judiciary Budget Rules and Administration Environment and Public Works Veterans Affairs Appropriations Energy and Natural Resources
Slight (less than 29 percentiles)	Armed Services Small Business	Governmental Affairs Commerce, Science, and Technology Agriculture Finance

Source: Ornstein et al. 1984, 187–189, 193–195.

influencing congressional voting behavior. According to Ornstein and associates (1984, 171): "Presidential success is mainly a function of the number of seats in Congress held by the president's party." In the period from 1953 to 1983, the president with the highest success rate in congressional roll calls was John F. Kennedy, who "won" an average of 85 percent of the House and Senate roll calls on which he took a position in his three years in the White House. Other recent presidents rank as follows: Johnson, 83 percent over five years; Carter, 76 percent over four years; Reagan, 73 percent over three years; Eisenhower, 72 percent over eight years; Nixon, 67 percent over six years; and Ford, 58 percent over three years.

The best single year a president ever had in this period was 1965, when President Johnson enjoyed a 93 percent success rate. President Eisenhower recorded 89 percent in 1953, when his Republican party held narrow majorities in each chamber. Kennedy's high figure for both chambers combined was 87 percent in 1963. Reagan's 82 percent success rate in 1981 was the highest for a president whose party was not in control of both chambers. Reagan, as one would expect, fared consistently better in the Republican-controlled Senate (88, 83, and 86 percent in 1981, 1982, and 1983) than in the Democratic House (72, 56, and 48).

The president's position invariably coincides more frequently with the votes of members from the president's own party than with the votes of opposition party members (Ornstein et al. 1984, table 8-2, 180–181). Data for 1986, published in *Congressional Quarterly Weekly Report* (Oct. 25, 1986, 2691) show that forty Republicans voted for the president's announced position at least 70 percent of the time, while the remaining thirteen Republicans voted for the president from 30 to 70 percent of the time. Of the Democrats in 1986, three (Heflin of Alabama, Long of Louisiana, and Hollings of South Carolina) voted with the president at least 70 percent of the time, 24 voted with him from 30 to 70 percent of the time, and the remaining twenty voted with him less than 30 percent of the time.

PARTY PATTERNS IN ROLL-CALL VOTING

Legislative issues and the unpredictable nature of procedural developments can have strange effects on party regularity in congressional roll-call voting. There can be gradations in the degree to which a party divides on a given question. We will use such gradations to define five categories of roll calls (see table 10-7). The party may be 100 percent on one side of the question, or its dominant bloc may be either at the 80 percent level or barely at the 51 percent level. For purposes of this classification scheme and analysis, we will accept a party division of sixty-forty as the minimum condition of a substantial majority. Any roll call closer than sixty-forty to a perfectly even fifty-fifty split will be considered a split roll call for that party.

The first type of roll-call result is one where the substantial majority of both parties is on the same side of the issue; we refer to this as a type A roll call (Clem 1981, 69–71).

A type B roll call has substantial majorities of the two parties on opposite sides

Table 10-7. Five types of roll-call outcomes illustrated by hypothetical results in the Senate

Roll-call type	Votes	Majority party (Democrats) (n = 55)	Minority party (Republicans) (n = 45)	Total
A	Yes	50	40	90
	No	5	5	10
B	Yes	50	5	55
	No	5	40	45
C	Yes	29	22	51
	No	26	23	49
D	Yes	50	22	72
	No	5	23	28
E	Yes	29	40	69
	No	26	5	31

Note: See text for fuller explanation of the roll-call types.

of the question. This is the most "satisfactory" type of party pattern, since it reflects deep differences and genuine alternatives between the parties. A type C roll call is one on which both parties are considerably split. A type D roll call is one in which the majority party has a substantial majority on one side, while the minority party is split. A type E roll call (quite dangerous to the legislative goals of the majority party) occurs when the majority party is split on the question, while the minority party produces a substantial majority on one side.

Table 10-8 categorizes all congressional roll calls of 1985 on the basis of these five types. The most common type of roll call in 1985 was type B. Roll calls with both parties voting on the same side (type A) were next most frequent in occurrence. Comparatively few roll calls caused one or both of the parties to split. Interestingly, the minority party in both chambers split its vote (type D) more often than the majority party (type E). The rarest pattern was type C, where both parties split their vote. The frequency order of the five roll-call types—namely, B, A, D, E, and C—was the same in both chambers.

Table 10-8. A count of five roll-call types in the House and Senate, 1985

Roll-call type	House Number	House Percent	Senate Number	Senate Percent	Total Number	Total Percent
A	136	31.0	149	39.1	285	34.8
B	230	52.4	151	39.6	381	46.5
C	10	2.3	6	1.6	16	2.0
D	41	9.3	39	10.2	80	9.8
E	22	5.0	36	9.4	58	7.1
Total	439	100.0	381	99.9[a]	820	100.2[a]

Note: See text for explanation of roll-call types.
[a]Rounding error.
Source: Calculated by the author from roll-call information provided throughout the year in *Congressional Quarterly Weekly Report.*

Further investigation of type B, C, and E roll calls reveals that on several occasions the minority party's position won the day against a majority party, which took the opposite position or split its vote. In the House, the Republican minority position prevailed against the majority party on 27 roll calls (type B), and the Republicans also prevailed on 19 roll calls when the Democratic party was split (type E). For example, on May 9, Rep. Danny Burton (R.–Ind.), moved an amendment to delete from the State Department authorization bill funds designed to provide special religious sensitivity instruction for U. S. foreign service officers. The Burton amendment was adopted 224 to 189 in a type B roll call when Republicans divided 145 to 30 (a net yes margin of 115 votes) and the Democrats divided 79 to 159 (a net no margin of 80 votes). A type E example in the House was the June 6 vote to adopt the amendment offered by Rep. Bob Edgar (D.–Penn.) to amend the amendment offered by Rep. Jamie Whitten (D.–Miss.). (Edgar's motion was to reduce from $150 to $51 million the funds added for water projects of the U. S. Army Corps of Engineers.) The Edgar amendment passed by one vote, 203 to 202, with Republicans favoring it 108 to 69 (a net yes margin of 39 votes) and Democrats opposed 95 to 133 (a net no margin of 38 votes).

In the Senate, the Democratic minority carried the day on 32 roll calls in opposition to the Republican majority (type B) and on another 35 roll calls when the Republicans split (type E). For example, a type B roll call occurred October 10 on a motion by Sen. Bob Packwood (R.–Ore.) to table, or kill, the amendment by Sen. John Glenn (D.–Ohio) to affirm an existing requirement that presidential budgets include proposals for eliminating any gap (deficit) between spending and revenues and to bar such budgets, beginning in F. Y. 1987, from proposing increases in the federal debt for that purpose. The Packwood motion was rejected 33 to 65, the Republicans dividing 33 to 18 (a net yes margin of 15 votes), and the Democrats cast all 47 of their votes against the motion. A Senate type E roll call developed on September 26 on the amendment by Sen. James Abdnor (R.–S.D.) to add $1.5 million to the appropriation for the Office of Management and Budget, restoring the full amount of the administration's request. The Abdnor amendment was defeated 24 to 72, the Republicans dividing 24 to 27, while the Democrats were entirely on the negative side, 0 to 45.

On two Senate roll calls where both parties split their vote (type C), the minority Democratic margin established the winning side. An example occurred September 24 on the amendment proposed by Senator Abdnor to exempt fertilizer, animal feed, and any raw material used in their production from the superfund excise tax. Abdnor's amendment was narrowly defeated, 46 to 48, with Republicans giving it a six-vote yes margin (28 to 22) and the Democrats an eight-vote no margin (18 to 26).

As a general rule, type A, B, and D roll calls can be considered victories for the majority leadership. It should be noted that a type B roll call, depending on the way two parties split their votes, could provide the minority side with a victory. The type D result is perhaps the most impressive majority party success, since it means the majority has succeeded in splitting the minority party while keeping itself at least reasonably cohesive. A type C roll call represents somewhat of a failure for both parties, though perhaps the minority side can regard it as something of a moral victory. A type E roll call is the best sort of victory the minority party can hope for and represents a debacle for the majority party.

In the previous chapter, the legislative history of P. L. 99-17, which provided for the construction of twenty-one MX missiles, was presented as an example of how a bill moves through Congress on its way to becoming a law. We return again in the case that follows to the resolution of the MX missile issue in 1985 to give a particular example of an important congressional activity: the process of deciding whether to vote for or against a specific proposition. No single vote is typical. Analysts of legislative voting behavior are particularly interested in deviations from consistency with party, ideological, or regional groupings on the part of individual members. This example uses the Senate vote on final passage of the MX measure to focus our discussion of legislative voting behavior on specific issues and legislators and suggests how unpredictable are the motives and pressures that influence members' voting decisions.

Senate Voting Behavior
on the 1985 MX Missile Issue

The Senate vote on the MX missile issue was a general, though not perfect, party vote: 82 percent of the Republicans voted for the construction of the missiles, while 82 percent of the Democrats opposed construction (see table 10-9). However, about one out of five members of each party voted irregularly, and the question arises as to why these eighteen senators voted as they did against the majority of their party colleagues.

Comparing the distribution of Republican senators in table 10-9 with table 10-1 shows that all eight of the dissident Republicans on the MX vote had scores in the middle or lower ranges in the party-unity scale (see table 10-1). Senator Kassebaum was the only dissident Republican whose party unity score was above 50. But at the same time, there were a large number of Republicans on the low end of the scale in table 10-1 who voted for the MX missile: D'Amato, Packwood, Chafee, Kasten, Heinz, Specter, and Mathias, to name a few. Similarly, eight of the ten dissident Democrats were in the lower half of the Democratic party unity scale, and the other two were between the 60 and 80 percent marks. Several other Democrats with comparatively low party-unity scores voted against the missile.

A similar degree of relationship existed between ideology (shown in table 10-3) and the MX vote. The Republican dissidents were all on the more liberal side of their party, and the dissident Democrats were all on the more conservative side of their party.

As to region, none of the Republican dissidents came from the southern

Table 10-9.   The Senate vote on the MX appropriation bill (S. J. Res. 75), March 1985

Vote	Republicans	Democrats
Yes	Denton AL, Danforth MO, Evans WA Murkowski AK, Hecht NV, Gorton WA Stevens AK, Laxalt NV, Kasten WI Goldwater AZ, Humphrey NH, Simpson WY Wilson CA, Rudman NH, Wallop WY Armstrong CO, Domenici NM Roth DE, D'Amato NY, East NC Hawkins FL, Helms NC, Nickles OK Mattingly GA, McClure ID, Packwood OR Symms ID, Heinz PA, Lugar IN Specter PA, Quayle IN, Chafee RI Dole KS, Thurmond SC, McConnell KY Abdnor SD, Cohen ME, Gramm TX Mathias MD, Garn UT, Hatch UT Boschwitz MN, Trible VA, Cochran MS Warner VA	Heflin AL DeConcini AZ Nunn GA Long LA Stennis MS Zorinsky NE Boren OK Gore TN Bentsen TX Byrd WV
No	Weicker CT, Grassley IA Kassebaum KS, Durenberger MN Andrews ND, Hatfield OR Pressler SD, Stafford VT	Bumpers AR, Levin MI, Pryor AR Riegle MI, Cranston CA, Eagleton MO Hart CO, Baucus MT, Dodd CT Melcher MT, Biden DE, Exon NE Chiles FL, Bradley NJ, Inouye HI Lautenberg NJ, Matsunaga HI, Bingaman NM Dixon IL, Simon IL, Moynihan, NY Burdick ND, Harkin IA, Glenn OH Ford KY, Metzenbaum OH, Pell RI Johnston LA, Hollings SC, Mitchell ME Sasser TN, Sarbanes MD, Leahy VT Kennedy MA, Rockefeller WV, Kerry MA Proxmire WI

Note: phi = +0.64.
Each senator voted the same way on S. J. Res. 71, the MX authorization bill, as on the above appropriations resolution.
Source: Calculated by the author from data in *Congressional Quarterly Weekly Report,* Mar. 23, 1985, 553.

part of the country. Most of the Democratic dissidents were southerners, the exceptions being DeConcini of Arizona, Zorinsky of Nebraska, and Byrd of West Virginia.

Twenty-one states had senators who split their votes on the MX question, thereby cancelling each other out. In thirteen of these states, the senators were of opposite parties. In four states (Kansas, Minnesota, Oregon, and South Dakota), Republican senators split their votes. The same thing happened with the two Democratic senators of another four states (Louisiana, Nebraska, Tennessee, and West Virginia).

Nine states had senators who voted on the same side of the MX question in spite of the fact that they were not members of the same party: Alabama, Arizona, Mississippi, Oklahoma, and Texas voted pro, and Connecticut, Iowa, North Dakota, and Vermont voted con. Map 10-1 shows the sectional distribu-

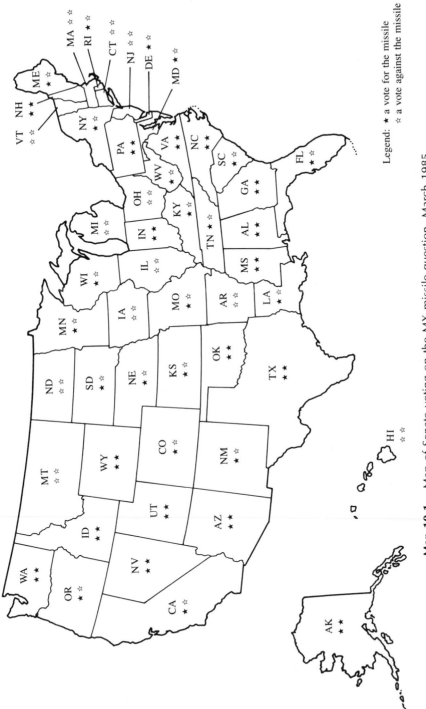

Legend: ★ a vote for the missile
☆ a vote against the missile

Map 10-1. Map of Senate voting on the MX missile question, March 1985

tion of support for and opposition to the missile construction program. MX supporters were in the majority in the southern (eighteen to six) and western (eighteen to eight) states, while MX opponents were in the majority in the eastern (fourteen to ten) and midwestern (seventeen to nine) states.

The sectional support pattern shown in the map on Senate voting is largely confirmed when House voting is studied. The southern state representatives supported the MX authorization strongly, eighty-nine to thirty-two; those from the western states supported it by a narrow margin, forty-three to forty-two. There was more opposition to than support for missile construction among representatives from eastern (thirty-eight to sixty-nine) and midwestern (forty-nine to seventy) states.

Besides party affiliation, ideology, and section, several other possible influences on voting can involve the desire (1) to support the president's program, (2) to reinforce a colleague's position (given no other compelling reasons),[2] (3) to help the economy of the home state, and (4) to increase chances of reelection. Reelection considerations are of particular importance to senators serving the last two years of a term. In this example, the voting behavior of the dissident Republicans certainly does not betray any special sensitivity because of an impending reelection. Of the eight senators voting against the MX program, two were scheduled to be up for reelection in 1986, three in 1988, and three in 1990. Investigations of voting behavior would be aided if legislators would, or could, reveal the factors that most influence their personal voting decisions. Even if such data could be obtained, questions might be raised about the legislators' awareness of personal motivations or about their candor in making such motivations public.

SUMMARY

Members' political party attachments are generally the most powerful predictor of how they will vote on a roll-call question, but many competing sources of influence over voting behavior exist. Since members cast several hundred recorded votes each year and since each vote could turn out to be highly important to some segment of their constituency, members are under considerable pressure when voting. The White House, members' party leader, caucus, committee chair, close friends, and powerful individuals and groups in the constituency are among the most important potential influences on voting decisions; seldom will members be able to cast votes that do not offend or displease some significant actor in their political environment.

NOTES

1. *Congressional Quarterly* analysts note a relative weakening of the conservative coalition in 1987 (Davis, 1988). The coalition appeared on only 8.3 percent of roll calls in the two chambers, but it was successful 93 percent of the time when it did appear.

2. In discussing voting cues, Cherryholmes and Shapiro (1969) note that party, ideology, committee, section, and other variables predispose most legislators when voting on a particular measure. But when these predisposing factors are weak, contradictory, ambiguous, or indecisive, legislators naturally seek cues from colleagues to whom they feel close. Legislators' voting decisions, according to the Cherryholmes-Shapiro model, thus can be divided into predisposition and conversation phases.

REFERENCES

CHERRYHOLMES, CLEO H., and SHAPIRO, MICHAEL J. *Representatives and Roll Calls*. Indianapolis, Ind.: Bobbs-Merrill, 1969.

CLAUSEN, AAGE R. *How Congressmen Decide*. New York: St. Martin's Press, 1973.

CLEM, ALAN L. *American Electoral Politics: Strategies for Renewal*. New York: D. Van Nostrand, 1981.

DAVIS, JOSEPH A. " 'Conservative Coalition' No Longer a Force." *Congressional Quarterly Weekly Report* (16 January, 1988):110–114.

FROMAN, JR., LEWIS A. *Congressmen and Their Constituencies*. Skokie, Ill.: Rand McNally, 1963.

HINCKLEY, BARBARA. *Coalitions and Politics*. San Diego, Calif.: Harcourt Brace Jovanovich, 1981.

KINGDON, JOHN W. *Congressmen's Voting Decisions*. New York: Harper & Row, 1973.

MATTHEWS, DONALD R., and STIMSON, JAMES A. *Yeas and Nays*. New York: Wiley, 1975.

MAYHEW, DAVID R. *Congress: The Electoral Connection*. New Haven, Conn.: Yale University Press, 1974.

ORNSTEIN, NORMAN J., MANN, THOMAS E., MALBIN, MICHAEL J., SCHICK, ALLEN, and BIBBY, JOHN F. *Vital Statistics on Congress, 1984–1985*. Washington, D. C.: American Enterprise Institute, 1984.

SHAFFER, WILLIAM R. *Party and Ideology in the United States Congress*. Lanham, Maryland: University Press of America, 1980.

XI GOVERNMENTAL CONNECTIONS

Congress does not work in a political vacuum. The issues it argues and the decisions it makes must be viewed in a larger context. What Congress does and does not do affects and is affected by forces and actions outside the first branch of government.

This chapter and the next will, in turn, discuss the roles and activities of five elements outside the legislative branch: in the governmental sector, the executive branch, the judicial branch, the fifty state governments; in the nongovernmental sector, interest groups and the news media. Sometimes relationships are so close between Congress and certain of these elements that we have to remind ourselves that the elements are not formally part of Congress. At the same time, there are strong and recurring tensions between Congress and each of these elements.

CONGRESS AND THE EXECUTIVE BRANCH

Congress Versus the President

Through the 1980s the president and many, if not most, members of Congress felt that the Sandinista government in Nicaragua represented a Communist beachhead in Central America that gravely threatened our national security. Accordingly, they strongly advocated support for the Contra movement in order to undermine the Sandinistas. But many other members of Congress regarded military aid (in the form of weapons and advisers) and even humanitarian aid (food and medical supplies) to the Contras to be attempts to prop up an undesirable, unpredictable, and unrepresentative insurgency. Many members found themselves in the uncomfortable and unenviable position of seeing some truth to both sides of the argument; as a result, these members vacillated between expanding and reducing U. S. involvement in Nicaragua.

This is just one example of a highly visible issue on which political leaders have taken diametrically opposed stands and argued for them eloquently and persistently. The Nicaraguan situation was just one chapter of a seemingly endless saga of tension between the legislative and executive branches of the federal government. One branch is charged with establishing policy; the other branch is charged with carrying policy into effect. But the functions cannot be completely separated. In delivering the annual messages to Congress on the state of the union, the economy, and the budget, the president becomes a legislative leader. And, in a negative way, the exercise of the veto allows the president to enter into the legislative process. Congress, on the other hand, spends considerable effort overseeing how laws are carried out. Conflict and confusion are inevitable in a system purposefully set up to divide power and responsibility. But cooperation between the two branches occurs frequently, reflecting the fact that lawmakers and administrators share fundamental responsibilities and aspirations in making laws workable and feasible. Cooperation is obviously more likely when the leaders in the two branches belong to the same political party.

Contact between Congress and the executive establishment occurs at many levels. At the very top, there are occasional, highly visible confrontations between the president and the speaker of the House or the majority leader of the Senate as in Speaker Jim Wright's involvement in the Nicaraguan peace negotiations in late 1987 (Sidey 1987, 16). At the next levels are contacts between (1) cabinet secretaries and committee chairs having responsibilities in the same policy areas and (2) agency heads and subcommittee chairs or individual legislators. Meetings of these officials are most likely to take place in committee or subcommittee hearings on Capitol Hill, but they also take place on public affairs programs (such as "Meet the Press" and "Face the Nation") and at public symposia arranged by academicians, public interest groups (such as the League of Women Voters), or journalists.

The president has several legislative powers. The president's signature is necessary to enact laws, and several presidents have made extensive use of the power to veto legislation. Notably active in using the veto have been Presidents Grover Cleveland (584 vetoes in 8 years), Franklin Roosevelt (635 in 12 years), and Harry Truman (250 in 8 years). Cleveland had only 7 of his vetoes overridden by Congress; Roosevelt, only 9; and Truman, 12. Among the least successful vetoers were Andrew Johnson, who had 15 of his 25 vetoes overridden, and Gerald Ford, who had 12 of his 66 vetoes overridden (see Davidson and Oleszek 1985, 293–296; Jones 1982, 344–349; and Keefe and Ogul 1985, 328–329). David Rohde and Dennis M. Simon (1985) studied the degree to which the outcomes of veto efforts have been affected by four factors: (1) the proportion of congressional seats controlled by the president's party, (2) the level of public support enjoyed by the president at the time, (3) the policy domain of the vetoed legislation, and (4) the voting alignment that prevailed at the time of passage.

Another question is the controversy over the item veto. Some feel that the president should have the power to approve part of a bill while vetoing another part. Many proponents of the item veto see it as a device to control federal spending, while others see it as a way to eliminate "pork barrel" projects that have little value to the nation. But opponents of the item veto believe it would further weaken Congress as the central policy-making institution and would increase the imperial nature of the presidency.

A dramatic veto battle occurred on September 26, 1986, when President Reagan vetoed a measure (H. R. 4868) that imposed stiffer economic sanctions against the Union of South Africa because of its apartheid policies. The Democratic-controlled House overrode the veto on September 29 by a vote of 313 to 83, and the Republican Senate followed suit on October 2 by a vote of 78 to 21. Public opinion and most Republican leaders in the House and Senate seemed to agree that strong measures were called for, in spite of the president's assertions that the sanctions would hurt the people they were intended to help.

The president is a major factor in setting the congressional agenda. A large percentage of the bills Congress considers originates in the White House or in one of the executive agencies. The annual budget is prepared in the President's Office of Management and Budget (OMB) and formally submitted to Congress in the annual budget message, as will be detailed in a later section.

For its part, Congress affects the execution and administration of laws in many ways. It defines the mission of each administrative unit, from the Department of State to the U. S. Merit Systems Protection Board (created by P. L. 95-454) or the Advisory Council on Historical Preservation (created by P. L. 89-665). Congress provides the money to run every governmental program through the fiscal processes of authorization, appropriation, and budget and also determines the tax system that enables the federal government to collect revenues.

Furthermore, Congress writes the rules governing the hiring, promoting, and firing of personnel in all branches of the federal government. The Pendleton Act of 1883 (which based the employment of government workers on merit rather than on party patronage) and the Hatch Act of 1939 attempted to insulate Civil Service workers from partisan pressures to contribute money to or engage in partisan political activity. Congressional committees exercise legislative oversight by holding hearings to investigate allegations of conflict of interest, criminal activity, or disloyalty on the part of officials serving in the executive branch.

Congressional–presidential relations have long been characterized as a continuing duel for political, if not constitutional, primacy. In *Congressional Government,* first published in 1885, Woodrow Wilson saw Congress as predominant, whereas a generation later in *Constitutional Government in the United States,* published in 1908, he saw the president "at the front of affairs" (Wilson 1956, 7). As Lippmann wrote in his introduction to a new edition of *Congressional Government* in 1956: "The fact is that at times the system works as he (Wilson) describes it in this book *(Congressional Government)* and at other times it works as he describes it in the second book *(Constitutional Government)*" (Wilson 1956, 8).

Legislative Oversight of the Administration

Legislative oversight is a routine, ongoing function of congressional committees. The purpose of such oversight is to ensure that the laws passed by Congress are being consistently and properly administered. It is not a simple task for a few hundred Capitol Hill staff members to oversee the work of the 2 million individuals who make up the federal bureaucracy. In just one year, the Defense Department supplied Congress with 20,000 pages of justifications for the money it had requested for the 1985 defense budget, and in 1983 alone, witnesses from that department provided at least 1,453 hours of testimony before 91 congressional committees and subcommittees (see Hiatt and Atkinson 1985, 6). That is a lot of information to digest.

Two devices help Congress control the executive branch in its administrative work. "Sunset laws" specify terminal dates for new programs at the time the programs are authorized; the program may be continued beyond the original "sunset," or concluding, date only if Congress passes continuing legislation to that effect. The intent of sunset legislation is to reduce, if not eliminate, the number of programs that have outlived their usefulness. The second device is the legislative veto, under which certain administrative agencies are given authority to make policy decisions that would remain in effect unless Congress were to reject, or veto, such decisions. Three types of legislative veto have been established: those allowing one chamber to stop an executive action, those requiring agreement of both chambers to stop an executive action, and those allowing a specified congressional committee to exercise the veto.

In a 1983 decision (*Immigration and Naturalization Service* v. *Chadha*), the Supreme Court declared the legislative veto as used in certain circumstances to be unconstitutional. Congress, in Section 244(c)(2) of the Immigration and Naturalization Act, used the following language to assign deportation functions, subject to review by either chamber of Congress:

> (2) In the case of an alien specified in paragraph (1) of subsection (a) of this subsection—if during the session of the Congress at which a case is reported, or prior to the close of the session of the Congress next following the session at which a case is reported, either the Senate or the House of Representatives passes a resolution stating in substance that it does not favor the suspension of such deportation, the Attorney General shall thereupon deport such alien or authorize the alien's voluntary departure at his own expense under the order of deportation in the manner provided by law. If, within the time above specified, neither the Senate nor the House of Representatives shall pass such a resolution, the Attorney General shall cancel deportation proceedings.

The Supreme Court's decision concluded:

> The veto authorized by § 244(c)(2) doubtless has been in many respects a convenient shortcut; the "sharing" with the Executive by Congress of its authority over aliens in this manner is, on its face, an appealing compromise. In purely practical terms, it is obviously easier for action to be taken by one House without submission to the President; but it is crystal clear from the records of the [Constitutional] Convention, contemporaneous writings and debates, that the Framers ranked other values higher than efficiency. The records of the Convention and debates in the States preceding ratification underscore the common desire to define and limit the exercise of the newly created federal powers affecting the states and the people. There is unmistakable expression of a determination that

legislation by the national Congress be a step-by-step, deliberate and deliberative process.

The choice we discern as having been made in the Constitutional Convention imposes burdens on governmental processes that often seem clumsy, inefficient, even unworkable, but those hard choices were consciously made by men who had lived under a form of government that permitted arbitrary governmental acts to go unchecked. There is no support in the Constitution or decisions of this Court for the proposition that the cumbersomeness and delays often encountered in complying with explicit Constitutional standards may be avoided, either by the Congress or by the President. See *Youngstown Sheet and Tube Co.* v. *Sawyer,* 343 U. S. 379 (1952). With all the obvious flaws of delay, untidiness, and potential for abuse, we have not yet found a better way to preserve freedom than by making the exercise of power subject to the carefully crafted restraints spelled out in the Constitution.

V

We hold that the Congressional veto provision in § 244(c)(2) is severable from the Act and that it is unconstitutional.

In effect, the Chadha decision said, Congress should stick to the work of writing laws and separate itself from the work of executing them. In spite of the Chadha decision, the legislative veto remains an important facet of legislative-executive relations. Among the major laws containing legislative veto provisions are the War Powers Act, the Arms Export Control Act, and the Congressional Budget and Impoundment Control Act.[1]

Congressional committees and executive agencies whose responsibilities lie in the same policy area inevitably work together closely in writing and implementing laws. As noted in chapter 8, there is considerable variation among the policy areas in terms of the degree of conflict and cooperation between legislators and administrators. The policy networks that exist in Washington also include private interest groups that have a stake in the same policy area. Triangular relationships among congressional committees, executive agencies, and lobbyists, whether cozy or contentious, have much to do with the shaping and execution of governmental programs (see Jones 1982). Two examples of these "iron triangles," or tripartite subgovernments, may help convey their scope. In the area of agricultural policy, the Department of Agriculture would be the executive point of the triangle, the agricultural committees on the Hill would be the legislative point, and the major farm interest groups (notably the American Farm Bureau Federation and the National Farmers Union) would be the final corner. Agriculture's triangle could be further reduced into separate triangles for specific commodities (cotton, feed grains, food grains, dairy, tobacco, etc.), with commodity-specific executive services, legislative subcommittees, and interest groups working together to establish and monitor policies. In the area of education policy, the Department of Education, the Senate Labor and Human Resources and House Education and Labor committees, and the National Education Association (NEA), among others, would constitute the corners of the policy triangle.

The principle of separation of powers is often written about, but it is not as simple as it may sound. The principle is quite complex, and continues to produce confusion and conflict. In his study of major trends in congressional history, James Sundquist (1981) notes a number of ambiguities with which the Constitution has saddled our nation's political leaders. Congress was to write the laws, but the president was given several roles directly affecting the legislative power, namely, the responsibility for recommending, approving (or vetoing), and administering laws. On the other hand, while the president was made the head of the executive branch, Congress was given the power to vote funds and authorize programs that the executive branch was to administer. Further, Congress was given the power to establish the shape and functions of the various parts of the federal administrative apparatus and to ensure that laws were administered as intended. Sundquist notes five particular constitutional ambiguities.

1. Legislative initiation and leadership. How much involvement by the president in urging legislation and setting the legislative agenda is proper, beyond the president's clear duty to recommend legislation?

2. The veto. Should the president use the power to veto legislation freely, as some presidents have done, or with restraint, as other presidents have done?

3. The scope of executive power. The Constitution does not define the executive power exercised by the president (the legislative powers of Congress are expressly and considerably limited), so in how broad an area can the president operate independent of any real congressional control? Foreign policy crises and control over the military and executive establishments are particularly important areas of ambiguity.

4. Congressional control of administration. The Constitution states that the president has the duty to "take care that the laws be faithfully executed," but Congress has many opportunities for involving itself in the inner workings of the bureaucracy, as in confirming (or withholding confirmation of) nominations of top administrators or in prescribing administrative organization and procedures (not to mention funding executive agencies).

5. The congressional right to information. The right of Congress to investigate activities in the executive branch was established early, but there is at the same time a long tradition of executive privilege, the right of the president to withhold information if its publication might endanger national security or compromise the independence of the executive branch. Watergate was by no means the first time a president said that other branches have no right to see presidential documents.

Sundquist (1981, 18) concludes his discussion of these constitutional ambiguities with these words:

> . . . when the Founders separately interpreted the [Constitution] they had together written, they often disagreed. James Madison and Alexander Hamilton had both been at Philadelphia, and they had collaborated on *The Federalist,* yet they had profoundly different conceptions as to how the new government should evolve.

. . . enough checks and balances had been created to safeguard against either legislative or executive despotism; the exact balance of power would have to be worked out by reasonable men striving together to make the structure that was given them succeed.

In the wake of disclosures in late 1986 concerning the Iran/Contra affair (the complex and covert operations involving arms sales to Iran, release of hostages in the Near East, and aid for the Contras in Central America), the attention of congressional probers, journalists, foreign observers, and American citizens was focused on two fundamental questions: First, how is American policy established? Second, can Congress effectively oversee the administration of American national security policy? Some of the controversy was due to the peculiar nature of foreign policy questions, for under the Constitution the president has special functions and authority, notably the roles as commander-in-chief of the armed forces and as chief diplomat, the official who receives foreign ambassadors to the United States and appoints U. S. ambassadors to other nations. These roles give the president special opportunities for foreign policy initiative and influence. One theme in the testimony on the Iran/Contra affair was that Congress had been slow, uncertain, ambiguous, and inconsistent in providing guidelines for national security policy. The congressional hearings throughout 1987 at least had the effect of reminding us of several realities: (1) that political problems are complex; (2) that there is a fine line between establishing policy and implementing it; (3) that even though many members of Congress have become expert in particular policy fields, they are generally not as experienced and specialized (and numerous) as those in the executive branch; (4) that national security policy is a special case wherein the president is expected to take the initiative; and (5) that policy makers seem to spend more time, and to gain more publicity, in reactive policy making (responding to a crisis that has already exploded) than in active policy making (attempting to solve a problem before it has reached crisis proportions).

The Budget Process

Perhaps no better example exists of the inherent complexities of coordination of policy making (by Congress) and policy execution (by the executive branch) than the budget process. Fiscal power—including both the power to raise revenues through taxes and to spend money through appropriations—is a fundamental legislative power, and the Constitution establishes Congress's fiscal preeminence in two provisions of Article I: (1) "All bills for raising revenues shall originate in the House of Representatives" (Section 7), and (2) "No money shall be drawn from the treasury, but in consequence of appropriations, made by law" (Section 8, subsection 7). Revenue bills must originate in the lower chamber and, by tradition, appropriations bills do so as well, giving the fiscal committees of the House something of an advantage in the process.

There are many stages and a considerable lapse of time between legislative approval of spending and administrative certification that services have been rendered and bills may be paid. The great growth in the size of federal government activity in this century has further complicated this massive process.

The Budget and Accounting Act of 1921 attempted to make the federal budget process more responsible and efficient. It provided (1) that an executive budget was to be prepared under the aegis of the president, (2) that a budget office be set up in the executive branch to collect new spending requests from executive agencies and to account for agency adherence to their respective budgets during the fiscal year, and (3) that Congress would, as before, debate budget proposals and make final budget decisions.

A continuing problem centered on Congress's piecemeal approach to the budget process. For one thing, one set of committees—Ways and Means in the House and Finance in the Senate—was determining revenue policy, while another set of committees—the two Appropriations committees—was determining spending policy. There was no certainty, therefore, that the amount of federal revenues for a given fiscal year would bear any relation to levels of federal spending. For another thing, the Appropriations committees were split into several subcommittees, each responsible for particular agencies and programs, and therefore an additional element of uncertainty was inherent in the budgeting system.

For these and other reasons, a second major piece of budget legislation was passed in 1974 that created a new annual budget timetable and established new standing committees on the budget in each chamber, as well as a Congressional Budget Office. The federal fiscal year was changed; formerly it had run from July 1 to July 30, and now it was to run from October 1 to September 30. The president still was to present the budget message to Congress early in the calendar year, but now there was to be a little more time—the three months from July 1 to October 1—for Congress to make its final budget decisions. The Appropriations committees, taking into consideration the programs authorized by the standing committees as well as the agency recommendations contained in the president's budget message, were to spend several weeks adjusting estimates and report to the floor of their respective chambers a recommendation that would become, by May 15, the first budget resolution. This first budget resolution would focus on such basic fiscal considerations as how large a deficit will be allowed, how much the national debt will grow, and what percentage of the gross national product the federal government will spend. Throughout the summer months, congressional committees continue to refine their estimates, and eventually by September 15 a second budget resolution is due. After that, minor adjustments and reconciliations are to be made, resulting in a final budget for the new fiscal year beginning October 1. This process is not as automatic and easy as it may sound, and the period of late September and early October is often filled with last-minute threats and compromises and stop-gap measures that allow the government to continue to pay its bills and perform its functions.

Legislation known as Gramm-Rudman-Hollings attempted to reduce federal deficits by means of a complex and controversial mechanism; that of setting a series of deficit reduction targets over a period of several years until the annual deficit was eliminated entirely. If Congress failed to meet the Gramm-Rudman-Hollings time-table, this would force automatic, across-the-board, proportional cuts in all pro-grams sufficient to reduce the deficit to Gramm-Rudman-Hollings standards. Con-gress could come up with no better method of forcing the federal government to "live within its income" and thereby to stop contributing each year to the increasing national debt.

A strong case can be made that the budget process makes the president the main initiator of policy—not only of fiscal policy but of policy in every area requiring the expenditure of public funds—and the main agenda setter for the nation. The essence of budgetary debate and decision making on Capitol Hill is determined by what the president has emphasized in the original budget message to Congress.

Table 11-1 shows the general shape of estimated outlays for F. Y. 1988 and illustrates the relative priorities that have been placed by Congress on various activities of the federal government. Figure 11-1 illustrates the fact that program activities are spread out over multiyear periods, so that what is spent in a given fiscal year is a combination of funds provided in enactments passed over several years.

TABLE 11-1.   The culmination of the budget process: federal outlays by function, F.Y. 1988 (estimated)

Function	*Outlay (billions of dollars)*
National defense	299.1
International affairs	18.3
General science, space, and technology	9.3
Energy	4.5
Natural resources and environment	11.8
Agriculture	19.7
Commerce and housing credit	3.8
Transportation	24.1
Community and regional development	5.5
Education, training, employment, and social services	26.3
Health	36.7
Medicare	76.0
Income security	123.1
Social security	226.1
Veterans benefits and services	26.9
Administration of justice	7.0
General government	5.7
General purpose fiscal assistance	1.8
Net interest	145.1
Allowances and undistributed offsetting receipts	(−46.4)
Total	1,026.8

Source: The United States Budget in Brief, Fiscal Year 1987. Washington, D. C.: Office of Management and Budget, 1987.

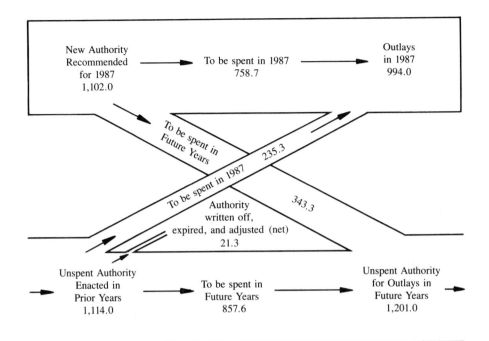

Figure 11-1.   Relationship of budget authority to outlays, (in billions of dollars), 1987

Note: This illustration, from p. 71 of the booklet, *The United States Budget in Brief, Fiscal Year 1987,* shows the incremental nature of the annual budget. New spending authority passed by Congress in a given year may be scheduled for spending over several fiscal years. That is, what is actually spent (outlays) in a given fiscal year will have come from budget authority measures passed over the course of several years.

Source: The United States Budget in Brief, Fiscal Year 1987. Washington, D. C.: Office of Management and Budget, 1987.

Capitol Hill developments in December, 1987, illustrate continuing serious problems with the budget process. The general problems were the need to reduce the deficit for F. Y. 1988 in order to meet Gramm-Rudman-Hollings limits and the on-going disputes between Democrats and Republicans, liberals and conservatives, and congressional and administration leaders over the huge fiscal package (Wehr 1987, Calmes 1987). A massive bill which the president was to sign finally emerged from Congress, but no one was very happy with the result (Hook 1988, Hornblower 1988, Lamar 1988). The comments of three members of the House are particularly relevant to the evaluation of the budget process (Calmes 1987, 3117):

> Minority Leader Robert Michel (R–Ill.): Some of the most important questions of our time are reduced to a simple, binary question: yes or no.
> William Natcher (D–Ky): If I were the president, I'd feel the same way he does.
> . . . When you put in all thirteen [programs] together, it's not the proper manner to do it.

Vic Fazio (D–Calif.): There's been a revulsion against the process this year. . . .
We're already talking about how we can prevent it in the future.

Only time will tell whether serious efforts will emerge to improve the budget system, or if the problems will be forgotten after the passions and frustrations of the moment have cooled.[2]

CONGRESS AND THE JUDICIAL BRANCH

Congress's interactions with the judicial branch are less frequent than those with the executive branch, but they are perhaps more dramatic when they occur. The basis for legislative-judicial relations can be simply stated: The courts have the power to declare legislative acts to be unconstitutional. Congress, on the other hand, has some control over the jurisdiction and membership of the federal courts and, to some degree, can bend the effect of court decisions.

A number of Supreme Court decisions in the past half century have had a dramatic impact on the powers and decisions of the other two branches of government. Several decisions either upheld or crippled fundamental New Deal programs. The steel seizure decision in 1952 rebuked President Truman and reasserted Congress's lawmaking prerogatives, while the reapportionment decisions of the 1960s asserted among other things, that congressional districts within a state must be substantially equal as to population. Some of the most notable decisions affected state laws or local government practices; examples of such decisions include strengthening the rights of accused persons, desegregating schools, ruling against prayers in public schools, allowing abortions, and regulating actions discriminatory to minorities. All of these decisions sparked heated public debate and in several instances led to congressional efforts to overturn or reduce their effect. The Supreme Court does not always have the last word. A hostile Congress can consider new legislation to rectify the point on which the Court has ruled a law or an action to be unconstitutional. Much effort has been expended, unsuccessfully to be sure, in the past two decades to amend the Constitution so as to, in effect, overturn Supreme Court rulings on school prayer and abortion. Other approaches available to Congress in dealing with the courts would be to pass new legislation changing the jurisdiction of various federal courts, the structure of the federal court system, or the size of the Supreme Court (and thus its ideological character). This is what President Roosevelt attempted to bring about in the late 1930s in his famous "court-packing" scheme, an effort unsuccessful in the short run but eventually made unnecessary because enough vacancies opened up due to retirements so that the president, through new appointments, could obtain a majority supportive of his innovative programs.

The president appoints all federal judges, including Supreme Court justices, subject to confirmation by the Senate. In making such appointments, the president exercises "senatorial courtesy," clearing judicial appointees with senators from the appointee's state. Most appointments are confirmed by the Senate, but occasionally the Senate thwarts the president's plans. Republicans and a few Democrats in 1968 used the threat of a filibuster to delay confirmation of President Johnson's nomination of Justice Abe Fortas to succeed retiring Chief Justice Earl Warren, thereby allowing the new president, Richard Nixon, in 1969 to designate the new chief justice, Warren Burger. But two of Nixon's next Supreme Court nominees, Clement Haynesworth and G. Harold Carswell, were rejected by the Senate. President Reagan's nomination of Associate Justice William Rehnquist to succeed retiring Chief Justice Burger in 1986 and his 1987 nomination of Robert Bork to fill the seat held by retiring Associate Justice Lewis Powell were resisted vehemently by many senators. In such confirmation proceedings, the Senate Judiciary Committee plays a central role, holding hearings and then recommending action to the Senate. The same committee would play a central role in the event of impeachment of a federal judge. Impeachment of a judge (or a president) is voted by the House, where the Judiciary Committee would play the leading role, and the trial would occur in the Senate. In the event of an impeachment trial involving the president, the chief justice of the Supreme Court would preside over the Senate proceedings.

Impeachments of federal judges are almost as rare as presidential impeachments. Until 1986 only five judges had ever been convicted, the last one being fifty years ago. Then on July 22, 1986, the House voted four articles of impeachment against U. S. District Judge Harry E. Claiborne, who was at that time serving a prison term for tax evasion while continuing to draw his judicial salary. The first two articles of impeachment concerned Judge Claiborne's underreporting of income for 1979 and 1980, the third article said he should be removed from office because of his conviction for tax evasion, and the fourth article stated that he had brought the federal judiciary into disrepute and had betrayed the people's trust. After proceedings in the Senate during which Congressman Peter Rodino of New Jersey, chair of the House Judiciary Committee, presented the impeachment case, the Senate on October 9, 1986, convicted Judge Claiborne on three of the four articles. On the first article of impeachment, eighty-seven senators voted "guilty" and ten voted "not guilty," with Senator Stevens of Alaska voting "present" and Senators Symms of Idaho and Garn of Utah not voting (the three followed the same pattern on the other three articles). On the second article, the vote was ninety "guilty" to seven "not guilty." On the third article, there were forty-six "guilty" votes and seventeen "not guilty" votes, with thirty-five senators voting "present." (Several of these senators said they did not wish to establish a precedent that conviction on a criminal charge would automatically result in conviction in an impeachment trial or, on the other hand, that a verdict of innocent in a criminal trial would lead to an unsuccessful impeachment effort.) The vote on the third article was less than the required two-thirds for conviction. On the fourth article, the vote was eighty-nine "guilty" to eight "not guilty." (The eight senators voting "not guilty" included four Republicans—Hatfield of Oregon, Hatch of Utah, Evans of Washington, and Laxalt of Nevada—and four Democrats—Pryor of Arkansas, Long of Louisiana, Bingaman of New Mexico, and Metzenbaum of Ohio.)

CONGRESS AND STATE GOVERNMENTS

While many programs of the federal government are carried out in foreign nations, U. S. territories, or the District of Columbia, most of them are carried out in one or another of the fifty states. As a general rule, federal programs are considered to be beneficial: The local area is helped by the dams, highways, bridges, and federal buildings that are constructed and by the salaries earned by the people who build them or work in them. From the beginning of the republic, there has been competition among the states to obtain a generous share of federal largesse. This competition has, if anything, been heightened in the twentieth century as the federal government has become more and more deeply involved in many totally new programs or in programs formerly financed by state or local government units alone.

In the early decades of the republic, there was frequent debate over the extent to which state governments should attempt to instruct or bind the state's members of Congress. Of course, as long as U. S. senators were chosen by the state legislatures—that is, until adoption of the Seventeenth Amendment in 1913—the opportunity to bind senators was clearly present. There may have been considerable philosophical discussion of the primary responsibility of representatives—to the nation, the state, the district, or to their own consciences. But what the debate soon boiled down to, as a matter of political practice, was that members of Congress were expected to bring home to their districts a large share of federal programs and dollars. Members from a particular state habitually work together "for any program that benefits any part of the state" (Woll 1985, 183).

Geography is a powerful unifying force on Capitol Hill. One of the most pervasive bases for informal social and political activity in Congress is the state. State delegations—all the senators and representatives from a given state, irrespective of their party affiliation—may not be tightly organized (Clapp 1964, 47) but they constitute, in Charles Jones's (1982, 238) words, a "natural organizational group" and on many issues attempt to find a common ground that will give the delegation greater bargaining leverage (Kingdon 1981, 89). Members do not want to be consistently out of step with other members of the state delegation.

State and local government officials frequently make contact with the state's congressional delegation to protect or enhance the state's "parochial interests" (Jones 1982, 238). And many of the state delegations meet with some regularity on Capitol Hill in order to maintain communication and to keep the members in step with one another on issues important to the state.

On occasion, serious and persistent clashes of personalities and political ambitions can occur within a state's congressional delegation, and sometimes the state's governor or other prominent state political leaders may become involved in such personal clashes or campaign confrontations.

Illustrating the growing importance of state government policy decisions— and, for that matter, of a new breed of political consultants and lobbyists concentrating their attentions on state governments—was a conference held in Washington, D. C., in December 1986 entitled "New Strategies for State Government Relations," sponsored by *Congressional Quarterly*. Among other things, the conference addressed such questions as: What is the difference between state government activity now and in the recent past? How does an organization get the most effective state relations program for the least investment? What do the differences between state legislative and congressional members and committees mean to an organization's government relations planning? How can an organization influence the political process in the states? Among the expert speakers and panelists scheduled to appear were the president of a public affairs consulting firm in Albany, New York, an executive of a private government relations firm with a fifty-state network of professional lobbyists, the vice-president for corporate relations for a tobacco company, the director of state government relations for TRW, and a regulatory attorney with International Playtex.

SUMMARY

This chapter has elaborated on the basic constitutional division of power and authority among the legislative, executive, and judicial branches and to a lesser extent between the federal and state governments. All these constitutional relations bring with them conflicts and tensions. The most important tension is that existing between Congress and the president. That tension is affected, first, by the style, goals, and personality of the person in the White House, and, second, by the balance of partisan control between Congress and the White House and between the two chambers of Congress. In its relations with the executive branch, Congress fluctuates between an emphasis on giving policy direction through enactment of new laws and on overseeing the administration's execution of laws already in effect. The standing committees and other oversight elements often spend more time on oversight activities than on proposing, amending, and passing legislation.

NOTES

1. For a fuller discussion of the legislative veto decision and possible alternatives, see "Court Bans," 1986.
2. See Elizabeth Wehr, "As Dust Settles from Battle to Cut Deficit . . . Second Thoughts on Budget Summitry." *Congressional Quarterly Weekly Report* (26 December 1987): 3188–3189.

REFERENCES

ARNOLD, R. DOUGLAS. *Congress and the Bureaucracy: A Theory of Influence*. New Haven, Conn.: Yale University Press, 1979.
BURNS, JAMES MACGREGOR. *Presidential Government*. Boston: Houghton Mifflin, 1966.

CALMES, JACQUELINE. "Fights on Contra Aid, Fairness Doctrine: Big Spending Decisions Go Down to the Wire." *Congressional Quarterly Weekly Report* (19 December 1987): 3117–3119.

CLAPP, CHARLES. *The Congressman: His Work as He Sees It.* Garden City, New York: Anchor Books, 1964.

"Court Bans Legislative Veto, but Congress Finds Alternatives." *Spring 1986 Guide, Current American Government.* Washington, D. C.: Congressional Quarterly Press, 1986.

DAVIDSON, ROGER H., and OLESZEK, WALTER J. *Congress and Its Members.* Washington, D. C.: Congressional Quarterly Press, 1985.

EDWARDS III, GEORGE C. *Presidential Influence in Congress.* New York: W. H. Freeman, 1980.

FISHER, LOUIS. *The Constitution Between Friends.* New York: St. Martin's Press, 1978.

FISHER, LOUIS. *The Politics of Shared Power: Congress and the Executive.* Washington, D. C.: Congressional Quarterly Press, 1987.

FREEMAN, J. LEIPER. *The Political Process: Executive Bureau-Legislative Committee Relations.* rev. ed. New York: Random House, 1965.

HIATT, FRED, and ATKINSON, RICK. "Joint Chiefs of Congress: Bombing the Pentagon with Paper Work." *Washington Post* (national weekly edition) (12 August 1985): 6.

Immigration and Naturalization Service v. Chadha, 462 U. S. 919 (1983).

HOOK, JANET. "Survey Shows Members Angry at Gridlock." *Congressional Quarterly Weekly Report* (16 January 1988): 126.

HORNBLOWER, MARGOT. "The Budget's Hidden Horrors: How Congress Tucked Goodies into its Christmas Pie." *Time* 131 (18 January 1988).

JONES, CHARLES O. *The United States Congress.* Homewood, Ill.: Dorsey Press, 1982.

KEEFE, WILLIAM J., and OGUL, MORRIS S. *The American Legislative Process: Congress and the States.* 6th ed. Englewood Cliffs, N. J.: Prentice-Hall, 1985.

KING, ANTHONY (ed.). *Both Ends of the Avenue.* Washington, D. C.: American Enterprise Institute, 1983.

KINGDON, JOHN. *Congressmen's Voting Decisions.* New York: Harper & Row, 1981.

KOENIG, LOUIS W. *The Chief Executive.* 4th ed. San Diego, Calif.: Harcourt Brace Jovanovich, 1981.

LAMAR, JR., JACOB V. "Taking a Scalpel to the Budget: Could a Line-Item Veto Reduce Federal Spending?" *Time* 131 (1 February 1988), 17.

LIGHT, PAUL C. *The President's Agenda.* Baltimore, Md.: Johns Hopkins University Press, 1982.

MILLS, G. B., and PALMER, J. L. *Federal Budget Policy in the 1980s.* Washington, D. C.: Urban Institute Press, 1985.

NEUSTADT, RICHARD E. *Presidential Power: The Politics of Leadership from FDR to Carter.* New York: Wiley, 1980.

POLSBY, NELSON W. *Political Innovation in America.* New Haven, Conn.: Yale University Press, 1984.

ROHDE, DAVID W., and SIMON, DENNIS M. "Presidential Vetoes and Congressional Response: A Study of Institutional Conflict." *American Journal of Political Science* 29 (August 1985): 397–427.

SIDEY, HUGH. "The Presidency: The Speaker's Itch for Power." *Time* 130 (November 1987): 16.

SUNDQUIST, JAMES L. *Decline and Resurgence of Congress*. Washington, D. C.: Brookings Institution, 1981.

WEHR, ELIZABETH. "Conferees Push to Finish Deficit-Reduction Bill: Bitter Disputes Delay Adjournment." *Congressional Quarterly Weekly Report* (19 December 1987): 3115–3116.

WILSON, WOODROW. *Congressional Government*. New York: Meridian Books, 1956. (Originally published 1885)

WOLL, PETER. *Congress*. Boston: Little, Brown, 1985.

XII INTEREST GROUPS AND THE MEDIA

Interest groups and the news media play crucial, if extraconstitutional, roles in the day-to-day work of Congress. They exert special pressures on Congress, of course, but they also contribute importantly to the quality of Congress's decisions. They provide sophisticated information Congress might not be able to obtain in any other way; they help Congress reach reasonable and agreeable consensus on many seriously controverted issues; and they describe, evaluate, and, in a sense, justify to the public the decisions of Congress. In these and other ways, interest groups and the news media help legitimate the entire representative system.

It is difficult to imagine what the nation's capital or the public's awareness of government would be like without the ubiquitous lobbyists and journalists. As Nelson Polsby (cited in Mann and Ornstein 1981, 13) writes, it is "the mandarins of the high-priced law firms, and the gurus of the Washington press corps, who give continuity and whatever it has in the way of corporate ideology to the Washington political community."

CONGRESS AND INTEREST GROUPS

Washington is the center of government. It is also the center of interest group activity in the United States. Thousands of interest groups maintain large offices, and sometimes national headquarters, in the nation's capital city. Lobbying organizations occupy generous and ornate suites in modern office buildings, especially along K and M streets and from 14th through 18th streets in northwest Washington and also along Connecticut and Massachusetts avenues. In some cases, the interest group itself owns the building it occupies.

Although there is room to list only a few of the many interest groups that operate in Washington, table 12-1 identifies major policy fields and names the interest groups, administrative and regulatory agencies, and congressional committees most prominently associated with each field. These three elements constitute an "iron triangle" (some say a cozy triangle) in each policy area. Some interest groups are concerned with a limited range of policy questions directly affecting their membership; many have an interest in a broader range of issues; and some, such as the American Federation of Labor/Congress of Industrial Organizations (AFL/CIO), the Chamber of Commerce of the United States, the League of Women Voters, the Americans for Democratic Action, and the National Association of Manufacturers, are interested in almost every legislative proposal.

Lobbyists are employed by interest groups to maintain close and continuing contact with Congress and are particularly interested in the specific arguments being made for and against proposed legislation that might conceivably affect their groups. Some interest groups are essentially "defensive," to use David Truman's (1971) terminology, in the sense that they are primarily concerned with protecting their present advantageous situation against any kind of threatening change. Other groups are "offensive" in that they seek changes in laws and programs in the hopes of improving their situation. Some groups are passive on some issues and active on others. For instance, organized labor is passive in its approach to labor-management or collective bargaining regulations, being concerned with maintaining labor's hard-earned status vis-a-vis employers. The labor movement at the same time is active in continuing to push for expansion or adoption of a wide range of welfare, unemployment, poverty, education, antidiscrimination, and job-training programs it feels would benefit its members and society generally.

Interest groups try to directly influence congressional decision makers and administrative officials in shaping and executing laws. Lobbyists are the contact people. They find the critical access points where decisions on legislation are most likely to be made. Such access points include those majority and minority party members on the committee of jurisdiction with the greatest influence over their colleagues' attitudes and decisions. Attention to the agenda is important, too. Knowing when a bill will be brought up in committee or on the floor is important in planning how to present the interest group's arguments and in determining which members are likely to be most receptive to those arguments.

Lobbyists testify in committee hearings; share information and plans with members and staffers in Capitol Hill offices and corridors; and track legislative debate and progress on bills they are concerned about from the House and Senate galleries and through the pages of the *Congressional Record,* the newspapers, the calendars, and the committee hearings and reports. Lobbyists are particularly adept at developing or responding to new arguments, ideas, and facts that might persuade members to change their minds about pending legislation.

Contrary to what many citizens seem to believe, interest groups are not always successful in pushing their special interests. As Paul Glastris (1987, 52, 56) puts it in a review of a book[1] about the Tax Reform Act of 1986: "Tax reform was the first dramatic confrontation in more than a decade in which the special interests, and the politics of selfishness they represent, lost to the public interest." Glastris comments that it required great imagination and leadership by, among others, Sen. Bill Bradley (D.–N.J.) to achieve the public interest against representatives of powerful special interests and concludes that the success of tax reform "has widened the boundaries of the politically possible."

Interest groups and Congress exist in a state of what biologists refer to as

Table 12-1. Policy areas and associated interest groups, administrative agencies, and congressional committees

Policy field	Affected interest groups (selected)	Administrative or independent agencies	Congressional committees	
			House	Senate
1. SECURITY				
National security	Arms Control Assn., Council for a Livable World, Navy League	Defense	Armed Services	Armed Services
Foreign policy	American Peace Society, World Federalists, United Nations Assn., Council of the Americas	State	Foreign Affairs	Foreign Relations
Law and order, crime control	American Bar Assn., American Civil Liberties Union, Natl. Council on Crime and Delinquency, Internatl. Assn. of Chiefs of Police	Justice	Judiciary	Judiciary
2. FISCAL				
Taxes	National Assn. of Manufacturers, Tax Foundation, Public Citizens	Treasury	Ways and Means	Finance
Monetary policy, budget, banking, inflation	U. S. Chamber of Commerce, American Enterprise Inst., American Savings and Loan League	Treasury, Office of Management and Budget, Federal Reserve System	Budget, Banking, Finance, and Urban Affairs	Budget, Banking, Housing, and Urban Affairs
3. REGULATORY				
Consumer protection	Consumers Union of the United States, Public Citizens, American Retail Federation	Federal Trade Commission, Consumer Product Safety Commission	Energy and Commerce	Commerce, Science, and Transportation
Regulation of commerce, stock market	National Assn. of Securities Dealers	Commerce, Interstate Commerce Commission, Security and Exchange Commission	Energy and Commerce	Commerce, Science, and Transportation

(continued)

Table 12-1. *(continued)*

Policy field	Affected interest groups (selected)	Administrative or independent agencies	Congressional committees House	Senate
Regulation of common carriers	Assn. of American Railroads, Transportation Assn. of America, Air Line Pilots Assn.	Civil Aeronautics Board, Interstate Commerce Commission	Public Works and Transportation	Commerce, Science, and Transportation
Regulation of power, fuels	American Gas Assn., American Petroleum Inst., American Public Power Assn.	Energy, Nuclear Regulatory Commission	Energy and Commerce	Energy and Natural Resources
Regulation of media	National Assn. of Broadcasters, American Civil Liberties Union, Accuracy in Media, American Newspaper Publishers Assn.	Federal Communications Commission	Judiciary	Jucidiary
Regulation of elections	Americal Federation of Labor/Congress of Industrial Organizations Committee on Political Education, League of Women Voters, Americans for Democratic Action, Americans for Constitutional Action	Federal Elections Commission	House Administration, Judiciary	Rules and Administration, Judiciary
Regulation of labor-management relations	Americal Federation of Labor/Congress of Industrial Organizations, National Assn. of Manufacturers	National Labor Relations Board, Occupational Safety and Health Administration, Equal Employment Opportunity Comm.	Education and Labor	Labor and Human Resources
Promotion of commerce, transportation, and communication	American Maritime Assn., American Road Builders Assn., American Truckers Assn., American Automobile Assn.	Small Business Administration, Transportation, Commerce	Small Business, Energy and Commerce, Public Works and Transportation	Small Business, Commerce, Science, and Transportation

Continued

Table 12-1. (continued)

Policy field	Affected interest groups (selected)	Administrative or independent agencies	Congressional committees House	Senate
4. ENVIRONMENT				
Food production and agriculture	American Farm Bureau Federation, National Farmers Organization, National Farmers Union	Agriculture	Agriculture	Agriculture
Timber conservation	Sierra Club, Wildlife Management Institute	Interior, Agriculture, Environmental Protection Agency	Agriculture, Interior and Insular Affairs	Agriculture, Energy and Natural Resources
Soil conservation	Friends of the Earth, Izaak Walton League	Interior, Agriculture, Environmental Protection Agency	Agriculture, Interior and Insular Affairs	Agriculture, Energy and Natural Resources
Water conservation	Environmental Defense Fund, National Waterways Conference	Interior, Agriculture, Environmental Protection Agency	Agriculture, Interior and Insular Affairs	Agriculture, Energy and Natural Resources
Mineral conservation	American Mining Congress, United Mine Workers	Interior, Agriculture, Environmental Protection Agency	Agriculture, Interior and Insular Affairs	Agriculture, Energy and Natural Resources
Air pollution control	National Clean Air Coalition	Interior, Agriculture, Environmental Protection Agency	Agriculture, Interior and Insular Affairs	Agriculture, Environment and Public Works
5. HUMAN				
Civil rights and liberties	American Civil Liberties Union, National Congress of American Indians, National Urban League	Justice	Judiciary	Judiciary
Education	National Education Assn., National Congress of Parents and Teachers, American Assn. of Christian Schools	Education	Education and Labor	Labor and Human Resources
Health	American Medical Assn., American Hospital Assn., American Public Health Assn., Insurance Institute of America	Health and Human Services	Education and Labor	Labor and Human Resources
Welfare and social security	Salvation Army, National Assn. for the Advancement of Colored People, National Organization for Women, Volunteers for America	Health and Human Services	Ways and Means, Education and Labor	Finance, Labor and Human Resources

symbiosis; that is, they are separate organisms living together in close association for mutual benefit. Interest groups frequently become deeply involved in congressional campaigns. Since the 1970s, as a result of laws written to reform political campaign finance activities, much of the campaign effort formerly made by interest groups has been transferred to political action committees (PACs). Those PACs that contribute to five or more candidates for federal office have several distinct advantages that allow the committees to play a significant role in congressional elections. As long as a PAC does not coordinate its campaign activities with a candidate in any way, the PAC is unlimited in the amount it can spend on behalf of that candidate (see Conway 1983, 127).

The 1984 campaign operations of the political action committee of the Veterans of Foreign Wars (VFW-PAC) is an illustration of electioneering efforts by powerful, well-organized interest groups in recent years. VFW-PAC is a separate corporation that is controlled by the VFW. About 5 percent of its membership, or 100,000, contributed money to VFW-PAC in 1984. This money was then contributed to incumbent members of Congress who asked for it and who had voted in agreement with VFW positions on recent congressional roll-call votes. The VFW generally favored increasing veterans' benefits and assistance to their survivors and increasing American national defense capacity. Incumbents who voted with the VFW over 60 percent of the time thereby qualified for $500 in VFW-PAC support, and those who voted with the VFW 90 percent of the time received another $500. In 1984 Republican and Democratic incumbents all together received about the same amount of support from VFW-PAC. Very few challengers or contenders for open seats received VFW-PAC help. Members of the veterans affairs committees were especially likely to receive funds. A large number of relatively liberal Democratic members won VFW-PAC endorsements and contributions on the basis of their support for veterans benefits rather than for a stronger national defense (see Rubinoff 1985, 8–10).

Interest groups do not restrict activities to Washington or to election contests but also work back home in the congressional districts, putting indirect but often highly effective pressure on members of Congress. An example was the pressure brought to bear by the National Rifle Association (NRA) in 1986 against a coalition of major law enforcement groups, including the National Sheriffs Association and the Fraternal Order of Police, regarding proposed legislation to regulate firearms. The NRA adamantly opposed any further tightening of handgun control, while the law enforcement professionals were concerned about dangers to police and the public from the easy availability of small weapons. Especially noteworthy was the NRA's effort in Tennessee to discredit Rep. Jim Cooper (D.–Tenn.) because of his failure to sign a petition to discharge the NRA's proposal from the Judiciary Committee and bring it directly to the floor (see Cohodas 1986).

Interest groups carry out general information campaigns by way of advertising, direct mail, public meetings, and inspired (pre-arranged, but appearing spontaneous) demonstrations or communications, attempting to shape public opinion and to focus attention on the political issues of great concern to them. In this way, through news accounts, letters from individual constituents, and even contacts from party leaders and other political influentials back home, members are kept aware of interest group concerns.

There is considerable variation in the size, effectiveness, goals, economic bases, and operating styles of interest groups. Washington lobbyists may work for law or public relations firms, corporations, labor unions, or associations representing a number of organizations mutually interested in broad or narrow ranges of policy questions. The following vignette explores the work of an experienced lobbyist, James Mack. Mack knows the political ropes in Washington and around the country and his organization, the National Machine Tool Builders Association, is an alliance of specialized manufacturers interested in a fairly large number of policy issues whose interconnections may not be obvious. Among other things, this vignette shows that effective professionals on Capitol Hill must have a wide and changing range of acquaintances; a vast store of knowledge about congressional procedure as well as the major influentials in the policy field in question; the ability to negotiate, placate, and educate; and the energy to work effectively and persistently under sometimes inhuman timetables.

Lobbyist James Mack and the National Machine Tool Builders Association

The National Machine Tool Builders Association (NMTBA) is a trade association composed of about 250 companies in approximately 400 U. S. plants concentrated in New England, New York, and the Great Lakes area. The association was founded in 1902 when seventeen lathe manufacturers gathered in New York City to discuss the need for standards that would permit their customers to interchange common tooling components. The organization quickly developed industry standards for such components as face plates, chucks, tool holders, T-slots, and spindles. The association even created an industrywide paint color known as "machine tool gray." Members of the association today produce about 90 percent of the U. S. total machine tool output. Most of the member companies employ fewer than two hundred workers. Their common and characteristic activity is the production of machines that cut, shape, and form metal. The industry's economic situation is cyclical; 1986 found the industry badly affected by recession and competition from increased imports.

At its headquarters in McLean, Virginia, a Washington suburb, the NMTBA occupies its own modernistic office building and has a staff of about fifty persons. It has a political action committee called "MACHINE TOOLPAC" to enhance the industry's voice by contributing campaign funds to congressional candidates who support the objectives of the machine tool industry. NMTBA's public affairs department is responsible for conducting the industry's government relations program. Other NMTBA departments promote exports for its member companies and run the nation's largest industrial trade show every two years in September at McCormick Place in Chicago. The public affairs division is composed of four professionals and two secretaries, and its director is James H. Mack.

Mack was raised in Wisconsin; studied history, English, and politics at Wisconsin State University, LaCrosse; and then went to law school at the University of Wisconsin, where one of his close friends was William Steiger, later a Republican congressman from Wisconsin. Mack became involved in Republican party politics in Wisconsin, went into government relations work for the Illinois Tool Works in Chicago, and was campaign director for a series of major Republican candidates in Illinois in 1968, 1970, and 1972. He joined the NMTBA in 1975.

The original industry standards concerns of eighty-five years ago have given way to broader public policy issues in NMTBA priorities. In the mid-1980s, the NMTBA's principal legislative concerns were trade policy reform, the status of depreciation in new tax legislation, and product liability. Mack argued on Capitol Hill for three major items, the first being Reagan administration approval of NMTBA's national security import relief petition, which argued that the United States needed to maintain an up-to-date and efficient machine tool industry to protect its national security. (Although NMTBA's petition runs counter to the free trade preferences of the Reagan administration and the laissez-faire school of economic thought, the administration announced its intention to negotiate machine tool import limits with Japan on May 21, 1986, culminating three and a half years of NMTBA effort.) The second item was maintainence of liberal depreciation rules in corporate income tax legislation in order to encourage companies to modernize and expand their equipment. Finally, Mack pushed for control of the size of court settlements in product liability cases, particularly for companies producing equipment used in a workplace where equipment is often very old or has been insufficiently maintained by its owner. (This would provide some degree of liability protection to machine tool builders while reducing the success ratio and size of awards to individuals claiming injury.)

What follows are a few highlights from several days of Jim Mack's congressional activity in late April and early May 1986. In this particular time period, Mack focused his energies on four projects. One was the NMTBA's trade petition. He met with the staff of Rep. Lynn Martin (R.–Ill.) on this subject at 9 A.M. Tuesday, April 29, and he also discussed with them the possibility of securing partial funding by the Department of Defense for a machine tool research and development facility. An hour later he met with the staffs of

Republican Senators John Heinz of Pennsylvania, Charles Grassley of Iowa, and John Danforth of Missouri (who was then chair of the Commerce Committee) concerning trade petition strategy. The next evening (April 30) he contacted Commerce Secretary Malcolm Baldrige on the same subject.

A second project was the general trade legislation being drafted in the House Ways and Means Committee and the Senate Finance Committee. Mack met with Rep. Barbara Kennelly (D.–Conn.) on the Ways and Means Committee's trade bill late Tuesday morning (April 29), had a working lunch in a House cafeteria with his NMTBA coworkers on the trade markup, and spent most of the afternoon watching the Ways and Means Committee markup session. Monday morning, May 5, he had breakfast with John Hall, Senator Danforth's trade legislative assistant, on the Finance Committee trade hearings.

A third area of concern was the tax reform bill, which had passed the House in December 1985, and was pending in the Senate Finance Committee. On Monday, May 5, Mack attended a Finance Committee tax markup session from 7:30 to 10 P.M., then spent about an hour in a strategy session with Senator Heinz and several staff members, and over the midnight hour had cocktails and discussed the tax markup issue with staff members of Sen. Max Baucus (D.–Mont.). Most of the next day was spent in more Finance Committee markup sessions.

Of particular interest to Mack in the spring of 1986 was the connection between equipment depreciation in new tax legislation and the minimum tax idea. He talked with Senator Heinz about this at 2 P.M. Monday, May 5, and again at 8:30 A.M. the next morning, having prepared talking points and a briefing paper.

A third project was the Reagan administration's product liability bill. Mack met Wednesday morning, April 30, with Sen. Bob Kasten (R.–Wisc.) and several staff members concerning the proper tactics for Kasten's introduction of the administration bill. He had an extended meeting at 5:00 P.M. the next day with David Zorensky, counsel for the Senate Commerce Committee, on the product liability question. He met again with Zorensky on Thursday, May 8, concerning Senator Danforth's new product liability draft, and then later that evening discussed the Danforth draft with Victor Schwartz, an attorney and business tax consultant. On May 9 he met again with Zorensky on some technical changes in the draft, and that afternoon met with Senator Kasten's staffers and insurance industry lobbyists concerning connections between product liability and workers' compensation in product liability legislation.

All of these major lobbying activities were conducted in the midst of professional travel, office work, and family routines. On a typical morning in Washington, Mack would leave home at 7:30 A.M., heading either for NMTBA headquarters or Capitol Hill. Frequently there would be breakfast, lunch, or dinner meetings with members of Congress or their staff, allied lobbyists, or committee counsels; some would be formal meetings with speeches or presentations of some kind, and all would involve work. Mack's two-week diary shows he once returned home as early as 5:30 P.M., four other evenings by 8 P.M., and three other evenings by 11 P.M. Of course, even on these "early" nights, there were working papers and documents to be studied and plans to be made for the next day. One evening his arrival time was 1:15 A.M., after midnight cocktails at the Monocle restaurant; on another occasion it was 3 A.M., after Senate Finance Committee markup sessions that lasted until 2 A.M.

Mack's life as a lobbyist is busy and demanding. It requires sensitivity to the economic problems of machine tool builders; understanding of the objectives and resources of the trade association itself; knowledge of the law and lawmaking processes; reasonably friendly working acquaintances with scores of officials on the Hill; and the ability to manage one's own time in a frantic, constantly changing, and challenging work environment.

CONGRESS AND THE MEDIA

An important attribute of a truly democratic system is that citizens know what their government is doing. After all, government by the people is not very meaningful unless the people know which parties or officials are responsible for the decisions the government makes. The public has a stake in keeping its government visible. The visibility of government—federal, state, or local as well as legislative, executive, or judicial—basically depends on the independence, intelligence, and diligence of the press.

News media representatives are among the most numerous and busy denizens of Capitol Hill. They include reporters working for daily newspapers, wire service reporters, reporters who represent news services that provide Washington news coverage for groups of smaller newspapers, magazine editors and writers, and television reporters and camera technicians. The news media are provided with space in the House and Senate press galleries, places to keep equipment and write and transmit articles, and rooms in which interviews with members can be taped or filmed. Table 12-2 lists the larger press groups whose members are entitled to admission to the Capitol's press galleries.

Various news media produce different kinds of news. There is up-to-the-minute news—brief, urgent paragraphs that are meant to be transmitted to all parts of the nation—and deeper, more comprehensive reports filed at the end of a reporter's daily shift. There are short reports (for instance, on the fate of a tax bill in the Ways and Means Committee) that are designed for insertion in the network's nightly news program, and there are hour-long daily programs (such as the Mac-Neil-Lehrer report on public television) that probe the deeper implications of each day's developments through live interviews with experts who express at least two sides of the question being discussed. Generally speaking, the broadcast media report briefly and quickly on each day's events. The major daily newspapers report

Table 12-2.   Larger news media groups on Capitol Hill, 1985–1986

NEWSPAPERS AND SERVICES (NUMBER OF REPRESENTATIVES)

Washington Post (110)	Agence France-Presse (16)
Associated Press (91)	*Baltimore Sun* (15)
United Press (76)	*Chicago Tribune* (14)
Congressional Quarterly News Service (58)	*Daily Traffic World* (14)
Wall Street Journal (54)	Cox Newspapers (13)
The New York Times (50)	*Education Daily* (13)
Gannett News Service (40)	Knight-Ridder Financial News/CNS (13)
Washington Times (37)	Fairchild Publications (11)
Reuters (35)	*New York Journal of Commerce* (11)
Knight-Ridder Newspapers (33)	*St. Louis Post-Dispatch* (11)
Scripps-Howard News Service (33)	Washington Merry-Go-Round (11)
Los Angeles Times (29)	*Boston Globe* (10)
Newhouse News Service (25)	*Christian Science Monitor* (10)
States News Service (18)	

PERIODICALS OR PERIODICAL PUBLISHERS (NUMBER OF REPRESENTATIVES)

BNA Publications (138)	Kiplinger Washington Editors (29)
U. S. News and World Report (102)	Commerce Clearing House (28)
McGraw-Hill Publications (72)	*FDC Reports* (28)
Army Times Publishing Company (60)	*Newsweek* (28)
Time (42)	*National Journal* (27)

NETWORKS, STATIONS, AND SERVICES (NUMBER OF REPRESENTATIVES)

NBC News (168)	Associated Press Radio (60)
CBS News (102)	Mobile Video Services (48)
ABC News (96)	WTTG-TV (40)
National Public Radio (72)	WRC (38)
Cable News Network (66)	C-SPAN (37)
Mutual Broadcasting System (65)	Voice of America (36)
WJLA-TV (63)	WDVM (34)

Source: Congressional Directory, 99th Cong., 1985–1986, pp. 898–1004.

more comprehensively on many significant developments in committees and on the floor of the two chambers, also including related happenings in the executive branch and elsewhere. News magazines and opinion journals and the weekly interview broadcasts (such as "Meet the Press" and "Face the Nation") generally have more time and space available and thus present a more exhaustive and deliberate picture of current issues.

Congress is only one of many Washington institutions covered by the press corps. According to Stephen Hess (1981, 48–49), Congress ranks fourth out of thirteen Washington "beats" in terms of the percentage of reporters assigned to it and is among the "medium-prestige beats." The stories filed by Washington reporters are often given the foremost place of honor (the top of the right-hand column on page 1) by newspaper editors.

Research by Hess (1981, 94–95) showed that stories from Washington got the place of honor 45 percent of the time, home state stories 19 percent, local stories 18 percent, international stories 11 percent, and stories from another state, 7 percent. Most newspaper and television stories about Congress concerned committee and floor action; less attention was given to introduction of bills, action by sub-committees, or action by conference committees. As to policy fields, the most frequently mentioned subjects in both newspaper and television stories were foreign policy and economics/finance (109).

Hess also notes the "unusual personnel pattern" in Washington reporting (127–128). Relatively few journalists seem to make their Washington assignments their life's work. Journalism is a relatively easy field to get into, since it does not require academic credentials or professional certification; at the same time it provides opportunities to move into other careers. The excitement and drama of the field wear off for most journalists after a few years. Few journalists (and few politicians) can maintain the vigorous, zestful approach they brought to their work at the start of their careers.

Media exposure is obviously a good way for a member of Congress to gain attention, credibility, and power; thus, to some extent, stories and ideas come to the reporter rather than having to be sought out. As one member of the House told Larry Warren (1986, 43) of KUTV, Salt Lake City, during Warren's stint as a congressional intern:

> There are two ways around here to get power. I can hang around here half my life and maybe twenty years from now I'll be a committee chairman. Or I can get my face on TV a lot. I want whatever's hot that day, get on TV about it, and then get on to the next thing that's news. I'm not interested in sitting through hearings all day and getting buried in all that legislative stuff—I want to get on TV!

Some observers criticize reporters for placing so much emphasis on dramatic incidents and oversimplifying events. Richard Fenno, Jr. (1986, 14) was struck by the difference between the perspectives and interests of the typical journalist and the typical political scientist.

> There is a huge corps of journalists who observe politics every day. They do it very well. And we are already heavily dependent on what they tell us about our politicians. If we do not do it, they will do it for us. But it is in the nature of their occupation that they have neither the training, nor the patience, nor the interest to conduct a dialogue with political science theorizers. Journalists are not conceptualizers or generalizers. They are more interested in episodes than regularities.

The vignette that follows concerns Steve Berg, a news representative on Capitol Hill and an educated and experienced journalist who writes for a major regional newspaper and is interested in personalities and issues of particular relevance to one part of the country. As with successful lobbyists, effective media professionals must be ambitious, critical, tireless, widely acquainted, and knowledgeable. They cannot afford to waste time or pursue too many false trails. Berg and his employers hope that his energy, experience, and intelligence will enable him to cover his beat better than such competitors as television reporters, national news services, or correspondents for other newspapers.

Correspondent Steve Berg
of the *Minneapolis Star and Tribune*

The *Minneapolis Star and Tribune* maintains a news bureau in Washington consisting of three reporters. One covers the Supreme Court and the regulatory agencies and their hearings—the Federal Aviation Administration, Securities and Exchange Commission, Federal Trade Commission, and so on. A second reporter covers national politics and agriculture. (The newspaper's two main agriculture reporters work in the Twin Cities, Minneapolis and St. Paul, Minnesota). The other reporter is Steve Berg, whose beat is Congress exclusive of agriculture issues. The three colleagues share office space with the Washington news bureau of the *Des Moines Register* at 1317 F Street, N.W., the old *Baltimore Sun* building in downtown Washington.

Berg was born and raised in Fargo, North Dakota; received his bachelor's degree at the University of North Dakota in Grand Forks in 1968; served an army tour in Germany; and entered the graduate mass communications program at the University of North Carolina, where he was awarded a master's degree in 1971. He worked for the *Raleigh News and Observer* from 1971 to 1976, specializing in state government and energy and environmental issues. Then he joined the *Minneapolis Star and Tribune* in 1976 as a feature writer on entertainment, social trends, Hollywood stars, and celebrities. In 1980 he graduated to more serious work, reporting on projects such as the Mount St. Helens eruption, the possible discontinuance of Amtrak service and its impact, and the decline of the auto industry in Detroit. In 1981 he accepted the Washington assignment. The move meant considerable professional dislocation for his wife, a public relations consultant. The couple in 1986 lived with their two young children in Chevy Chase, Maryland. Many mornings Berg took the older child to school. He generally rode the Metro to and from work.

Berg found that it was harder to get the information needed for his stories in Washington than it had been in the Twin Cities or in state capitals such as Raleigh or Pierre. Even so, sources and newsworthy developments were abundant, and Berg each day spent considerable time deciding what to write up and what not to develop. The question frequently on his mind was: Which of thirty possible stories should I do now?

Another notable thing about journalistic work in Washington was that Berg was not protected, as he had been back home, by work-hour limitations specified in the Newspaper Guild labor contract. The working day was typically very long in Washington.

The work of many newspaper correspondents in Washington is aided by two regular, informal symposia, both held at the Sheraton Carlton hotel north of the White House on 16th Street in northwest Washington. The Godfrey Sperling breakfast, organized by the *Christian Science Monitor,* is held up to four times each week, and the *Wall Street Journal* luncheon occurs once a week (with people like David Broder and Roger Mudd in regular attendance). Both groups prorate expenses among attendees, and membership is by invitation only. At both symposia, "important people" come to talk informally about current affairs. For "second-echelon reporters," as Berg describes himself, the symposia are more important for offering access to decision makers and major communicators than for the specific news acquired.

Berg prepared a professional log covering fourteen working days in March 1986, from which the following selections have been drawn.

Monday, March 10

I arrive at the office about 9:45. I've read *The New York Times* on the subway, so I look over the *Washington Post,* the *Wall Street Journal,* and several recent issues of the *MS&T.*

I call the usual cast of suspects on my beat: Karen Doyne, press secretary to Sen. Dave Durenberger (R.–Minn.); Mary Lahr, press secretary to Sen. Rudy Boschwitz (R.–Minn.); Devin Bonderud, press aide to Rep. Martin Sabo (D.–Minn.); and Shirley Geer, press secretary to Rep. Bruce Vento (D.–Minn.). Shirley says she will send over a copy of my long story about the Amhoist company's move from Minnesota to Wilmington, North Carolina, which she had helped me with last week; she thinks it was a good story. I also call Karen Chandler from Congressman Gerry Sikorski's office. With all these people I talk about the week and what will be happening on the Hill.

Durenberger will be making a speech on tax-exempt bond financing in the afternoon before the National Conference of Mayors. It sounds like a yawn. One of my colleagues has covered the material in his Monday morning column.

I return a phone call from someone at the University of Minnesota. The message apparently has been on my desk for days. It is about a speech Rep. Bill Gray, (D.–Pa.) is making in Minneapolis. He is chairman of the Budget Committee and one of the most influential and interesting people in the House. I'm planning to write a profile on him.

After lunch I return to the office and check out the mail. An item catches my attention. Bill Gray will be holding a Budget Committee hearing in Worthington, Minnesota, on Friday, in the district of Republican Congressman Vin Weber. It is a hard-pressed farm district. Is Gray trying to embarrass Weber, who has been close to Reagan? Or did Weber somehow trick Gray into holding a hearing in his district, enabling Weber to continue to distance himself from Reagan on farm issues? Sounds like a potentially good political tale.

My bureau chief, Finlay Lewis, comes into my office and asks me to attend a press briefing the next day. A group of Harvard health policy people is proposing big changes in the Medicare system. I know little about Medicare, but I should be more clued in, particularly because Durenberger is so big in the health field.

Colleague Dave Phelps comes in to say he has heard a blurb on ABC radio that Vento, who is chairman of a national parks subcommittee, has put the stop on a plan to make a national shrine of Richard Nixon's birthplace, and a similar move to erect a shrine in Plains, Georgia, honoring Jimmy Carter. Sounds like a good story. I call Vento's office. Shirley Geer says Vento will call back. She punches up an Associated Press report of Vento's move on her computer and telecopies a copy to me.

It could be a good little story with a funny touch. Richard ("You won't have me to kick around much longer") Nixon gets kicked around again. Vento saying, "Let me make one thing perfectly clear, no shrine for Tricky Dicky."

I gather file information of proposals to make Nixon's birthplace into a national attraction. At 5:00 I call Geer; she's been unable to get to Vento. He won't be able to call me until 6:00 or 6:30. Most days I would wait. But I've been away from my family for days. To me, the story doesn't seem that worthwhile. I call the desk in Minneapolis to let them know I've changed my mind on doing the story. I head for home about 6:00 P.M.

Tuesday, March 11

After checking the mail and papers, I go to the Harvard brunch at 11:00 A.M. Sounds like a good story to develop. At noon I leave the session early and take a cab to the Hill. At 12:15 I'm in Sen. Jim Abdnor's office for a lunch date with his top aide, Tom Mason. While waiting for Mason, I call Karen Doyne in Senator Durenberger's office, telling her that I have a copy of what Harvard is proposing to do with Medicare. She says the senator is interested, and I say I'll drop by later with a copy and check with Chip Kahn, his expert on health care policy. The study has an embargo on it, meaning that we can't print a story on it until Thursday morning.

Mason and I have lunch in the Senate dining room in the Capitol. We talk about Abdnor's primary race against Republican Governor Bill Janklow. We talk about Congressman Tom Daschle's strategy (he's the South Dakota Democrat who is running for Abdnor's Senate seat). Mason concedes the campaign is having money problems and will hold a fund-raiser in Minneapolis next week sponsored by two prominent Democrats, Curt Carlson and Carl Pohlad, banker and owner of the Minnesota Twins. I tuck that information away for my weekend column.

After lunch I head for Durenberger's office and chat with Doyne and Kahn about the Medicare story; we agree to talk later about reactions to Harvard's recommendations.

I hop the tram back to the Capitol to check out the action on the House and Senate floors. I talk to colleagues in the Senate press room for awhile. The Senate is still debating a constitutional amendment to balance the budget, an idea that has always seemed headed nowhere but seems suddenly headed for more credibility following passage of Gramm-Rudman. Still, I'm not interested; it can't pass the House.

I head to the House side. They're talking about money to appease land claims involving the White Earth Indian Reservation in Minnesota. But Phelps has been covering that story, and he's on the scene.

I go to the House office buildings to chat with Democratic aides about Congressman Gray's big budget and farm hearing in Worthington later in the week.

By 3:30 I'm back in my office. LeAnn Buttrick of Congressman Tim Penny's office calls. She kids me for mistakenly identifying Penny as a Republican in a column in last Sunday's paper. I ask her if the Worthington meeting is an attempt to embarrass Weber; she says no, it will turn out to be the opposite. Weber is overjoyed because it will give him an opportunity on his own turf to blast Reagan's farm policy and solidify his chances in November.

I call Weber. He calls back. He tells me why he's happy that Gray is holding a hearing in his district and gives me a preview of what he'll talk about.

Gloria Halcomb, our news assistant, tells me that Gray will be the guest at tomorrow's *Christian Science Monitor* breakfast. Would I like to go? Yes! It will be a great chance to ask him why he's going to Worthington to help a Republican!

Bonderud calls to tell me that Congressman Sabo, one of the staunchest Norwegians in the House, will sponsor a congressional commemoration of Swedish immigration. It could be a funny story. I file it away for the weekend column. I begin assembling ideas for the column. By 7:00 P.M. I am heading for home.

Wednesday, March 12

At 7:55 I arrive at the Sheraton-Carlton hotel for the *Christian Science Monitor* breakfast. About twenty other reporters attend. Most of the discussion is about the budget and taxes. I ask Gray my question about the hearing in Weber's district. A friend from Knight-Ridder tells me he thinks he recalls Weber recently badmouthing the idea of Gray holding field hearings. That intrigues me. I realize that I need to write the story for Thursday morning, not Friday morning as I had previously thought.

By 9:15 I'm back in the office making phone calls like mad. I call the Democratic Congressional Campaign Committee and ask if its chairman, Congressman Tony Coelho of California, has received pressure from the Minnesota Democratic delegation to block the Worthington event. I ask if Coelho has spoken to Gray about the matter. It is well known that Coelho and Weber do not like one another, particularly since Weber supposedly called Coelho "sleazy" one day on the House floor. Mark Johnson on Coelho's staff says he will check it out and call me back.

I call other Hill sources, including aides to Congressmen Sabo, Vento, Oberstar, and Sikorski. Sikorski has apparently played a key role in letting Coelho and Gray know that Minnesota Democrats don't like the Worthington hearing. But Sikorski and his people aren't willing to talk much about that.

I place calls to Dave Johnson, the candidate running against Weber next fall. I leave messages. I run to lunch with Dave Phelps and colleagues from Knight-Ridder. We talk about a racy story that the *Washington Times* has written on Durenberger.

After lunch, I head for the *Baltimore Sun* offices. I want to check out its coverage of a Republican conference in Baltimore at which Weber allegedly badmouthed the idea of Gray's field hearings. I chat with Paul West, the paper's chief political writer. I place a call to Nancy Swertzler, the writer who covered the Baltimore conference. I can't get her. I take the train to the Hill. I talk with Democratic aides about their objections to the Worthington hearing. I ask Congressman Sabo about his feelings. He doesn't like the fact that I have picked Michigan to win the NCAA basketball tournament. We both would rather see Duke win, however.

I go to Sikorski's office, trying to track down who pressured whom on the Worthington matter. I get nowhere.

I call Doyne at Durenberger's office. We talk about the story in the *Washington Times*. She has had better days. Another part will run tomorrow. I won't have time to do the Harvard Medicare story, I tell her. She says fine.

I return to the office by 3:00 P.M. I call some political consultants working for Dave Johnson. They tell me what they know about Worthington. I try again to call Johnson. This time I chat with his staff people about the situation. He will call later. I call Mark Johnson at the Democratic Congressional Campaign Committee; he says he will call back. I begin writing the story. Mark Johnson calls with information from Coelho. Dave Johnson calls and we talk for about fifteen minutes. I transcribe my tape from the Gray interview that morning and the story begins to take shape. A woman from the publication *Human Events* comes in to get clips of my stories on Durenberger. The Evans and Novak people have called, too, wanting clips on Durenberger. Apparently, the right wing is planning a big assault on the senator, trying to make it appear that he is emotionally unfit to head the intelligence committee and thus have access to national secrets. My bureau chief, Finlay Lewis, comes in. We talk about a future story about all the attention Durenberger's life is drawing from the rightist press. We wonder how to approach doing such a story. By 8:00 P.M. my Worthington story is finished and by 8:45 I'm home. Both kids are in bed already.

Thursday, March 13

I arrive at 10 A.M., upset because I have left my umbrella on the train and it's supposed to rain hard this afternoon. The second installment of the *Washington Times* story on Durenberger has been worse than the first. I feel somewhat guilty for starting all this. I call Doyne and we chat. I ask for a breakfast with Durenberger. No story. Just a breakfast. She says Durenberger will talk about Senator Bob Packwood's tax proposals this afternoon. I tell our tax expert, Dave Phelps, and he'll cover the Durenberger event.

I begin reading about the Contra aid controversy, still wondering how to cover it next week. One of my Minneapolis editors, Sherrie Marshall, calls, wondering what I've got for her today and for the weekend. I say I'm struggling with Nicaragua ideas and will have a column for Sunday.

I decide that I want to speak with Durenberger about Central America, so I tag along with Phelps to the Durenberger event. After he talks about taxes, I ask about Nicaragua. I get some interesting answers. I also ask about a report floated to Congress by the White House that appears to be a repudiation of the so-called Kirkpatrick Doctrine—that dictatorships of the left are worse than those of the right, no matter the human rights violations.

I go back to the office and begin assembling the column. I leave early for a change. I'm home by 6:30.

What ultimately happens to Berg's prose depends, of course, on editorial decisions made in Minneapolis. Berg's stories may be run virtually as written by him, or they may be considerably shortened, split into two or three separate pieces, incorporated with dispatches written by other reporters or press services, or cut entirely. Some stories may be worked on at several different times and places over a period of several weeks. Others may be written at one time. Some stories are straight description—reports of what someone said or did— while other stories are more subjective or interpretive, probing the underlying causes of political activity or the connections between seemingly unrelated events. The following headlines are from some of the articles by Berg that were published in the *Minneapolis Star and Tribune* in March 1986: "Snag in Amhoist Move Perplexes Wilmington," March 9; "Congressional Hearing Will Give Farmers—and Weber—a Forum," March 13; "Reagan Policy Shift on Dictators Strikes a Familiar Note at Durenberger's Office," March 16; "Rural Congressmen Confront Contra Issues," March 19; "HUD Asks U. S. to Sue Amhoist in Grant Dispute," March 21; "Contra Aid Bill: Frenzel Casts Uneasy Vote Against Reagan," March 21; "Contra Aid Approval Would Deal 'Mortal Blow' to Peace, U. S. Told," March 22; "Four State Congressmen Resist Nuclear-Waste-Site Choices," March 26; "In Seeking Contra Aid, White House 'Cuts Out' Durenberger," March 29.

SUMMARY

Major interest groups compete for the attention of members and committees, and, for their part, members regulate interest groups' opportunities for access to their staff and their own time. Interest groups, especially political action committees, use several avenues—contributions to campaign treasuries, information about problems in the constituency, and information about proposed legislation—to improve their access to members. Members also receive many contacts from various media representatives and find it difficult to provide information and statements to the press without losing control of what the press has to say about current legislative activity. Reporters must regularly struggle to give the proper balance of air time or newspaper space to Congress vis-a-vis the executive branch or to the committees and members who have messages to communicate through the mass media.

NOTE

1. The book being reviewed was Jeffrey H. Birnbaum and Alan S. Murray's *Showdown at Gucci Gulch* (New York: Random House, 1987).

REFERENCES

BIRNBAUM, JEFFREY H., and MURRAY, ALAN S. *Showdown at Gucci Gulch*. New York: Random House, 1987.

CATER, DOUGLASS. *The Fourth Branch of Government*. New York: Vintage Books, 1959.

COHODAS, NADINE. "House Under Pressure: NRA, Police Organizations in Tug of War on Gun Bills." *Congressional Quarterly Weekly Report* (1 March 1986): 502–504.

CONWAY, M. MARGARET. "PACs, the New Politics, and Congressional Campaigns." In Allen J. Cigler and Burdett A. Loomis (eds.). *Interest Group Politics*. Washington, D. C.: Congressional Quarterly Press, 1983.

FENNO, JR., RICHARD F. "Observation, Context, and Sequence." *American Political Science Review* 80 (March 1986): 14.

GLASTRIS, PAUL. "Inside Tax Reform: How the Good Guys Got the Bad Guys to Do the Right Thing." *Washington Monthly* 19 (June 1987): 52, 56.

HESS, STEPHEN. *The Washington Reporters*. Washington, D. C.: Brookings Institution, 1981.

HESS, STEPHEN. *The Ultimate Insiders: U. S. Senators in the National Media*. Washington, D. C.: Brookings Institution, 1986.

MANN, THOMAS E., and ORNSTEIN, NORMAN J. (eds.). *The New Congress*. Washington, D. C.: American Enterprise Institute, 1981.

MILBRATH, LESTER. *The Washington Lobbyists*. New York: Rand McNally, 1963.

RUBINOFF, MICHAEL. "VFW-PAC." *The Political Report* (11 January 1985): 8–10.

SABATO, LARRY J. *PAC Power*. New York: Norton, 1984.

SCHLOZMAN, KAY, and TIERNEY, JOHN. *Organized Interests and American Democracy*. New York: Harper & Row, 1986.

TRUMAN, DAVID. *The Governmental Process*. 2nd ed. New York: Knopf, 1971.

WARREN, LARRY. "The Other Side of the Camera: A TV Reporter's Stint as a Congressional Aide." *PS* 19 (Winter 1986): 43.

XIII ETHICS, PERFORMANCE, AND REFORM

Americans find it easy to be critical of Congress. We hear more about its faults than about its virtues. Congress is slow, uncertain, contentious, undignified, unresponsive, secretive, unimaginative, dominated by special interests, and tolerant of unethical behavior among its members. So goes the litany from congressional critics.

Examples of timidity, evasion, and moral laxity on the part of Congress continue to occur. The *Chicago Tribune,* criticizing Congress's failure to write stiffer gun control laws, referred to Congress as a "life-sized jelly mold" ("The Guns and the Gutless," 1986). Objecting to efforts for a constitutional amendment to require balancing the federal budget, Sen. Lowell Weicker (R.–Conn.) (*Congressional Record,* 1986, S2244–2245) told his colleagues:

> We can balance the budget right now. . . . All the authority that is needed is here to balance the budget.
>
> Many of my colleagues who advocate a balance-the-budget constitutional amendment, when it comes time for specific votes to balance the budget, will not do it.
>
> . . . My God, this place does not even have the courage to go ahead by simple majority and vote taxes.

The House Committee on Standards of Official Conduct in early 1986 determined that one member should not be punished by the House even though he violated federal laws and House rules in accepting free plane rides from a defense contractor while billing the government as if he had made some of the trips by automobile (see Calmes 1986).

An ineffective Congress means that critical national decisions are being made more and more often by bureaucrats, judges, and special interest groups. Policies increasingly reflect selfish and parochial interests, rather than broad national ones.

In considering such pervasive charges against Congress, this concluding chapter reviews questions of unethical conduct on the part of individual members, reflects on the institution's corporate effectiveness in performing its basic functions, and ponders the objectives and efficacy of reform efforts.

THE PROBLEM OF CONGRESSIONAL ETHICS

The political philosophers of the late 18th Century were well acquainted with the weaknesses of humanity. The *Federalist Papers* (Number 51) said that governments are necessary only because men are not angels (Hamilton 1911, 264). Edmund Burke noted that political leaders possess contradictory instincts, some of them positive and some of them negative: "Men are in public life as in private, some good, some evil" (Burke 1907, 33). Though there may be more good than bad, the latter seems to have more impact on public opinion, in a manner reminiscent of Gresham's Law: "Bad money drives out good."

News about a few rotten apples in the congressional barrel affects the public's perception of the entire institution. Too frequently, life on Capitol Hill is "hot" enough to compete with the fictional plots of TV shows such as "Dallas," "Falcon Crest," and "Dynasty." If all one knew about Congress came from the tabloid press, one could readily believe that most members spend their days chasing secretaries around the office and their evenings splashing around in the Tidal Basin, occasionally accepting payoffs in unmarked bills from mysterious emissaries. Actual cases of such activities have deservedly damaged the reputation of members and of Congress. But such cases are not representative of the ethics or behavior of the majority of members nor are they descriptive of the way Congress habitually operates. Such cases do continue to occur, however, which suggests that Congress's efforts to police itself have not been—and perhaps cannot be—very effective. William Keefe and Morris Ogul (1985, 8) note that many observers feel that American legislatures, including Congress, are "not sufficiently attentive to the need for developing and maintaining high standards of rectitude" for their members.

The ethics and morality of Congress must be a critical part of any evaluation of that institution. Three questions provide a framework for discussing congressional ethics.

First, what kinds of ethical problems affecting members of Congress and their staffs most commonly arise? Conflicts of interest, where a member's votes or influence may be personally beneficial, may arise at many stages in the process of handling legislation and might include securing favorable government treatment on government contracts, gaining inside information about future government programs or even of criminal activity. A recent example is the case against Congressman Fernand St. Germain (D.–R.I.). The *Wall Street Journal* in September 1985 alleged that St. Germain used his congressional office and his position as chair of the House Banking, Finance, and Urban Affairs Committee to build his personal financial portfolio. More specifically, the *Journal* charged St. Germain with intervening with the Federal Home Loan Bank Board to help a business associate, who chaired the Florida Federal Savings and Loan, to obtain almost 100 percent financing from Rhode Island lending institutions to purchase International House of Pancakes restaurants; and with benefiting from real estate investments built by a developer who would profit from federally subsidized housing project contracts that

St. Germain helped obtain. The House Ethics Committee in April 1987 unanimously found that St. Germain had violated federal ethics laws and House rules dealing with financial disclosure and acceptance of gift trips. The committee concluded that allegations of abuse of office for personal gain "were not sustained by clear and convincing evidence." The committee findings did not mention allegations of bribery and tax shelter abuses against St. Germain. The Ethics Committee declined to recommend any punishment, and St. Germain issued a press release saying the committee's action confirmed that he had "adhered to the highest standard of conduct in both public office and private business affairs" (see Calmes 1987, 713–714).

Another form of conflict of interest involves the misappropriation of public funds to a member or an associate; this was part of the case against former Representative Adam Clayton Powell, (D.–N.Y.). Powell was a flamboyant Harlem clergyman, first elected to the House in 1944, who rose in seniority to become by the 1960s chair of the Education and Labor Committee. As chair, he placed his wife on the committee payroll and took vacations with her and others in the Bahamas at government expense. In early 1967 the House Committee on House Administration, chaired by Rep. Wayne Hays of Ohio, determined that Powell had misused House funds. Meanwhile, the New York state courts had issued a warrant for Powell's arrest to serve a thirty-day contempt-of-court citation, so that, as a fugitive, Powell could only visit his district on Sundays when warrants were not in effect. In the midst of public outcries over these highly publicized charges, Powell was ordered, following the election of 1966 in which he was reelected, by H. Res. 1 to step aside while the House members were sworn in, pending investigation of the charges against him. The select committee chaired by Rep. Emanuel Celler (D.– N. Y.) was directed to consider the question of Powell's continuance. The committee voted on February 23, 1967, to recommend to the House that Powell be seated, fined $40,000, and stripped of his seniority. But the House on March 1, 1967, went further and instead adopted H. Res. 278 by a vote of 307–116 to exclude Powell, that is, refuse him his seat. A special election was called for April 11, 1967, and, to no one's surprise, Powell's district once again elected him to the House— illustrating the intense loyalty of some constituents for their representative, regardless of his or her disreputable behavior. Powell was reelected again in 1968 and was seated in 1969, contingent on payment of a fine of $25,000. He was defeated for renomination in 1970. Meanwhile, Powell appealed his ouster, which was affirmed by the federal district and circuit courts. On June 16, 1969, the Supreme Court in *Powell* v. *McCormack* ruled by a 7 to 1 vote that exclusion was not the proper course of action for the House to have taken, since there was no irregularity charged as to the manner of Powell's election. Rather, said the court, the House could have seated Powell and then voted to expel him. Such expulsion action would have required a two-thirds majority rather than the simple majority required for exclusion.

In December 1987, Representative Austin Murphy (D.–Pa.) was formally reprimanded by the House because he diverted government resources to his former law firm, allowed another member to vote for him on the House floor, and kept a "no-show" employee on his payroll (Hook 1987, 3134).

Bribery was at the heart of the Abscam episode of 1979–1980. FBI agents designed a crime and then enticed Sen. Harrison Williams (D.–N. J.) and four representatives into committing it. Some colleagues resented the entrapment of their colleagues by an executive agency and attempted to defend the culprits and excuse their behavior. But other colleagues insisted that members of Congress must remain above reproach. "My conscience," said Sen. Howell Heflin of Alabama (Ehrenhalt 1982, 655) "dictates faithful adherence to the notion that in conducting ourselves in office, we aspire to meet a higher standard." Another colleague, Sen. Thomas Eagleton (Arieff 1982, 557) of Missouri, was terribly critical of Williams in the course of debate on expulsion in March of 1982.

> I ask ninety-eight of my colleagues, would any of you have engaged in this tawdry, greedy enterprise? If your silent answer of inner conscience is in the affirmative, then do your soul a favor by serving out your term and passively fading into deserved oblivion.
>
> Senator Williams has not had the good grace and good judgment to withdraw from this body. We should not perpetrate our own disgrace by asking him to stay.

Charges of election irregularity, corrupt electoral practices, and of immoral or unbecoming conduct are other categories of unethical behavior; examples include Senators Smith of Iowa and Vare of Pennsylvania in the 1920s, Congressman Theodore Bilbo of Mississippi in 1946, and Congressmen Wayne Hays of Ohio and Wilbur Mills of Arkansas in the 1970s. Another kind of problem that involves ability to serve rather than moral turpitude involves questions of mental, physical, or psychological disability.

Second, what kinds of punishments or sanctions can Congress itself impose on inappropriate behavior? Either chamber of Congress may expel a member, and this requires a two-thirds vote. Senator Williams resigned in 1982 in the face of what appeared to be an inevitable expulsion. Either chamber, by a majority vote, may exclude a person from being sworn in. Under the Supreme Court's decision in *Powell* v. *McCormack,* the exclusion motion must be based on basic qualifications for office, such as citizenship, residence in the state, age, loyalty, or character. Beyond expulsion and exclusion, Congress may invoke lesser penalties, such as levying fines; stripping the member of a place on a committee or of seniority; or censuring, denouncing, or reprimanding the member. Members of Congress may be prosecuted in the judicial branch on criminal charges.

Third, what rules and procedures has Congress established to eliminate or at least reduce future ethics scandals? Each chamber has a committee with special jurisdiction over ethics cases—the Ethics Committee in the Senate (which is not a standing committee) and the Standards of Official Conduct Committee in the House. Contrary to the practice with most congressional committees, these committees are made up of equal numbers of Democrats and Republicans. Assignment to these committees is not sought. Election contests fall under the jurisdiction of the House Administration Committee and the Senate Rules and Administration Committee. Ethics legislation, much of it passed in the 1970s, has (1) provided for full financial disclosure by members and staff earning $25,000 or more per year (including spouses and dependents) of income, assets, holdings, transactions, and liabilities; (2) prohibited gifts worth $100 or more from lobbyists; (3) limited outside earnings; (4) prohibited the practice of a profession such as law during regular office hours or use of congressional powers or facilities in such professional work; (5) prevented a former member from becoming a lobbyist within one year of departure from Congress; (6) eliminated unofficial office accounts (slush funds) or the use of campaign funds for personal purposes; (7) prevented a member in the final weeks of service from traveling overseas at government expense without action by Congress or presidential request; and (8) prohibited mass mailings at public expense within sixty days of a primary or general election.

The public is properly appalled when political figures lapse into venality, avarice, and dishonesty but its view may be distorted by the news media's tendency to chronicle errors, excesses, stupidities, and inconsistencies while ignoring the occasions in which honesty, common sense, goodwill, and the public interest prevail.

EVALUATING CONGRESSIONAL PERFORMANCE

When attempting to evaluate the members and work of Congress, the question should be asked, "Compared to what?" The president is usually a more satisfactory target for criticism because he or she is clearly and solely responsible for the executive branch and the administration of the laws. Responsibility in Congress is, in contrast, more diffuse; we can believe it is at fault, but we cannot identify an individual to take the blame. How do the organization and output of Congress compare with that of state legislatures? Are congressional procedures slower, more complicated, or less visible? Are debates more trivial, less profound, less relevant, less noble in sentiment and expression? Are the members less wise, less statesmanlike, less just? Is Congress relatively successful or something of a failure when compared to the national parliaments of the United Kingdom, Brazil, the Union of South Africa, India, Israel, Italy, or the Philippines? Are we any better or worse at identifying the national problems that cry for attention or at devising solutions to those problems?

While it is possible for scholars to reduce at least some of these questions to testable hypotheses and to gather hard data to test those hypotheses, the uniqueness of Congress's position would make comparisons tentative and of doubtful utility. Evaluation of Congress requires sober reflection of what our nation's policy problems are and on what Congress is doing, if anything, to investigate and resolve them. Evaluation also requires that Jeremy Bentham's sobering thought of two centuries ago about possibly harmful legislation be kept in mind (Bentham 1931, 48):

Every law is an evil, for every law is an infraction of liberty. Government . . . has but the choice of evils. In making that choice, what ought to be the object of the legislator? He ought to be certain of two things: first, that in every case the acts which he undertakes to prevent are really evils, and, second, that these evils are greater than those which he employs to prevent them.

He has then two things to note—the evil of the offence, and the evil of the law; the evil of the malady, and the evil of the remedy.

Evaluation of Congress might be clarified by considering five discrete manifestations of that institution: individual members, powers, structures, procedures, and outputs.

Members

The Constitution determines the length of members' terms and the methods by which they are to be chosen. There continue to be suggestions that the quality or behavior of members would be improved if the terms of representatives were lengthened and if there were limitations on the number of consecutive years or terms an individual member could serve. Congress itself by law determines to a large degree the attractiveness of service, since it sets its own pay and establishes other perquisites, including a generous pension. Taken together, these constitutional and statutory provisions make congressional service a reasonably attractive vocation and at the same time provide opportunity for a graceful exit. The basic requirement for a member is a reasonable degree of popularity, without which election would be unlikely. There is a perhaps universal public desire for members who are intelligent, honest, selfless, and aggressive, but the election process does not guarantee that these qualities will be abundant in Congress.

Major laws were passed in the 1970s that regulated and publicized political contributions and campaign spending. Federal subsidies are now provided to underwrite presidential campaigns and the presentation of national party nominating conventions, but Congress has not seen fit to provide subsidies for its own elections. Nomination processes for senatorial and congressional candidates vary widely from state to state and even, in some cases, from party to party. Congress has shown little inclination to establish national standards with respect to party and election systems. The settlement of contested congressional elections, as in the case of Indiana's 8th district in 1984, is still basically at the whim of whichever party happens to be in control of the chamber. Some more neutral agency would produce a more acceptable result, and the House might consider assigning responsibility for the handling of disputed elections to a committee on which both parties are equally represented (the Standards of Official Conduct Committee, for instance), thus taking jurisdiction away from the House Administration Committee.

Powers

Little can be done about the fundamental powers of Congress except by constitutional amendment. In the beginning, this book stressed that Congress was purposely given limited lawmaking powers. To broaden these powers at the expense of the executive or judicial branches, state governments, or individual citizens would be a chancey and no doubt unpopular proposal. There have been statutory attempts to "adjust" or modify some of these powers, as in the case of the legislative veto, the War Powers Resolution, and impoundment legislation. Many reform efforts have been directed at slowing down the long-standing accretion of power to the executive branch. Other kinds of external reforms have had the intention of restructuring the party system, notably the various efforts to produce more responsible parties or, alternatively, to induce party members in Congress to follow the lead of their president. Many members of Congress have opposed such changes, since the changes would limit the options members now enjoy and make them more dependent on national party leaders.

Structures

The structures of Congress have long invited the attention of journalists and scholars. The basic feature, bicameralism, is mandated by the Constitution and practically untouchable. Each chamber divides into two party caucuses, which make basic leadership decisions for each new biennium, and the standing committees, which assume control of legislation in their respective areas of policy jurisdiction. Both party caucuses and legislative committees have become more open and permeable in the past ten or fifteen years. The structures of Congress seem to be stable, useful, and capable of responding to new conditions.

Procedures

Procedural devices and rules change in limited ways, and over the years their rate of usage may change. Taken together, they allow the minority to speak, oppose, amend, and delay while ensuring that the majority will eventually prevail. Two qualifications should be noted. First, where augmented majorities are required—the 60 percent required in the Senate to invoke cloture against a filibuster, the two-thirds vote for Senate approval of treaties, and the two-thirds vote required in each chamber to override a presidential veto or to propose an amendment to the Constitution—a minority has the power to dispose of a matter. Second, to be effective in passing legislation, the majority must sustain itself through at least five critical stages (House committee, House floor, Senate committee, Senate floor, conference committee).

Many proposals for procedural reform are aimed at achieving more efficiency, promptness, or thoroughness in handling bills. Other proposals in this area aim at making internal leadership decisions more democratic. Adoption of the secret ballot in party caucuses is one way in which members can vote on their leaders without worrying about reprisals if they vote the "wrong" way. The larger the number of leadership decisions made by the party caucus, the less important is seniority in advancing an individual member's congressional career. A member's attitude about seniority, and about changing the power structure, is likely to reflect the member's relative level of seniority.

Outputs

Congressional outputs is an area that is always ripe for discussion. To evaluate the outputs of Congress presupposes some preference as to the goals of the government, for it is largely by new legislation (rather than by more vigorously applying old legislation in the executive branch or by adjudicating legislation in some new way in the judicial branch) that we expect the federal government to respond to newly critical problems that inevitably arise. Several general, widely desired objectives of governmental policy are identifiable: equality, democracy, unity, liberty, national and domestic security, morality, conservation of natural resources, opportunity for economic advancement and investment, quality of life and health, governmental efficiency, and justice. But some of these desirable objectives may be beyond the power of government programs to achieve. We are told that you cannot legislate morality and that if government tinkers too much with the economy, the economy will suffer. While many citizens want Congress to try to solve problems—airline safety, farm price stability, drug control, human rights at home and overseas, education quality—many others are convinced that governmental actions are likely to make matters worse and at the same time add to the annual federal deficit. In several cases, reaching one of these desired goals might imperil the achievement of other goals. Politicians often feel themselves to be participating in zero-sum games, where if one interest wins, some other interests must lose. It is, in short, difficult to agree on how well Congress is working unless there is some consensus as to which goals are paramount. In a democratic system, it is both tempting and consistent to resort to public opinion measurement[1] to determine, at a given time, how positive the citizens feel about the nation and how those same citizens would prioritize the policy issues awaiting congressional attention.

Its effectiveness in making policy is the most crucial aspect on which congressional evaluation should be based. How well Congress performs its policy-making function depends, of course, on the perspective of the investigator. Bee-keepers and petroleum producers will give Congress good marks if the laws written by Congress benefit their economic activities and status. Whatever one's policy preferences might be, to evaluate the effectiveness of congressional policy making would involve analysis of the proposals that are advanced on the congressional agenda and of the substantive policy decisions that emerge. The volume of legislation passed is not a criterion of the quality of laws. Professor Irving Younger (Younger, 1985) comments on the inflation of legislation. He feels we have too many laws and suggests, somewhat facetiously, that Congress's lawmaking powers be limited by the following four conditions:

1. No bill can become law unless all members voting for it have read it.
2. No bill can become law unless its content is "knowable," that is, capable of being understood. (Younger cites the internal revenue code as an example.)

3. No bill can become law unless both its ends and means are clear and understood, for "not all difficulties are problems with solutions," Congress does not know how to ameliorate the perplexities of life, and legislation does not have unlimited efficacy.
4. No bill can become law unless its provisions apply to Congress as those provisions apply to others; congressional self-exemption would be outlawed.

By comparing the policy preferences of the public, as revealed in scientific polls, with the statutes Congress enacts, some conclusions can be drawn as to how closely the laws follow public opinion.[2] But beyond the desires of the citizens and the legislative decisions of Congress lies a third critical factor in evaluating Congress's work, namely, the national interest. Deciding national interest is a matter of wisdom and of subjective, normative, individual judgment. As David Vogler (1977, 3–6) notes, evaluation by informed and uninformed alike is necessarily based on the evaluator's information about Congress and the evaluator's values and expectations as to how Congress should behave and what goals it should strive to attain.

Citizens, students, journalists, and scholars will do well to remember the differences between empirical and normative approaches. The lesson is not that one approach is better or more valid than the other but that the tenets of democracy, and the continuing success of the American democratic experiment, require us to use both.

Performance by Congress of its basic functions other than policy making can be quickly summarized. Congress continues to adjust its fiscal and budget procedures. The budget reforms of the 1970s gave Congress better methods and procedures for determining revenue and spending levels, but in spite of these advances, our annual deficits and therefore our national debt have continued to grow at alarming rates because the government continues to spend far more money than it takes in each fiscal year. The Constitution clearly gives Congress control over both revenues and expenditures. Congress may have a clearer picture than it formerly did of the size and causes of the debt burden, but whether current deficit-reduction programs such as Gramm-Rudman-Hollings will be successful will not be known for several years. Today's Congress inherited this problem from previous Congresses, and no single Congress can resolve it. Efforts in Congress to enact a fiscal program that will control deficits will be resisted by the continuing demands of interest groups and government agencies for expenditures.

As to the representative function, Congress does a good job, by all accounts, of satisfying constituents, so good a job that separate and special interests get most of what they expect at the expense of the nation and the general consumer. So, reverting to Edmund Burke's (Burke, 1907) prescriptions on representation, there is a definite need for more statesmanship, that is, protection of the general interests of the nation, and for less emphasis on parochial interests. The election system is such that it makes members of Congress primarily dependent on the constituencies rather than on the party, president, or congressional leadership.

Congress spends considerable time in oversight activities. The Constitution provides that Congress have all the legislative powers of the federal government. But real legislative initiative, as many observers have said, comes from the executive branch and interest groups, leaving Congress with an essentially passive role. No government program can exist, though, unless it is authorized by Congress, and no money may be spent unless it is appropriated by Congress. Congress uses committee hearings, press releases, and floor debates to oversee administrative agencies, and this process is generally public, frequent, constant, and critical. But it is also an uneven process across policy fields, and oversight depends in many cases on the unpredictable interests and ambitions of committee chairs, presidential candidates, executive agency heads, and interest group leaders.

The review of presidential nominations and treaties is probably most thoroughly performed when the White House and the Senate are controlled by different political parties. But a cooperative spirit can exist when party control is divided, and there can be bitter legislative-executive conflict when the same party is in control of both the presidency and the Senate. Certainly the review function is performed in the most satisfying way when the emphasis is on impersonal, objective evaluation of personal qualifications of nominees or of the wisdom of treaty provisions rather than on purely partisan considerations. The president is more limited in his nomination options when confronted by a hostile Senate. When nominations become highly controversial, as with Supreme Court nominees Fortas, Haynesworth, Carswell, Bork, and Ginsburg, the chances for presidential success are reduced (see chapter 11).

Which of its several functions is most critical in the evaluation of Congress? It can be argued that the most valid test of a representative system is not how wise, just, efficient, or egalitarian its laws may be, but how representative and democratic the institution is. Congress is generally given high marks for its vigorous representation of constituents. But Congress was also intended to be a lawmaking machine, and its performance of this function has not been so clearly successful.

The bottom line in evaluating Congress is, after all, the opinion of the citizens it serves. Congress as an institution has consistently received low marks from public opinion, lower than marks received by the courts and almost all major occupational groups, and usually below the president. In the 1970s, "this negative evaluation of Congress by the public . . . hovered around the 75 percent mark" (Vogler 1977, 3). Numerous measures of public opinion published in the past decade confirm the continuance of this negative public evaluation of Congress.[3]

CONGRESSIONAL REFORM

Proposals to reform Congress are as numerous as the criticisms of its operations and outputs. Although many people think of Congress as an institution stubbornly impervious to change, it has at times made significant adjustments. In the 1970s, for instance, the budget process was modernized (although as we have noted severe problems remain) and in the House, the majority party caucus gained in influence over the standing committees.

Most reform proposals aim at improving specific functions. Sometimes, two reform proposals work at cross purposes to each other; the solution to one problem produces a new problem. Making Congress more efficient, for example, might at the same time make it less democratic. As Leroy Rieselbach (Rieselbach 1986, 148–149) writes, some reforms are aimed at producing a "centralized, more responsive institution" while other proposals stress a "free and open deliberative process." Because there is no "widely shared vision of what the legislature should be," he notes, "reform is likely to be episodic and incremental."

The budget imbroglio of December, 1987, was caused by what columnist James Kilpatrick called "an indefensible, indigestible, indescribable mess" of a bill which Congress presented to the president for approval. Such crises induce observers to consider how deadlocks on massive bills might be avoided. Several options suggest themselves.

First, the president might be given the power of the item veto, which would of course greatly strengthen his role as a legislative leader. However, since Section 7 of Article I of the Constitution did not mention a presidential power to approve or reject part of a bill, this would seem to require passage of a constitutional amendment.

A second option—changing to a parliamentary form of government so that the executive authority would be responsible to and chosen by the legislative branch, producing far greater party cohesion than we have known—would involve a far more substantial constitutional change than the first option. This proposal sounds unrealistic if not downright "un-American," but several thoughtful observers have suggested it.

A third option—choosing a president and congressional majority of the same party—is within the power of America's voters now, but since World War II they have divided power between the two parties as often as not. Changes in party control of the White House have been frequent, and every new president has different priorities from his predecessor, even when they have belonged to the same party. Changes in party control of Congress have been much less frequent, and Congress seems to look and act much the same from one term to the next. Within this context, certain differences between the two chambers have considerable significance. The Senate seems to be a more changeable body than the House, and it may therefore hold greater promise than the House of finding remedies for the ills of Congress. Senators themselves are more visible as individuals and more interesting as a group. Their election campaigns, while less frequent, are far more intensely contested and competitive, with the result that a smaller ratio of Senators win reelection. The most obvious result, of course, is the fact that while party control of the House has not changed since 1954, party control of the Senate has changed twice, and the minority party is often within a handful of votes of obtaining control. Senate campaigns, which are conducted statewide, are more likely to center on general or national issues than are the more localized House campaigns. Whether these differences will cause the Senate to take the lead in efforts to improve congressional performance remains to be seen.

A fourth option would be for Congress to avoid writing bills that contain unrelated material, including spending bills that contain too large a slice of the fiscal pie. Why couldn't major functional areas of the budget—national defense, foreign aid, space and technology, energy, environment and national resources, agriculture, commerce and transportation, education and training, health, Social Security, Medicare, government pensions and unemployment compensation, veterans' benefits—each be the subject of a separate bill? Why couldn't each chamber produce bills that do not combine unrelated matters, and, whenever its sister chamber attempts to slip such combinations through conference, refuse to compromise? And why couldn't congressional leaders schedule legislation so as to avoid, or at least significantly reduce, logjams at session's end?

Wall Street Journal reporter Albert R. Hunt, writing "In Defense of a Messy Congress," advised reformers to avoid five things: adopting a European-style parliamentary system, changing the length of House terms, limiting the number of terms or committee assignments for an individual member, repealing the reforms of the 1970s, and trying to elect brighter or better members (in Davidson and Oleszek 1987, 235–246). Then on a positive note Hunt suggested half-a-dozen improvements that should be sought: publicly financed congressional campaigns, restructuring committees, reducing congressional staff by one-fifth, reducing the amount of legislation and encouraging more oversight, enacting more sunset legislation to make programs more controllable, and devising a new way to set congressional salaries and allowances.

To that list might be added three reform ideas that seem particularly important as of the late 1980s: first, establishment of a party-neutral, objective, and prompt method for judging disputed congressional election contests; second, establishment of a more effective, critical, and demanding method of reviewing ethics and morals charges, and of disciplining members for unethical or immoral actions; and third, development of a more rational and timely congressional budget process.

CONGRESS ENTERS ITS THIRD CENTURY

Each biennial election has changed Congress to some extent, and the one-hundredth election in 1986 was no exception. Every two years some members retire and a few others are defeated in their reelection attempts. But 87 percent of the senators and 89 percent of the representatives serving in the 100th Congress (1987–1988) had served in the previous Congress. The electoral success rate of incumbents remained high—75 percent in the Senate, 98 percent in the House.

In November of 1986, the Democratic party regained its accustomed status as the majority party in both chambers of Congress, and this meant there would be changes in Capitol Hill gamesmanship. Disarmament, relations with Central America and the Middle East, protection of the environment, the structure of the tax system, health care, and welfare reform were debated and resolved in a new political context. In this sense, the 100th Congress marked a break with its immediate predecessors. But even so, what Stephen Bailey called the "inverted coalition" (Bailey 1970, 39)[4] would still prove in many cases to be more determinative of congressional outcomes than the simple count of Democratic and Republican members.

Congress is a large and diverse body, a collection of very independent politicians. Lacking strong central leadership and any real sense of group responsibility, it is not surprising that Congress is deliberate in all of its processes, from writing laws to disciplining its members. It hears all sides of an issue and listens to every relevant proposition before taking final action on a bill. Like the large population it represents (though not in equivalent proportions), Congress contains many kinds of people—urban and rural, male and female, sophisticated and plain, young and old, black and white, rich and not so rich, reactionary and radical—who themselves have many widely different ideas about the nation's problems and how they should be solved. The composition of Congress and the expectations Americans have of it produce a situation where, too often, the citizens who observe the partisan wrangling on Capitol Hill become disenchanted, impatient, and disgusted. Perhaps that is part of the price of democracy. Kings, philosophers, judges, bishops, and field marshals may be more impressive individually and collectively but they are not elected by the people.

It is not in the nature of large organizations such as Congress to respond confidently and consensually to immediate crises. The nature of the president's constitutional functions and responsibilities—and the expectations of the public—clearly demand that the president take the lead in handling emergencies. But it can also be said that Congress in its deliberations and decisions will determine how sensible, just, fair, open, and responsible our nation's government will be.

It should be remembered that a democratic society is expected to make decisions that satisfy a majority of the public as well as a majority of Congress. It takes time to establish majority support for any disputed proposition, so we should not be surprised when Congress seems to move ponderously or uncertainly. Democracy also requires a full discussion of policy options, and certainly Congress meets that requirement. Striking a balance between prompt response to current problems and full discussion of alternative ways to respond to these problems is a continuing tension with which members of Congress are familiar. When the balance between expression and resolution is maintained, all participants in the policy process, winners and losers alike, are willing to accept the legitimacy of the system and the finality of its decisions. This is the way Congress in its work helps to maintain the stability and thus the strength of a highly diverse nation.

The wisdom of Congress's policy outputs depends both on the quality of its members and on their ability to organize, discipline, manage, and motivate themselves effectively. The important faults of Congress lie less in the quality of its members than in the complexity of its structures and procedures and in the vacillation and ambiguity of its leadership. Considered as discrete individuals, members are generally diligent, ambitious, and concerned about the people and interests they represent and the nation they serve. It is in the management and organization of its corporate work that Congress is most likely to falter. Its most demanding and important work is to identify, confront, and solve, or at least ameliorate, the host of challenging problems that face the nation at any given time. A democratic body may not be as effective or as efficient in performing these policy functions as we would sometimes wish, and as a result substantive solutions may be slow and unsure in coming, but those makeshift decisions and halting processes may well turn out to be better than any alternatives in the long run for the largest number of citizens.

NOTES

1. *Public Opinion* magazine has reported on the level of what it calls the "Gross National Spirit" several times over the past few years.
2. Several considerations limit the utility of measures of the public's policy preferences as guides for policy making, notably question wording, the effects of polarization, and low public information or attentiveness. For a recent commentary, see Ladd 1987, 59.
3. For a provocative essay about how recent Congressional activities have further eroded public trust in representative democracy, see John Alvis, "Willmore Kendall and the Demise of Congressional Deliberation," *The Intercollegiate Review*, Spring 1988, 57–66.
4. *Congressional Quarterly* uses the phrase "conservative coalition" to refer to this combination of Republicans and southern Democrats.

REFERENCES

ALEXANDER, HERBERT E. *Financing Politics: Money, Elections, and Political Reform.* Washington, D. C.: Congressional Quarterly Press, 1984.

ARIEFF, IRWIN B. "Williams Resigns Senate Seat to Avert a Vote to Expel Him; Chapter on Abscam is Closed." *Congressional Quarterly Weekly Report* (13 March 1982): 555–559.

BAILEY, STEPHEN K. *Congress in the Seventies.* 2nd ed. New York: St. Martin's Press, 1970.

BEARD, E., and HORN, STEPHEN. *Congressional Ethics: The View from the House.* Washington, D. C.: Brookings, 1975.

BENTHAM, JEREMY. *The Theory of Legislation.* (ed.). C. K. Ogden. London: Routledge and Kegan Paul, Ltd., 1931.

BOLLING, RICHARD. *House Out of Order.* New York: Dutton, 1965.

BURKE, EDMUND. "Thoughts on the Cause of the Present Discontents." In *The Works of Edmund Burke,* Vol. II. New York: Oxford University Press, 1907.

CALMES, JACQUELINE. "Panel Says Daniel Erred, Urges No Sanction." *Congressional Quarterly Weekly Report* (15 February 1986): 312–313.

CALMES, JACQUELINE. "House Ethics Committee Clears St. Germain." *Congressional Quarterly Weekly Report* (18 April 1987): 713–714.

CLARK, JOSEPH S. (ed.). *Congressional Reform: Problems and Prospects*. New York: Crowell, 1965.

Congressional Record, 99th Cong., 2nd sess., Mar. 1986, S2244–2245.

DAVIDSON, ROGER H., KOVENOCK, DAVID, and O'LEARY, MICHAEL. *Congress in Crisis: Politics and Congressional Reform*. Belmont, Calif.: Wadsworth, 1966.

DAVIDSON, ROGER H., and OLESZEK, WALTER J. (eds.) *Governing: Readings and Cases in American Politics*. Washington, D. C.: Congressional Quarterly Press, 1987.

DE GRAZIA, ALFRED (ed.). *Congress: The First Branch of Government*. Garden City, New York: Anchor, 1967.

DODD, LAWRENCE C., and OPPENHEIMER, BRUCE I. *Congress Reconsidered*. 2nd ed. Washington, D. C.: Congressional Quarterly Press, 1981.

EHRENHALT, ALAN. "Harrison Williams and the New Senate." *Congressional Quarterly Weekly Report* (20 March 1982): 655.

"The Guns and the Gutless." *Chicago Tribune* (12 April 1986) sec. 1:8.

HAMILTON, ALEXANDER, MADISON, JAMES, and JAY, JOHN. *The Federalist or The New Constitution*. Everyman's Library ed. New York: Dutton, 1911. (Originally published 1787–1788)

HOOK, JANET. "Panel Considers Expulsion for Biaggi: House Punishes Rep. Murphy, Prepares to Act on Other Cases." *Congressional Quarterly Weekly Report* (19 December 1987): 3134–3135.

HUNT, ALBERT R. "In Defense of a Messy Congress." In *Governing: Readings and Cases in American Politics*. Roger H. Davidson and Walter J. Oleszek (eds.). Washington, D. C.: Congressional Quarterly Press, 1987.

KEEFE, WILLIAM J., and OGUL, MORRIS S. *The American Legislative Process: Congress and the States*. 6th ed. Englewood Cliffs, N. J.: Prentice-Hall, 1985.

LADD, EVERETT CARLL. "Where the Public Stands on Nicaragua." *Public Opinion* 10 (September/October 1987): 2–4, 59–60.

LOCKARD, DUANE. *The Perverted Priorities of American Politics*. New York: Macmillan, 1976.

LOWI, THEODORE. *The End of Liberalism*. New York: Norton, 1969.

ORNSTEIN, NORMAN (ed.). *Congress in Change: Evolution and Reform*. New York: Praeger, 1975.

Powell v. *McCormack,* 395 U. S. 486 (1969).

RIESELBACH, LEROY N. *Congressional Reform*. Washington, D. C.: Congressional Quarterly Press, 1986.

SHEPPARD, B. D. *Rethinking Congressional Reform: The Reform Roots of the Special Interest Congress*. Cambridge, Mass.: Schenkman, 1985.

SUNDQUIST, JAMES L. *The Decline and Resurgence of Congress*. Washington, D. C.: Brookings, 1981.

VOGLER, DAVID J. *The Politics of Congress*. 2nd ed. Newton, Mass.: Allyn & Bacon, 1977.

VOGLER, DAVID J., and WALDMAN, SIDNEY R. *Congress and Democracy*. Washington, D. C.: Congressional Quarterly Press, 1985.

YOUNGER, IRVING. Speech on the limited efficacy of legislation. 12 April 1985, Sioux Falls, South Dakota.

APPENDIX
RESEARCH EXERCISES

These research exercises are suggested for students who want to actively engage in original, empirical analysis of legislative structure and behavior. The exercises are individually lettered and are listed below with the chapter to which their subject relates.

Exercise A (chapter 1). The Powers of Congress

Read and summarize the essential points expressed in a Supreme Court decision concering the powers of Congress or the separation of powers concept. Some examples: *Youngstown Sheet and Tube Company* v. *Sawyer* (343 U. S. 579 [1952]); *Powell* v. *McCormack* (395 U. S. 486 [1969]); *McGrain* v. *Daugherty* (273 U. S. 135 [1927]); *Gravel* v. *United States* (408 U. S. 606 [1972]); *Hutchinson* v. *Proxmire* (443 U. S. 111 [1979]); and *Immigration and Naturalization Service (INS)* v. *Chadha* (462 U. S. 919 [1983]).

Exercise B (chapter 2). Foreign or State Law

Investigate and describe an example of an important law written by a foreign national legislature or an American state legislature.

Exercise C (chapter 2). Parliamentary Coalitions

Describe the formation of a multiparty parliamentary coalition in any foreign nation since 1960.

Exercise D (chapter 3). Drawing Congressional Districts

Consider a state having from four to twelve congressional districts and, using recent election data in Richard Scammon's biennal *America Votes* volumes (Washington, D. C.: Congressional Quarterly Press), create an alternative districting system gerrymandered in favor of the Democratic party. Then do another districting scheme attempting to maximize the number of Republican districts.

Exercise E (chapter 4). District Topography and Economy

Describe any congressional district, other than a district covering an entire state, in terms of topography and the district's important economic activities and ethnic groups.

Exercise F (chapter 4). Incumbents and Challengers

Trace the origins and election campaigns of any U. S. representative who has served more than three terms, paying particular attention to the closeness of the voting outcomes and the quality and background of the various challengers that have confronted the member over the years.

Exercise G (chapter 5). Campaign Organization

Describe the organization and management of any candidate's campaign for election to Congress in the past ten years, noting especially how the candidate appointed, supervised, and worked with the campaign manager.

Exercise H (chapter 5). Factors in Recent Campaigns

Compare a set of recent campaigns in five or six congressional districts in terms of their relative emphasis on party loyalty, ideology, issues, and candidate personality.

Exercise I (chapter 6). Congressional Staff Organization

Describe and analyze the background, organization, and functions of the staff of any U. S. senator or representative. Interviews or correspondence with members or staffers will be necessary to carry out this exercise.

Exercise J (chapter 6). How Members Spend Their Time

Describe and comment on how a particular U. S. senator or representative spends his or her work time for a given day, week, or longer period of time. Interviews or correspondence with members or staffers will be necessary to carry out this exercise.

Exercise K (chapter 7). Selection of a Leader

Describe in as much detail as you can the process by which any important congressional or state legislative leader was chosen by his or her respective party caucus. Newspaper accounts, magazine articles, interviews, and correspondence will provide helpful insights and details.

Exercise L (chapter 8). Committee Membership Changes

Prepare a table and comment on the changes in membership and individual ranking over a period of at least five terms for any standing committee of the Senate or House or of a state legislature. Committee lists can be obtained from the *Congressional Directory*.

Exercise M (chapter 8). Voting Patterns on a Committee

Describe voting patterns in markup sessions of a congressional or state legislative committee. Articles in the *Congressional Quarterly Weekly Report* or the *National Journal* will occasionally present the committee voting record on important legislation. Such information might also be available from the committee staff. One could also study how members of a given standing committee vote on the committee's legislation, or other legislation, when bills go to the floor.

Exercise N (chapter 9). A Day in the House or Senate

Write a summary description of what the Senate or House did on a given day (Tuesday, Wednesday, or Thursday are most likely to have significant action) and outline at least one important colloquy among members. Use the *Congressional Record* as a source.

Exercise O (chapter 9). Motions on a Particular Bill

Chart and locate by page in one day's *Congressional Record* all motions made on a particular bill. Record the outcome of each motion and do so in terms of yes-and-no voting by party where that information is given in the *Record*.

Exercise P (chapter 10). Congressional Voting Patterns in a Recent Year

From data in *Congressional Quarterly*, make a five-column by two-column cross tabulation showing various categories of voting support for the president, the majority party, or the conservative coalition in the House or Senate for any recent year.

Exercise Q (chapter 10). Factors Affecting a Particular Roll-Call Vote

Analyze any roll-call vote in the U. S. Senate in the past two years to show the impact of party and one other factor (ideology, region, occupation of member, age of member, seniority of member) on the outcome, using the cross-tabulation format and the phi coefficient to show degree and direction of influence.

Exercise R (chapter 11). Testimony from the Executive Branch

Use committee records, hearings, and reports to analyze the quantity and quality of appearances by officials from the various executive departments before an assigned House or Senate committee in a recent year.

Exercise S (chapter 12). Testimony from Special Interest Groups

Use the records, hearings, and reports of an assigned committee to identify the interest groups that appear most frequently in a given year or congressional biennium. Why are these particular groups interested in the committee's legislation?

Exercise T (chapter 12). Description of an Interest Group or News Unit

Describe the office management, operations, special equipment, and objectives of any news organization or lobbying organization in Washington or in a state capital city.

Exercise U (chapter 13). How to Improve Congress

Write an essay of from 500 to 1,000 words describing what you believe is the most serious problem with the organization or operation of Congress and suggest an approach for solving that problem.

INDEX